READING IN THESE TIMES

SEMEIA STUDIES

Jacqueline M. Hidalgo, General Editor

Editorial Board:
L. Juliana M. Claassens
Rhiannon Graybill
Raj Nadella
Emmanuel Nathan
Kenneth Ngwa
Shively T. J. Smith
Wei Hsien Wan

Number 103

READING IN THESE TIMES

Purposes and Practices of Minoritized Biblical Criticism

Edited by

Tat-siong Benny Liew and Fernando F. Segovia

SBL PRESS

Atlanta

Copyright © 2024 by SBL Press

All rights reserved. No part of this work may be reproduced or transmitted in any form or by any means, electronic or mechanical, including photocopying and recording, or by means of any information storage or retrieval system, except as may be expressly permitted by the 1976 Copyright Act or in writing from the publisher. Requests for permission should be addressed in writing to the Rights and Permissions Office, SBL Press, 825 Houston Mill Road, Atlanta, GA 30329 USA.

Library of Congress Control Number: 2024932875

This volume is fondly dedicated to one of our colleagues, Hector Avalos, who passed away during the process of composition and publication. He left us, alas, at a most productive stage of his life and his career, depriving us of so much work and so much wisdom still in the offing. We count ourselves, however, most fortunate in having his study in the volume. His work was always solid, sharp, and challenging. We shall miss his voice and his face. We are most grateful for his multiple contributions to both the field of biblical studies and the movement of minority studies.

Contents

Acknowledgments ix
Abbreviations xi

Part 1. Introductions

Reading in These Times: Contexts of Minoritized Biblical Criticism
   Fernando F. Segovia 3

Temporal Boomerang: Reading and Writing of the Bible ...
in These Times
   Tat-siong Benny Liew 61

Part 2. Naming and Facing the Times

Struggling with Culture: African American Biblical Hermeneutics
in These Times of HIV and AIDS
   Cheryl B. Anderson 93

Minoritized Biblical Scholarship as Christian Missiology and
Imperialism
   Hector Avalos..105

Bordered Hospitality and "the Least of These": The Bible as a Tool
of Citizenship Excess in the Contemporary US Immigration Crisis
   Jacqueline M. Hidalgo 125

Passed On and Passing On: Reading John's Affective Transfer
   Tat-siong Benny Liew 141

Of Escoffier, *Gastronomie*, Craft, and Canon
   Yii-Jan Lin 169

viii   Contents

Confronting Christian Identity, Chosenness, and Violence in a
Predominantly African American Graduate Theological Center
    Vanessa Lovelace 189

Whose Recognition? Latino/a Studies and the Need to Belong
    Francisco Lozada Jr. 207

Unsettled Homecomings: A Repatriate Reading of Ezra-Nehemiah
    Roger S. Nam 235

Négritude and Minoritized Criticism: A Senegalese Perspective
    Aliou Cissé Niang...257

Ticketing, Signaling, and Watching: A Reading Strategy for
Times like These
    Hugh R. Page Jr..279

Leer Para Hacer Lío/Reading to Raise a Ruckus: The Critical
Task of Disruptive Reading in These Times
    Jean-Pierre Ruiz..287

Arrested Developments: Dismantling the Disciplinary Network
of a Surveillance State
    Abraham Smith 303

"Talkin' 'bout Somethin'": Scripturalization—Or, a Transgressive
Politics of the Word
    Vincent L. Wimbush...337

Part 3. Conclusion

On the Threshold of End Times: Paths and Agendas of
Minoritized Criticism
    Fernando F. Segovia 359

List of Contributors...399
Names Index 401
Subject Index...409

Acknowledgments

This volume has been made possible due to the assistance and support of a good number of people, to whom we are deeply indebted and most thankful. First and foremost, to all those who took part in the project, for their gracious acceptance of our invitation and fine contributions. Second, to Dr. Jacqueline M. Hidalgo, general editor of Semeia Studies, for her full support of this project, and to Dr. Gregory A. Cuéllar, the board editor for the volume, for his keen and gracious review of the volume. Third, to Olubunmi Adegbola and Ludwig Noya for their work on preparing the indexes. Finally, to the publications staff of SBL Press for their assistance throughout the process of publication.

Abbreviations

ABDIJ	*African and Black Diaspora: An International Journal*
AcBib	Academia Biblica
Achill.	Dio Chrysostom, *Achilles* (*Or.* 58)
AfrAmRev	*African American Review*
AJS	*American Journal of Sociology*
ALH	*American Literary History*
AmerJ	*Amerasia Journal*
BCS	*Buddhist-Christian Studies*
Bell. jug.	Sallust, *Bellum jugurthinum*
BFHSP	*Bulletin of Friends' Historical Society of Philadelphia*
BibInt	Biblical Interpretation Series
BibRec	*Biblical Reception*
B.J.	Josephus, *Bellum judaicum*
BSNA	Biblical Scholarship in North America
BZAW	Beihefte zur Zeitschrift für die alttestamentliche Wissenschaft
Cat.	Cicero, *In Catalinam*
CBQ	*Catholic Biblical Quarterly*
C&C	*Christianity and Crisis*
CI	*Critical Inquiry*
CollEng	*College English*
CommQuart	*Communication Quarterly*
CRIT	*Concilium: Revista Internacional de Teología*
CSA	Cultural Studies of the Americas
CSSH	*Comparative Studies in Society and History*
CultAnthr	*Cultural Anthropology*
DDD	*Dictionary of Deities and Demons in the Bible.* Edited by Karel van der Toorn, Bob Becking, and Pieter W. van der Horst. Leiden: Brill, 1995. 2nd rev. ed. Grand Rapids: Eerdmans, 1999.

xii   Abbreviations

ECN	*Estudios de Cultura Náhuatl*
EGP	*Ethics & Global Politics*
ESV	English Standard Version
FAT	Forschungen zum Alten Testament
GlobS	*Global South*
HistTheor	*History and Theory*
HTR	*Harvard Theological Review*
IGSAP	*Intersections: Gender and Sexuality in Asia and the Pacific*
IJLC	*International Journal of Law in Context*
IMR	*International Migration Review*
Int	*Interpretation*
JAH	*Journal of American History*
JAR	*Journal of Africana Religions*
JBL	*Journal of Biblical Literature*
JCLC	*Journal of Criminal Law and Criminality*
JHCPU	*Journal of Health Care for the Poor and Underserved*
JLE	*Journal of Latinos and Education*
Jorn	*La Jornada*
JSH	*Journal of Social History*
JSNT	*Journal for the Study of the New Testament*
JSNTSup	Journal for the Study of the New Testament Supplement Series
JSpecPhil	*Journal of Speculative Philosophy*
JWCCC	*Journal of White Collar and Corporate Crime*
JWCS	*Journal of Working Class Studies*
LatSt	*Latino Studies*
loc.	location
LXX	Septuagint
Metam.	Ovid, *Metamorphoses*
MonthRev	*Monthly Review*
Mor.	Pseudo-Plutarch, *Moralia*
MQR	*Michigan Quarterly Review*
M&W	*Man and World*
NEQ	*The New England Quarterly*
NLR	*New Left Review*
NovT	*Novum Testamentum*
NPT	*New Perspectives on Turkey*
NRSV	New Revised Standard Version

Abbreviations

Off.	Cicero, *De officiis*
PB	*Policy Brief*
P&G	*Politics and Governance*
PJ	*The Prison Journal*
PMLA	*Proceedings of the Modern Language Association*
PresAfric	*Presence Africaine*
PsychDial	*Psychoanalytic Dialogues*
PTMS	Princeton Theological Monograph Series
PublCult	*Public Culture*
QH	*Quaker History*
QJS	*Quarterly Journal of Speech*
Rep	*Representations*
Res gest. divi Aug.	Res gestae divi Augusti
RFBC	*Review (Fernand Braudel Center)*
RSV	Revised Standard Version
SAQ	*The South Atlantic Quarterly*
SCID	*Studies in Comparative International Development*
SecCent	*Second Century*
SemeiaSt	Semeia Studies
SocRes	*Social Research*
StImp	Studies in Imperialism
SymS	Symposium Series
T@C	Texts @ Contexts
TCL	*Twentieth-Century Literature*
TCS	*Theory, Culture & Society*
TheatJ	*Theater Journal*
TiA	*Theory in Action*
TSWL	*Tulsa Studies in Women's Literature*
UMLR	*University of Miami Law Review*
USQR	*Union Seminary Quarterly Review*
WUNT	Wissenschaftliche Untersuchungen zum Neuen Testament
YJC	*Yale Journal of Criticism*
YJLF	*Yale Journal of Law & Feminism*

Part 1
Introductions

Reading in These Times:
Contexts of Minoritized Biblical Criticism

Fernando F. Segovia

Introduction

This exercise in biblical criticism, which bears the title *Reading in These Times*, presents the question of critical posture—the vision and the mission of the critic in contemporary society and culture—as the topic of inquiry. The problematic of critical identity and function can be pursued from any number of perspectives and in any number of contexts. Like any other exercise along these lines, therefore, the present undertaking does so in certain circumscribed ways. What these are can be ascertained from its setting within a broader and ongoing project of research and publication, within which it stands as a third phase of development. The project as a whole has to do with the conception and practice of minoritized ethnic-racial criticism. Such, then, is the framework for the present exercise. Consequently, its distinctive character with regard to the problematic—its delimitation by way of perspective and context—can be determined by examining its position in the overall sequence of the project.

In its initial phase of development, the project addressed the fundamental question of critical definition: the conceptualization and formulation of minoritized ethnic-racial criticism within the field of studies. The volume sought to analyze key components of this critical approach: underlying framework, defining contours, operative dynamics (Bailey, Liew, and Segovia 2009). This it did by calling on minoritized voices from throughout the United States, including a set of scholars from other areas of studies, both within and outside Christian studies, who served as consultants to this venture. This quest was conveyed by the subtitle of the volume: *Toward Minority Biblical Criticism*.

-3-

In a second phase of development, the project concentrated on the question of critical wherewithal: the dynamics and mechanics at work in minoritized criticism. The volume set out to examine the ways in which minoritized criticism envisioned and executed its work: theoretical models and analytical approaches (Liew and Segovia 2022). This it carried out by bringing together minoritized voices from throughout the world, though mostly from the United States, to bear on the same texts, four in all, both by way of individual interpretation and by way of group interaction. This search was signified by the subtitle of the volume: *Pursuing Minoritized Biblical Criticism*.

With this third phase of development, the project turns to the question of critical posture: the problematic of identity and function envisioned in and for minoritized criticism. The volume seeks to ascertain how minoritized critics view their métier and their task, an objective that the title presents by way of a metaphor: *Reading in These Times*. This it pursues by drawing on critical voices from a variety of minoritized formations in the United States—African Americans, Asian Americans, Latinx Americans. This perspective and this context account for its distinctive approach to the problematic of posture. To wit, what are the vision and the mission of ethnicized-racialized critics in the contemporary social-cultural context of the United States? This undertaking is set forth by the subtitle: *Purposes and Practices of Minoritized Biblical Criticism*.

Retaking the Problematic

In taking up the problematic of posture, the volume harks back to and follows up on recommendations from the first phase of the project. In addressing the question of critical definition, the project invited a set of voices, three in all, from outside the field of biblical criticism as external consultants. These scholars hailed from a variety of fields of studies, inside as well as outside Christian studies—all representatives of different ethnic-racial formations in the country and in the academy. They offered a number of critical directions for the future pursual of the project—all quite to the point and very much worth pursuing, indeed even today, more than a decade later. They all emphasized the need to move beyond the given focus on texts and approaches of the inquiry, the dynamics and mechanics of criticism, and onto the broader dimensions of interpretation, the underlying discourses and contexts of criticism. This they did from the different perspectives of their respective fields of studies and from their particular angles of vision within such studies—calling for due attention to the religious-historical, the political-pedagogical, and the political-national frameworks behind interpretation. Such recommendations are worth recalling.

From the field of Christian theological studies, Mayra Rivera Rivera (2009) urged minoritized critics to be up front about the religious-theological foundations and ramifications of their work: to surface their operative constellation of beliefs and to examine the relation between their proposals for minoritized criticism and their systems of beliefs. Grounded in the field of Christian practical theology, specifically the realm of religious education, Evelyn L. Parker (2009) pressed minoritized critics to analyze the political-pedagogical contours and consequences of their task: to bring to light the foundational philosophy and practice of white supremacy and to forge instead an alternative philosophy and practice of color consciousness, with close attention to such matters as the underlying historical-political context, the driving orientation and expression of impartation, and the animating political objectives. From the field of ethnic studies, James Kyung-Jin Lee (2009) asked minoritized critics to examine the political-national parameters and consequences of their work: to expose the cultural logic of the state regarding dominant-minority relations and minority status and to work toward alternative constructions of the cultural logic.

While the second volume on critical wherewithal did not follow up on any of these recommendations, given a perceived and pressing need at the time to expand on the dynamics and mechanics of interpretation, the present volume does. This it pursues in indirect rather than direct fashion. In effect, given its goal of pondering the problematic of critical posture in these times, the volume takes up suggestions ventured by Parker and Lee. Thus, while not explicitly addressing the political-pedagogical project of whiteness regarding the assimilationist process of hegemonic formation, the volume, in analyzing the vision and mission of minoritized critics in our times, cannot but deal with questions of context, mode, and objectives in criticism—along the political lines marked by Parker. Similarly, although not explicitly entertaining the political-national cultural logic of the state regarding the dialectical process of minoritized formation, the volume, in examining the identity and function of minoritized critics in these times, cannot but contend with the question of models for approaching dominant-minority relations and minority status in criticism—along the national lines traced by Lee. Such broader concerns do arise without

6 Fernando F. Segovia

fail, in one way or another and to one degree or another, in all contributions to this volume. To the extent that they do, the critical directions for expanding the horizons of minoritized criticism have been heeded.

Refining the Problematic: A Call for Further Delimitation

Despite the circumscribed version of the problematic outlined above, the question as posed remains, to my mind, much too general. One can immediately raise questions regarding both dimensions of the exercise, as signified by the title—a gerund phrase consisting of a present verb form, "reading," and a modifying prepositional phrase, "in these times." Thus, with respect to the gerund, which advances the element of critical program as such, no further indications are provided. Nothing is said, for example, about a particular focus of attention or a specific mode of analysis. Similarly, with respect to the phrase, which introduces the element of critical context, no further markers are given. Nothing is offered regarding, say, a concrete demarcation of the present in view or a distinct angle for the period in mind. As a result, the dimension of identity and function as well as the dimension of span and slant remain quite open-ended. Consequently, the task undertaken by this exercise—reflecting on the vision and mission of minoritized criticism in the United States today—would benefit from further delimitation, paying close attention to and providing pointed responses to such questions.

Such a call for a refining of the problematic applies not only to each contribution to the exercise but also to the exercise as a whole, as a project venue for such contributions. This latter reflection I propose to undertake in my introductory and concluding essays to the volume. Toward this end, a preliminary word of explanation regarding such questions is in order. Certain clarifications regarding both the verb form and the prepositional phrase, I find, prove helpful. These allow for a more precise articulation of what reading in these times—the problematic revolving around the identity and function of the minoritized biblical critic in the United States today—envisions and entails. This description, in turn, allows for an appropriate course of action regarding my proposed reflection on the exercise as a whole.

Recasting the Problematic: A Call for Channeling

In terms of the gerund *reading*, first of all, two clarifications are to the point—the focus and the mode of critical program. A first delimitation concerns the reach of the inquiry. While grounded in the context of the United States, the question of shape would benefit from further specification. The spectrum of possibilities is expansive, from the more exclusive to the more inclusive. Various points of reference come to mind: pursuing a particular group agenda, adopting a minoritarian perspective in general, following a national framework, embracing a global perspective. A second delimitation has to do with the approach to the inquiry. While based in the tradition of ethnic-racial criticism, the question of procedure stands to benefit from further definition. The range of options is broad, from the more focused to the more intersectional. A number of combinations is possible: using the lens of a specific ethnic-racial area of study, drawing on minority studies, appealing to various fields of study.

In terms of the phrase *in these times*, two clarifications are also in order: the duration and slant of the times. A first delimitation has to do with the span of time to have in view. While regarded as present and ongoing, the question of a point of departure stands to benefit from greater precision. The spectrum of options is broad, from the more proximate to the more distant. A number of key divisions readily suggest themselves: a pivotal event in the first two decades of the century, the beginning of the century, the end of the Cold War in 1989–1991, and the fundamental social-cultural shift signified by the 1960s–1970s. The second delimitation concerns the angle of the times to have in mind. While viewed as active and impinging, the question of social-cultural dimension would benefit from closer identification. The range of possibilities is expansive, from the more focalizing to the more totalizing. A number of angles can be immediately identified: a particular crisis in the social-cultural matrix; a broader confluence of crises affecting the matrix; a specific dimension of the matrix, materialist or discursive; and the totality of the social-cultural matrix.

Concluding Comment

In light of the preceding observations, my critical reflection on the exercise as a whole will proceed in four steps. To begin with, I examine the attitude toward critical posture in the history of the field of studies. Second, I revisit an earlier attempt on my part to attend to the problematic of critical identity and function. Such revisiting will yield, primarily for reasons of length, a formal separation of the question of reading and the question of context. The former, the exposition of the reading in question, I take up in the concluding essay, by way of a joint conversation with the contributors to the volume. The latter, the explication of the times in question, I develop here. Out of such revisiting will come a revisioning of the problematic. Third, I proceed to unfold a theoretical model for pursuing the dimension of context, taken from the social sciences. Last, I conclude with a word on the demands and challenges of context in these times for the future of ethnic-racial criticism.

Critical Posture in Biblical Studies

The question regarding the identity and function of the critic has seldom, if ever, been regarded as a topic for discussion in biblical studies. Such has been the norm regardless of academic-intellectual orientation, whether religious-theological or secular-humanist. Before addressing the question of the why, a look at how these different frameworks cohere and function is in order. I do so as follows: first in terms of the umbrella fields of study within which biblical criticism is placed and how such umbrella fields approach the status of the Bible, then in terms of how biblical criticism, so situated, relates to other areas of study within the umbrella fields in question.

Biblical studies can be linked to Christian studies or religious studies. From the religious-theological perspective, the field is conceived as an area of study within the umbrella field of Christian studies. So placed, the field subscribes—in some respect and to some extent—to a view of the Bible as a sacred writing, Scripture or the Word of God. As such, questions of revelation, inspiration, and authority hover in the background. The spectrum of positions varies widely: at one end, overt acknowledgment and active engagement, as pursued by more conservative ecclesial traditions; at the other end, implicit acceptance and working distantiation, as followed in the more liberal ecclesial traditions. From the secular-humanist perspective, the field is construed as an area of study within the umbrella field of religious studies. So situated, the field adheres—in some form—to a view of the Bible as a document of antiquity, a product of human beings. Consequently, no formal or necessary connection would be made to the umbrella field of Christian studies or the question of Scripture; however, an informal or logical association may be granted and perhaps even broached. A spectrum of positions may be drawn in terms of primary focus: toward one pole, questions of literary import, broadly conceived; toward the other, matters of historical interest, similarly conceived in broad terms.

In accord with such placement, biblical studies is associated with different sets of areas of studies that, taken together, are seen as constituting the umbrella field of studies. When taken as an area within Christian studies, biblical criticism is set within an academic-ecclesial framework of some sort: an undergraduate department in religiously affiliated university, a professional school (independent seminary, university-related denominational divinity school, university-related nondenominational divinity school), a graduate program in religiously affiliated university). While the areas in question vary according to ecclesial-institutional tradition, a core is discernible throughout: historical studies, theological studies, moral studies, and practical studies. When taken as an area within religious studies, biblical criticism is set within an academic-secular context of some sort—an undergraduate department in a secular university or a graduate program in a secular university. Two possibilities can be readily identified. First, and more narrowly so, it may be seen as related to other areas of study with a similar focus on religious traditions with a scriptural foundation, such as, say, Islamic studies or Buddhist studies. Second, and more broadly, it may be viewed as related to other areas of study having to do with religious traditions, such as, say, traditional religions of Africa or native religions of the Americas.

Regardless of academic-intellectual orientation, as stated earlier, the culture of silence regarding critical posture remains in force. Behind such a modus operandi, there lies, I would argue, a sense of the question as settled, whether consciously or unconsciously. The identity and function of the critic are taken as a given, not as a problem, and hence no trajectory of discussion on this topic, no sense of a problematic, is to be found. In effect, what critical posture presupposed, whether along religious-theological lines of the Bible as a sacred writing or along secular-humanist lines of the Bible as a document of antiquity, was set by a historicist-contextualist tradition of interpretation going back to the formation of the field as field and holding sway through the mid-1970s. What such a tradition demanded of the critic was to serve as an intermediary between the past and the present: to revisit and to recover, to go back to and to make present, the texts and contexts of the biblical world.

This task the critic would perform by re-creating the meaning of the ancient texts and reconstructing the contours of the ancient contexts, using each to shed light on the other. Toward this end, there was a set of guiding principles in place, grounded in established procedures of academic-intellectual inquiry. Among these, two stand as foundational. With regard to

10 Fernando F. Segovia

the past, the critic would follow a realist-empiricist view of history: a sense of the historical as out-there and in-itself, independent of observation, yet opaque, due to a number of factors, such as the loss of information or the change in context. With regard to the present, the critic would embrace an objectivist-disinterested view of historiography: a claim to impartiality in the retrieval of the past, whether by way of discursive recreation or material reconstruction, grounded in principles and strategies of scientific research.

Disciplinary Turns

This culture of silence endured into the mid-1970s, when biblical studies began to undergo a series of theoretical and methodological developments that posed fundamental challenges to the historicist-contextualist tradition in place. These developments, it should be noted, actually reflected what was taking place across the entire spectrum of the academy, in the social sciences and the human sciences alike. Each development brought about a problematization of long-standing and deep-rooted principles and habits of the discipline. As such, they may be appropriately characterized as turns. Among them, I would highlight the following: the discursive and the materialist, the contextual and the ideological, the populist and the culturalist. These I have organized in terms of primary orientation; the result is a division of three sets of critical turns and foci of attention. While the first two sets take place in the circles of academic criticism, the third set occurs outside such circles.

Discursive-Materialist

The first set has to do with the realm of professional criticism, with a primary focus on the past—the texts and contexts of antiquity. Here I have placed the discursive turn as well as the materialist turn. This mode of analysis does have an impact on the other two sets of turns as well: (1) the present of professional criticism, the agents and contexts of interpretation; and (2) the world of nonacademic criticism, the alternative loci and traditions of interpretation. In effect, what applies to the linguistic-literary and social-cultural analysis of the past also stands true, mutatis mutandis, with regard to the other dimensions of interpretation as well, so that attention to discursivity and materiality is imperative at all times.

With the discursive turn two developments are to be noted. First, there emerged a view of language as constructed and indeterminate, rather than mimetic and stable. Such a position required overt consideration and specification of meaning throughout, without ever escaping the presence of ambiguity. Second, there also emerged a view of texts as literary and rhetorical worlds in themselves, involving dynamics and mechanics of construction and argumentation. This position demanded explicit attention to aesthetic and communicative models and strategies of production. As a result, the connection to historical-contextual reality turned into a problem, while the mode of representation of such reality became the focus of interest.

With the materialist turn there came a view of society and culture as constructed and structured, neither natural nor disparate. This position called for conscious examination of social systems and cultural traditions. Texts turned thereby into social and cultural worlds of their own, adopting and adapting available models of social frameworks and strategies of cultural frameworks. Consequently, the study of the sociocultural dimensions of texts in terms of their relation to historical-contextual reality and experience became not only highly problematic but also highly complex.

Contextual-Ideological

The second set of turns involves, as in the case of the first set, the world of professional criticism, but with a primary focus on its present dimension— the agents and contexts of interpretation. Here I have set the contextual turn and the ideological turn. This angle of analysis also has a bearing on the other two sets of turns: the past of formal criticism, the texts and contexts of antiquity; and the world of nonacademic criticism, the alternative loci and traditions of interpretation. Thus, again, what is said of the present with regard to the importance of location and perspective applies, mutatis mutandis, to the other dimensions of interpretation, with the result that consideration of setting and standpoint is crucial throughout.

The contextual turn emphasized the role of the critic as a situated and circumscribed agent, by no means free-floating and universal. This stance called for a vision of the agent of interpretation as shaped and moved in some way by the social and cultural frameworks within which they found themselves and operated. Such an approach required detailed exposition and analysis of such frameworks. The ideological turn highlighted the role of the critic as an active and perspectival agent, not simply passive and determined. This stance called for a corresponding vision of the agent as inserted into and speaking from, in multiple and imbricated ways, a

12   Fernando F. Segovia

network of unequal formations and relations of power—status sets—constitutive of all frameworks. Such an approach demanded close surfacing and scrutiny of these differential webs of power.

Popular-Culturalist

The third set of turns comprehends the realm outside professional criticism—alternative loci and traditions of interpretation. In this set I have placed the popular turn and the culturalist turn. This type of analysis does have an effect as well on the other sets of turns: the past and the present of professional criticism, the texts and contexts of antiquity as well as the agent and contexts of interpretation. Here, once more, what stands true of the popular and culturalist trajectories of reception applies, mutatis mutandis, to the other dimensions of interpretation, so that attention to multiplicity of readings and diversity of appropriation remains essential throughout.

With the popular turn arose a view of all readers and readings, whether as individuals or as groups, as valuable signifiers of meaning and hence as worthy of consideration. This position required the placement of interpretations ventured by everyday readers and study groups, across space and time, alongside those advanced from within the circle of learned critics. This move yielded a considerable expansion of the object of study in criticism. With the culturalist turn came to the fore a view of readings tendered outside the religious-theological domain as important markers of meaning, and thus as worthy of note. This position demanded the placement of interpretations adopted in both social arenas (e.g., politics and economics) and cultural arenas (e.g., literary arts and visual arts) side by side with those forged within the religious-theological realm. Such a move led to further and significant expansion of the object of study in criticism. What both turns indicated was, in effect, that any reading, no matter where it took place, had much to say about the way in which texts and contexts were activated and applied.

Interdisciplinary Turn

There is yet another turn that I would characterize as the interdisciplinary or multidisciplinary. Technically speaking, this development could be placed within the second set of turns delineated above, since its conceptualization and formulation took place within the world of academic criticism. Practically speaking, however, it is more appropriate to approach it as a different category, a seventh turn, insofar as it constitutes an integral dimension of all three sets and all critical turns in question. In effect, its thrust grows out of and turns back onto each and every critical turn. What the interdisciplinary turn signified was the need, indispensable and pressing, for engagement with and integration of other fields of study in the pursuit of interpretation—in all of its dimensions, whether inside or outside academic criticism.

This need entailed two interrelated moves. On the one hand, it called for informed recourse to the critical repertoire at work in these fields: adequate mastery of the concepts and the terms, the models and the strategies, of analysis as employed and defined. On the other hand, it called for a solid grasp of the scholarly trajectories behind such fields: appropriate acquaintance with ongoing developments, conflicted discussions, and shifting stages regarding the concepts and terms as well as the models and strategies in use. It is not difficult to see how such moves apply across the various sets of turns outlined.

In the case of the first set, it would be entirely unsatisfactory to entertain the elements of discursivity and materiality without a close dialogue with fields of study that attend to matters linguistic and literary as well as social and cultural. Similarly, in terms of the second turn, it would prove no less unthinkable to examine the dimensions of setting and standpoint without a thorough engagement with the various fields of study that pursue matters of contextual and ideological configuration. Last, in the case of the third turn, it would be thoroughly inappropriate to consider the issues of multiplicity of readings and diversity of appropriations without a solid conversation with fields of study that address the production and consumption of social and cultural expressions.

Such a modus operandi should not be surprising. Biblical criticism has held close ties before with a number of other fields of study. Among these, historical studies, classical studies, and ancient Near Eastern studies feature prominently. Indeed, these represent the fundamental conversation partners within the historicist-contextualist paradigm of interpretation. However, the interdisciplinary turn under discussion signifies a radical heightening of such ties, and this on various counts. Several such ramifications readily come to mind.

First, this development brings about considerable expansion regarding the scope of the critical task—the range of fields to be engaged and integrated. Whatever a critic seeks to analyze is taken as ensconced within

14 Fernando F. Segovia

a particular academic-scholarly framework, or set of frameworks, that requires careful consultation. Second, such a turn yields thorough complexification with respect to the mode of the critical task—the status of each and every framework to be engaged and integrated. Whatever a critic wishes to express in analysis is seen as demanding strict sifting and determination, given the highly sophisticated, sharply disputed, and ever-changing composition of all such frameworks. Third, this turn results in profound transformation regarding the scholarly trajectory behind the critical task—the nature of the conversation with the traditional dialogical partners. Whatever a critic seeks to argue in analysis along such lines—historical, classical, Near Eastern—is viewed as in urgent need of theoretical updating as well, since the changes introduced, the driving concerns and markers, by the new turns in criticism have also affected and presently crisscross the traditional links of research.

A Concluding Comment

While all such turns have brought about wide-ranging and far-reaching changes in the ways of interpretation, the culture of silence regarding posture has endured nonetheless. The question regarding the identity and the function of the critic has remained either not addressed at all or decidedly underaddressed in the field. There have been, to be sure, occasional musings and tentative approximations in this regard. These have touched, fleetingly, on various aspects of this problematic: the who of identity and the what of concentration, the wherefore of motivation and the whereto of objective, the where of placement and the how of implementation. There has been, however, no sustained and systematic discussion to be found as such.

Revisiting and Revisioning Criticism in Critical Times

In both regards, the lack of significance attached to the question of critical posture in the field of biblical studies and the dearth of attention devoted to its analysis in the history of scholarship, I had found myself going in the opposite direction. The reasons for such a contrarian position on my part I am able to discern more clearly now, with the benefit of hindsight. I should like to bring these to the fore and to show how such concerns led to a particular course of action at a key moment of academic-professional life. Thereupon, I will expand on the parameters of such a move, which set the stage for the pursuit of a theoretical model suitable for understanding and analyzing our critical times.

The insouciance regarding the figure of the critic in society and culture had haunted me for quite some time. This was due, I now see, to a radical experience of transnational and transgeopolitical migration. This took place at an early stage in my life, when I was still in my early teens and hence at the onset of adolescence. Its impact, alas, has perdured through the decades and still makes itself felt today, at an advanced stage of life. The experience involves a twofold process of translation from one world to another. To begin with, there is a foundational passage of dislocation and relocation, marked by profound conflict and utmost uncertainty. This was a brief phase, highly traumatic. I would describe it in terms of exilic disorientation and existential redirection. Subsequently, protracted subjection to otherization takes place, by way of both ethnic minoritization and imperial peripheralization. This has been a long phase, still ongoing. I would characterize it in terms of latinization and primitivism, respectively. My preoccupation with posture was clearly rooted in and nourished by this experience of migration—a need to know who I was as a historical subject.

The vacuum regarding the discussion of this question in the field had troubled me for quite some time as well. This was due, I realize now, to a thorough integration on my part of the academic-intellectual habitus of theorization, which was becoming ever more highly refined in the wake of the multiple turns impacting on the field. This habitus entails a process of appropriation and channeling of experience through insertion into and engagement with appropriate frameworks of discourse. From such a perspective, any reflection regarding the figure of the critic would demand critical encounter not only with other such pointed reflections but also with the full tradition of reflection as well. My frustration with theoretical silence on posture was grounded in and pressed by this quest for explicit and precise articulation—a need to define who I was as a critical subject.

Upon election as president of the Society of Biblical Literature for 2014, I decided to avail myself of the unique opportunity afforded by the presidential address to wrestle with this long-lingering, twofold specter in my life as a critic. I resolved, on the one hand, to address directly the question of critical identity. I sought thereby to clear a space, to carve out a point of departure, for a path of scholarship along these lines, one that would draw on a variety of scholarly trajectories outside the field. This aspect of my decision I signified by way of the subtitle, "Reflections on

Vision and Task." I further resolved, on the other hand, to attend to the forces and currents that I had come to view by then as critical for society and culture. I regarded these as bearing directly on the configuration of the first resolve and hence as essential for the proposed theorization of critical posture. This aspect of my decision I conveyed by way of the title, "Criticism in Critical Times."

Several years later now, as I reflect again on critical posture for this volume on reading in these times, now within the context of a project on ethnic-racial minoritized criticism, I find it imperative to begin by revisiting and revisioning this initial venture of mine. Only then can I advance the inquiry onto a new level of discussion. Such rereading I undertake in two steps. I begin by repositioning—recalling and reevaluating—the critical times in question; then, I continue by recalibrating—re-viewing and reorienting—the task of criticism in new times.

Repositioning Critical Times

The decision to use the presidential address as a crucible for engaging the problematic of critical posture was gradually propelled and shaped by the realization that my tenure as president would coincide with a number of anniversaries having to do with key periods of time in both the world and the country, and that it was incumbent on me to take these into consideration in my address. All such periods represented critical times not only in terms of their own distinctive configurations but also in terms of their consequences for later times, including our own times. Indeed, such consequences would leave an imprint on my own life in direct and weighty ways. These consequences, furthermore, I could detect in the forces and currents that had come to frame my vision of our critical times. This process of discovery and integration on my part involved three more or less sequential moves: historical-political, as a child from outside the West; spatial-geopolitical, as a child from the Global South; and spatial-geographical, as a child of migration from the America of the Global South.

From the historical-political point of view, I saw that my tenure would mark a number of anniversaries having to do with global conflicts involving the West over the course of the twentieth century. Such conflicts moved from the First World War (1914–1918), through the Second World War (1939–1945), to the Cold War (1947–1988/91). From this trajectory of warfare, which drew in and affected the rest of the world throughout, it was the descent into hell, by way of ever more extreme violence, material and discursive alike, that captured my attention. This downward spiral in military-technological destruction and nationalist-supremacist barbarism, I argued, would bring the West to an ever more profound crisis of identity. Years later now, to my mind, this crisis of identity the West faces, alongside the rest of the world, more starkly than ever before.

From the spatial-geographical standpoint, I observed that my term of office would match the sixtieth anniversary of the contentious rise of the Third World as agent, material and discursive alike, in its own right (1952–1955). This period comprised such key events as the defeat of the French imperial forces in Vietnam (1954) and the first gathering of the former European colonies of Africa and Asia as new nations at Bandung, Indonesia (1955). From this path of awakening, which expanded and intensified throughout the Global South, I was particularly struck by the sense of resistance and affirmation in the face of highly unequal relations between North and South. This process of conscientization, I proposed, would lead to ever more trenchant critique and would move, as a result of wave upon wave of migration, into the very heart of the Global North itself. At this point, several years afterwards, this dialectic of North-South inequality stands as more visible and more vulnerable than ever before.

From the spatial-geographical point of view, I saw that my tenure would mark the fiftieth anniversary of a conflictive period in relations between the United States and Latin America and the Caribbean (1963–1965). Such tension was signified by the military coup d'état staged in Brazil (1964), which was the first of many to follow and which brought untold grief on the region for decades, and by the Immigration and Nationality Act of 1965, which opened the gates of immigration beyond the northern-western European favoritism in place and led to massive migration from the Global South, especially from Latin America and the Caribbean in a flight from dark times. From this policy of active interventionism and border relaxation, which together altered radically the demographic composition of the country, it was the ever greater expansion and distribution of this diaspora that I found remarkable. This burgeoning presence of the America of the South—alongside similar flows from the rest of the Global South—in its midst, I argued, would bring the United States to an ever more severe crisis of identity. Years later now, to my mind, such Latinx ascendancy, ever more numerous and ever more influential, the country finds even more unsettling, more disruptive, and more threatening than before.

18 Fernando F. Segovia

From all three directions, therefore, I realized how imperative it was to expose and to name as well as to dissect and critique the state of affairs in our own times. On a historical-political key, as an outsider-insider in the West, buffeted about by the contrary winds of the Cold War, the world of today in 2014 I saw as acutely critical. Such times exceeded the critical times that revolved around the global conflicts of the West through the twentieth century—utterly devastating as these were. On a spatial-geopolitical key, as a product of the Global South in the North, caught in a never-ending web of colonial and decolonial ruminations, I also looked on the world of today in 2014 as decidedly critical. These times outdid the critical times that accompanied the coming-to-be of the Third World around the mid-1950s—highly turbulent as these were. On a spatial-geographical key, as a native of the America of the South in the North, tossed into the vortex of dislocation and relocation by migration, the world of today in 2014 I again viewed as acutely critical. Such times surpassed the critical times that surrounded the state of relations between the two Americas around the mid-1960s—profoundly consequential as these were.

Recalibrating Criticism

The decision to imagine criticism in the critical times of today led to a variety of theoretical moves. Among these, two stand as foundational. It is imperative, on the one hand, to surface and to name the major crises of our times. Critics must discern and identify the salient critical developments that bear on the contemporary world. It is essential, on the other hand, to expose and to dissect such crises by means of appropriate critical tools. Critics must outline and analyze their dynamics and mechanics, by themselves and as a set, by way of informed critical approaches, sound theoretical models and methodological apparatuses. These two moves are interdependent: critical developments and critical tools go hand in hand. Several years later now, it is this twofold task of unveiling and explicating our times that stands in need of refinement. The times of today are simply, and remarkably so, not the times of 2014.

Critical Developments

I argued then that our times should be seen as constituting the era of the post–Cold War. Speaking twenty-five years later, I posited the rupture in 1989 of the bloc of socialist nations, under the aegis of the Union of Soviet

Socialist Republics, as the point of departure for a new historical-political era. This collapse of the East, reaffirmed by the dissolution of the USSR itself in 1991, brought to an end the long span of the Cold War (1945–1989)—the binomial confrontation between East and West. In this new historical-political era, three crises struck me as overriding: global economics, climate change, and worldwide migration. Speaking in the wake of the Great Recession of 2008, I highlighted the economic crisis as pivotal and developed it at length. A number of other major crises I mentioned in passing as well: the emergence of geopolitical multipolarity, the rise of national-political breakdown, and the explosion of multidimensional social violence. All these crises, furthermore, I described not only as individual developments but also as interlocking phenomena, bringing about a crisis in and for the world as a whole.

This diagnosis of our critical times clearly reflected my process of gradual conscientization regarding the major anniversaries that would coincide with my term as president and the critical times that lay behind them. As such, the diagnosis reflected as well the forces and currents that such critical times left in their wake, which had come to envelop the course of my life and to color my vision of the world. In every instance, the diagnosis has changed since its first formulation in 2014, for the worse and decidedly so.

Thus, the crisis of global economics links up with the dialectic of inequality that marked relations between the Global North and Global South, implanted throughout the long process of colonization, yet sustained, though sharply confronted, in the era of decolonization. Such a relation of structural inequality I now view as turning far more pronounced and destructive in the contemporary world. Similarly, the crisis of climate change relates to the crisis of identity at the heart of the West that followed a long path of devastation, facing the dire aftereffects of untrammeled industrial development, signified by deforestation and pollution. Nowadays, I regard such a state of ecological degradation in the world at present as fast veering toward a doomsday scenario. Last, the crisis of worldwide migration connects with the extraordinary process of population translation from the America of the Global South to the United States that was propelled by sustained political-economic interventionism, yielding ever sharper demographic transformation and ever stronger resentment. (This, I hasten to point out, was not the only translation from the Global South to the United States, or to the Global North for that matter, yielding even more consternation and insecurity.) Such an exploding diasporic presence

20 Fernando F. Segovia

of Latinx America I now see as pushing headlong into a climactic situation of nativism and xenophobia in the contemporary world.

Critical Approaches

I affirmed two directions. Along particularist lines, I demonstrated the need for appeal to and use of models and trajectories from other fields of study having to do with each crisis in question. Along generalist lines, I called for a similar recourse to and application of models and trajectories from other fields of study that could address the various crises as a set, as interconnecting and interfeeding developments that together constituted a systemic crisis. In all such endeavors, I regarded interdisciplinary work, sophisticated and rigorous, as of the essence. In effect, criticism would have no choice but to enter into conversation with any number of complex and conflicted fields as well as with a variety of approaches, no less complex and conflicted, that addressed the concept of a world system.

In terms of distinct fields of study, having foregrounded economics, I availed myself of the work of Alfred J. López (2011) on the master narrative of globalization, the ideological matrix of neoliberalism. Such work outlined a threefold development at work: first, construction—implantation of the model; second, deconstruction—implosion of the model; next and now, alternatives—quest for other models. In the wake of disastrous failure, such work called for a new master narrative. This López envisioned as a postglobal discourse that would address head-on the abysmal differential inequalities of the model and promote instead the welfare of all, especially the untold many left behind by globalization—the subalterns. Such discussions would be necessary for criticism in critical times to master and integrate. The same type of work would be required with regard to all other major crises. Indeed, the ideal throughout would be not to follow one analytical model but rather to acquire a sense of the scholarly discussion.

In terms of systemic approaches, what I did was to point the way, to find and suggest a critical framework that would keep the conjunction of the crises foremost in sight. This would require, I argued, a recourse to world theory, and for this awareness of and acquaintance with global studies would be in order. Here two directions present themselves: one emerging from social theory in the Global North, dealing with theories of world order; the other forthcoming from social theory in the Global South, attending to epistemologies of the South in pursuit of a better world. These discussions are indispensable for criticism in our critical times to learn and appropriate thoroughly. The ideal would be to look both ways, to the Global North and the Global South, and to acquire throughout a broad sense of the scholarly discussion.

A Path Forward

I noted before that for me the task of unveiling and explicating our times stands in need of refinement, both regarding the major crises having a marked impact on the world and regarding the analytical tools deployed for proper assessment of and reaction to such crises. The former task, the comparative evaluation of historical developments, I take up in the concluding essay. There I set forth a revised reading of our times at this point, in the wake of the year 2021, which represents for me a turning point in multiple and profound ways. I also draw on the studies of this volume to design a mapping of the major developments ethnic-racial critics have in mind as they ponder the problematic of critical posture. In so doing, I seek to forge a critical conversation on these times within minoritized ethnic-racial criticism. The latter task, the appropriate selection of critical models, I pursue in the section that follows.

World Order in Turmoil

Writing in 2014, I could not even begin to foresee the swift and acute deterioration of the global situation that was forthcoming soon thereafter. For this turn of affairs, I find the historical-political framework provided by the presidential term of office of 2017–2021 in the United States to be a perfect marker. What happened in the course of this quatrennium, the administration of Donald J. Trump, signifies a before and an after. This I find to be so on two counts. First, the tenor of this presidency—its mixture of ignorance and arrogance, braggadocio and deception, spite and vitriol—stands as altogether beyond equal, with disastrous consequences for national as well as international affairs. Second, a number of developments came together toward its final days that prove utterly alarming, serving as a sort of apocalyptic overture or harbinger. The resulting state of affairs changes altogether, to my mind, any reflection on critical posture—including my own.

Indeed, what I had anticipated before as a work in waiting, engagement with world theory and hence with global studies, now presented itself as a work of utmost urgency. As already noted, such dialogue demands much work as well as much patience, for this field of studies is extensive and convoluted. What I undertake here is consequently but a beginning step. I lay out two accounts of world order as theorized from the Global North and the Global South, respectively. Such a course of action calls for an account of its theoretical foundations and its particular configuration. For this I draw on the overarching and incisive account of Steven Seidman (2013, 158), professor of sociology at the State University of New York–Albany, regarding the historical trajectory of social theory. This path is presented in four phases: the rise of the classical tradition, rethinkings of the classical tradition, revisions of and revolts against the classical tradition as established and rethought, and the rise of postdisciplinary theory. What Seidman does, in effect, is to provide a reading of these times through the optic of social theory.

In his account of the third stage, Seidman describes three reactions to the rethinking of the classical tradition that had been taking place in two different contexts, the tradition of American sociology and the tradition of European theory. These revisions and revolts begin to emerge in the 1950, in the aftermath of the Second World War, and to call into question the long-standing project of the Enlightenment and its corresponding vision of modernity, which had been forged in and had become the ethos of the West. At the heart of this vision, there lies, argues Seidman (157), "a deep, abiding faith: with the aid of science and democratic institutions, humans could create a world of freedom and justice for all."[1] In the postwar period, given the many wide-ranging and far-reaching transformations that were taking place in the world, a number of social thinkers, he continues, begin to push for a thorough revision of theory, and with it a fundamental revision of the project of the Enlightenment as well.[2] "A new world order was in the making," Seidman writes, "a world at once modern and postmodern." In effect, this was the advent of the postmodern era (158).

---

1. Such faith included a set of postulates: the objectivity of science, a coupling of scientific and social progress, the unity of humankind, the evolution of humanity from East to West, and evolution from oppression to freedom (Seidman 2013, 157).

2. Among such developments Seidman (2013, 158) lists a postindustrial economy, a world society, a media-saturated culture, and multiculturalism. The result was the decline of driving notions of modern theory: the primacy of the nation, the primacy of the individual, the superiority of the West, and the story of progress.

Reading in These Times

All three reactions advance a critique of modernity. This they do, however, not so much by way of radical opposition, espousing rejection of its values along the lines of antimodernity, but rather by way of thorough recasting, addressing shortcomings of such values—be they contradictions, omissions, or ramifications—along the lines of postmodernity. This project they carry out from different perspectives and with different programs—all postmodern, in a broad sense of the term. The first challenge is designated as "The Postmodern Turn," thus invoking a narrower sense of the term, which undermines the teleological drive of modernity. The second is characterized as "Identity Politics and Theory," which calls into question the unitary mode of modernity. The last challenge is described as "Theories of World Order," which challenges the political worldview of modernity. Such reactions I do not read as independent and self-contained, mutually exclusive; I see them, rather, as having much in common, despite a distinctive angle of vision in each case, also quite varied in its own right.

What Seidman brings together under "The Postmodern Turn" are theorists who seek to reimagine various core understandings of modernity—its conception of self and identity, its approach to knowledge and society, and its view of history and freedom. Its representatives are identified according to three strands of thought: (1) advancing visions of the postmodern world—Jacques Derrida, Jean-François Lyotard, Jean Baudrillard; (2) unfolding the notion of the disciplinary society—Michel Foucault; and (3) undertaking the sociology of postmodernity—Zygmunt Bauman. What they propose as a set may be captured as follows: (1) a sense of the human self as a social product, with multiple and unstable identities; (2) an approach to knowledge as related to power and hence as involving moral consequences; and (3) a vision of society as highly diverse and highly conflicted. What characterizes each strand is its particular take on the social world today: the demise of the notion of progress, the rising power of the media, and the proliferation of ruling powers outside the realms of law and government. What such proposals envision is no longer the modernist dream of a final attainment of "freedom and justice for all" (Seidman 2013, 157). It is, rather, "a permanent struggle for gains in pleasure, choice, self-expression, social bonding, and justice" (199).

Under the designation of "Identity Politics and Theory," a variety of critical developments are listed, with a slash relating yet separating the subordinate and dominant dimensions of the axis of identity in question: (1) feminist theory/masculinity studies; (2) critical race theory/white studies; (3) lesbian, gay, and queer theory/heterosexual studies; and (4) colonial discourse studies. What unites these theorists, all products of the social conflicts raging throughout the West and the world in the 1960s, is a critique of the liberal order regarding its core tenet of identity—the social aspects bypassed and the social inequalities embodied, whether along the lines of class in Europe; the triad of race, gender, and sexuality in the United States; or the role of empire throughout the world. This critique these theorists carry out by way of both calls for inclusive reforms and demands for radical reconstitution. What differentiates them is the focus of the critique, which is organized along the lines of group identity, out of which emerge "new subjects of knowledge" and "new knowledges," previously outside the purview of classical theory (Seidman 2013, 264). What such proposals entertain ceases to be the modernist dream of scientific objectivity. What emerges, rather, is a view of science as political, "entangled in social practices of exclusion, marginalization, and devaluation," not to be "dismissed as evil" but to be "used to combat" such omissions and inequalities (265).

What Seidman includes under the category of "Theories of World Order" are theorists who seek to transform yet another core tenet of modernity—the exaltation of the nation-state as the basic unit of social life. Its advocates are presented according to different schools of thought: (1) expanding analysis from internal-national to external-global frameworks—David Held and Mary Kaldor, (2) foregrounding the globalization of capitalism—Immanuel Wallerstein and Manuel Castells, and (3) insisting on the ongoing role of imperial frameworks—Michael Hardt and Antonio Negri alongside David Harvey and Michael Mann. What they share in common is the need to reconceptualize the primacy accorded to the nation-state in modern social theory, not by discarding altogether the fundamental significance of the nation-state but rather by attending to social frameworks and dynamics beyond. Where they part ways is in the particular scenario and processes emphasized—the spread of global networks, the emergence of a world-economy, and the assertion of imperial power. What such proposals address is no longer the modernist dream of "reliance on international institutions and law to create civil order and peace across the globe" on the part of sovereign nation-states (Seidman 2013, 270). It is now a "global order" with direct consequences for nation-states: the need for "global regulation," the spread of "global social inequality," and the pressure of imperial realities, whether by way of diffuse control of "world order" or the exercise of "imperial ambitions" (301).

Reading in These Times 25

All of these reactions to the vision of modernity borne by the project of the Enlightenment are worth analyzing and integrating into any quest for a critical posture proper to these times, including that of minoritized ethnic-racial criticism. For evident reasons, this can only be done one step at a time. Given my focus on the conjunction of major crises in our world, I should like to draw initially on the category of "Theories of World Order," in particular on the work of Wallerstein regarding global capitalism and the concept of a world-system. What Wallerstein shows for me, among many things, is the need to think beyond my previous designation of our context as the era of the post–Cold War. At the same time, it is clear from a reading of Seidman that, with the exception of one strand of thought within the category of "Identity Politics and Theory," the path of social theory drawn is overwhelmingly from the Global North, not only in terms of theorists but also in terms of focus. I should therefore like to balance the choice of Wallerstein with that of Boaventura de Sousa Santos, whose work, although he himself hails from the Global North, has been consistently on social theory from the Global South. What de Sousa Santos impresses on me, again among many things, is the need to think in truly global fashion.

Through the Global North: Immanuel Wallerstein

Immanuel Wallerstein (1930–2019) was a leading figure of social theory through the latter half of the twentieth century and into the twenty-first century. He was a scholar of many interests and pursuits, among which the following are often highlighted: economic history, political sociology, and geopolitical studies. He was a public intellectual with a panoramic view of the world and a political commitment to its marginalized. All of these elements de Sousa Santos, a close colleague for many years, brings out in pointed fashion in an eulogistic obituary, brief and personal, written in his memory. Characterizing his death as an "irreparable loss for the social sciences," de Sousa Santos (2019) describes his academic-professional standing as "the most important American sociologist of the twentieth century and the one with the greatest international projection" and his social-cultural stance as a "sociologist committed to the fate of the world and, above all, to the fate of the most vulnerable populations"—"the disinherited of the earth."[3]

---

3. This is my translation of the obituary, published in the Argentinian leftist daily *Página12* (de Sousa Santos 2019), which was itself translated into Spanish from the Portuguese original by Antoni Aguiló. My first citation is taken from the first

26   Fernando F. Segovia

In another obituary, this one academic and expansive in nature, another close colleague of his, Çağlar Keyder (2019), provides an insightful outline of Wallerstein's professional and academic trajectory.[4] Various phases can be readily discerned. The first, extending from 1958 to 1971, is represented by his initial appointment in the Department of Sociology at Columbia University, where he had pursued his entire undergraduate and graduate education (PhD, 1959). During these years, and reflecting the times in question, the convulsive decade of the sixties, his work centered on Africa, thus continuing the focus of his dissertation on nationalist movements in West Africa. Such work dealt with the legacy of colonialism, the struggles for decolonization, and the triad of race-class-nation.[5] These early concerns with issues of domination and exploitation on a global scale, Keyder argues, served as markers throughout the whole of Wallerstein's life and work.

A second phase, encompassing 1971 through 1976, involves his tenure as professor in the Department of Sociology at McGill University in Mon-

---

two sentences, which read as follows: "La muerte de Immanuel Wallerstein supone una pérdida irreparable para las ciencias sociales. Sin lugar a duda, fue el sociólogo estadounidense más notable del siglo XX y el de más proyección internacional." My second citation is taken from the final sentence, which proceeds as follows: "La mejor manera de honrar la memoria de Immanuel Wallerstein es continuar nuestro trabajo sin olvidar ... la forma brillante con la que logró combinar la objetividad científica y el compromiso con los desheradados de la Tierra." This last expression is clearly a reference to the title of Franz Fanon's (1961) last volume, *Les damnés de la terre*, with whom he was acquainted and who was an enduring influence on his thinking.

4. Keyder is professor of sociology at the State University of New York in Binghamton and at Koç University in Istanbul. He traces his relationship to Wallerstein to the latter's years at McGill University (1971–1976). This was followed by invitations to visit SUNY Binghamton: first, at the Fernand Braudel Center, and then as an adjunct at the Department of Sociology. In 1982 he became a full member of the faculty there, where he was in residence one semester every year.

5. From this focus on Africa, two salient developments should be noted. First, in 1960 Wallerstein met Franz Fanon, when the latter was appointed as ambassador to Ghana for the Provisional Government of the Algerian Republic. This was the year before Fanon's death to cancer and the publication of *Les damnés de la terre*. The two, Wallerstein (2009a) recounts, held many discussions on the state of world affairs. Second, in 1973 Wallerstein was elected president of the African Studies Association, a learned society of scholars from the United States and Canada with an interest in Africa, established in 1957. His presidential address was on Africa and capitalism (Wallerstein 1973).

tréal, Canada. It is here that his signature concept of and project on the modern world-system began to take shape, yielding the publication of the first volume of *The Modern World-System*, with a focus on the emergence of the capitalist economy in Europe out of the crisis of feudalism (1400–1640; Wallerstein 1974a).[6] A third phase, encompassing 1976 through 2000, stands as the apex of his career, revolving around his long tenure at the State University of New York at Binghamton, both as distinguished professor of sociology and as director of the Fernand Braudel Center for the Study of Economies, Historical Systems, and Civilization. The latter was a research institute for the pursuit of the ambitious project on the modern world-system from inception through the present.[7]

This was a time of expansion, in multiple directions, of earlier proposals and themes, led by the publication of two more volumes of *The Modern World-System*. These traced the continuing development of the capitalist economy: the second volume, with regard to its solidification in northern Europe (1600–1750); the third, with respect to its further consolidation throughout Europe (1730s–1840s) (Wallerstein 1980, 1989).

The final phase, extending from 2000 to 2019, takes up his years of retirement in New Haven, during which time he held an appointment as senior research scholar at Yale University. This period witnessed the publication of many projects as well. These included a general introduction to world-systems theory and the fourth volume of *The Modern World-System*, which brought the project to the end of the First World War, tracing the spread of the capitalist economy around the globe (Wallerstein 2004, 2011). Keyder highlights distinctive aspects of his work during these years: the decline of the United States as a hegemonic power, the future of capitalism as world-system, and the pursuit of his role as public intellectual by way of regular commentaries on world affairs. The latter, published biweekly on his website (iwallerstein.com) and distributed by Agence

---

6. In addition to this volume, two articles are published that summarize the overall parameters of the world-systems approach (Wallerstein 1972, 1974b).

7. What the center provided for many years, since its inception in 1976, was the opportunity to bring together a number of scholars who would dedicate themselves to the study of the modern world-system. This the center pursued, beyond faculty appointments, in a number of ways, as outlined on its webpage: allowing for visits and presentations by scholars from around the world, organizing conferences and meetings, launching research initiatives by way of working groups, and undertaking an active program of publication. The center, it should be noted, closed on 30 June 2020—less than a year after the death of Wallerstein.

28 Fernando F. Segovia

Global, lasted from 1998 through 2019 and numbered five hundred in all. The final contribution, bearing the title of "This Is the End; This Is the Beginning," appeared but a few weeks before his death (Wallerstein 2019).[8]

World-System in Place

The core concept of the world-system, a driving feature of his work for over forty years (1974–2019), is lucidly summarized by Wallerstein (2004) in his general introduction to the project published thirty years after its launching, *World-Systems Analysis*. It may be approached in terms of five key dimensions. Two of these have to do with the notion of the world-system as such, both in general terms and with reference to its different configurations. Two others focus on one of these variations in particular, the world-economy, addressing aspects of its dynamics and mechanics. The last dimension involves the historical trajectory proposed with regard to this variation, given its long-lasting and ever-expanding duration, its complex and differential organization, and its conflictive and shifting composition.

On the notion of the world-system, there is the question of definition and the element of typology. With regard to the former feature, a world-system signifies a network of individual societies that are linked and interact with one another by way of political and economic relations. It is this interrelated and interconnecting social network, rather than individual societies, that is taken as the primary unit of social analysis.[9] Here

---

8. In this final commentary, Wallerstein describes the format of these pieces and the norms of distribution. What the title signifies by "end" is that there will be no more: they all stand together from now on as an archive, "a community of commentaries." What the title conveys by "beginning" is the future of the world-system. While "inherently unknowable," he holds out the possibility, given the structural crisis underway, of a "transformatory use of a 1968 complex," a "transformatory change," but only after much time has elapsed, without a sense of its actual shape, and with but a fifty-fifty chance of success.

9. The introduction includes a useful glossary of terms (Wallerstein 2004). These are worth noting. The term *system* is defined as "some kind of connected whole, with internal rules of operation and some kind of continuity" (98). The term *world-system* is presented as "the unities of social reality within which we operate, whose rules constrain us" (98). Wallerstein (98) goes on to add that a world-system is "not the system of *the* world" but rather "a system that is a world," most commonly "located in an area less than the entire globe."

Wallerstein breaks with traditional social theory and its focus on individual societies. With respect to the latter feature, two types of world-system are identified: world-empire and world-economy.

On the one hand, the model of world-empire represents a social network of individual societies marked by political centralization, alongside an economic division of labor, exercised by a dominant society.[10] In this category, Wallerstein places a variety of examples: from ancient times, the Roman Empire, and from recent times, the Ottoman Empire. On the other hand, the model of world-economy constitutes a social network of individual societies characterized by an economic division of labor, alongside political plurality, involving a variety of leading societies.[11] For Wallerstein (2004, 92), there has been but one instance of this category: capitalism, a system revolving around the market and having profit and growth as driving goal—"the priority of the *endless* accumulation of capital." In this division of world-systems, it should be noted, there is a chronological component at work: the phenomenon of world-empires is viewed as receding with the advent of the world-economy.

On the model of the world-economy, there is the issue of structuration and the mode of relationality. With respect to the former feature, this type of social network has yielded a set of fairly distinctive economic and political zones. Within such zones, the various individual societies can be situated and analyzed. Further, in each case, these zones largely account for the potential for economic development and the profile as political configurations of the societies in question. For Wallerstein, the set of zones constitutes a triad: core, semiperiphery, and periphery. With regard to the latter feature, this type of social network is driven by the economic exploitation of the periphery by the core, sustained by political dominance, which is in turn exercised by means of a wide array of social and cultural ways. For Wallerstein, this central impulse yields inequality: a periphery marked by poverty and weakness, and a core characterized by wealth and power.[12]

---

10. The glossary describes the term *world-empire* as a "large bureaucratic structure with a single political center and an axial division of labor, but multiple cultures" (Wallerstein 2004, 99).

11. The glossary explains the term *world-economy* as a "large axial division of labor with multiple political centers and multiple cultures" (Wallerstein 2004, 99).

12. The semiperiphery stands between the core and the periphery as a set of individual societies that share constitutive elements of both zones. As such, they possess

On the historical path of the world-economy, there is the problematic of rivalry. Within the core zone of the world-economy, given the presence of political plurality rather than centralization, a number of dominant societies exist. These are in competition with one another in the quest for endless accumulation of capital, and hence in the exploitation of the societies in the periphery. At times, one of these rival societies attains hegemony over the others, achieving supremacy in the economic sphere and dominance across the political sphere.[13] However, hegemonic status proves inherently unstable and inevitably temporary, given not only the competitive character of the core zone but also the shifting nature of the triad as a whole. For Wallerstein, it is this process of ascendancy and decline of hegemonic societies within the core that provides the foundations for charting the historical path of the modern world-system of capitalism.

In broad strokes, this trajectory unfolds as follows.[14] At the beginning, between 1600 and 1750, capitalism flourished in northern Europe. At this point, within a core zone constituted by the United Kingdom, the Netherlands, and Belgium, it was the Netherlands that gained the role of hegemonic power. Subsequently, through the end of the nineteenth century, capitalism extended to other parts of Europe and was brought to many areas of the world. During this period, the United Kingdom emerged as the hegemonic society, displacing the Netherlands but in competition with France throughout. Then, by the middle of the twentieth century, capitalism ruled the entire globe. Toward the early part of the century, Germany and Japan vied for world hegemony. By midcentury, however, after World War II, it was the United States that became the hegemonic power, replacing the United Kingdom but in competition with the Soviet

---

a differential economy: development in one area and underdevelopment in another. In the glossary, Wallerstein (2004, 97) explains that their production involves a "fairly even distribution" of "core-like and peripheral-like products": trading the former to the peripheral zone and the latter to the core zone. They also possess a "special kind of politics": a central position that serves as protection for the core from the periphery.

13. In the glossary, Wallerstein contrasts his narrower definition of the term with the looser definition of Antonio Gramsci, for whom hegemony involved rule of the dominant with the consent of the population. In world-system theory, he explains, it refers to situations "in which one state combines economic, political, and financial superiority over other strong states, and therefore has both military and cultural leadership as well" (Wallerstein 2004, 94).

14. Here I follow the summary provided by Seidman 2013, 285.

Union throughout the Cold War. For Wallerstein, the decade of the sixties signified the initial undoing of such hegemonic status, due to a variety of global developments. This, in turn, set in motion a crisis of the world-system that perdures to our days—despite the cessation of the Cold War in 1989, the dissolution of the Soviet Union in 1991, and the resultant position of the United States as the sole superpower.

World-System in Crisis

Wallerstein describes the crisis of the world-system as a long-lasting and ever-worsening process. It begins after some twenty-five years of global order and stability, from 1945 to about 1970, following the conflagration and devastation of the Second World War. Such a state of affairs was secured and maintained by the rise of a new hegemon on the world scene, the United States. This twofold process of hegemonic consolidation and decline is portrayed by Wallerstein in several pieces published in the *New Left Review* in the early years of the century. The first, "The Curve of American Power," appeared shortly before the Great Recession of 2008, while the second, "Structural Crises," followed not long thereafter (Wallerstein 2006, 2010). As such, both were written from within the vortex of a world-system perceived as under intense duress—marked by a twofold sense of encroaching decline regarding the past and growing uncertainty regarding the future.

Both pieces address the same phenomenon; they do so, however, in different ways. They proceed from different perspectives. The earlier analysis is more historical in orientation. It sets forth the crisis underway in terms of three geopolitical phases: (1) 1945 to 1970—a period of unquestioned hegemony, grounded in economic and political dominance; (2) 1970 to 2000—a time of relative decline, brought about by fundamental transformations; and (3) 2001 to 2025—a period of attempted hegemonic reversal, undermined by serious miscalculations and resulting in greater decline. The later analysis has a more structural orientation. It approaches the crisis from three different perspectives: (1) economics, (2) geopolitics, and (3) ideology. The two pieces also adopt different approaches. While the earlier one recurs to a wealth of detailed description, the latter emphasizes overarching scenarios. What they do possess in common is the point of departure: the relatively short-lived era of the United States as hegemonic power—a quarter-century marked by economic supremacy, geopolitical primacy, and ideological confidence.

32   Fernando F. Segovia

Such status, to be sure, was not unquestioned. The United States was haunted and challenged throughout by the presence of a powerful and determined adversary, the Soviet Union.[15] Its overall hegemony prevailed nonetheless, due to a deal forged between the two rivals: (1) a division of the world into corresponding spheres of influence—ruled by tacit agreement not to upset such bifurcation through direct military force; (2) the creation of two separate economic zones—a capitalist interstate system led by the United States and a collective protectionist system led by the USSR; and (3) an agreement to engage in ideological denunciations of one another—a rhetorical separation of the world into free and totalitarian (US) or bourgeois and socialist (USSR) camps. Despite the fundamental agreement in place, there were ups and downs throughout. These Wallerstein (2006, 4) refers to as "flies in the ointment": (1) the economic recovery of Europe and Asia, within the capitalist sphere; and (2) the geopolitical assertion of the Third World, beyond the imposed spheres of influence. By and large, however, the agreement kept, under the threat of mutual nuclear annihilation.

In what follows, I summarize the course of the world-system in terms of the historical phases outlined in the earlier study (Wallerstein 2006). In so doing, I follow the overarching scenarios laid out in the later study, though with the earlier piece and its wealth of information in mind throughout (Wallerstein 2010).

Phase 1: Unquestioned Hegemony

From 1945 to 1970, Wallerstein argues, a conjunction of three pivotal developments involving the United States took place. First, from the point of view of economics, these years witnessed a process of unprecedented expansion—"the most expansive Kondratieff A-upturn that the capitalist world-economy had ever known" (Wallerstein 2010, 133).[16]

---

15. Such contestation is present even in the first phase of unquestioned hegemony (Wallerstein 2010, 2). While wielding economic supremacy and geopolitical primacy, even cultural centrality, the military domain proved troubling. With a large standing army and a growing nuclear arsenal, the USSR challenged any dominance in this regard.

16. In the glossary of terms, Wallerstein (2004, 96) provides a succinct explanation of Kondratieff cycles: "the basic cycles of expansion and stagnation in the capitalist world-economy." Each is said to last from fifty to sixty years, involving an

During this time, the United States attained and exercised economic dominance through a quasimonopoly of the leading products behind the expansion.[17] Such a position yielded considerable profits and hence a vast accumulation of capital.[18] Second, from a geopolitical perspective, this period represented an era of overall order and peace—"a relatively stable situation required for profit-making" (134). During this time, the United States achieved and maintained global dominance through a quasimonopoly of geopolitical power. Such a position allowed it to "set the rules by which the interstate system operates, to assure its smooth functioning and to maximize the flow of accumulated capital to its citizens and productive enterprises" (134).[19]

Last, from the point of view of ideology, these years witnessed a process of unprecedented success for the antisystemic movements comprising the old left (communists, social democrats, national-liberation movements)—the attainment of "a position ... of political centrality and considerable strength around 1950," reflecting a "summit of their mobilizing power

---

A-phase of expansion and a B-phase of stagnation. They are so named after the figure of Nikolai Dimitriyevich Kondratieff (1892–1938), a Russian economist who became a very influential figure in Soviet economics but who eventually fell out of favor with the authorities and was ultimately executed during the Great Purge of Joseph Stalin (1934–1939).

17. The reason is evident (Wallerstein 2006, 2). At the end of the Second World War, the industrial plants of the major industrial powers stood largely in ruins, save for that of the United States, which remained not only untouched but actually strengthened. This situation allowed it to produce all key industrial products without any real competition from its would-be rivals. Further, given the devastation, "many of these countries suffered from food shortages, unstable currencies, and acute balance of payment problems"—and they looked to the US for assistance.

18. This period, argues Wallerstein (2006, 7), "was buoyed by the concept of 'development'—the idea that somehow, by adopting the right state policy, every country could achieve the standard of living of the wealthiest countries." Such was the goal, with variations, pursued by all geopolitical divisions—the United States, the Soviet Union, and the Third World. The "path to a promised land of prosperity" was well laid out: industrialization, urbanization, better methods of agriculture as well as education, and short-term protectionism.

19. In contrast to a Kondratieff cycle, Wallerstein (2010, 134) points out, a hegemonic cycle entails a far longer period of time. It is marked by "a long struggle with other potential hegemons," from which the hegemonic power emerges upon the attainment of economic superiority over its rivals and the waging of a "thirty years' war" with its major rival. In the case of the United States, the thirty years' war is identified as 1914–1945, the period comprising the two world wars.

34   Fernando F. Segovia

... from 1945 to 1968" (135). During this time, the United States, acting from a position of strength and seeking to preserve it, opted for certain strategic decisions that allowed for a consolidation of such forces. In the economic realm, it did so via concessions to worker demands for material improvement—over costly interruptions to the process of production. In the geopolitical realm, it proceeded via concessions to colonial demands for decolonization—over costly recourse to repressive measures. By the mid-1960s, "the Old Left movements," states Wallerstein, "had achieved their historic goal of state power almost everywhere."[20]

Phase 2: Relative Decline

This state of affairs began to unravel in 1965–1970, ushering in a time of profound transformations during the last three decades of the twentieth century, 1970 to 2000. From an economic angle, these years mark the onset of the Kondratieff B-downturn, as expansion turned to stagnation. "The problem for capitalists is that all monopolies are self-liquidating, due to the fact that new producers can enter the world market" (Wallerstein 2010, 134), and, as a result, "the degree of competition rises, prices go down and therefore profits go down too." That is precisely what began to happen at this point.[21] From a geopolitical standpoint, this period also signals the start of hegemonic decline. "The problem for the hegemonic power is the same as that facing a leading industry: its monopoly is self liquidating"

---

20. The signs adduced for such success are worth mentioning (Wallerstein 2010, 136). First, with regard to communists, one-third of the world was now under the rule of communist parties. Second, with respect to social democrats, in another one-third of the world, they now either ruled or alternated rule, while their model of the welfare state was adopted even by conservative parties. Third, with regard to national-liberation fronts, power was now in their hands throughout most of the colonial world, while populism reigned in Latin America.

21. The ideal of developmentalism from the 1960s yielded to the adoption of an alternative "path to the promised land" in the 1980s: the Washington consensus and the neoliberal agenda of inversion regarding developmentalist principles and objectives (Wallerstein 2008, 8). In the midst of severe economic difficulties, new dogmas were formulated, as the "'market' rather than the welfare of the population now became the measure of all appropriate activity of the state." While the role of the state sector was downplayed and gutted, that of the private sector was praised and stimulated. The regimes of Margaret Thatcher in the United Kingdom (1979–1990) and Ronald Reagan (1981–1989) in the United States led the charge.

(134). Just as inevitable military interventions bring about loss of capital and lives within the hegemon, so does the steadily rising power of competitors lead to self-assertion and resistance abroad. "The hegemon," declares Wallerstein (134), "enters into a process of gradual decline relative to the rising power."[22]

From an ideological angle, these years further mark the beginning of decline for the old left and with it for the ideological foundation upholding the world-system. "The world revolution of 1968," which Wallerstein (136) sees as comprising 1966 to 1970, "changed all that."[23] In addition to the United States, the revolutionaries had three major targets in sight: (1) the USSR, for its role in maintaining the global status quo; (2) the old left, for its failure to change the world upon accession to power, as promised; and (3) the old left, again, for bypassing the marginalized by reason of ethnicity, gender, race, and sexuality. The revolution itself proved fleeting: "It rose like a phoenix, burned bright across the globe, but by the mid-1970s seemed to be extinguished everywhere" (136–37). However, its accusations were destructive and its consequences momentous. On the one hand, the antisystemic movements of yore would no longer be able to mobilize any degree of fundamental social change. On the other hand, centrist liberalism would no longer be able to function as the foundational ideology behind the world-system. In short, Wallerstein (136) concludes, the revolution of 1968 was "both an enormous political success and an enormous political failure."

Most momentous still is a third consequence of the revolution. Given the economic turn to stagnation, the geopolitical onset of decline, and the ideological collapse of the status quo, through the undermining of the old left and the displacement of centrist liberalism, the "world right," long under the constraints imposed by the hegemonic system, proceeded to launch a project of its own, what would become known as the model

---

22. The objective of the United States during this period was to manage and thus slow down the decline of hegemony (Wallerstein 2008, 9). This it sought to accomplish in three ways: (1) partnering with allies in constructing a global geopolitical policy—partly successful; (2) working against the proliferation of nuclear weapons—partly successful; and (3) extending economic and financial involvement in the Third World—most successful.

23. Wallerstein (2008, 6) defines it as a "world revolution" for two reasons: (1) it took place throughout the world, and (2) it took on the entire geopolitical division of the world in place—the West, the Soviet bloc, and the Third World.

36 Fernando F. Segovia

of neoliberal globalization. Its goal was the reversal of "all the gains of the lower strata during the Kondriateff A-phase"; as such, it sought "to reduce the costs of production, to destroy the welfare state and to slow the decline of US power" (Wallerstein 2010, 137).[24] At first sight, the year 1989 appeared to signify—given the disbanding of the Eastern bloc and the subsequent dissolution of the Soviet Union in 1991—the culmination of the project, bringing about a sense of triumphalism in such circles through the 1990s. However, as with the revolution of 1968, Wallerstein (137) classifies this much longer crusade of the world right as "both a great success and a great failure."

Phase 3: Attempted Restoration and Greater Decline

Writing in 2010, with the effects of the Great Recession still very much in evidence all around, Wallerstein ventures a critical assessment of the first quarter of the century, 2001 to 2025. He surveys what has transpired and weighs what is yet to come. Such analysis focuses, quite understandably, on economics. On the one hand, the "great success" of the world right comes about in the accumulation of capital through financial speculation rather than productive efficiency. In this regard, as in all Kondratieff-B phases, "the key mechanism has been the fostering of consumption via indebtedness; this time, however, this strategy has accounted for the 'biggest speculative mania' ever" (Wallerstein 2010, 137). On the other hand, its "great failure" is signified by the recurring financial bubbles of the system. These surface from the 1970s, through the 1980s and 1990s, and into the 2000s, with the crash of 2008 as a nadir in this regard (240).

The result has been the onset of "systemic gridlock, from which exit will be extremely difficult" to secure—an era marked by ever greater fluctuations, ever greater fear, and ever greater alienation (137). Such gridlock constitutes a "structural crisis," brought about by three key developments: (1) the sheer magnitude of the "economic collapse" of 2008, (2) the

---

24. This program would be internationalized in the Third World through the World Trade Organization, with demands for deregulation and privatization. The result proved quite contrary to the promise: "the disappearance of safety nets, increasing rates of unemployment, and declining currencies" alongside the creation of spectacular wealth in elite circles (Wallerstein 2008, 13). "The picture," argues Wallerstein (13), "was one of greatly increased internal inequalities in the less developed countries of the world."

increased pressure on profit-making and capital accumulation within the system by the relative growth of Asia and the rapid expansion of China, and (3) the most dramatic rise ever in the production costs (personnel, inputs, taxation) of the world-economy (240). This crisis brings about, in turn, a "bifurcation of the systemic process": raising the question of systemic replacement rather than mending and creating "an arena of struggle for the successor system," with no clear vision of outcome (140).

In the earlier piece of 2006, Wallerstein had provided a geopolitical assessment of the times. During the triumphalist decade of the 1990s for the world right, a neoconservative movement came together in the United States in a think tank known as the Program for the New American Century. This group rejected the previous approach in place, managing the relative decline of American hegemony, and proposed instead a vigorous path toward hegemonic reversal and restoration. Toward this end, the program called for the United States to abandon multilateralism for unilateralism in dealing with its allies. The problem behind relative decline had to do with political timidity and bumbling, not with structural changes. Consequently, they advanced a three-pronged strategy, grounded in intimidation: (1) adherence to nuclear nonproliferation by resisting countries, alongside freedom for the United States to expand its own arsenal of weapons; (2) abstention from participation in international treaties that would limit the national interests of the country; and (3) removal of Saddam Hussein from power in Iraq. With the election of President George W. Bush in 2000, many of these individuals were appointed to positions of power in government, and, with the attack of al-Qaeda on 11 September 2001, their proposal for the new American century became the hallmark of the Bush presidency (2001–2009).[25]

On all three fronts, argues Wallerstein, the grand strategy backfired. With regard to the initial move, Saddam Hussein was indeed ousted, and swiftly so. Afterward, however, the United States found itself trapped in

---

25. Wallerstein (2008, 15) describes the grand strategy as follows: begin with the overthrow of Hussein; then, move on to control all major threats to hegemony through the power of intimidation: claims to greater autonomy on the part of Western Europe; nuclear proliferation by Iran and North Korea; and resistance to a resolution of the Israeli-Palestinian conflict by the Arab states. The rationale is well captured: "If they could achieve these three objectives rapidly and conclusively, all serious opposition to the US hegemony would disintegrate and the world would enter a 'new American century'" (15).

a costly and protracted military as well as political venture. With respect to the perceived threats to its hegemony, the outcome was no less counterproductive, in the wake of failure in Iraq. First, the reaction of Europe was to exert even greater autonomy—"a degree of political independence unknown since 1945" (Wallerstein 2006, 15). Second, the response of the would-be nuclear proliferators, Iran and North Korea, was to press ahead with their nuclear programs—"the surest defense of the existing regimes was to speed up the acquisition of a nuclear arsenal" (16). Third, the reaction of the Arab countries was to continue the same course of ambiguity as before—"aghast at the political consequences of the invasion of Iraq—both for Iraq and for their own countries" (16). In addition, an economic consequence is ventured. The failure in Iraq also affected the neoliberal model prior to the crash of 2008, as the countries of the South showed greater resistance to its economic objectives and policies.

In sum, the grand strategy of reversal and restoration launched during the Bush presidency only served to "accelerate the decline of US hegemony rather than reverse it" (17). Just as the collapse of economic policy brought about a "structural crisis," so did the collapse of geopolitical policy bring about "a relatively unstructured, multilateral division of geopolitical power" (17). Just as the economic crisis leads to the question of systemic replacement and a struggle for power, so does the geopolitical backfiring yield "a number of regional centres of varying strength manoeuvering for advantage," with "no overwhelming superiority … in any one of these centres" (17). In both pieces Wallerstein weighs a number of possible scenarios for the future.

Beyond the World-System

A few years later, during the latter half of the 2010s, Wallerstein (2015, 2018) revisited the crisis of the world-system by way of two commentaries, first in 2015 and then in 2018. Both underline the steep hegemonic decline of the United States and the resultant turmoil in the world-system. In the earlier commentary, "It Is Painful to Live amidst Chaos," the focus is on both economics and geopolitics; the verdict is clear: "The world-system is self-destructing." The economic order is marked by wild swings across all measures (markets, employment rates, exchange rates, energy costs), bringing "pain to the vast majority of the world's population." The geopolitical order reveals ever-shifting alliances among a number of powers vying for autonomy, yielding a highly unstable "multipower world." As it

Reading in These Times

stands, therefore, the world-system "cannot survive"; only the question of replacement is appropriate. In the later commentary, "Twenty-First Century Geopolitics: Fluidity Everywhere," the focus lies solely on geopolitics; the verdict is no less trenchant: "overall chaotic zigzagging." This geopolitical order is traced throughout the world, as countries pursue their own interests (most pointedly so with respect to Russia and China), yielding a situation of "great danger," especially in the face of "nuclear accidents, or mistakes, or folly."

In describing the world-system as having reached a point of bifurcation, where reform is altogether out of the question and a new system is urgently in order, it is imperative to analyze the alternatives in play. Toward this end, Wallerstein identifies two key features of structural transition, both ideological in character. First, in such circumstances, small social mobilizations can unleash considerable repercussions, as "political agency prevails over structural determinism" (Wallerstein 2010, 141). Second, in such circumstances, core groups within the alternative projects find it hard to dictate the way to the ranks or to persuade others to join, given "multiple players, advocating different emphases" (141). The alternatives are laid out at the conclusion of "Structural Crises" (Wallerstein 2010).

On one side, named as the "spirit of Davos," the successor system envisioned would follow or sharpen the lines of the present capitalist system—"hierarchical, exploitative, polarizing" (140). On the other side, named as the "spirit of Porto Alegre," the successor system would adopt radically different lines—"relatively democratic and relatively egalitarian" (141). Given the limited power attributed to core groups, a division is identified within each alternative. Among followers of Davos, the contrasting tendencies are depicted as follows: a repressive system in which the rule of leaders over subjects is emphasized alongside a meritocratic system in which a sizable number of subjects are co-opted by leaders. Among followers of Porto Alegro, the contrasting tendencies are portrayed as follows: a decentralized system in which innovation is allowed without the creation of a class of experts removed from society alongside an integrated system in which innovation flows from a class of experts on top. Rather than two alternatives, therefore, Wallerstein unfolds an array of four options.

Given such analysis, the structural transition underway will involve not only struggle between the opposing camps but also struggles between contending tendencies in each camp. In effect, he states, "This is a confusing situation, morally and politically; the outcome is fundamentally uncertain" (Wallerstein 2010, 142). What is to be done? Not long before

40 Fernando F. Segovia

death, Wallerstein offered a set of practical suggestions, all grounded in the tradition(s) of antisystemic movements, and hence in the spirit of Porto Alegre. These may be approached in terms of immediacy. At the most pressing pole of the spectrum, steps must be taken to minimize the pain caused by the crisis—aiding those most in need, protecting judicial and political rights, attending to the environment. Next, the struggle against inequality along the various axes of human identity must continue to be waged—gender, class, race-ethnicity, and religion. Next, the development of alternative modes of production must be entertained and pursued—away from profit as the driving force and toward a model of sustainable growth. At the most distant pole of the spectrum, earnest discussion must take place, in comparative fashion, regarding the successor system espoused—drawing its would-be contours and outlining working strategies while on the way. In the end, Wallerstein gives the spirit of Porto Alegre "at best a fifty-fifty chance of creating a better world system." Not a bad chance in itself, but one that must be taken anyway, "even if it escapes us"; indeed, "What more useful thing can any of us do?"

From the Global South: Boaventura de Sousa Santos

Like Wallerstein, de Sousa Santos (1940–) has played a leading role in social theory from the last decades of the twentieth century into the first decades of the twenty-first. Despite varying academic foundations, theoretical orientations, and intellectual emphases, the two share many critical traits in common as well. Three of these I should like to highlight here. To begin with, the range of interests and pursuits exhibited by de Sousa Santos has been similarly expansive. Among these, the following feature prominently: sociology of law, geopolitics of epistemology, and economics of globalization. In addition, de Sousa Santos qualifies, and eminently so, as a public intellectual. His critical voice has displayed a wide-ranging grasp of the world, with an unrelenting focus on the divide between Global North and Global South and a corresponding commitment to the silenced and overridden lands and peoples of the Global South. Last, the work undertaken by de Sousa Santos has been similarly shaped by his early experience in the crucible of the sixties. Such was the case not only with regard to his formation in the First World but also with respect to his encounter with the Second World and his involvement in the Third World.

For a critical overview of his role and voice in social theory, a trajectory of his academic-professional life is to the point. This trajectory,

Reading in These Times 41

which is perforce limited given the vast output of his scholarly work and the countless number of academic achievements, can be outlined, for analytical purposes, in terms of three major periods.[26] These can be described as follows: to begin with, an expansive pursuit of postgraduate education, thoroughly international in scope and decidedly formative in character (1960–1973); then, a long, close, and varied professional association with the University of Coimbra (1973–2001); and last, a division of academic residence between Portugal, continuing thereby his long-standing relationship with Coimbra, and the United States, opening a new relationship with a major school of law (2001–present).

The first period involves an extended and distinguished process of advanced education. Having earned a degree in law from the University of Coimbra, Portugal, in 1963, he pursued postgraduate studies in law in West Germany, Portugal, and the United States. First, in the early 1960s, he undertook studies in the philosophy of law at the Free University of Berlin (1963–1964). Then, in the mid-1960s, he focused on criminal law at Coimbra (1964–1965), while serving as assistant professor in the law school (1964–1969). Subsequently, in the late 1960s and early 1970s, he specialized in the sociology of law at Yale University (1969–1973), obtaining a master of law degree on the way to a doctor of the science of law degree in 1970 and 1973, respectively.

The second period revolves around major lines of development at Coimbra, two of which I single out. First, upon his return, he was instrumental in launching a school of economics, which included a component in social theory. Within this department, he began as associate professor (1973–1987), continued as professor until retirement, and since then holds the rank of professor emeritus. Second, from 1978 through 2019, he served as director of the Centre for Social Studies. This was designed as a research and training institution, geared toward inter- and transdisciplinary work—involving the human sciences, the arts, and the social sciences—and toward critical knowledge in quest of a world marked by inclusivity and justice.[27] The third period brings a transcontinental

---

26. This trajectory I take from his own webpage. See de Sousa Santos 2021.

27. On this critical orientation, the self-description of the center is worth noting. Its mission, from inception, is made explicit: "Since its foundation, in 1978, CES has been conducting research with and for an inclusive, innovative and reflexive society by promoting creative critical approaches in the face of some of the most urging challenges of contemporary societies." Likewise, the edge of such research is pointedly

42 Fernando F. Segovia

commitment. Following a number of visiting appointments, he accepted an annual, half-year position as distinguished legal scholar in the Law School of the University of Wisconsin at Madison. This appointment he has held from 2001 through today.

The formative period proved crucial for all that followed. This de Sousa Santos explains in the course of an interview, conducted by Aram Ziai (2013), for the journal *Development and Change*, published by the International Institute of Social Studies at The Hague. With regard to his sojourn in the Federal Republic of Germany, he offers a revealing two-fold reflection. On the one hand, this experience affirmed for him the privileges afforded by an open, democratic society. Having come from the context of an "obscurantist dictatorship" in his native Portugal, he notes, West Berlin represented "a university community that bred democratic values."[28] On the other hand, this experience reinforced the specter cast by a closed, authoritarian society. As a frequent visitor to East Berlin, he mentions the "stark contrast" provided by the Stalinist élan of the time in the German Democratic Republic, which "strengthened my democratic ideals and prevented me from becoming a communist." To his studies in Germany, therefore, he traces his commitment to democratic principles and his rejection of communist ways.

With respect to his stay in the United States, he again offers a keen twofold insight. On the one hand, while studying at Yale itself, he witnessed the multiple social upheavals that were raging across the country. This context, he points out, led him to Marxism, whereby he devoted himself to "participating in study groups to read and discuss *Das Kapital.*" On

---

described: "CES scientific strategy aims to democratize knowledge, revitalize human rights and to contribute to the establishment of science as a public commodity. We pursue this mission by continuously reshaping our research fields in a response to the needs of the society." Further, its scope is outlined: "Our work covers a wide range of scientific activities and scope, at the national and international level, with particular focus on the North-South and South-North dialogues."

28. The reference here is to the Estado Novo in Portugal and the dictatorship of António de Oliveira Salazar (1933–1974). In a sharp analysis of its political and ideological origins, Ernesto Castro Leal (2016, 129) describes the political culture of the Estado Novo as "conservative, nationalist, anti-liberal and anti-democratic, integrating elements of totalitarian political regimes"—single party, political police, political courts, political prisons, concentration camp, official censorship, idolatry of the chief, state propaganda, a civil militia, and official youth organizations. This model was advanced in reaction to the profound crisis of the First Republic (1910–1926).

the other hand, while doing field work in Brazil for his doctoral research, he encountered abject marginalization and poverty, at the time already within the historical-political period of the military dictatorship (Napolitano 2018). In his role as participant observer in one of the many *favelas* surrounding the city of Rio de Janeiro, he witnessed the struggles "for the decency and the dignity of their lives" among those living "in the most degrading and undignifed conditions." This context, he declares, brought about a decisive change in his life, "not just in terms of my political and theoretical preferences but also in terms of the epistemological and existential foundations of my identity as a scholar-activist." To his studies in the United States, therefore, he dates his turn to Marxist theory and his commitment to engaged criticism.

This life of activism is well captured in a review piece by José-Manuel Barreto (2017), a Colombian scholar similarly active in the areas of international law, decolonial theory, and ethics of emotions. Barreto identifies three paradigm shifts in the thought of de Sousa Santos, which lead to three radical transformations in legal and social theory: the postmodern, the postcolonial, and the emotional-aesthetic. These three phases are presented as sequential in nature, but by no means as mutually exclusive.[29] The first, postmodern turn centers on the philosophy of law. Barreto describes de Sousa Santos as "one of the first and the few" to undertake a critique of the principles underlying modern jurisprudence and to introduce a set of concepts toward a postmodern reconfiguration.[30] A second, postcolonial turn presents a much broader scope, encompassing both the realm of the law and that of society. Its ramifications affect epistemological models, critical theory, and Eurocentric vision. The third, emotional-aesthetic turn bears a twofold dimension. The emotional concern, conveyed by the notion of the Global South, addresses the suffering brought by colonialism on so many peoples. The aesthetic concern, channeled through adoption

---

29. This overview of de Sousa Santos's (1995) work takes as point of departure his volume *Toward a New Common Sense*, which Barreto describes as the "culmination" of the first, postmodern stage. At the same time, he notes, "some themes of the current post-colonial moment are already present there."

30. The critique touched on such modern staples as "universals, foundationalism, progress, rationalism, the state and individualism." The proposal argued for such postmodern concepts as "difference, scale, margins, plural legal orders, transnational law, multiculturalism ... and constructivism," along with "the spatial turn and the argumentative strategy of mapping" (Barreto 2017, 558).

44 Fernando F. Segovia

of hip-hop, attends to the use of the arts in movements of social protests. The earlier turns, it should be noted, anticipate the later ones, while the later ones expand on the earlier turns.

The postcolonial shift is worth amplifying insofar as it gives rise to central features of the project advanced by de Sousa Santos. With regard to the theory of knowledge, de Sousa Santos follows historical materialism and postmodern thinking in moving away from the dominant tradition of subjectivism.[31] While the former emphasizes economics and history and the latter contingency and solidarity in relation to knowledge, he foregrounds a connection with politics. This move calls for an ecology of knowledges, with particular attention to popular and resisting knowledges that have been suppressed or subordinated—the concept of epistemologies of the Global South. With respect to critical theory, he calls for a different type of emancipatory discourse, given the crisis brought about by the use of Marxism in support of oppression and by the collapse of real communism. This move envisions the transformation of social structures, national and global alike—the notion of intercultural human rights. With regard to Eurocentric vision, de Sousa Santos follows the path of various lines of thought—such as subaltern studies in India and the geopolitics of knowledge in Latin America—in calling for a reformulation of hegemonic thought. This move argues for the adoption of decolonizing knowledge— the concept of epistemic justice.

In this last respect, Barreto (2017, 559) places de Sousa Santos within a broad-sided critical movement intent on exposing "the historical bias" and "the intellectual limits" of Eurocentric knowledge. Such a path entailed a perspectival move from the Global North to the Global South, signified by attention to the history of colonialism as well as to the divide (economic, political, epistemic) between the two realms. What emerged therefrom is a critique of the hierarchical conception of knowledge at the core of modernity: the North as "universal, objective, and valid" and the South as "local, subjective, and false"—the notion of abyssal thinking. The way out of this oppositional abyss lies not in reversal but in deconstruction, through a coming together where both perspectives "are equally valid and converge

---

31. This tradition Barreto traces from the seventeenth century through the twentieth century, from René Descartes (1596–1650) to Edmund Husserl (1859–1938). It is defined as the search for truth, within the relation between subject and object, "by breaking with the worldly conditions of the process of knowledge and relying on universal or a priori notions"—hence an idealist reflection (Barreto 2017, 558).

in a horizontal and intercultural dialogue." Such dialogue has direct economic and political consequences, addressing the process of globalization from above and seeking justice on a global scale.

Abyssal Line in Place

The core concept of the abyssal line, present widely throughout his work, is pointedly addressed by de Sousa Santos (2018b) in the introduction to *The End of the Cognitive Empire*, "Why the Epistemologies of the South?" Here he presents the project of Western modernity—well captured elsewhere as "the Eurocentric socio-cultural, capitalist and colonialist project of the modern period" (Ziai 2013, 728)—as having drawn an abyssal line between the Global North and the Global South. This line bears economic and political as well as scientific and legal dimensions. Its trajectory is traced from the fifteenth century through our times, yielding three major developments in all.

First, since the fifteenth century, the line has been marked by the rule of patriarchy as well as by the spread of capitalism and colonialism. Second, with the seventeenth century, it is intensified through the development of modern science and modern law, leading to an emplacement of an epistemic abyss as well, a division between the epistemologies of the North and the epistemologies of the South. Here the term *epistemology* is taken to signify "the conditions of identification and validation of knowledge in general, as well as justified belief" (de Sousa Santos 2018b, 2). Such emplacement constitutes a project of epistemicide, that is, a sustained and systematic attempt to annihilate the epistemologies of the Global South. Third, in the twenty-first century, the line remains in place, but in an ever-sharper state of fundamental crisis.

For de Sousa Santos, it should be noted, these designations constructed by the abyssal line laid down by the modern project are primarily epistemological, nongeographical, in nature. However, they are also said to bear a prominent geographical dimension, given the "uneven development of capitalism and the persistence of Western-centric colonialism" (de Sousa Santos 2018b, 2). There is, therefore, a partial overlap between the epistemological and the geographical significations. In effect, the epistemological North may be found in the geographical South, just as the epistemological South may be found in the geographical North. Consequently, just as there are many Norths or "little Europes," often occupying positions of dominance, throughout Africa, Asia and Oceania, and Latin

46 Fernando F. Segovia

American and the Caribbean, so are there many Souths, often waging struggles of resistance, throughout Europe and North America (2).

What is the nature of this epistemic abyss? While there are many epistemologies of the North, a common set of assumptions is said to underlie them all (de Sousa Santos 2018b, 6). These may be grouped around three categories representing key dimensions of the epistemic process: the constitution of reality, the nature of knowledge, and the conception of science. On the view of reality, the following stand: (1) a perception of nature as res extensa or the material world as a whole, (2) an understanding of time as linear, and (3) a definition of truth as the representation of reality. Regarding knowledge, one finds (1) a clear distinction between agent and object, knower and known; (2) a stance of universalism, whereby validity is altogether divorced from context; and (3) the espousal of neutrality in matters social and political as essential for objectivity. On the view of science, the following belong: (1) its definition as rigorous knowledge, on the basis of which it is granted absolute priority; (2) an explanation of rigor in terms of determination; and (3) a sense of progress by way of academic disciplines and critical specialization.

This privileged validity accorded to the rigorous knowledge embodied in modern science is further explained as grounded in two premises (de Sousa Santos 2018b, 5). On the one hand, such knowledge, based as it is on close observation and controlled experimentation, is accepted and circulated as the unique creation of the West. As a result, the scientific knowledge produced by the West is utterly differentiated from all scientific knowledges produced outside the West. On the other hand, such knowledge, given its rigorous character and its instrumental potential, is advanced and proclaimed as superior. As such, the scientific knowledge pursued by the West is utterly differentiated from all other ways of knowing, whether lay or popular, practical or commonsensical, intuitive or religious.

The combined effect of such epistemic assumptions and such scientific claims is to create a dialectic of superiority and inferiority, yielding a definition of the Other by way of a definition of the self. The result is what de Sousa Santos (2018b, 5) describes as "the exceptionalism of the Western world vis-à-vis the rest of the world."[32] Such a sense of exceptionalism

---

32. Since the seventeenth century, the division created by the abyssal line is also described in terms of two social groups: the fully human and the subhuman. For the

has rendered the scientific knowledge of the North as dominant and normative. As such, it grounds its representation of the world as universal, justifying thereby any transformation in terms of its own needs and projects. Similarly, it sets its forms of social relationships as universal, defining thereby the canons of validity, normality, and ethicality. In so doing, given the dialectic, it approaches any knowledge of the South as ignorance or superstition. Thereby, it denies the South any power of representing and transforming the world as well as of setting and defining the forms of sociability in its own terms. As a result, argues de Sousa Santos (6), "The South is the problem; the North is the solution."

For de Sousa Santos, as anticipated earlier, this abyssal line wrought by capitalism and colonialism, patriarchy, and modern science and modern law is by no means a thing of the past but has remained firmly entrenched through present times. Throughout, it has been responsible for systematic "injustice, oppression, and destruction" of the South (de Sousa Santos 2018b, 1). For the last forty years, under the guise of neoliberalism, this state of affairs has not changed; to the contrary, the abyss has been reinforced and expanded, yielding even greater devastation. Indeed, ours are times in which "the most morally repugnant forms of social inequality and social discrimination are becoming politically acceptable," insofar as the modern forces of resistance and visions of alternatives have waned, finding themselves "everywhere on the defensive" and "largely coopted by neoliberalism" (de Sousa Santos 2018a, vii).[33] Ours, therefore, are times in which utopias cannot even be imagined. Nonetheless, de Sousa Santos argues, such a sense of heightened and teleological exceptionalism has entered into a definitive state of crisis and cries out for radical transformation.

Abyssal Line in Crisis

This scenario de Sousa Santos has recently approached from the perspective of the Covid-19 pandemic of 2019 and its ongoing aftermath. This he has

---

former, the latter are dispensable. This division represents a fragmentation of humanity as a whole. See Fontevecchia 2022.

33. These forces had been at work since the beginning of the twentieth century: one was the way of swift revolution and the other the way of gradual reform. For both, social transformation was the aim—the vision of a society more just and less violent. In their absence, what prevails instead is no hope and much fear—a sense that things are bad today and will turn worse tomorrow. See Fontevecchia 2022.

48 Fernando F. Segovia

done by way of op-ed pieces and extended interviews. Here I draw on two in particular, both appearing in leftist Argentinian dailies: an interview in *Perfil* on the legitimacy of the neoliberal model, and a column in *Página12* on the future of the model (Fontevecchia 2022; de Sousa Santos 2020). These reflections provide a critical analysis of the neoliberal order that has embodied and upheld the abyssal line since the 1980s. I would highlight three concerns: the breakdown of established certainties, the emergence of a fraught period of transition, and the call for a particular path forward. While the pandemic provides the central angle of vision, it is also placed within a broader background. It also constitutes a major economic crisis, the second since the start of the century, following the Great Recession of 2008. Further, it bears large-scale political consequences as well.

With regard to established certainties, de Sousa Santos identifies a set of four pillars fundamental to neoliberalism. First, the tenet that capitalism has achieved a decisive and definitive triumph over Soviet socialism, its major historical rival. Second, the priority of markets in both the economic realm and the social sphere, yielding a variety of results: privatization and deregulation of economic and social policies alongside reduction of the role of the state in the regulation of collective life. Third, the globalization of the economy based on comparative advantages in production and distribution. Last, the flexibilization of labor relations for the sake of employment and economic growth, yielding a brutal precariousness in the labor market. This neoliberal order, he argues, has fed on the disorder of human lives throughout, with disastrous consequences for many, especially so for those who entered the labor force in the 2000s.

What the pandemic brought to this order was a radical exposé of acute deficiencies and failures in the model. Such a state of affairs led, in turn, to a return of various principles, long silenced and discarded, regarding the disposition of the political-economic realm. First, the state alone, and not the markets, is able to protect the lives of the citizenry. Second, globalization can place the survival of the citizenry in danger, given the inability of countries to produce their own essential goods. Third, workers in precarious jobs prove to be the most vulnerable, since, upon termination, they lack any source of income as well as any umbrella of social protection. Finally, social-democratic and socialist alternatives are in order, on two counts: the ecological destruction wrought by capitalism has reached extreme limits, and countries that have not privatized or decapitalized their laboratories, such as China and Russia, have proved to be the most effective in producing and distributing vaccines.

Reading in These Times 49

The joint effect provided by the shaking of the fundamental pillars behind neoliberalism and the revival of repressed political-economic alternatives has yielded, among proponents of the model, a sense that the world has entered a new era—an era of disorder.[34] On the one hand, de Sousa Santos (2020) declares himself in full agreement with this appraisal. "The diagnosis that they offer is quite lucid," he states, "and the preoccupations that they reveal are real" (translation mine).[35] All the evidence presented to this effect, therefore, he accepts, declaring that disorder does indeed represent the order of the day. On the other hand, he finds, unlike such voices, a range of possibilities for the times beyond, from within the vortex of disaster. Such paths he classifies as "options more decisive and less comfortable that those that have prevailed in the last decades" (translation mine).[36]

Beyond the Abyssal Line

The spectrum of possibilities is drawn with the neoliberal model in mind: its platform for human development as well as its legacy of disasters unleashed on human lives. Its range extends from continued adherence to substantial change, with moderate adjustment in the middle. What the

---

34. This era of disorder is further described as one marked by weighty questions and weak answers (de Sousa Santos 2022). This evaluation regarding the state of present-day critical theory is altogether in line with his position on the waning of the traditional lines of opposition from the past and the turning to the path of transitionism for the future.

35. The originals are as follows: "El diagnóstico que hacen es muy lúcido y las preocupaciones que revelan son reales." Seven such preoccupations are highlighted, and they are worth listing here. (1) Workers' salaries in the Global North have not increased for thirty years, while social inequalities have continued to climb. (2) In their final stages of decline, empires tend to produce caricature leaders, who only serve to hasten the end. (3) The external debt of many countries has become unsustainable and unpayable, as has the credit debt of many families. (4) A number of countries have opted for the way of tourism, a path that is subject to permanent uncertainty. (5) China has hastened its trajectory toward becoming the first economy of the world. (6) The second wave of capitalist globalization (1980–2020) has reached its end, and no one knows what will follow. (7) The era of privatization in the social realm for the sake of profit seems to have reached its end.

36. The original runs as follows: "Estos diagnósticos, a veces esclarecedores, implican que entraremos en un período de opciones más decisivas y menos cómodas que las que han prevalecido en las últimas décadas."

model preached is clear: unlimited exploitation of nature and humans, infinite economic growth, priority of individualism and private property, and secularism. What the model produced is no less clear: impressive technological advances, certainly, but also contrary results—benefits for some social groups alongside exclusion for most social groups. Such inequality it created through domination: exploitation of workers—capitalism; oppression of races deemed inferior through appropriation of resources and knowledges—colonialism; and devaluation and oppression of women—patriarchy.[37] All such relations of inequality the pandemic rendered far more pronounced.

At one pole of the spectrum, there is the path of negationism. The sense of a new era of disorder is not accepted: neoliberalism will continue as the dominant model. The economic order has actually been strengthened rather than weakened by the crisis, while the social order, under duress, can be contained through an enhanced system of law and order on the part of the state. Given the threat from China, the model will likely undergo change, along the lines of a variation on *tribalismo nacionalista* ("national tribalism"; de Sousa Santos 2020). At the other pole, there lies the way of transitionism. The reality of a new era of disorder is not only accepted but accentuated: neoliberalism is no longer viable as a model. The pandemic is viewed as having brought the order in place, economic and political, since the sixteenth century to an end, as evidenced by a vast number of contrarian reactions. Such disorder is taken to signify a transition to other models of civilization. In the middle, there stands the path of reformism. A new era of disorder is readily acknowledged but viewed as manageable: neoliberalism can continue to function, to produce capital, but changes to the model are in order. In the economic sphere, a reduction in social inequalities is deemed imperative, but without changes to the core of the system. In the political realm, a continued alliance with low-intensity democracy is advocated, allowing for some human rights but without challenging the social order.

For de Sousa Santos (2020), as noted by Barreto, transitionism provides the only way forward, as the most hopeful and least harmful option for life human and nonhuman alike. It views the reigning disorder as an

---

37. For de Sousa Santos, all the forces of domination are coordinated and work together in drawing and maintaining the abyssal line. Consequently, no one force, not even capitalism, as was the case in former times, should be seen as primordial and grounding. See de Sousa Santos 2022.

era of "transición paradigmática hecha de varias transiciones"—a paradigmatic transition consisting of various transitions. What does such a transition imply? On the one hand, a dominant mode of individual and collective life—created by a particular economic-social-political-cultural system—begins to show growing difficulties in reproducing itself. On the other hand, more and more signs and practices begin to germinate within this mode of life—and underlying system—that point toward other, qualitatively different, forms of life. As such, transitionism implies a slow and difficult process.

Various characteristics are noted. First, a transition is intensely political, insofar as it presupposes an option between two horizons, the dystopian and the utopian. Over against the doing nothing of negationism or the doing little of reformism, it envisions a utopian future, which, by definition, bears infinite possibilities for doing. Second, it proves impossible to identify with certainty when a transition begins and ends. Present times may indeed be evaluated quite differently from a future perspective, perhaps even pointing to the transition as having begun much earlier. Last, a transition is not very visible for those who find themselves within it. It can be fully identified only after it has run its course. The description of the process is quite effective: "Es un tiempo de prueba y error, de avances y contratiempos, de cambios persistentes y efímeros, de modas y obsolescencias, de salidas disfrazadas de llegadas y viceversa" (de Sousa Santos 2020).[38]

In this way forward, tentative and uncertain as it is, the epistemologies of the South are to be used as beacon and resource. Such epistemologies survived the crusade of epistemicide and are already providing a vast number of opposing reactions, foci of resistance and alternatives, to the dominant model. Their expressions are many: (1) ecological activism of urban youth; (2) resistance to the invasion of territories and abandonment of the state on the part of peasants, peasants, indigenous and Afrodescendant groups, forest and river peoples; (3) reinvindication of the importance behind the multiple tasks performed by women; and (4) a new rebellious activism in the arts, especially so in the peripheries of large cities throughout the

---

38. No translation can capture the sense of searching and wandering conveyed by de Sousa Santos: "It is a time of trial and error, of advances and setbacks, of changes persistent and ephemeral, of fashions and obsolescences, of departures disguised as arrivals and vice versa."

world.[39] It is, therefore, out of the silenced and repressed Global South that a way out of the order imposed by the Global North is to be found. Not, however, by way of an inversion of the dialectic; rather, by way of mutual engagement in the face of disorder, as humanity sees "la flecha de la catástrofe ecológica viniendo hacia nosotros"—the arrow of ecological catastrophe coming our way. As rallying cry de Sousa Santos (2022) suggests the notion of "common goods," but this is a topic for another time.

A Concluding Comment

In searching for a critical posture suitable for these times, I called for recourse to social theory in the delineation of our times. In the light of my assessment of these times as critical, given a conjunction of major crises bringing about a crisis of the world-system as a whole, I appealed first, among the four currents of postmodernist social theory outlined by Seidman, to that strand whose focus revolves around world order. This I have done above, in counterbalancing fashion, through the choice of Wallerstein and de Sousa Santos. Wallerstein's analysis centers on the Global North, with due consideration of repercussions for the Global South, while de Sousa Santos's analysis focuses on the Global South, with due attention to implications for the Global North. Both approaches proceed along the historiographical lines of the Annales school: analysis from the perspective of *la longue durée* (Wallerstein 2009b). As such, they trace the long-range historical-political and social-cultural frameworks for the project of modernity. These approaches allow me to review and recast my own analysis of our critical times, which I had traced to the beginning of the post–Cold War period and which I have viewed as reaching a culmination with the fateful events of 2021.

On the one hand, with a driving focus on the North, Wallerstein traces the world-system of the world-economy, the capitalist model of endless profit and growth, to the foundations of the modern project in the fifteenth century. In this process of "long duration," involving a variety

---

39. A fundamental problem for de Sousa Santos (2022) is that such forces and visions are not, unlike those of domination, coordinated but fragmented, making it impossible to articulate and pursue a unified struggle against domination—against the dominant model of humanity not as one but as divided between the fully human and the subhuman. For this, the answer lies in promoting greater interknowledge among the various movements of the oppressed.

Reading in These Times 53

of hegemonic successions, he foregrounds a period of about five years, from 1966 to 1970, as the beginning of what would turn into a protracted structural crisis. This crisis involves interrelated economic, geopolitical, and ideological developments, with primary emphasis given to the economic and geopolitical components. Wallerstein goes on to argue for a progressive deterioration of this crisis of modernity through both the last quarter of the twentieth century, a period of relative hegemonic decline, and the first quarter of the twenty-first century, a period of accelerated hegemonic decline.

On the other hand, with a leading focus on the South, de Sousa Santos traces the epistemological abyss within the world-system, the dialectical model of science and knowledge, to a later phase of the modern project in the seventeenth century. In this process of "long duration," encompassing a multiplicity of epistemological divisions, he highlights a period of about ten years, from 2008 to 2019, as the onset of what would become a sustained structural crisis. This crisis reflects the same triad of economic, geopolitical, and ideological dimensions, but now with primary emphasis placed on the ideological component. De Sousa Santos proceeds to argue for a pronounced deterioration of this crisis from the implosion of neoliberal ideology, with the economic recession of 2018, to the explosion of its aftereffects, with the viral pandemic of 2019.

The resultant state of global affairs is described by Wallerstein in terms of bifurcation and by de Sousa Santos as definitive. For both, this state of extreme tension and utter disarray generated by the exhaustion of the modern project creates an epoch-making moment of decision regarding the future of the world order. For Wallerstein, the structural crisis is without resolution as it stands. In the wake of the hegemonic vacuum left behind by the decline of the United States, a new world-system is inevitable but yet to emerge. At this point, it is necessary to analyze the array of discernible scenarios and then to advocate for the path favored. For Wallerstein, this lies in a quest for a model better than the world-economy of capitalism. Its main features are well-drawn: embracing decentralization and democracy, driven by sustainability and equality, and having the exploited and the marginalized foremost in mind. For de Sousa Santos, the structural crisis is also open-ended at this point. In the light of the disorder wrought by the ideology of neoliberalism, a new world-system is in order but not yet in sight. At this time, it is imperative to weigh the spectrum of possible scenarios and to press toward the path selected. For de Sousa Santos, this involves the pursuit of a model better than that of neoliberal ideology. Its distinctive features are well-delineated: espousing transformation and engagement, sustained by utopian hopes for the future, and keeping the silenced and the repressed foremost in mind. As a way to move beyond the structural crisis, therefore, Wallerstein looks to a spirit of innovation in conversation from all quarters, not just experts, while de Sousa Santos posits a spirit of knowledge from all sides in dialogue, not just southern or northern epistemologies.

Both analyses lead me, first of all, toward a far more expansive conceptualization and formulation of the systemic global crisis that I had first addressed in 2014 and that I have continuously revised ever since. Its constitutive components I can discern much more sharply now: (1) its intimate relation to the project of modernity, unfolding in steady and encroaching fashion since the fifteenth century; (2) its long trajectory of formation and development, involving a variety of hegemonic struggles as well as of epistemological divisions; (3) its point of unbearable tension and manifest exhaustion in our own times, rupturing along various structural lines in individual and joint fashion; and (4) its resultant state of disconcerting and depressing anxiety, beset by uncertainty on all sides. Both analyses lead me, furthermore, to a far more focused consideration of that most pressing question from this crisis: a vision and a mission for the future—a future that cannot but bear the deep scars of modernity but that must also move beyond the detritus roundabout. The various options I can discern much more sharply now: dogged intensification, strategic reformism, thorough overhauling.

In this regard, certain questions come immediately to the fore. In times of global structural bifurcation or transition—times beset by disasters on so many fronts, times tossed about by uncertainties in so many directions, times haunted by whiffs of extinction in so many ways—what is biblical criticism to do? More to the point, what is that strand of criticism long under the shadow of ethnic-racial minoritization and imperial-colonial peripheralization—represented by this volume and pursuing that strand of postmodernist social theory revolving around identity—to do? What do the various components of criticism—the texts and contexts of biblical antiquity, the traditions and approaches of biblical interpretation, the encounters and interactions of biblical criticism with other fields of study—have to offer? What might be, or should be, the response of criticism to the call for choice making and action taking issued by Wallerstein and de Sousa Santos with a better model of world order in view and presented as at once ineluctable and pivotal?

It would be interesting to consider such a response at length in terms of the three options outlined—intensification, reformism, overhauling. For now, I restrict myself to the present volume. Its driving spirit lies, I would argue, along the lines of overhauling. In effect, the project offers a panoply of visions and missions for the future: an array of critical paths for the times ahead in the light of critical overviews of the present—all from the epistemological standpoint of minoritized criticism. This undertaking the introduction by Tat-siong Benny Liew pursues at a concentrated theoretical level: foregrounding the problematic of time underlying the question of criticism in these times and doing so by drawing on any number of critical angles and voices. At the heart of the problematic, I discern three central components: (1) the indeterminacy and instability of the notion of time as such, (2) the configuration of time as an ideological exercise and production, and (3) the construction of time advanced by the neoliberal project of our times, which Liew dates to the period following World War II in general and to the decades of the 1980s and 1990s in particular.

Following the work of Mira Moshe, senior lecturer at Ariel University, Israel (Moshe 2019), Liew describes neoliberal time as driven by the goal of efficiency, as generating in the process a variety of new temporalities, and as claiming the banner of progress, an aura of inherent and constant improvement. While the variety of temporalities yields a sense of time that encompasses polychronicity and hybridity, the juxtaposition and intermingling of modes of time, the banner of progress sets forth a construction of time that involves closure and exclusion, preserving what proves bearable and convenient while sidelining what is embarrassing or contradictory. On such a foundation, then, Liew argues for a "temporal boomerang." Within this neoliberal configuration, within the framework of the United States though applicable as well throughout the world of neo-imperialism today, the response of the ethnic-racial minoritized biblical critic should be to pursue the discombobulation of dominant time.

Such a project would involve puncturing the narrative of progress and installing an alternative narrative of time. This would be done through the recuperation, by way of juxtaposition and intermingling, of the many narratives overridden along the way—whether altogether destroyed and buried, effectively silenced and excluded, or actively banned and persecuted. In this way, any pretense to "innocence and hegemony," any "desires for coherence, progress, and triumph," any "denials, disguises, or deflections," would be undone by recollections and recitations of the "various wreckages and numerous wounds," the "systemic theft and structural looting," lying behind the banner of progress. In the process, the project would expose how such traumas of the past remain very much alive at present, given "the contiguous and continuous nature of racism, imperialism, and neoliberal capitalism."

To my mind, the strategy of a temporal boomerang as a response to the global structural crisis of our times lies squarely within the model of overhauling rather than that of reformism. It involves not so much a strategic tinkering with the neoliberal model of the modern project as a thorough recasting thereof by way by way of exposé and critique. In terms of world theory, it may not be as forthcoming on overall visions of democracy and engagement, or on working ideals of equality and utopia, but it is very much in keeping with the insistence on having foremost in mind the Other—the exploited and the marginalized, à la Wallerstein, or the silenced and the repressed, à la de Sousa Santos. This path of "reading griefs," argues Liew, following the work of Sara Ahmed (2014), presently an independent scholar in the United Kingdom, can lead to a politics in solidarity with the grief of others and to a reading of emotion with the signs of texts. This path is one in which all contributors to this volume share—in one way or another, to one extent of another—in their respective reflections on the demands on ethnic-racial minoritized criticism in these times. They all surface recollections, personal and collective, of narratives overridden and griefs endured, exposing and challenging in the process the ways of dominant criticism.

From the perspective of world theory, as drawn above, all voices and angles represented in this volume come out, in one way or another, of the peripheral circles within the world-economy identified by Wallerstein and the southern knowledges within the epistemological abyss by de Sousa Santos. Such intrusions of the Other are imperative. They are so, first of all, because of the volatile nature of the times, a global state of affairs in structural or definitive crisis. In such times of bifurcation and transitionism, the voices of the many Others are needed toward the ideal of a better world for all. They are so, furthermore, because, in such defining times, the processes of peripheralization and minoritazion have by no means abated. To the contrary, they have in many ways gotten worse, as evidenced by the rise of national populism and its scapegoating of transnational migrants and minoritized formations. They are so, moreover, because all the major crises that underlie the crisis of the world system do not affect everyone in the same way. Indeed, each and every one of them affects the peripheralized and the marginalized in highly disproportionate fashion.

The present exercise in reading in these times from the standpoint of ethnic-racial biblical criticism represents a modest, but significant, step in such a need for intrusions of the Other, those from peripheral circles and southern knowledges, in dominant frameworks and discourses. Needless to say, much work remains to be done along these lines. In my own case, I find two tasks quite pressing in this regard: expanding the critical interaction with theories of world order and engaging the other strands of social theory dealing with the collapse of the modern project. There is much to be gained from such efforts, as this conversation with Wallerstein and de Sousa Santos has made evident in general and has shown me in particular.

Works Cited

Ahmed, Sara. 2014. *The Cultural Politics of Emotion*. 2nd ed. Edinburgh: Edinburgh University Press.

Bailey, Randall C., Tat-siong Benny Liew, and Fernando F. Segovia, eds. 2009. *They Were All Together in One Place? Toward Minority Biblical Criticism*. SemeiaSt 57. Atlanta: Society of Biblical Literature.

Barreto, José-Manuel. 2017. "Contextualising Boaventura de Sousa Santos's Post-colonial Legal Theory." *IJLC* 13:558–61.

Fanon, Franz. 1961. *Les damnés de la terre*. Paris: Maspero.

Fontevecchia, Jorge. 2022. "Boaventura De Sousa Santos: 'El neoliberalismo dejó de ser legítimo en el mundo luego de la pandemia.'" *Perfil*. 25 February. https://tinyurl.com/SBLPress06106c7.

Keyder, Çağlar. 2019. "Obituary: Immanuel Wallerstein, Public Intellectual and Leader of Progressive Social Science, Passes." *NPT* 61:5–8.

Lee, James Kyung-Jin. 2009. "The Difference That Damage Makes: Reflections of an Ethnic Studies Scholar on the Wabash Consultation." Pages 347–64 in *They Were All Together in One Place? Toward Minority Biblical Criticism*. Edited by Randall C. Bailey, Tat-siong Benny Liew, and Fernando F. Segovia. SemeiaSt 57. Atlanta: Society of Biblical Literature.

Liew, Tat-siong Benny, and Fernando F. Segovia, eds. 2022. *Reading Biblical Texts Together: Pursuing Minoritized Biblical Criticism*. SemeiaSt 98. Atlanta: SBL Press.

López, Alfred J. 2011. "The (Post) Global South." *GlobS* 1:1–11.

Moshe, Mira. 2019. "Neo-Liberal Effects on Time Perception: When 'Time Is Money' Turns Into 'Hybrid Time.'" Pages 119–35 in *Neoliberalism in Multi-disciplinary Perspectives*. Edited by Adrian Scribano, Freddy

Timmermann Lopez, and Maximiliano E. Korstanje. Cham: Palgrave Macmillan.

Napolitano, Marcos. 2018. "The Brazilian Military Regine, 1964–1985." *Oxford Research Encyclopedia, Latin American History.* https://doi.org/10.1093/acrefore/9780199366439.013.413.

Parker, L. Evelyn. 2009. "Teaching for Color Consciousness." Pages 331–46 in *They Were All Together in One Place? Toward Minority Biblical Criticism.* Edited by Randall C. Bailey, Tat-siong Benny Liew, and Fernando F. Segovia. SemeiaSt 57. Atlanta: Society of Biblical Literature.

Rivera Rivera, Mayra. 2009. "Incarnate Words: Images of God and Reading Practices." Pages 313–30 in *They Were All Together in One Place? Toward Minority Biblical Criticism.* Edited by Randall C. Bailey, Tat-siong Benny Liew, and Fernando F. Segovia. SemeiaSt 57. Atlanta: Society of Biblical Literature.

Seidman, Steven. 2013. *Contested Knowledge: Social Theory Today.* 5th ed. Malden, MA: Wiley-Blackwell.

Sousa Santos, Boaventura de. 1995. *Toward a New Common Sense: Law, Science and Politics in the Paradigmatic Transition.* New York: Routledge.

———. 2018a. *The End of the Cognitive Empire: The Coming of Age of Epistemologies in the South.* Durham, NC: Duke University Press.

———. 2018b. "Introduction: Why the Epistemologies of the South? Artisanal Paths for Artisanal Futures." Pages 1–16 in *The End of the Cognitive Empire: The Coming of Age of Epistemologies in the South.* Durham, NC: Duke University Press.

———. 2019. "Immanuel Wallerstein, objetividad científica y compromiso social." *Página12*, 3 September. https://tinyurl.com/SBL06106a.

———. 2020. "El futuro del orden neoliberal después de la pandemia." *Página12.* 29 October. https://tinyurl.com/SBLPress06106c6.

———. 2021. "Bonaventura de Sousa Santos, Curriculum Vitae." https://tinyurl.com/SBL06106bg.

Wallerstein, Immanuel. 1972. "Three Paths of National Development in Sixteenth-Century Europe." *SCID* 7.2:95–101.

———. 1973. "Africa in a Capitalist World." *Issue* 3.3:1–11.

———. 1974a. *Capitalist Agriculture and the Origins of the European World-Economy in the Sixteenth Century.* Vol. 1 of *The Modern World-System.* Berkeley: University of California Press.

———. 1974b. "The Rise and Future Demise of the World Capitalist System: Concepts for Comparative Analysis." *CSSH* 16.4:387–415.

———. 1980. *Mercantilism and the Consolidation of the European World-Economy, 1600–1750.* Vol. 2 of *The Modern World-System.* New York: Academic Press.

———. 1989. *The Second Great Expansion of the Capitalist World-Economy, 1730–1840s.* Vol. 3 of *The Modern World-System.* San Diego: Academic Press.

———. 2004. *World-Systems Analysis: An Introduction.* Durham, NC: Duke University Press.

———. 2006. "The Curve of American Power." *NLR* 40:77–94. Page references in citations are to the version available at https://tinyurl.com/SBL06106c1.

———. 2009a. "Reading Fanon in the Twenty-First Century." *NLR* 57 (May–June): 117–25.

———. 2009b. "Braudel on the Longue Durée: Problems of Conceptual Translation." *RFBC* 32.2:155–70.

———. 2010. "Structural Crises." *NLR* 62:133–42.

———. 2011. *Centrist Liberalism Triumphant, 1789–1914.* Vol. 4 of *The Modern World-System.* Berkeley: University of California Press.

———. 2015. "It Is Painful to Live amidst Chaos." *Commentary* 393 (15 January). https://tinyurl.com/SBL06106b.

———. 2018. "Twenty-First-Century Geopolitics: Fluidity Everywhere." *Commentary* 467 (15 February). https://tinyurl.com/SBL06106c.

———. 2019. "This Is the End; This Is the Beginning." *Commentary* 500 (1 July). https://tinyurl.com/SBL06106d.

Ziai, Aram. 2013. "Boaventura de Sousa Santos." *Development and Change* 44:727–38.

Temporal Boomerang:
Reading and Writing of the Bible ... in These Times

Tat-siong Benny Liew

As the title of the two-volume work edited by Fernando F. Segovia and Mary A. Tolbert (1995a, 1995b)—*Reading in This Place*—makes clear, where a reader of the Bible stands affects the way this reader will interpret and make sense of the Bible. While there are undoubtedly colleagues in the guild who are still stubbornly holding on to the noble dream of historical objectivity or interpretive neutrality, most have by now embraced the understanding that all readings are contextual, so readings vary depending on who is reading and from where (Novick 1988). The inability or unwillingness to consider social location in one's interpretive practice—and hence the ability and will to avoid examining the specificities of what, how, and why one chooses to read from the Bible— effectually denies one's ethical responsibility and political agency as a critic of the Bible.

The language of social location—or, in Segovia and Tolbert's shorthand, place—connotes a spatial focus. Where and how one stands, however, may change with time, and context is always socio-geographical as well as historical. We all "need to understand how a place on the map is also a place in history" (Rich 1986, 212). Martin Heidegger (1962) has, of course, argued that we as human *beings* are moved and animated by time. Regardless of one's opinion on Heidegger's existentialist philosophy, one must admit that people are interested in or perhaps even obsessed with time, though the focus may range from the time of the end to the end of time to endless time. Given the presence of an apocalypse in both the Hebrew Bible and the New Testament, biblical scholars should already be cognizant of time's significance in the Bible. Time, however, should also be important in how biblical scholars read the Bible.

According to Roland Barthes (1972, 260), "Criticism is not an homage to the truth of the past or to the truth of 'others'—it is a construction of the intelligibility of our own time." The link Barthes makes between criticism and time can also be argued on the etymological links that exist between the words *criticism, critique, critical,* and *crisis.* An African American literary critic, Hortense Spillers (2020, 681), observes that critical theory "witnesses its most impressive moments of efflorescence in times of crisis." Crisis or not, how would minorized scholars think about biblical criticism if "we" were to give a greater or an equal emphasis on the temporal reality of "our" readings—though I would note that crisis may well be ordinary time for minorized people and community (Berlant 2011, 101)? To what critical tasks should minorized scholars of the Bible attend or apply "ourselves" in this first quarter of the twenty-first century?

Contributors to this volume—the third installment in a set on minority or minorized biblical criticism—will problematize Barthes's singular understanding of time and respond to these questions in different ways (see Bailey, Liew, and Segovia 2009; Liew and Segovia 2021). Writing about these times is, of course, a tricky endeavor. As Steed Davidson reminds me, times may change quickly. By the time this volume appears in print, what it has to offer—like Hegel's (1991, 23) owl of Minerva, which "begins its flight only with the onset of dusk"—may well be late and untimely. However, as I hope to show in this essay, just keeping up with the times can be problematic, and "untimeliness deployed as an effective intellectual and political strategy [can be] a bid to reset time" (Brown 2014, 44).

In this general reflection on reading and writing today, I will proceed in three steps. I begin with an analysis of these times. I then go on to discuss the significance of how temporality may be understood, lived, and employed differently, emphasizing particularly the need to attend to these times without losing sight of the past. I conclude with a focus on a politics of mourning, especially for minorized populations in these times.

These Times of Neoliberalism

I used to joke that 2020 would be the year of perfect vision, but I had no idea what it would end up bringing so clearly into my focus. From the fire in Australia, to COVID-19 becoming a pandemic, to the brutal and global structural virus of anti-Blackness, just to list a few problems that have occupied news headlines, the year 2020 seemed to be a time of deaths and losses. I have not even mentioned the damage the incompetent but impetuous and imperialistic Trumpian regime has done to the people and the environment of this country and around the world since 2016. While Trump is no longer the president of the United States, one must keep in mind that Trumpism is not ending any time soon. More importantly, Trumpism is not an exception but a more extreme or most explicit expression that proves the rule of these times.

In ways that recall the Bush administration's refusal to join the International Criminal Court, Trump authorized sanctions against the International Criminal Court for investigating war crimes committed in Afghanistan by various parties (including those committed by the US). The global militarism of the United States—whether through military aid and training or direct military interference—under the banner of promoting development and protecting democratic freedom is, likewise, a long state tradition (Latham 2011; Bacevich 2013; Brooks 2016). This military or militaristic tradition fights not only overseas. Like the militarization of the police in its (anti-Black and anti-Brown) war against drugs, the Department of Homeland Security's wars against undocumented migrants and terrorists (and often undocumented migrants *as* terrorists) have been militarizing its agents to fight—and terrorize—"enemies within" (Meads 2016; Stohl 2012; Hacker et al. 2012; Marquez 2015). Trump's personality aside, his policies on the economy, on the military, and on race in general are in many ways continuations of past practices and symptomatic of a deep-rooted white supremacy. I say this not to minimize the harms that Trump has brought about but to maintain that the end of Trump's presidency merely means a changing of the guard; it does not necessarily mean a changing of the times.

Checking the Times

In contrast to Jacques Derrida's (2000, 143, 145) claim that "it is always war that makes things change," the United States is only interested in "keeping the change" through wars (both external and internal). As "one of the most aggressive arms salesmen in history," Trump, as others before and after him, knew that wars could bring obscene amounts of money (Hartung 2019). Although those who advocate a so-called America First policy like Trump continue to lament the offshoring of so-called American jobs, jobs on military bases of the United States around the world are mostly contracted to private companies that have been known to employ and exploit people of many nations to maximize profit (Coburn 2018).

This outsourcing practice on the part of the government is, of course, similar to that of the private business sector.

Despite a populist and protectionist rhetoric, there is therefore a consistent implementation of the neoliberal project in every sphere of life, both within and beyond the borders of the United States (Braedley and Luxton 2010; Ventura 2012; Scott 2018; Snider 2020). As Maria Ryan (2019, 214) points out, "Trump's most ostensibly radical commitment ... to economic protectionism ... was not a wholesale rejection of neoliberal trade in all circumstances." Pointing to "four elements of the neoliberal project: 'post truth,' disaster capitalism, individualism, and the dumbing down of society," Wesley C. Marshall (2018, 58) declares "Donald Trump as man of his times, in many ways a singularly precise personification of today's neoliberal inspired zeitgeist." As Trump's comments about taking or keeping the oil in Iraq and in Syria show, military might and money are, for him and his supporters who continue to promote Trumpism, interrelated if not exactly interchangeable. After all, the so-called freedom that the United States is protecting and promoting in these times under a different president is still the freedom of capital to move around the globe and the freedom to consume mindlessly.

The policies of neoliberalism are well-known: privatization, corporatization, deregulation, subsidization of transnational business but withdrawal from the service sector by the state, suppression of labor unions, predation of public and common goods, emphasis on "individual responsibility," and elevation of the market as the ultimate standard for measuring and organizing societies. These have led not only to the undoing of democracy in the geopolitical West (Brown 2015, 2019), but also to an even larger wealth gap, greater social fragmentation, and wider environmental destruction across the globe (Johnston, Taylor, and Watts 2002; Greenhouse 2010; Dooling and Simon 2012; Islam 2013; Zarembka 2014; see also Slobodian 2020).[1]

This outsourcing of neoliberalism—in the doubled sense of making neoliberalism global and relocating industries offshore—inevitably means that people of the Global South are supplying many of the necessary services,

---

1. Referring to Michel Foucault's (2004) work on governmentality, Wendy Brown (2015, 79–111) also emphasizes how liberal subjects become *homines oeconomici* who are committed to investing in and marketing *themselves* as commodities even as they commit themselves to investing in markets and consuming commodities. See also Scharff 2016.

including, particularly for women, the provision of affective labor and surrogacy services (e.g., Boris and Parreñas 2010; Kang 2010; Rudrappa 2015; Padios 2018). Because of the negative impacts I mentioned above on income parity, community, and ecology—as well as capital's capriciousness and hence sudden market crashes—neoliberal economies bring about not only global movement of companies, goods, and services but also mass displacement of people. Predictably, the poor, especially those of the Global South, are the most affected; their financial precarity often necessitates their migration for the sake of survival (Gutiérrez-Rodríguez 2010; Bahng 2018; Kikon and Karlsson 2019). Whether as a cause or an effect of a neoliberalism that reduces "all of human life to economic calculation"—or most likely both—a plutocracy exists now in which the wealthiest class of people rules the world at the expense of much of the world's population (Davies 2017, xxii; see Duménil and Levy 2005).[2]

It is important to note, however, that, if the lassitude toward the coronavirus crisis indicates that many leaders and citizens of the United States value the economy over humanity, their response to the protests for Black lives against police brutality in various cities demonstrates a readiness to use violence or even the military to safeguard and (r)e(i)nforce their business-first policies.[3] Although neoliberalism appears to function within a democratic political regime, it often "depends on authoritarian institutions [and personalities] to implement its program measures" (Scribano 2019, 5). Here is one of the many paradoxes of neoliberalism: "in the name of liberty it increases control" (11). As Wendy Brown (2019, 15; see 11–13) explains, neoliberalism in our twenty-first century is a "markets-and-morals project" that not only frees capital to run amok but also reaffirms and restores hierarchical orders, such as those based on gender, race, and/or religion. One of the most ancient hierarchical orders is, of course, that of the sovereign over its subjects, with the former often being supported by another hierarchical order: the military. It is little wonder why people like Trump have continued to condemn Colin Kapernick's kneeling gesture as a disrespect of both the national flag and the United States military (14).

---

2. Let me clarify that I am not suggesting that neoliberalism is the sole and direct cause of every and all socioeconomic ailments but that "nothing is untouched by a neoliberal mode of reason and valuation" (Brown 2019, 8).

3. The way certain politicians prefer to handle both the coronavirus crisis and the Black Lives Matter protests reveals a necropolitics that sanctions the death of poor people and Black people. For an exposition of necropolitics, see Mbembe 2019.

The close connection among capitalism, militarism, and racism in the United States—a kind of unholy trinity, if you will—has long been recognized by people of color (e.g., Du Bois 2003; King 1986). Sadly, we also have in these times a group of neoliberal, neo-authoritarian, and neomilitaristic rulers around the world. The combination of neoliberal capitalism and state terrorism are wreaking havoc far and wide. With various shitstems (to use a parlance from reggae) that make everything and everyone merely instrumental to economic efficiency and utility maximization, numerous persons outside the plutocrats' circles of wealthy friends are feeling anxious about their work or job prospects; they become what Andrew Ross calls "precariats" (Ross and Smith 2011, 254). Worse, millions today are living as "undocumented," "stateless," or "uncounted" people who do not or no longer have what Hannah Arendt calls the "right to have rights" (Arendt 1976, 296; Cobham 2020; see Brysk 2002, 10–14). Precarities of livelihood in the Global North and of life in the Global South result in widespread worries and insecurities.

Akin to the threat of terrorism's so-called invisible enemies, the unknowns and uncertainties caused by neoliberalism trigger a social sentiment of fear that also allows a more authoritarian culture of oppression, colonization, and exploitation to develop (Korstanje 2019, 78–84; see also Robin 2004; Skoll 2016). As many media pundits have pointed out, Trump's election in 2016 had partly to do with his self-projection as a "strong man" who could alleviate people's anxieties about terrorism, offshoring job loss, queer sexuality, *Roe v. Wade*, and/or illegal immigration.[4] There is indeed a "crisis in the world system" that plagues both the Global North and the Global South (Segovia 2015, 25).

Things got even worse with the COVID-19 pandemic, although some managed to seize the pandemic as another opportunity for profit in what Naomi Klein (2007, subtitle) calls "disaster capitalism" by marketing hydroxychloroquine, other experimental medicine, or designer face masks. The pandemic not only exposed but also was exacerbated and mediated by existing socioeconomic inequalities. I do not think I am exaggerating to say that there is much dread, including the dread of death, in these times, when our world is confronted by what Segovia (2015, 26) correctly calls a "convergence of crises."

---

4. The media is itself by no means innocent when it comes to the spread of fear with its infotainment profit structures and programs.

This sense of dread is arguably even heavier in the United States. The coronavirus crisis has brought to the surface the deep-rooted racial/ethnic prejudice and socioeconomic inequities of this nation. All one needs to do is to look at who gets blamed for causing the virus, who must report to work despite the virus, and whose lives are disproportionately extinguished because of the virus. Mass shootings have been averaging more than one per day five years in a row, and there have been more than six hundred cases per year in the last four years (Boschma, Merrill, and Murphy-Teixidor 2023).[5] The lack of a social safety net and the cost of health care mean that homelessness is a near and present danger for a good proportion of the population (Desmond 2016). Decades of aggressive drilling and fracking have polluted our waters, soils, and even air (e.g., Wylie 2018). If one wants to talk about climate change and the ecological crisis, one may even say that the planet we call home is running out of time. Times of "neoliberal fantasies" are fragile times (Connolly 2013).

Thinking about these times reminds me of the scholarly conversations that have been taking place about the interregnum. While interregnum originated as a Roman law authorizing the senate to exercise power in the absence of the consuls, it has received much academic attention as a way to think about times of political imbalance, including, particularly for my purposes here, why people support right-wing authoritarian movements (Theophanidis 2016, 112). Two tantalizing reflections on interregnum merit particular mention in my view.

First, Zygmunt Bauman (2012, 49) proposes that we recognize the "planetary condition" of the twenty-first century "as a case of interregnum." Referring to the Roman understanding of interregnum as "a time-lag separating the death of one royal sovereign from the enthronement of the successor," Bauman (49, 51) goes on to characterize the interregnum as "a condition" or "a time" in which "the rulers no longer *can* rule while the ruled no longer *wish* to be ruled." In the Ten Years of Terror project to reflect critically on the decade since 9/11, Bauman likens the powerlessness people feel in the interregnum to being in a plane in midair only to learn that there is no pilot and the plane is heading to a yet-to-be-built airport (Evans and Critchley 2011; see Theophanidis 2016, 114).

---

5. Mass shooting is defined as a shooting that involves "a minimum of four victims shot, either injured or killed, not including any shooter who may also have been killed or injured in the incident" (https://www.gunviolencearchive.org/explainer).

68 Tat-siong Benny Liew

Second, Antonio Gramsci, whose thoughts on the interregnum Bauman (2012, 49) also references, presents the interregnum as a time of crisis when the ruling class has basically lost its legitimacy. As a result, it is "no longer 'leading' but only 'dominant,' exercising coercive force alone," and "the great masses have become detached from their traditional ideologies, and no longer believe what they used to believe previously" (Gramsci 1972, 275–76). He goes on to suggest that this crisis situation "consists precisely of the fact that the old is dying and the new cannot be born; in this interregnum a great variety of morbid symptoms appear" (276). These symptoms, as summarized so succinctly by Philippe Theophanidis (2016, 112; see Gramsci 1972, 276), manifest themselves "physically (depression), epistemologically (skepticism with regard to all theories), economically (poverty), and politically (cynicism)."

I find Bauman's and Gramsci's respective readings of the interregnum uncannily and disturbingly relevant in the seemingly perpetual interregnum of these times in the United States.

It Is about Time

If the interregnum is a helpful way for us to think about these times, it is important to consider how neoliberalism itself has also much to do with time. Pointing to neoliberalism's emphasis on (1) compressing time (and space) to make things instantaneously available and (2) measuring everything "through the quantification of time through money," Adrian Scribano (2019, 8–9) understands neoliberalism "as a proposal to manage and control the experience of time." For Mira Moshe (2019), human understandings of and relations with time change in neoliberalism, with efficiency becoming the desired goal and time being monetized as money. Since time and money should not be wasted, Moshe suggests, neoliberal subjects, organizations, and systems value keeping and following a schedule over being spontaneous with their use of time. Furthermore, new ideas about temporality are generated in connection with neoliberalism. These include "squeezed time" (so more can be done in limited time), "speeded-up time" (so people communicate with each other as well as change jobs, relationships, and addresses more quickly and more frequently), "flexible time" (so the best time can be released for the most profitable activities), and "eternal time" (with the here and now becoming the only concern).

Moshe shares two additional thoughts about neoliberal temporality that particularly interest me. She talks about polychronic time—that is, the coexistence of a variety of times (such as premodern, modern, and postmodern times; or secular and religious times)—and hence also the possibility of hybrid time that "mixes various kinds of times and tempos" (Moshe 2019, 126–27). At the same time, she suggests that many assume neoliberalism represents a time of progress, since "constant improvement is a 'natural' phenomenon" (120).

Moshe's mention of progress and multiple temporalities reminds me of what Dipesh Chakrabarty says about Europe's (read: white and dominant) historicism (see Hegel 1956). According to Chakrabarty (2000, 7–8), this historicism

> say[s] that the "country that is more developed industrially only shows, to the less developed, the image of its own future" ... [and] consigned Indians, Africans, and other "rude" nations to an imaginary waiting room of history. In doing so, it converted history itself into a version of this waiting room. We were all headed for the same destination ... but some people were to arrive earlier than others. That was what historicist consciousness was: a recommendation to the colonized to wait.... This waiting was the realization of the "not yet" of historicism.

As Chakrabarty (2000, 6) explains, the temporal structure can be summarized in the statement, "First in the West, and then elsewhere," or by what Johannes Fabian (1983, 1–69) calls "the denial of co-evalness" in the discipline of anthropology.[6] The waiting room is therefore where multiple temporalities can be found, though progress or something such as a unified and linear development is assumed. Also assumed is the structural privilege and power for one group of people to tell other groups of people that they must wait—or, if and when it fits the purposes of the dominant group, that these racialized others simply lack the desire to catch up. Both Gayatri Chakravorty Spivak (1988, 281) and M. Jacqi Alexander (2005, 189–96; see Kim 2020, 86–87) use the image of a palimpsest to point to the continuing if covered-over reality of (neo)colonialism and (neo)imperialism in a (neoliberal) linear temporality of progress.

With what she calls "racial time," Neda Atanasoski explains that at the so-called end of the Cold War the United States needed a new nar-

---

6. Pointing to the museum as an example, Chandra Talpade Mohanty (1987, 30) also criticizes a teleological view of history as Eurocentric, because "progress is defined as the ordained linear movement ... [so] other civilizations or tribal cultures are seen as 'contemporary ancestors,' the past the West has already lived out."

rative to justify its national and neocolonial interests. Some began to present the backwardness of peoples in the Eastern Bloc, Africa, Asia, and the Middle East—namely, their racism, sexism, authoritarianism, religionism, and "[premodern] view of history [which] was stagnant, cyclical, and incongruous with democratic development"—as the new threat after communism (Atanasoski 2013, 34). With these peoples representing "an anachronistic reflection of a pre–civil rights era of U.S. racist past," the United States, with its present "freedom, mobility, and rights," continues its militaristic neocolonialism in the name of humanitarianism (36). Racial exploitation and control are justified by, in, and through this linear temporality of progress (Hanchard 1999). It also means that, in terms of the nation's population, "becoming less white would involve moving backwards in time" (Ahmed 2014, 3). This narrative provides also, then, a clear rationale for a certain kind of national policy that causes particular bodies to do time in prisons and immigration detention centers.

Chakrabarty's image of the waiting room therefore tellingly signifies not only, as Chakrabarty (2000, 8) points out, the "not yet" of the others and their need to wait but also the arrival of the dominant self. It is simultaneously a not-so-subtle put-down of others and a blatant buildup of oneself. While others have long denounced theories of underdevelopment for actually causing and continuing underdevelopment, I want to highlight instead how the temporal structure of a developmental narrative or a progress plot enables the powerful to emphasize closure and claim that the nation has gotten over and moved on from, perhaps even transcended, a less-than-desirable past (Amin 1974; Faría 2011; Leary 2016). As Joseph R. Winters (2016, 4) writes, "The pervasive commitment to the idea of progress in American culture … mitigates experiences and memories of racial trauma and loss" to protect its myth of exceptionalism.[7] We see this, for example, in the white and dominant perspective that slavery

---

7. Commitment to this progress idea is also consistently present in the rhetoric of President Obama (see Leeman 2012; Winters 2016, 187–207). I think the same can be said of President Joe Biden. Notion and rhetoric of progress can also be found in liberation movements, including the civil rights movements in the US. Besides the need to differentiate usages of these notions to challenges the status quo from those that seek to reinforce the status quo, one also needs to attend to blind spots within movements that belong to the former category. Liberation movements are not always or necessarily immune from acts of marginalization or contradiction.

Temporal Boomerang 71

is over, that the internment of (Japanese American) citizens is no more, that affirmative action is obsolete, or that the Cold War has ended. Referring to this cultural habit to "repress" and "forget troublesome details of the national memory," Ralph Ellison (1964, 250) proposes that "more than any other people, Americans have been locked in a deadly struggle with time, with history."

Alternative Temporality: The Past in These Times

What if we read the history of the United States as a palimpsest in which what was written or done in the past cannot be cleanly wiped out or completely covered over? What if we cease trying to erase or explain away tragedies of the past and try instead to bring these memories to the fore and into focus? As the many works of historian Dominick LaCapra (1985, 1994, 1998, 2014) show, psychoanalysis has taught us that there is no getting over the past or what we call history. The past will keep on returning, and history has effects and consequences.

Seemingly eschewing the apocalyptic and teleological triumph of a proletarian revolution, Walter Benjamin (2007, 257–58), a Marxist historian, writes:

> A Klee painting named *Angelus Novus* shows an angel looking as though he is about to move away from something he is fixedly contemplating. His eyes are staring, his mouth is open, his wings are spread. This is how one pictures the angel of history. His face is turned toward the past. Where we perceive a chain of events, he sees one single catastrophe which keeps piling wreckage upon wreckage and hurls it in front of his feet. The angel would like to stay, awaken the dead, and make whole what has been smashed. But a storm is blowing from Paradise; it has got caught in his wings with such violence that the angel can no longer close them. The storm irresistibly propels him into the future to which his back is turned, while the pile of debris before him grows skyward. This storm is what we call progress.

Through this famous musing on a 1920 painting by Paul Klee, Benjamin not only recommends that we must linger to attend to the past rather than assume progress and take flight into the future but also turns any promised salvation history into cycles of catastrophe.

What might this alternative temporality—or cyclical and catastrophic view of history—imply about my reading of and in these times? What if tragedies of the so-called past are not over and done but are constitutive of our present? What if this neoliberal, neo-authoritarian, and neomilitaristic interregnum is not merely an in-between time that will transition to a better time of stability, safety, and salvation but one that keeps piling wreckages of the past onto the present and the future?[8] What if returning to the past may actually be necessary for and helpful to the imagination of a different future?

Times That Remain

To understand these times in the United States as "*relatively* novel," we must not disavow the effects of the past on the present (Brown 2019, 10; emphasis added). The basic blueprint for the neoliberal society was already laid out by Friedrich Hayek and the Mont Pelerin Society in the 1940s; it was then actively implemented by Margaret Thatcher and Ronald Reagan in the 1980s as well as through the so-called Washington consensus of the mid-1990s (Harvey 2005; Olsen 2019; Brown 2019). In fact, as seen in the English and Dutch East India Company and the Hudson's Bay Company, transnational companies and the practice of outsourcing have been a significant element in capital- and empire-building since the seventeenth century (Phillips and Sharman 2020). Of course, empire can never be built without military force at the ready.[9] Many people across the globe did not have to wait until the beginning of neoliberalism or what the world has come to know as 9/11 to know what it means to live in fear and anxiety.

While empires do succeed one another, they also build on one another. For instance, Japan's (settler) colonialism in the twentieth century was not only informed by Thomas Malthus's political economic theory but also influenced by the (settler) colonialism of the United States. At times, it was also facilitated and even carried out by Japanese Americans (Azuma 2019;

---

8. In his helpful discussion of the interregnum, Theophanidis (2016, 117, 119) also questions the common desire among theorists to present the interregnum as "a situation we need to exit ... to move through and out of ... to attain a new, better political order," and wonders whether "the interregnum could itself become the name of an alternative form of political synthesis." Unfortunately, besides a brief mention of a lecture by Giorgio Agamben, Theophanidis does not really elaborate on what he himself has in mind for this "alternative form of political synthesis."

9. The ability to employ military power is one of the reasons why Andrew Phillips and Jason C. Sharman (2020, 1, 5–9) use the term *company-states* to refer to the transnational companies that practiced outsourcing as early as the seventeenth century.

Lu 2019). After the Second World War, the United States, in turn, used the colonial order that Japan had set up to facilitate its own Cold War politics and neocolonial programs in Asia (Kim 2019, 47; see Hasegawa 2011; Li 2018). As Ann Laura Stoler (2013, 2016) argues, "imperial debris" from the past signal and enable "imperial durabilities" into the present. Empire lives on in different forms or by different names, and imperial damages do not necessarily have expiration dates.

Anti-Black structures and practices were not eliminated with the first memorialization of Juneteenth, the delegalization of Jim Crow, or the election of President Barack Obama. This anti-Black problem does not belong to "a dark and distant place in time, but [is] a burden that we still carry and [is] a history that [most] have not agreed to face or acknowledge as a source of our subjectivities" (Hale 1999, 295). Similarly, Korea is still divided, and nuclear warfare still a threat despite the so-called ending of the Cold War.[10] The Cold War has not only led to migrants from Asian countries such as Korea, Vietnam, Cambodia, and Laos becoming minoritized subjects of the United States but also facilitated the extraction of raw materials from, and outsourcing of jobs to, these Asian countries.

The confluent impacts of white supremacy and imperial domination—what Nikhil Singh (2017, 18, 19, 32) famously calls "the inner and outer wars" of the United States—are long and deep. Neither will disappear, even though they may function differently and more subtly with a different person in the White House in 2021. Racial time and "racial management" will continue to be significant in the neoliberal United States of the twenty-first century, since such a state, like a "traffic cop," is primarily concerned with directing the smooth flow of capital—and hierarchical chains of command—both at home and abroad, even, or especially, as it celebrates that its racist past is over (Brown 2019; Goldberg 2009, 327–76).

State attempts to create narratives to assert simultaneously its innocence and hegemony, as well as to safeguard a triumphalist plot with its notion of progress, are not surprising. Those in power will also do what they can to make things unknown and forgotten by erasing or covering up other narratives. Trump's regime has shown us how easy it is to do so by creating "alternative facts" and its own "fake news." Judith Butler

---

10. It is reported that there are "ghost flames" at massacre sites in South Korea's Gyeongsang province, because the remains of the large number of buried bodies "have [supposedly] changed the chemical makeup of the earth, causing the soil to ignite" (Cho 2008, 16).

74   Tat-siong Benny Liew

(1997, 2004) points out that public space is needed for collective grieving, but public grieving for certain lives is prohibited by the state. Who knows how many "forgotten wars," "disappearing acts," or "hidden wounds" there have been for the United States to have its "century" and counting (Pfaelzer 2008, subtitle; Cho 2008, subtitle; Taylor 1997; Berry 2010; see McCoy 2017)? Whether understood in terms of a second murder—since "*even the dead* will not be safe"—or "double oblivion" when we forget that we have forgotten, we need to be aware that the so-called national history of the United States often silences or leaves behind what may be incoherent with a notion of progress and triumph (Benjamin 2007, 255; emphasis original; Casey 1992, 282).

While desires for coherence, progress, and triumph are understandable, they can cause us to become, wittingly or unwittingly, blind to injuries, deaths, or other damages. As Lisa Lowe (2015; see Rogin 1996) brilliantly shows, liberal ideas such as freedom usually have an underside, so what is called progress is also often dependent on the enslavement and exploitation of others, especially those who have been made into an underclass because of race, class, and/or gender. If neoliberalism has taught us anything, it is that unregulated capitalism relies on networks to perform systemic theft and structural looting. By denials, disguises, or deflections, various wreckages and numerous wounds are written out of our country's narratives and collective memories, even or especially if those damages are fundamental and foundational to the building of our "forgetful nation" and its myths (Behdad 2005).[11]

Racial histories are very much embedded in the present, but normative whiteness is partially constructed by "hidden affect and disavowed social loss," or with guilt and denial that Toni Morrison (1989, 11) calls "the ghost in the machine" (Singleton 2015, 14). This explains why when Linda Chavers (2020) was writing in the *Boston Globe* in June 2020 that students' "knowledge about this country's past and present terrorization of Black people is grossly insufficient," Trump was tweeting that we all need to be "proud" of "the American story" on 10 July. We see this also in the 1776 Commission as a reaction to the 1619

---

11. Similar dynamics may also operate in our personal lives. Even one's maturation entails loss, including that of innocence. For an example through a good short story, see Jen 1999, 37–48. For those of us who are minoritized scholars, we know that "education can also alienate individuals from communities that have historically been denied access to institutions of higher learning" (Winters 2016, 70).

Temporal Boomerang

Project (Solender 2020). With what Diana Taylor (1997, 119–38) calls "percepticide," we as part of the general population may willfully blind ourselves to disavow or (dis)miss not only sights and scenes of past and present injustice but also the continuations of past traumas into the present.

My point here is not that these times are just the same as those times of the past, but that these times cannot be read in myopic isolation. Myopia will not help us see broader structure or systems. For example, we will not understand the prison industrial complex as a "new Jim Crow" if we have a focused view only on the twenty-first century (Alexander 2010). We must question "the apparent closure of our understanding of historical progress and ... contribute to what Michel Foucault has discussed as a historical ontology of ourselves, or a history of the present" (Lowe 2015, 3; see Foucault 1988).[12] As James Baldwin (2017, 105) writes,

> History is not the past.
> It is the present.
> We carry our history with us.
> We *are* our history.
> If we pretend otherwise, we literally are criminals.

For the same reason, Frantz Fanon (1967, 49) writes to offer his French friend a dossier of hard and painful memories before his departure from Algeria:

> I offer you this dossier so that no one will die, neither yesterday's dead, nor the resuscitated of today.
> I want my voice to be harsh, I don't want it to be beautiful, I don't want it to be pure, I don't want it to have all dimensions.
> I want it to be torn through and through, I don't want it to be enticing, for I am speaking of man and his refusal, of the day-to-day rottenness of man, of his dreadful failure.
> I want you to tell.

This emphasis is, of course, going against the neoliberal temporalities that I discussed earlier through the work of Moshe (2019), but the need for it is as timely as news and tweets that we read in these times.

---

12. Foucault (1998, 369) himself explains his genealogy as a commitment to "record ... what we tend to feel is without history."

Let me also clarify that I am not trying here to normalize death and dread or turn them into a spectacle but to explain what I am starting to understand and feel as "a hope not hopeless but unhopeful" (Du Bois 1907, 209; see Tumarkin 2005). Just like having a shortsighted view, wearing rose-colored glasses to rush into the future is a hermeneutical trap for our reading of and in these times. In the words of Ralph Ellison (1952, 5), "that ... is how the world moves. Not like an arrow, but a boomerang," so one has to "keep a steel helmet ready."

Reading Griefs

If the history of exponential wreckage is long and an old wound can boomerang back in a new disguise, how will we be able to "seize hold of a memory as it flashes up at a moment of danger" (Benjamin 2007, 255)? Instead of downplaying or drowning out injuries and losses of the past, we must become attuned to them so we can expose and encounter the contiguous and continuous nature of racism, imperialism, militarism, and neoliberal capitalism (see Kendi 2019, 151–63). "Layered histories," as Jinah Kim (2019, 57) puts it, "can be razed but not erased." I do not mean here that we are imprisoned in the past or that we have no agency to make changes, but only that we cannot live without the past and that our agency is always exercised within inherited power structures. We have here what David Kyuman Kim (2007) calls "melancholic freedom": an agency that is not immune from but is in tandem with having endured loss and suffered violence. This agency or freedom is melancholic, because melancholy is "a *continuous* engagement with loss and its remains" (Eng and Kazanjian 2003a, 4, emphasis added).

Melancholy is what Anne Anlin Cheng (2001) uses to describe the ongoing grief that cannot be addressed or resolved through grievance, especially in the experience of minoritized people in the United States of America. As Cheng points out, an Asian American cannot "approximate an ideal [of whiteness] that one has already failed," not to mention the loss of "Asianness, home, and language" (Ahmed 2014, 150; Eng and Han 2000, 667). Denied of their full subjectivities, Asian Americans occupy "a truly ghostly position in the story of American racialization" (Cheng 2001, 23). Cathy Park Hong (2020, 55) also talks about how minoritized persons develop what she calls "minor feelings," which include "paranoia, shame, irritation, and melancholy," especially when an "American optimism" that contradicts their racialized reality is being imposed on them. In addition to articulating melancholia "as a uniquely-suited means through which to explore racism" as a collective "structure of feeling," Cheng argues that this melancholy or ongoing grief can actually serve as a productive basis to construct an identity for minoritized communities and a politics of resistance (Kaplan 2007, 514; Williams 1975).

In the last couple of decades, there has been much scholarly investigation of melancholy or unfinished grief as a "politics of mourning" (Eng and Kazanjian 2003b, subtitle). Mourning takes place "under conditions in which history, and the narrative coherence and direction it once promised, has been shattered" (Butler 2003, 471). Instead of accepting a dominant drive to make racialized subjectivities whole and known, minoritized scholarship in the larger world of literary and cultural studies has argued for a greater acknowledgment of and more conversations about loss. Latinx scholars have done so by reevaluating Lacanian psychoanalysis (Viego 2007). Others have done so by looking in various directions: African American cultural productions; Asian Americans of Generations X and Y who grew up not only with the pressure to be a model minority but also in the midst of a global neoliberalism and an intensifying rhetoric regarding colorblindness; Korean American and Japanese American literature, art, and films as responses to the trans-Pacific militarism and imperialism of the United States; and José Clemente Orozco's *Epic of American Civilization*, a twenty-four-panel mural cycle that Orozco painted at Dartmouth College (Holloway 2003; Singleton 2015; Winters 2016; Eng and Han 2018; Kim 2019; Coffey 2020).[13]

As a politics that minoritized people use to perform, rather than repress, their disappointments and pain, unresolved mourning keeps alive and renders memorable the "waste" and "excess" that do not fit a plot of progress but unsettle us with the need to re-cognize realities that we would rather forget or deflect onto other nations or peoples (Winters 2016,

---

13. All of these studies simultaneously refer to and revise Sigmund Freud's (1953–1974, 14:243–58) well-known essay, which presents mourning in terms of a successful recovery from suffering a loss, and pathologizes melancholia as a failure to get over a loss. Besides making Freud's work more social and more explicitly political, these studies correctly problematize Freud's binary understanding between a positive mourning and a negative melancholia. As Judith Butler (2004, 20–22) insightfully argues, Freud's assumption that objects are interchangeable and hence his understanding that persons can replace a lost object, overcome a loss, and resolve their grief successfully is highly questionable.

101). Commenting on Benjamin's (1998, 126) comparison of mourning to "the lining of a dress at the hem or lapel," Butler (2003, 470) suggests that mourning is "a presence ... that undoes what appears." By providing reminders of "duress" and preserving remainders of "debris," unfinished griefs have the potential to haunt us into a "sociological imagination" of "what could have been" (Stoler 2013; Gordon 1997, 2011).[14] Mourning past wounds and losses can help us think of—or help make us aware of— unrealized dreams, missed opportunities, foreclosed alternatives, or what normative politics see as impossible or impractical (see Eng and Kazanjian 2003a, 4–5). As Hannah Arendt (1961, 10–11) suggested over half a century ago, the future can drive us "back into the past."

Being intentional about attending to the past can correct not only amnesia but also myopia. Performing a politics of mourning here "functions as an episteme, a way of knowing" (Taylor 2003, xvi). It is also a politics of time by constantly referring and returning to the past. Jinah Kim (2019, 67) calls this "a melancholy temporality." In the words of Yên Lê Espiritu (2014, 23; emphasis original), "We [must] become tellers of *ghost stories*, ... pay attention to what ... history has rendered ghostly, and ... write into being the seething presence of the things that appear to be not there." A ghost, then, "is primarily a symptom of what is missing. It gives notice not only to itself but also to what it represents" (Gordon 1997, 63).

Referencing not only Freud's work on mourning and melancholia but also Butler's (1997; see 2004) insight that lives have to be recognized if their loss is to be grievable, Sara Ahmed suggests that a politics of queer grief is crucial despite certain pitfalls.[15] By publicly declaring that what others view as ungrievable losses are "*not only missing but also missed*," such a politics helps to keep pushing the question about whose lives count and what losses are grievable (Ahmed 2014, 157; see 155–61). Instead of seeing the griever and the grieved as victims, a politics of grief affirms both as subjects. It differs, therefore, from a wallowing in grief or what Edward W. Said (1993, 18) calls a mere "politics of blame." An enduring

---

14. Note that Avery F. Gordon (2011, 1) also pinpoints two specific causes for her work on loss and haunting: "racial capitalism" and "monopolistic and militaristic state violence."

15. For Ahmed (2014, 162, 192–93), a politics of grief may cause people to pity the mourners as "lacking," to practice "charity," or even to attempt to rescue the mourners and/or their lost objects.

politics of grief that refuses to "let go" is, for Ahmed (2014, 159, 187), not only ethical by keeping the dead alive rather than "kill[ing] again" but also enabling for the grievers and the lost object to form new attachments.

Noting that a politics of grief can become narcissistic, Ahmed (159, 174) notes that this politics must also involve responding to the pain and loss of *others*. Given how lives of racialized people and poor people are unrecognized, Ahmed's suggestions have implications beyond queer communities. Winters (2016, 50), for instance, talks about how the spirituals written by those who survived the Middle Passage function to remember and recognize those who died in the journey. Jinah Kim (2020, 85) further calls those who mourn losses that are forbidden to be grieved by the state as engaging in acts of an "insurgent melancholia."

There is another aspect of Ahmed's work that is important for minoritized readers of the Bible in these times. Presenting emotion as providing "a script" that generates affects, Ahmed (2014, 12, 42–61, 177, 215) compares affect to a speech-act that is addressed to someone—and one that can potentially lead to an emergent collective or even "world."[16] Ahmed's (12) book on emotions actually focuses on reading texts by talking about "the emotionality of texts."[17] For her, texts are not "repositories of feelings and emotions," and emotions are not properties contained "in" texts (Cvetkovich 2003, 7; Ahmed 2014, 14, 19 n. 22). Instead, they are "objects of emotion" that can be circulated to generate affective effects. Emotions "work by working through signs," including language and literary texts (Ahmed 2014, 191). By extension, then, one can say that they also work through the Bible, especially since all the biblical writings were written in times of ancient colonial catastrophes. In these times of death and dread, I suggest that minoritized biblical scholars might read the Bible to circulate emotions, generate affects, and hence implement a politics of grief and mourning for the present. Readers will find within this volume my essay on John, which illustrates this reading practice.

---

16. "Working ... on bodies to materialize the surfaces and boundaries that are lived as worlds," emotions, according to Ahmed (2014, 191), have the power to generate and materialize things, including moving bodies into and out of communities. With the capacity of moving people into movements, affects are important sites of and for sociopolitical struggles (176). Following Ahmed (205–7), I refuse to make a rigid distinction between emotions and affects.

17. This does not imply that text is the only or even the best means to generate affect.

Conclusion

In light of the squeezed and accelerated time of neoliberalism, the decision not only to slow down but also to step back in time to reflect on an ancient collection of texts such as the Bible is itself a rather antiquated if not anachronistic act. However, anachronism is perhaps what we need if we are to reconsider what we have come to assume to be established and evident (see Moore 2019). As David Tracy (1981) suggested four decades earlier, there is a certain excess of meaning and timelessness to classic texts that can help open up new horizons in our present moments. This is even more so when we are dealing with grief that comes after loss, which "makes itself known precisely in and through the survival of anachronism itself" (Butler 2003, 468). Blatantly anachronistic readings of the Bible can be employed effectively today to disturb people's willful amnesia and myopia. Keeping alive losses of the ancient biblical past can help us remember what we have tried to forget in our own, more recent past. Doing so can also disrupt a plot of unified and linear progress. In fact, "variable temporalities" have been identified and said to be consistent in the "tradition of the oppressed" (Wehellye 2005). Mohanty (1987, 81) calls this "a temporality of *struggle*" against "the logic of linearity, development, and progress which are the hallmarks of European modernity." In a temporal boomerang, perhaps we can go back in time and borrow what Friedrich Wilhelm Nietzsche (1911, 14), a master of suspicion within Europe itself, wrote in 1886 to talk about reading in general and reading of the Bible in particular:

> One thing above all—to step to one side, to leave themselves spare moments, to grow silent, to become slow—the leisurely art of the goldsmith applied to language: an art which must carry out slow, fine work, … now more desirable than ever before; … the highest attraction and incitement in an age of "work": that is to say, of haste, of unseemly and immoderate hurry-skurry, which is intent upon "getting things done" at once, even every book, whether old or new … how to read well: i.e. slowly, profoundly, attentively, prudently, with inner thoughts, with the mental doors ajar, with delicate fingers and eyes … this book appeals … to readers … : *learn* to read me well!

In these times, we will do well to take time to read the Bible and reset time. As Baby Suggs in Morrison's (2004, 6) *Beloved* says, "Not a house in the country ain't packed to its rafters with some dead Negro's grief." One way to do so, then, among other possibilities, is with a rhetoric and politics of grief and mourning.

Works Cited

Ahmed, Sara. 2014. *The Cultural Politics of Emotion.* 2nd ed. Edinburgh: Edinburgh University Press.

Alexander, M. Jacqui. 2005. *Pedagogies of Crossing: Meditations on Feminism, Sexual Politics, Memory, and the Sacred.* Durham, NC: Duke University Press.

Alexander, Michelle. 2010. *The New Jim Crow: Mass Incarceration in the Age of Colorblindness.* New York: New Press.

Amin, Samir. 1974. *Accumulation on a World Scale: A Critique of the Theory of Underdevelopment.* 2 vols. New York: Monthly Review.

Arendt, Hannah. 1961. *Between Past and Future: Six Exercises in Political Thought.* New York: Viking.

———. 1976. *The Origins of Totalitarianism.* New York: Houghton Mifflin Harcourt.

Atanasoski, Neda. 2013. *Humanitarian Violence: The U.S. Deployment of Diversity.* Minneapolis: University of Minnesota Press.

Azuma, Eiichiro. 2019. *In Search of Our Frontier: Japanese America and Settler Colonialism in the Construction of Japan's Borderless Empire.* Oakland: University of California Press.

Bacevich, Andrew J. 2013. *The New American Militarism: How Americans Are Seduced by War.* Updated ed. New York: Oxford University Press.

Bahng, Aimee. 2018. *Migrant Futures: Decolonizing Speculation in Financial Times.* Durham, NC: Duke University Press.

Bailey, Randall C., Tat-siong Benny Liew, and Fernando F. Segovia, eds. 2009. *They Were All Together in One Place? Toward Minority Biblical Criticism.* SemeiaSt 57. Atlanta: Society of Biblical Literature.

Baldwin, James. 2017. *I Am Not Your Negro.* New York: Vintage International.

Barthes, Roland. 1972. *Critical Essays.* Translated by Richard Howard. Evanston, IL: Northwestern University Press.

Bauman, Zygmunt. 2012. "Times of Interregnum." *EGP* 5:49–56.

Behdad, Ali. 2005. *A Forgetful Nation: On Immigration and Cultural Identity in the United States.* Durham, NC: Duke University Press.

Benjamin, Walter. 1998. *The Origin of German Tragic Drama.* Translated by John Osborne. New York: Verso.

———. 2007. *Illuminations.* Translated by Harry Zohn. New York: Schocken.

Berlant, Lauren. 2011. *Cruel Optimism.* Durham, NC: Duke University Press.

Berry, Wendell. 2010. *The Hidden Wound.* Berkeley: Counterpoint.

Boris, Eileen, and Rhacel Salazar Parreñas. 2010. *Intimate Labors: Cultures, Technologies, and the Politics of Care.* Stanford, CA: Stanford University Press.

Boschma, Janie, Curt Merrill, and John Murphy-Teixidor. 2023. "Mass Shootings in the US Fast Facts." CNN. 4 October. https://tinyurl.com/SBLPress06106c5.

Braedley, Susan, and Meg Luxton, eds. 2010. *Neoliberalism and Everyday Life.* Montreal: McGill-Queen's University Press.

Brooks, Rosa. 2016. *How Everything Became War and the Military Became Everything: Tales from the Pentagon.* New York: Simon & Schuster.

Brown, Wendy. 2014. "Untimeliness and Punctuality: Critical Theory in Dark Times." Pages 41–58 in *Radical Future Pasts: Untimely Political Theory.* Edited by Romand Coles, Mark Reinhardt, and George Shulman. Lexington: University of Kentucky Press.

———. 2015. *Undoing the Demos: Neoliberalism's Stealth Revolution.* New York: Zone.

———. 2019. *In the Ruins of Neoliberalism: The Rise of Antidemocratic Politics in the West.* New York: Columbia University Press.

Brysk, Alison. 2002. "Introduction: Transnational Threats and Opportunities." Pages 1–16 in *Globalization and Human Rights.* Edited by Alison Brysk. Berkeley: University of California Press.

Butler, Judith. 1997. *The Psychic Life of Power: Theories in Subjection.* Stanford, CA: Stanford University Press.

———. 2003. "Afterword: After Loss, What Then?" Pages 467–73 in *Loss: The Politics of Mourning.* Edited by David L. Eng and David Kazanjian. Berkeley: University of California Press.

———. 2004. *Precarious Life: The Powers of Mourning and Violence.* New York: Verso.

Casey, Edward. 1992. "Forgetting Remembered." *M&W* 25:281–311.

Chakrabarty, Dipesh. 2000. *Provincializing Europe: Postcolonial Thought and Historical Difference.* Princeton: Princeton University Press.

Chavers, Linda. 2020. "What Too Many White People Still Don't Understand about Racism." *Boston Globe*, 9 June. https://tinyurl.com/SBL06106f.

Cheng, Anne Anlin. 2001. *The Melancholy of Race: Psychoanalysis, Assimilation, and Hidden Grief*. New York: Oxford University Press.

Cho, Grace M. 2008. *Haunting the Korean Diaspora: Shame, Secrecy, and the Forgotten War*. Minneapolis: University of Minnesota Press.

Cobham, Alex. 2020. *The Uncounted*. Medford, MA: Polity.

Coburn, Noah. 2018. *Under Contract: The Invisible Workers of America's Global War*. Stanford, CA: Stanford University Press.

Coffey, Mary K. 2020. *Orozco's American Epic: Myth, History, and the Melancholy of Race*. Durham, NC: Duke University Press.

Connolly, William. 2013. *The Fragility of Things: Self-Organizing Processes, Neoliberal Fantasies, and Democratic Activism*. Durham, NC: Duke University Press.

Cvetkovich, Ann. 2003. *An Archive of Feelings: Trauma, Sexuality, and Lesbian Public Cultures*. Durham, NC: Duke University Press.

Davies, William. 2017. *The Limits of Neoliberalism: Authority, Sovereignty and the Logic of Competition*. Rev. ed. Thousand Oaks, CA: Sage.

Derrida, Jacques. 2000. *Of Hospitality: Anne Dufourmantelle Invites Jacques Derrida to Respond*. Translated by Rachel Bowlby. Stanford, CA: Stanford University Press.

Desmond, Matthew. 2016. *Evicted: Poverty and Profit in the American City*. New York: Crown.

Dooling, Sarah, and Gregory Simon. 2012. *Cities, Nature and Development: The Politics and Production of Urban Vulnerabilities*. Burlington, VT: Ashgate.

Du Bois, W. E. B. 1907. *The Souls of Black Folk: Essays and Sketches*. Chicago: McClurg.

———. 2003. "Preface to the Jubilee Edition of *The Souls of Black Folk* (1953)." *MonthRev* 55.6 (November): 41–43.

Duménil, Gérard, and Dominiqué Levy. 2005. "The Neoliberal (Counter-) Revolution." Pages 9–19 in *Neoliberalism: A Critical Reader*. Edited by Alfredo Saad-Filho and Deborah Johnston. Ann Arbor, MI: Pluto.

Ellison, Ralph. 1952. *Invisible Man*. New York: Random House.

———. 1964. *Shadow and Act*. New York: Random House.

Eng, David L., and Shinhee Han. 2000. "A Dialogue on Racial Melancholia." *PsychDial* 10:667–700.

———. 2018. *Racial Melancholia, Social Dissociation: On the Social and Psychic Lives of Asian Americans*. Durham, NC: Duke University Press.

Eng, David L., and David Kazanjian. 2003a. "Introduction: Mourning Remains." Pages 1–25 in *Loss: The Politics of Mourning*. Edited by David L. Eng and David Kazanjian. Berkeley: University of California Press.

———, eds. 2003b. *Loss: The Politics of Mourning*. Berkeley: University of California Press.

Espiritu, Yên Lê. 2014. *Body Counts: The Vietnam War and Militarized Refugees*. Berkeley: University of California Press.

Evans, Brad, and Simon Critchley. 2011. "Ten Years of Terror." Histories of Violence. https://www.historiesofviolence.com/tenyearsofterror.

Fabian, Johannes. 1983. *Time and the Other: How Anthropology Makes Its Object*. New York: Columbia University Press.

Fanon, Frantz. 1967. *Toward the African Revolution: Political Essays*. Translated by Haakon Chevalier. New York: Grove.

Faría, Carlos Ramiréz. 2011. *The Origins of Economic Inequality between Nations: A Critique of Western Theories on Development and Underdevelopment*. New York: Routledge.

Foucault, Michel. 1988. "The Art of Telling the Truth." Pages 86–95 in *Politics, Philosophy, Culture: Interviews and Other Writings, 1977–1984*. Edited by Lawrence D. Kritzman. Translated by Alan Sheridan et al. New York: Routledge.

———. 1998. "Nietzsche, Genealogy, History." Pages 369–91 in *Essential Works of Foucault, 1954–1984*. Vol. 2, *Aesthetics, Method, and Epistemology*. Edited by James D. Faubion. Translated by Robert Hurley et al. New York: New Press.

———. 2004. *The Birth of Biopolitics: Lectures at the College de France*. Edited by Michel Sennelart. Translated by Graham Burchell. New York: Picador.

Freud, Sigmund. 1953–1974. *Standard Edition of the Complete Psychological Works of Sigmund Freud*. 24 vols. Edited and translated by James Strachey. London: Hogarth.

Goldberg, David Theo. 2009. *The Threat of Race: Reflections on Racial Neoliberalism*. Malden, MA: Blackwell.

Gordon, Avery F. 1997. *Ghostly Matters: Haunting and Sociological Imagination*. Minneapolis: University of Minnesota Press.

———. 2011. "Some Thoughts on Haunting and Futurity." *borderlands* 10.2:1–21.

Gramsci, Antonio. 1972. *Selections from the Prison Notebooks.* Edited and translated by Quintin Hoare and Geoffrey Nowell Smith. New York: International Publishers.

Greenhouse, Carol, ed. 2010. *Ethnographies of Neoliberalism.* Philadelphia: University of Pennsylvania Press.

Gutiérrez-Rodríguez, Encarnacion. 2010. *Migration, Domestic Work and Affect: A Decolonial Approach on Value and the Feminization of Labor.* New York: Routledge.

Hacker, Karen, Jocelyn Chu, Lisa Arsenault, and Robert P. Martin. 2012. "Provider's Perspectives on the Impact of Immigration and Customs Enforcement (ICE) Activity on Immigrant Health." *JHCPU* 23:651–65.

Hale, Grace Elizabeth. 1999. *Making Whiteness: The Culture of Segregation in the South, 1890–1940.* New York: Vintage.

Hanchard, Michael. 1999. "Afro-modernity: Temporality, Politics, and the African Diaspora." *PublCult* 11:245–68.

Hartung, William D. 2019. "Trump Is an Aggressive Arms Dealer. So Were His Predecessors." The Nation, 19 November. https://tinyurl.com/SBL06106g.

Harvey, David. 2005. *A Brief History of Neoliberalism.* New York: Oxford University Press.

Hasegawa, Tsuyoshi. 2011. *The Cold War in East Asia, 1945–1991.* Stanford, CA: Stanford University Press.

Hegel, Georg Wilhelm Friedrich. 1956. *The Philosophy of History.* Translated by John Sibree. New York: Dover.

———. 1991. *Elements of the Philosophy of Right.* Edited by Allen W. Wood. Translated by Hugh B. Nisbet. New York: Cambridge University Press.

Heidegger, Martin. 1962. *Being and Time.* Translated by John Macquarrie and Edward Robinson. New York: Harper.

Holloway, Karla FC. 2003. *Passed On: African American Mourning Stories.* Durham, NC: Duke University Press.

Hong, Cathy Park. 2020. *Minor Feelings: An Asian American Reckoning.* New York: One World.

Islam, Md Saidul. 2013. *Development, Power, and the Environment: Neoliberal Paradox in the Age of Vulnerability.* New York: Routledge.

Jen, Gish. 1999. *Who's Irish?* New York: Vintage.

Johnston, Ron J., Peter J. Taylor, and Michael J. Watts. 2002. *Geographies of Global Change: Remapping the World.* 2nd ed. Malden, MA: Blackwell.

Kang, Miliann. 2010. *The Managed Hand: Race, Gender, and the Body in Beauty Service Work.* Berkeley: University of California Press.

Kaplan, Sara Clarke. 2007. "Souls at the Crossroads, Africans on the Water: The Politics of Diasporic Melancholia." *Callaloo* 30:511–26.

Kendi, Ibram X. 2019. *How To Be an Antiracist*. New York: One World.

Kikon, Dolly, and Bengt G. Karlsson. 2019. *Leaving the Land: Indigenous Migration and Affective Labour in India*. New York: Cambridge University Press.

Kim, David Kyuman. 2007. *Melancholic Freedom: Agency and the Spirit of Politics*. New York: Oxford University Press.

Kim, Jinah. 2019. *Postcolonial Grief: The Afterlives of the Pacific Wars in America*. Durham, NC: Duke University Press.

———. 2020. "The Insurgency of Mourning: *Sewol* across the Transpacific." *AmerJ* 46:84–100.

King, Martin Luther, Jr. 1986. *A Testament of Hope: The Essential Writings and Speeches of Martin Luther King, Jr.* Edited by James M. Washington. New York: HarperCollins.

Klein, Naomi. 2007. *The Shock Doctrine: The Rise of Disaster Capitalism*. New York: Holt.

Korstanje, Maximiliano E. 2019. "Neoliberalism in the Culture of Terror." Pages 67–88 in *Neoliberalism in Multi-disciplinary Perspectives*. Edited by Adrian Scribano, Freddy Timmermann Lopez, and Maximiliano E. Korstanje. Cham: Palgrave Macmillan.

LaCapra, Dominick. 1985. *History and Criticism*. Ithaca, NY: Cornell University Press.

———. 1994. *Representing the Holocaust: History, Theory, Trauma*. Ithaca, NY: Cornell University Press.

———. 1998. *History and Memory after Auschwitz*. Ithaca, NY: Cornell University Press.

———. 2014. *Writing History, Writing Trauma*. Ithaca, NY: Cornell University Press.

Latham, Michael E. 2011. *The Right Kind of Revolution: Modernization, Development, and U.S. Foreign Policy from the Cold War to the Present*. Ithaca, NY: Cornell University Press.

Leary, John Patrick. 2016. *A Cultural History of Underdevelopment: Latin America in the U.S. Imagination*. Charlottesville: University of Virginia Press.

Leeman, Richard. 2012. *The Teleological Discourse of Barack Obama*. Lanham, MD: Rowman & Littlefield.

Li, Xiaobing. 2018. *The Cold War in East Asia*. New York: Routledge.

Liew, Tat-siong Benny, and Fernando F. Segovia, eds. 2021. *Reading Biblical Texts Together: Doing Minority Biblical Criticism.* SemeiaSt 98. Atlanta: SBL Press.

Lowe, Lisa. 2015. *The Intimacies of Four Continents.* Durham, NC: Duke University Press.

Lu, Sidney Xu. 2019. *The Making of Japanese Settler Colonialism: Malthusianism and Trans-Pacific Migration, 1868–1961.* New York: Cambridge University Press.

Marquez, John. 2015. "Latinos as the 'Living Dead': Raciality, Expendability, and Border Militarization." *LatSt* 10:473–98.

Marshall, Wesley C. 2018. "The Trump Administration and the Neoliberal Project." *TiA* 11.3:58–82.

Mbembe, Achille. 2019. *Necropolitics.* Translated by Steve Corcoran. Durham, NC: Duke University Press.

McCoy, Alfred W. 2017. *In The Shadows of the American Century: The Rise and Decline of US Global Power.* Chicago: Haymarket.

Meads, Mallory. 2016. "The War against Ourselves: Heien v. North Carolina, the War on Drugs and Police Militarization." *UMLR* 70:615–47.

Mohanty, Chandra Talpade. 1987. "Feminist Encounters: Locating the Politics of Experience." *Copyright* 1:30–44.

Moore, Stephen D. 2019. "The Rage for Method and the Joy of Anachronism: When Biblical Scholars Do Affect Theory." Pages 187–211 in *Reading with Feeling: Affect Theory and the Bible.* Edited by Fiona C. Black and Jennifer L. Koosed. SemeiaSt 95. Atlanta: SBL Press.

Morrison, Toni. 1989. "Unspeakable Things Unspoken: The Afro-American Presence in American Literature." *MQR* 28:1–34.

———. 2004. *Beloved.* New York: Vintage.

Moshe, Mira. 2019. "Neo-liberal Effects on Time Perception: When 'Time Is Money' Turns into 'Hybrid Time.'" Pages 119–35 in *Neoliberalism in Multi-disciplinary Perspectives.* Edited by Adrian Scribano, Freddy Timmermann Lopez, and Maximiliano E. Korstanje. Cham: Palgrave Macmillan.

Nietzsche, Friedrich Wilhelm. 1911. *The Dawn of Day.* Translated by John McFarland Kennedy. New York: Macmillan.

Novick, Peter. 1988. *That Noble Dream: The "Objectivity Question" and the American Historical Profession.* New York: Cambridge University Press.

Olsen, Niklas. 2019. *Sovereign Consumer: A New Intellectual History of Neoliberalism.* Cham: Palgrave Macmillan.

Padios, Jan M. 2018. *A Nation on the Line: Call Centers as Postcolonial Predicaments in the Philippines*. Durham, NC: Duke University Press.

Pfaelzer, Jean. 2008. *Driven Out: The Forgotten War against Chinese Americans*. Berkeley: University of California Press.

Phillips, Andrew, and Jason C. Sharman. 2020. *Outsourcing Empire: How Company-States Made the Modern World*. Princeton: Princeton University Press.

Rich, Adrienne. 1986. *Blood, Bread, and Poetry: Selected Prose 1979–1985*. New York: Norton.

Robin, Corey. 2004. *Fear: The History of a Political Idea*. New York: Oxford University Press.

Rogin, Michael. 1996. "The Two Declarations of American Independence." *Rep* 55:13–30.

Ross, Andrew, and Paul Smith. 2011. "Cultural Studies: A Conversation." Pages 245–58 in *The Renewal of Cultural Studies*. Edited by Paul Smith. Philadelphia: Temple University Press.

Rudrappa, Sharmila. 2015. *Discounted Life: The Price of Global Surrogacy in India*. New York: New York University Press.

Ryan, Maria. 2019. "'Stability Not Chaos'? Donald Trump and the World—An Early Assessment." Pages 205–26 in *The Trump Presidency: From Campaign Trail to World Stage*. Edited by Mara Oliva and Mark Shanahan. Cham: Palgrave Macmillan.

Said, Edward W. 1993. *Culture and Imperialism*. New York: Knopf.

Scharff, Christina. 2016. "The Psychic Life of Neoliberalism: Mapping the Contours of Entrepreneurial Subjectivity." *TCS* 33.6:107–22.

Scott, Catherine V. 2018. *Neoliberalism and U.S. Foreign Policy: From Carter to Trump*. Cham: Palgrave Macmillan.

Scribano, Adrian. 2019. "Introduction: The Multiple Janus Faces of Neoliberalism." Pages 1–20 in *Neoliberalism in Multi-disciplinary Perspectives*. Edited by Adrian Scribano, Freddy Timmermann Lopez, and Maximiliano E. Korstanje. Cham: Palgrave Macmillan.

Segovia, Fernando F. 2015. "Criticism in Critical Times: Reflections on Vision and Task." *JBL* 134:6–29.

Segovia, Fernando F., and Mary Ann Tolbert, eds. 1995a. *Reading from This Place*. Vol. 1, *Social Location and Biblical Interpretation in the United States*. Minneapolis: Augsburg Fortress.

———, eds. 1995b. *Reading from This Place*. Vol. 2, *Social Location and Biblical Interpretation in Global Perspective*. Minneapolis: Augsburg Fortress.

Singh, Nikhil. 2017. *Race and America's Long War*. Berkeley: University of California Press.

Singleton, Jermaine. 2015. *Cultural Melancholy: Readings of Race, Impossible Mourning, and African American Ritual*. Urbana: University of Illinois Press.

Skoll, Geoffrey R. 2016. *Globalization of American Fear Culture: The Empire in the Twenty-First Century*. London: Palgrave Macmillan.

Slobodian, Quinn. 2020. *Globalists: The End of Empire and the Birth of Neoliberalism*. Cambridge: Harvard University Press.

Snider, Laureen. 2020. "Beyond Trump: Neoliberal Capitalism and the Abolition of Corporate Crime." *JWCCC* 1.2:86–94.

Solender, Andrew. 2020. "Trump Launches 'Patriotic Education' Commission, Calls 1619 Project 'Ideological Poison.'" *Forbes*, 17 September. https://tinyurl.com/SBL06106h.

Spillers, Hortense. 2020. "Critical Theory in Times of Crisis." *SAQ* 119:681–83.

Spivak, Gayatri Chakravorty. 1988. "Can the Subaltern Speak?" Pages 271–313 in *Marxism and the Interpretation of Culture*. Edited by Cary Nelson and Lawrence Grossberg. Urbana: University of Illinois Press.

Stohl, Michael. 2012. "US Homeland Security, the Global War on Terror and Militarism." Pages 107–23 in *The Marketing of War in the Age of Neo-Militarism*. Edited by Kostas Gouliamos and Christos Kassimeris. New York: Routledge.

Stoler, Ann Laura, ed. 2013. *Imperial Debris: On Ruins and Ruination*. Durham, NC: Duke University Press.

———. 2016. *Duress: Imperial Durabilities in Our Times*. Durham, NC: Duke University Press.

Taylor, Diana. 1997. *Disappearing Acts: Spectacles of Gender and Nationalism in Argentina's "Dirty War."* Durham, NC: Duke University Press.

———. 2003. *The Archive and the Repertoire: Performing Cultural Memory in the Americas*. Durham, NC: Duke University Press.

Theophanidis, Philippe. 2016. "Interregnum as a Legal and Political Concept: A Brief Contextual Survey." *Synthesis* 9:109–24.

Tracy, David. 1981. *The Analogical Imagination: Christian Theology and the Culture of Pluralism*. New York: Crossroad.

Tumarkin, Maria. 2005. *Traumascapes: The Power and Fate of Places Transformed by Tragedy*. Melbourne: Melbourne University Publishing.

Ventura, Patricia. 2012. *Neoliberal Culture: Living with American Neoliberalism*. Burlington, VT: Ashgate.

Viego, Antonio. 2007. *Dead Subjects: Toward a Politics of Loss in Latino Studies.* Durham, NC: Duke University Press.

Wehellye, Alexander G. 2005. *Phonographies: Grooves in Sonic Afro-Modernity.* Durham, NC: Duke University Press.

Williams, Raymond. 1975. *The Long Revolution.* Westport, CT: Greenwood.

Winters, Joseph R. 2016. *Hope Draped in Black: Race, Melancholy, and the Agony of Progress.* Durham, NC: Duke University Press.

Wylie, Sara Ann. 2018. *Fractivism: Corporate Bodies and Chemical Bonds.* Durham, NC: Duke University Press.

Zarembka, Paul. 2014. *Sraffa and Althusser Reconsidered: Neoliberalism Advancing in South Africa, England, and Greece.* Bingley: Emerald.

Part 2
Naming and Facing the Times

Struggling with Culture:
African American Biblical Hermeneutics in These Times of HIV and AIDS

Cheryl B. Anderson

"Remembering is never a quiet act of introspection or retrospection." Rather, "it is a painful re-membering, a putting together of the dismembered past to make sense of the trauma of the present" (Bhabha 1986, xxii, xv). I was drawn to this quotation because it describes my goal in writing this reflection. Paraphrasing Homi Bhaba, my process of re-membering African American biblical hermeneutics is to make sense of a particular kind of trauma in the present. That particular trauma is the harmful ways in which people of African descent on both sides of the Atlantic interpret the Bible in the context of the HIV/AIDS pandemic.

To begin, I need to explain my hermeneutical starting point. When I started my doctoral studies in the Hebrew Bible over twenty years ago, a crucial shift in the field was already underway. Even at that point, the historical-critical approach was no longer the only method studied. For example, we were taught that no reading of the Bible was disinterested, which meant that the traditional distinction no longer held between "subjective" eisegesis (bad) and "objective" exegesis (good). Instead, we studied "biblical interpretations," that is, we used a term that is less value-laden. Furthermore, we were not limited to reconstructing ancient Israel or positing an implied reader. Instead, we were encouraged to engage flesh-and-blood readers and consider their—and our own—social locations. In addition, we were exposed to postmodern theory and its critiques of a hegemonic grand narrative, as well as the emerging analysis of the postcolonial impulse.

Fernando Segovia describes those shifts and the new world of biblical criticism that was emerging as one of "competing narratives" that had to

-93-

94 Cheryl B. Anderson

"engage in critical dialogue with one another." In such a world, biblical readers no longer just submit to the traditional hegemonic understandings of texts. In his words, the role of readers has to be considered in interpreting the text, along with engaging the text itself.

> Readers become as important as texts and ... models and reconstructions are regarded as constructions; [this is] a world in which there is no master narrative but many narratives in competition and no Jerusalem but many Jerusalems, a world in which the fundamental problem lies not in the translation and dissemination of a centralized and hegemonic message into other tongues but rather in having the different tongues engage in critical dialogue with one another. (Segovia 1995, 32)

While in graduate school, I naively thought that such counterhegemonic questioning and critical dialogues were taking place everywhere—including local churches. I was in for a rude awakening. Not long after completing my graduate program, I started doing congregationally based research on how Christians of African descent were reading the Bible in the context of HIV and AIDS. During these times of a pandemic that disproportionately affects Black people, it was clear to me that traditional interpretations (such as a focus on abstinence-only education for prevention) had to be questioned, because they actually contributed to rather than prevented high rates of HIV infection. Yet I found that such different interpretations, based on scholarly insights, were often resisted rather than embraced by affected Black communities. This reflection follows my search to understand why such resistance occurs.

The Trauma of the Present

It is worth repeating that the HIV/AIDS pandemic today disproportionately affects people of African descent. Two-thirds of all HIV-positive persons in the world are in sub-Saharan Africa; in the United States, African Americans are only 13 percent of the population but over 40 percent of those newly infected each year. While researching HIV and the Black Christian response, I spent time in South Africa, the country with the highest number of persons living with HIV in the world.

During one of those visits, I heard about an incident that has haunted me since then. It was a conversation with a Black South African pastor, and he was asked the following question: Would he teach his teenage son about condom use? The pastor's answer was that he would not, because his son knew that as a Christian he should abstain from having sex until he was married. Again, South Africa has the highest number of persons living with HIV in the world, and the area, KwaZulu-Natal, in which this conversation took place has the highest infection rates in South Africa. Additionally, the son is a teenager, and the twin dynamics of violence against females and sex between older men and younger girls (cross-generational sex) are so prevalent that "a schoolgirl in South Africa is thirteen times more likely to be infected with the virus than a sex worker in China" (Pisani 2008, 124–25). The person then asked the pastor another question: "But what if he has sex and becomes infected with HIV?" The pastor's response, about his own son, was, "Then he'll learn that the wages of sin is death."

Now, as a biblical scholar, I know that the pastor's use of Rom 6:23 in this way is a gross misinterpretation of the text. In the broader literary context, Paul is contrasting death (i.e., slavery to sin) with the new life believers gained through slavery to God (Kittredge 2014, 406). Therefore, the text refers neither to a physical death nor to divine punishment as the consequence of sin, as the pastor's statement implies. Yet that is not what concerns me most about that statement. To the contrary, my question is the following: How could a father apply the text in this way to his own son, even if that *were* the correct interpretation of Rom 6:23?

In the South African context, why was this pastor not able to resist what he assumed to be the meaning of this text for the sake of his own son's well-being? Although that was one of the first times I heard a Black person's damaging reading of the Bible in the context of the HIV/AIDS pandemic, it has not been the last. I have heard such harmful readings in the United States as well. As an African American biblical scholar, I know that, in earlier historical periods, we were able to read texts such as the exodus narrative in ways that speak to our own social conditions. Why are we not able to do those rereadings now at such a crucial moment in time?

History, Hermeneutics, and Context

That African Americans have questioned traditional interpretations and reinterpreted biblical texts to reflect their own social location is well established. Specifically, when enslaved African Americans embraced the religion of their slave masters, they reinterpreted biblical texts, as seen in the spirituals, and rejected readings of Pauline texts that would condemn them to slavery forever. Similarly, several African American scholars in

96 Cheryl B. Anderson

recent years have examined how the biblical exodus has served as a motif of resistance throughout our history for Black communities seeking their own freedom from captivity (Glaude 2000; Callahan 2006; Marbury 2015).

Although African Americans have tended to see the exodus story as our story, Randall Bailey writes that our story more closely resembles the story of the Canaanites, the indigenous people of the promised land. Bailey (2005b, 20–23) details how the Canaanites were labeled sexual deviants (such as in Lev 18:2–3), their faith practices were ridiculed and labeled "idolatry" (such as in Deut 12:2–4), and their intellectual property was destroyed (Judg 1:11, as discussed in Fewell 2007). Bailey convincingly argues that each of these aspects of destabilization and exploitation has been used against African Americans, and that the rationale with both the Canaanites and African Americans was to rationalize their oppression and their dispossession—all to the advantage of a dominant group.

Naturally then, the problem is when African American Christians see themselves as the privileged Israelites—just as privileged white Americans do in our more contemporary eras. Yet, we do not have the history of a privileged group, and to read the biblical text in this way means that we have to ignore our specific history. Bailey (1998, 78) describes that specific dynamic in the following way: "We read the text with the interests of whites, who are our oppressors, in mind. We, who have had our land stolen and have been enslaved by the people who stole our land, read the promise to Abraham to be given someone else's land and don't see our own story. We identify with Abraham."

For Black Americans to read the Bible as if we were white and privileged is particularly problematic in the context of HIV and AIDS. Remember that the HIV/AIDS pandemic disproportionately affects people of African descent on both sides of the Atlantic. If we read the Bible from the perspective of Abraham, Moses, and the Israelites, we cannot see our own story—or the disastrous consequences of that dominant narrative on our very existence. Therefore, Bailey's observation indicates why we need to reread the Bible in ways that reflect more accurately our current context, and his work indicates why we are unable to do so.

As I continued my quest to understand why Black Christians resist interpreting the Bible in different, more affirming ways, I remembered an article by Vincent Wimbush that was published before I entered graduate school. "The Bible and African Americans: An Outline of Interpretive History" was included in the groundbreaking volume *Stony the Road We Trod: African American Biblical Interpretation* (Felder 1991). Wimbush describes five different reading approaches over time that African Americans have used. In the earliest approaches, exemplified by the spirituals, Wimbush (1991, 88) concludes that there was "a hermeneutic characterized by looseness, even playfulness, vis-à-vis the biblical texts themselves," and he goes on to write that at these stages, "the interpretation was not controlled by the literal words of the texts, but by social experience."

In contrast, Wimbush notes, by the time of the fifth and final approach, in the last decades of the twentieth century, a fundamentalist approach was adopted by increasing numbers of African Americans. For Wimbush (96), this trend represented an "embrace of Christian tradition, specifically the attempt to interpret the Bible, without respect for the historical experiences of persons of African descent in this country," and, as such, it was a reading that "radically marks this reading and this period from the others." Such fundamentalist, more-literal readings of the biblical texts are still found today in the twenty-first century.

Yet, in the midst of a pandemic that disproportionately affects Black people, the need has never been greater for looseness and readings that take into account the social context of Black readers. However, that need has come at a time of increasing commitments to fundamentalist readings, resulting in inevitable conflict. As Bailey (2005a, 93) notes, "I contend that part of the problem in our addressing social justice issues in the church is this fundamentalist claim on the text, which prohibits us from reading the text through our own stories and prevents us from recognizing when the text itself is steering us away from social justice." In other words, Bailey is arguing that fundamentalist readings preclude social justice readings for people of African descent. I cannot think of a better example of this dynamic than the South African pastor who would hold to a supposedly literal reading of the text and, in so doing, ignore the context of the pandemic in which he and his son were situated.

Remembering Frantz Fanon

A shift toward more fundamentalist readings explains part of the resistance found to nontraditional approaches to the Bible, but I knew that at least one other factor existed. Since Black people have been oppressed historically, whether through slavery or colonization, I thought that the effect of such oppression was important to consider. For that reason, I returned to the writings of Frantz Fanon, which I first read in college. Fanon was born in 1925 on the Caribbean island of Martinique, studied psychiatry in France, and practiced in Algeria, where he was buried after his death in 1961. His work is best known in the fields of postcolonial theory and the development of the postcolonial nation state. Essentially, he wrote on the psychological impact of oppression on the colonized, and it is that aspect of his book *Black Skin, White Masks* and his other writings that I want to explore. As Henry Louis Gates Jr. (1991, 458) writes in his seminal article on Fanon, "Our current fascination with Fanon has something to do with the convergence of the problematic of colonialism with that of subject formation."

Specifically, Fanon argued that the Black man, *le Noir*, attempts to assimilate into the dominant culture through education, including learning the white man's language. But such a man's experiences force him to realize that he will never be accepted fully and that he will be rejected regardless of his efforts. That rejection eventually results in neurosis and alienation from self and others (Bergner 1995, 76). Alienation, helplessness, and an inferiority complex, according to Fanon, mark the internalized damage of colonial objectification of those with Black skins, and the result is an attempt "to run away from [their] own individuality, to annihilate [their] own presence" (Watkins and Shulman 2008, 113). I cannot help but wonder whether the pastor's ability to say that his own son must learn that "the wages of sin is death" exemplifies that kind of alienation and self-annihilation.

I see similar examples of that alienation and self-annihilation when I try to get African Americans to read the Bible differently using contextual Bible study. Several years ago, I learned how to lead contextual Bible studies from Sarojini Nadar, Isabel Phiri, Beverley Haddad, and Gerald West, who were my colleagues at the University of KwaZulu-Natal. Contextual Bible study is a process that allows readers to interpret the text based not just on spiritual needs but on their own socioeconomic realities. Contextual readings open up new insights and permit participants to reflect on the world around them in constructive ways. Some participants enjoy the process, but there are always some who question it and wonder whether we are doing something heretical. Simply by introducing new understandings of biblical texts and not reinforcing the traditional ones, they think we are being "unchristian," and that makes them uncomfortable.

However, Fanon (2008, 90) reminds me that such contextual readings are exactly what Black people need, given his observation that "the black man has no ontological resistance in the eyes of the white man." In other words, whites (the colonizers) will not consider the realities of Black

Struggling with Culture

people as different from their own, and, in turn, they can readily impose their civilization and perspectives on others. By implication, then, Black people must develop their own counterhegemonic readings of the Bible that do take their realities into account. We cannot wait for those who have developed the dominant readings to do that work for us.

Similarly, in his studies on the effects of colonization, Albert Memmi (1990, 157) writes, "The most serious blow suffered by the colonized is being removed from history and from the community," therefore preventing them from "contributing to [their] destiny and that of the world" and excluding them from "all cultural and social responsibility." As a result, Memmi (158) concludes that the colonized person becomes an object and not a subject, someone who "has forgotten how to participate actively in history and no longer even asks to do so." For me, a foundational Christian belief is the existence of a God who acts in history and sides with the oppressed. Yet if the colonized feel that *they* cannot act in history and offer resistance to the colonizer, it seems that their understanding of the divine is of one who cannot act in history, either—and certainly not act in history on their behalf. Alternatively, could it be that they *assume* God acts in history but that theological trends have shifted the way these groups see God at work?

There was a time, not too long ago, when the concept of a God who was on the side of the oppressed and who acted in history was more prevalent—as seen in the Kairos Document of South Africa, in the ministry of Martin Luther King Jr. in the United States, and in liberation theology in Central and South America. What happened? I think I found an answer in the work of Ignacio Martín-Baró. Martín-Baró was a psychologist and Jesuit priest who worked with the people in El Salvador. He was assassinated in 1989, but his work on the concept of a liberation psychology remains relevant.

According to Martín-Baró (1994, 140), the consequence of the changes brought by the Second Vatican Council and then the Medellín Conference meant that the marginalized no longer had to passively accept their conditions, and they had a religious basis for engaging social change:

> In El Salvador, the main consequence has perhaps been that the rural and urban working-class sectors most closely tied to the church have abandoned the traditional belief that their miserable oppressed situation is the will of God, or is at least tolerated by God, and have begun to think that faith in God should guide them toward the construction of a more just and humane society.

100   Cheryl B. Anderson

Martín-Baró (140) suggests that such comparable awakenings were viewed as a threat to the national security of local Central American governments, as well as the United States, and that their response was to engage in what he refers to as "a psychological war of conversion" by bringing in Pentecostal and fundamentalist groups that focused on individual, rather than systemic, change:

> [As a result,] Latin Americans were channeled toward the "true salvation" and the "true faith" grounded in individual change, leaving to God the task of transforming the "world of sin." The recourse to pentecostal fundamentalism, frequently imbued with intense anti-communism, was logical, since it entailed a religious world view that postulated direct intervention of the Holy Ghost in the solution of human problems.

The shift in theological emphasis that Martín-Baró outlines has two significant implications for this study. First, believers are taught that they do not have to solve human problems themselves, because God will intervene on their behalf. As a result, the faithful become passive again and no longer try to bring about socioeconomic change. Second, there is an emphasis on the individual and on one's own personal salvation and relationship to God, rather than on the community's material conditions.

Martín-Baró (141) observes that this "ideological counteroffensive" took the form of the charismatic renewal movement in the Roman Catholic Church, and he points out that the charismatic movement was similar in its beliefs and practices to evangelical Pentecostalism. Although he was describing the Central American context, the same shift in theological emphasis has occurred in the United States and South Africa. A theological focus on the individual, combined with the context of a globalized economic system, has given rise in both countries not only to Pentecostalism but to the popularity of the prosperity gospel, where individualism is emphasized, systemic social change is not sought, and interest in the community as a whole has diminished.

Earlier in this study, I asked a question: Why do Black Christians resist different but life-affirming biblical interpretations in the traumatic context of HIV and AIDS? Postcolonial theorists such as Fanon, Memmi, and Martín-Baró have helped me to answer that question. They describe the damaging patterns of colonialism, but for Black people those patterns have simply been replaced by the damaging patterns of global capitalism and increasing political marginalization. As a result, the psychological damage described by these theorists has not ended. Therefore, people of African descent remain alienated from a critical awareness of themselves and their surroundings, and they have embraced conservative evangelical and Pentecostal beliefs and practices that remove such considerations from their lives of faith. Consequently, Black Christians are not able to develop consistently the necessary theologies and biblical interpretations that would reflect their social and economic contexts.

On a more positive note, a Fanonian analysis can suggest measures that might cause the needed epistemological rupture for Black people. First, as one scholar reminds us, individual freedom and collective liberation are inextricably related; if this were recognized, it could help us counter the trends today where we have privatized the concept of liberation so that it has merely become "a question of getting rich" (Gibson 2011, vii). Similarly, Fanon's response, argues another scholar, would be for us to reclaim the concept of communalism, the importance of the well-being of the community to the well-being of the individual, "as an enduring cultural value orientation rooted in ancient African civilizations" (Gaines 1996, 30).

Second, according to Fanon, we must replace the logos of colonialism (which was to dominate and essentially erase the colonized) with "the logos of a new world" that will be shaped by "revolutionary language" using an "ancient language." That "revolutionary language" will occur when "the colonial monologue ends" and the voices of those now voiceless are heard (Renault 2011, 113). For Fanon, that "ancient language" was, as one would imagine, the French language. However, I think that the need for a new logos also applies to our traditional approaches to biblical interpretation. The logos of traditional interpretations has been a colonial monologue, if you will, and it needs to give way to a new logos that reflects the voices and concrete realities of African peoples.

Conclusions

Earlier I alluded to the exodus story as an example of Black Christians rereading the narrative in a way that spoke to their concrete realities as an oppressed group seeking freedom. However, even with that powerful motif of liberation, I have to recognize that its use has not resulted in greater freedom for all members of the Black community. For example, Irene Monroe notes that what could be the liberating message of the exodus narrative has been equated with only the struggles of Black heterosexual men and that such a limited reading has been justified by a patriarchal gender paradigm.

Consequently, she argues, Black women and LGBTQ persons have been kept in gender and sexual captivity (Monroe 2000, 89). As she describes it, "Policing women, lesbians, gays, bisexuals, and transgender people gives black heterosexual men what they could not have during slavery and what they only have nominally today: power" (90).

For the purposes of this reflection, Monroe's observation is significant because women and LGBTQ persons, the same people who do not benefit from traditional heteronormative readings of the exodus motif, are also those who are disproportionately affected by HIV infections. Along with other activists, I realize that the HIV/AIDS pandemic primarily affects those who are socially and economically marginalized, specifically, racial/ethnic groups, women, the LGBT community, and the poor. From this perspective, having the virus is not a sign of failed individual morality but rather an indication of far-reaching systemic disparities. As a result, if we are to prevent new infections, we need to see the spread of the virus as a social justice issue and work to eliminate those disparities. We are not likely to adopt a different strategy to HIV prevention, though, if we continue to tell our communities to "just abstain." The Christian approach to HIV prevention must be one of social justice, including comprehensive sex education.

Based on this reflection, I have reached two additional conclusions. First, Black Christians must realize that traditional biblical interpretations do not take their specific realities into account and therefore can be harmful to them in the context of the HIV/AIDS pandemic. Consequently, Black Christians must develop more contextually based biblical interpretations—and become comfortable with them. Second, in the traumatic context of a pandemic more than at any other time, the Black community must re-member itself and include those who are generally excluded from arenas of power or marginalized. Black Christian communities must have the courage to counter harmful biblical readings, whether those readings have their origins outside the community or within it.

Finally, Fanon's (2008, 206) *Black Skin, White Masks* ends with this plea: "O my body, always make me a man who questions." I cannot help but emend the sentence, as we often do in biblical studies, so that the current vocative becomes a prepositional phrase, and then modify the sentence so that it speaks to those who are Black and Christian. With these two changes, the plea becomes a prayer: "O God, for the sake of my body, always make me one who questions." Questioning, then, becomes the way to re-member Black bodies. Remembering Fanon, therefore, reminds us of the fundamental fact that our very existence as Black people depends on learning to question hegemonic theological and biblical norms.

Works Cited

Bailey, Randall C. 1998. "The Danger of Ignoring One's Own Cultural Bias in Interpreting the Text." Pages 66–89 in *The Postcolonial Bible*. Edited by Rasiah S. Sugirtharajah. Sheffield: Sheffield Academic.

———. 2005a. "The Biblical Basis for a Political Theology of Liberation." Pages 91–96 in *Blow the Trumpet in Zion! Global Vision and Action for the Twenty-First-Century Black Church*. Edited by Iva E. Carruthers, Frederick D. Haynes III, and Jeremiah A. Wright Jr. Minneapolis: Fortress.

———. 2005b. "He Didn't Even Tell Us the Worst of It!" *USQR* 59:15–24.

Bhabha, Homi K. 1986. "Remembering Fanon: Self, Psyche and the Colonial Condition." Pages vii–xxvi in *Black Skins, White Masks*, by Frantz Fanon. London: Pluto.

Bergner, Gwen. 1995. "Who Is That Masked Woman? Or, the Role of Gender in Fanon's *Black Skin, White Masks*." *PMLA* 110:75–88.

Callahan, Allen D. 2006. *The Talking Book: African Americans and the Bible*. New Haven: Yale University Press.

Fanon, Frantz. 2008. *Black Skin, White Masks*. Translated by Richard Philcox. New York: Grove.

Felder, Cain Hope, ed. 1991. *Stony the Road We Trod: African American Biblical Interpretation*. Minneapolis: Fortress.

Fewell, Danna Nolan. 2007. "Deconstructive Criticism: Achsah and the (E)razed City of Writing." Pages 115–37 in *Judges and Method: New Approaches in Biblical Studies*. 2nd ed. Edited by Gale A. Yee. Minneapolis: Fortress.

Gaines, Stanley O., Jr. 1996. "Perspectives of Du Bois and Fanon on Psychology of Oppression." Pages 24–34 in *Fanon: A Critical Reader*. Edited by Lewis R. Gordon, T. Denean Sharpley-Whiting, and Renée T. White. Cambridge: Blackwell.

Gates, Henry Louis, Jr. 1991. "Critical Fanonism." *CI* 17:457–70.

Gibson, Nigel, ed. 2011. *Fanonian Practices in South Africa: From Steve Biko to Abahlali baseMjondolo*. New York: Palgrave Macmillan.

Glaude, Eddie S., Jr. 2000. *Exodus!* Chicago: University of Chicago Press.

Kittredge, Cynthia Briggs. 2014. "Romans." Pages 325–426 in *Fortress Commentary on the Bible: The New Testament*. Edited by Margaret

Aymer, Cynthia Briggs Kittredge, and David A. Sánchez. Minneapolis: Fortress.

Marbury, Herbert R. 2015. *Pillars of Cloud and Fire: The Politics of Exodus in African American Biblical Interpretation*. New York: New York University Press.

Martín-Baró, Ignacio. 1994. *Writings for a Liberation Psychology*. Cambridge: Harvard University Press.

Memmi, Albert. 1990. *The Colonizer and the Colonized*. London: Earthscan.

Monroe, Irene. 2000. "When and Where I Enter, Then the Whole Race Enters with Me: Que(e)rying Exodus." Pages 82–91 in *Take Back the Word: A Queer Reading of the Bible*. Edited by Robert E. Goss and Mona West. Cleveland: Pilgrim.

Pisani, Elizabeth. 2008. *The Wisdom of Whores: Bureaucrats, Brothels, and the Business of AIDS*. New York: Norton.

Renault, Matthieu. 2011. "Rupture and New Beginning in Fanon: Elements for a Genealogy of Postcolonial Critique." Pages 105–16 in *Living Fanon: Global Perspectives*. Edited by Nigel C. Gibson. New York: Palgrave Macmillan.

Segovia, Fernando F. 1995. "'And They Began to Speak in Other Tongues': Competing Modes of Discourse in Contemporary Biblical Criticism." Pages 1–32 in *Social Location and Biblical Interpretation in the United States*. Vol. 1 of *Reading from this Place*. Edited by Fernando F. Segovia and Mary Ann Tolbert. Minneapolis: Fortress.

Watkins, Mary, and Helene Shulman, eds. 2008. *Toward Psychologies of Liberation*. New York: Palgrave Macmillan.

Wimbush, Vincent. 1991. "The Bible and African Americans: An Outline of an Interpretative History." Pages 81–97 in *Stony the Road We Trod: African American Biblical Interpretation*. Edited by Cain Hope Felder. Minneapolis: Fortress.

Minoritized Biblical Scholarship as Christian Missiology and Imperialism

Hector Avalos†

I have developed a very different perspective on minoritized approaches to biblical studies. I am a biblical scholar who happens to be identified as Latino, or Mexican American, and as an atheist. Since most members of the Society of Biblical Literature have religious affiliations, I may truly represent the most marginalized minority in the Society of Biblical Literature. I argue elsewhere that my experience with disability and my secularist stance, rather than my ethnicity or minority status, better explain the nature of my scholarship (Avalos 2015).

I am an anthropologist and biblical scholar by training, but I also teach and do research in ethnic studies. I founded the US Latino studies program at Iowa State University in 1994. In 2004, I edited a volume on the US Latino and Latina religious experience, while serving as editor of the Religion in the Americas series for Brill (Avalos 2004). In 2005, I published *Strangers in Our Own Land: Religion and U.S. Latina/o Literature*, and I still teach a course on Religion and US Latino/a Literature at Iowa State University. Those experiences have raised my awareness of both the benefits and disadvantages of looking at the Bible through what is being called "minoritized" criticism. Minoritized criticism centers on "'minoritization' or the process of unequal valorization of population groups, yielding dominant and minority formations and relations, within the context, and through the apparatus, of a nation or state as the result of migration, whether voluntary or coerced" (Bailey, Liew, and Segovia 2009a, ix).

An earlier version of this essay appeared as "Minoritized Biblical Scholarship as Christian Missiology and Imperialism." *The Bible and Interpretation*. August 2017. https://tinyurl.com/SBLPress06106c4. Used with permission.

106   Hector Avalos†

First, let me address the benefits. One benefit is raising awareness that European scholarship has been biased in a number of areas. In fact, detecting Eurocentric biases in biblical studies may be the single most important achievement of any minoritized biblical scholarship. Second, a minoritized approach also signals a more inclusive attitude toward scholars of non-European ethnicities and identities. That non-Europeans can be recognized as scholars in their own right is a welcome change. Despite these benefits, I view minoritized approaches as predominantly another form of Christian missiology and imperialism, rather than as a means to expose and undermine that imperialism.

Philosophical Problems with Minoritized Biblical Criticism

My main philosophical objection to minoritized biblical criticism is that most of it is incompatible with the idea of historical-critical biblical studies. Academic biblical studies should be an empirico-rationalist and secular enterprise that uses only methodological naturalism. This is not to deny that different ethnic groups may have a variety of approaches to the Bible. We certainly should study how different ethnic groups approach the Bible. However, I differentiate the study of how ethnic groups use the Bible from any program to develop or consolidate a uniquely minority or minoritized stance on biblical scholarship. For me, the study of how different minorities might approach the Bible is a sociological study rather than some constructive, ethno-theological program.

Historical findings about the Bible should not depend on ethnicity or religious presuppositions, any more than historical conclusions in any other field should depend on ethnicity or religious presuppositions. Martin Luther either wrote *On the Jews and Their Lies* in 1543 or he did not; our ethnicity does not change the result. We can either corroborate in textual and archaeological sources the presence of Alexander the Great in Mesopotamia or we cannot, regardless of ethnicity or religious presuppositions. Therefore, in some ways, minoritized approaches to the Bible are as useful as minoritized chemistry or ethnic Assyriology. These ethnic approaches inevitably lead to solipsism, because I can claim that there are individualized approaches just as there are ethnic group approaches to anything. If I am justified in using a group perspective, then I also should be justified in using an individual perspective on anything, so why privilege the group rather than the individual perspective (Bailey, Liew, and Segovia 2009b, 32)?

Indeed, ethnic identity is itself a construct, and identities are multiple and always evolving. Many times, minorities define themselves against a white or European culture that is itself diverse (Middleton, Roediger, and Shaffer 2016). We certainly can study how ethnic minorities interpret biblical texts without having to participate in some larger program to reify those interpretations as better or more suitable for any minorities.

Biblical studies should be an academic field much like all other academic fields in the humanities—much like classical studies, or Assyriology, or the study of English literature. My principal task is to discover, as best I can, what the intentions of authors were and the context in which they wrote their works. My secondary task is to explain how those ancient texts still exert influence in the modern world.

I try to identify Eurocentric biases in order to erase those biases. Replacing European biases with ethnic perspectives is equally objectionable. If I have a Latino ethnic bias, then I want to identify it in order to subvert it, much like any sort of personal bias should be subverted in history. Personal ethnic identity certainly can influence the subjects we choose, but it ought not influence results that should be based on evidence alone. This is not to deny that an ethnic identity may be useful for other purposes—just not for the purpose of doing historical or literary biblical scholarship.

Not all minoritized criticism involves theological approaches, but much of it certainly does. Given my commitment to empirico-rationalism as the only approach to historical or literary biblical studies, I hold that theological approaches are academically unsound, because I cannot evaluate theological claims. Theological claims are inherently undemocratic if they are based on nothing more than a theologian's word and on religious presuppositions that I do not share. In contrast, the use of empirico-rationalist methodologies rests on assumptions that can be shared by all. The main assumption would be that one or more of our natural senses and/or logic can give us reliable information about the world. To me, the most significant divide is not between some larger Eurocentric and a minoritized approach but between secular approaches and those that are religionist or bibliolatrous.

By *religionism*, I refer to a position that regards religion as useful or necessary for human existence and something that should be preserved and protected. Regardless of whether one has a Latino perspective, an Asian perspective, or an African perspective, I still see most biblical scholars engaged in minoritized criticism as trying to advance the idea that religion is good and necessary for human existence. I cannot recall any work of minoritized biblical scholarship that concludes that we must move past any sort of religious thinking. One may argue that assisting people to move past religious thinking is not the task of biblical scholars. Yet, many of the same scholars have no problem describing their task as advancing Christian principles or liberation-theological perspectives. By bibliolatry, I refer to the position that views the Bible as a privileged document that is worthy of more study or attention than many other ancient works that we can name. Promoting the Bible as important for our civilization is another self-interested project, because it also functions to preserve the employment of biblical scholars. I have written elsewhere on how the supposed relevance of the Bible in our civilization is an illusion created in part by biblical scholars, the professorial class, and ministers who wish to preserve their status in our society (Avalos 2007, 2010).

Minoritized Criticism as Colonialism and Missiology

In a well-known postcolonialist tome, *The Empire Writes Back: Theory and Practice in Postcolonial Literatures*, Bill Ashcroft, Gareth Griffiths, and Helen Tiffin (1989, 7) observe that the British Empire is now largely defunct, but "cultural hegemony has been maintained through canonical assumptions about literary activity, and through attitudes toward postcolonial literature which identify them as off-shoots of English literature." Similarly, although Christian empires may no longer be as politically powerful as they once were, they still exert their cultural hegemony by extolling the ethical and aesthetic superiority of their biblical texts over those of other cultures. Many biblical scholars can be viewed as agents of that effort to maintain Christian cultural hegemony even among underrepresented minorities today.

The attempt to understand other cultures and minorities within American culture is a standard part of Christian missiology. The integration of missiology with the effort to understand the Other is evidenced at Fuller Theological Seminary, which offers degrees in missiology. The description of the master of theology in intercultural studies states that it "equips pastors, mission and denominational leaders to meet the challenge of ministering in an increasingly complex, multiethnic, multinational world" (Fuller Theological Seminary n.d.).

In a broader context, minoritized biblical criticism can be viewed as part of the tradition of some of the early anthropologists whose aim was

Minoritized Biblical Scholarship as Christian Missiology and Imperialism 109

to understand other cultures in order to facilitate their conquest and colonization (Tilley and Gordon 2007). Instead of outright conquest, modern Christian missiology analyzes minority cultures to identify experiences that can facilitate extending Christianity and the authority of biblical texts to those cultures. Indeed, much of the minoritized biblical scholarship I read is predominantly a missiological and pastoral endeavor, meant to retain or recruit minorities by persuading them that the Bible offers them some comfort or analogy to their experience that can be beneficial. Therefore, minoritized biblical scholarship argues, ethnic minorities should still retain the Bible as some sort of authority to inform their experience. In his book on the Bible and migrants, Jean-Pierre Ruiz (2011, x) explicitly tells us, "I am convinced that the work of biblical studies and of theological scholarship is an ecclesial vocation, one that takes place at the heart of the church for the sake of its mission to witness to the goodness and the justice of God in the world." In so doing, Ruiz and most other advocates of minoritized biblical scholarship are still carrying out another version of the Great Commission in Matthew 28:19: "Go therefore and make disciples of all nations, baptizing them in the name of the Father and of the Son and of the Holy Spirit" (NRSV).

By "textual imperialism," I refer to the effort to promote the Bible as a privileged cultural text or as the standard by which minorities should guide their lives. These scholars are still trying to convince minorities that the Bible has a message that is relevant for them. Some of these scholars are explicit about their Christian agenda. One example is self-identified Latino scholar Ruben Muñoz-Larrondo (2014, 205), who states, "The theoretical framework envisioned for Latino/a hermeneutics involves five criteria." His first is "tuning our Christian identity beyond nationalist overtones," by which he means that Latinos should stress that they are Christian more than they are Mexican American, or Cuban, or some other Latino identity (205).

In my recent book *The Bad Jesus: The Ethics of New Testament Ethics*, I argue that the unwillingness to find any flaws in the ethics of Jesus betrays that most scholars of New Testament ethics—whether European, Latino, Asian, or African American—still view Jesus as divine and not as a human being whose ethics must be flawed somewhere. Religionism and bibliolatry are at the core of all Eurocentric approaches to the Bible historically (Avalos 2015). If that is the case, then most practitioners of minoritized criticism are not departing from Eurocentrism but rather developing an alternative form of Eurocentrism. Minoritized criticism is more about aes-

110   Hector Avalos†

thetics—it seeks to promote the appearance of diversity when it retains the core components of Christian textual imperialism.

Minoritized Criticism: Formal Thematic Features

When it comes to formal thematic features encountered in works of minoritized biblical scholarship, one finds at least these four: (1) experiential analogies, (2) ethno-theology, (3) representativism, and (4) the appeal to interpretive flexibility as a superior virtue of biblical texts. My aim is to show that these themes are simply religionist and bibliolatrous variants of, rather than radical or transformative departures from, Eurocentric or nonminoritized biblical criticism.

Experiential Analogy as Missiology

Scholars using minoritized approaches often seek some analogy in the Bible for the experience of minorities today. Particularly popular are analogies to the immigrant experience. This feature can be seen in the work of Gregory Lee Cuéllar and Gale Yee. In both cases, such experiential analogies are clearly announced in the titles of their work. In the case of Cuéllar (2008), this is explicitly conveyed in his volume *Voices of Marginality: Exile and Return in Second Isaiah 40–55 and the Mexican Immigrant Experience*. In the case of Yee (2009), it is no less evident in her article "'She Stood in Tears amid the Alien Corn:' Ruth, the Perpetual Foreigner and Model Minority."

Gregory Lee Cuéllar

In *Voices of Marginality*, Cuéllar seeks analogies between the themes of exile and return in Isaiah 40–55 and the Mexican American immigrant experience, especially as expressed in short narrative songs called *corridos*. For Cuéllar (2008, 68), these "*corridos* arise out of crisis and function to redress a social breach. They not only provide invaluable documentation of the Mexican migratory experience, but also serve as expressions of oppositional culture due to their message of resistance, empowerment and social critique." However, the very use of biblical texts to create analogies with Mexican American immigrants is already a very Christian missiological enterprise in this case. Indeed, there are more apt analogies in indigenous Mesoamerican literature that are com-

Minoritized Biblical Scholarship as Christian Missiology and Imperialism 111

pletely disregarded in favor of Second Isaiah, whose context is far more culturally removed from the experiences of Mexican immigrants, especially those who are undocumented.

Consider the bilingual (Spanish-Nahuatl) narrative known as *Crónica Mexicáyotl*, which dates to about 1609 and is attributed to Fernando Alvarado Tezózomoc, a Nahuatl indigenous writer who collected Nahuatl traditions. *Crónica Mexicáyotl* contains the story of how the Mexica people, from whom Mexican Americans derive part of their name, were exiled from many places before finally founding their core homeland of Tenochtitlan (in the middle of what is now Mexico City). The narrative begins as follows: "Here it is told, it is recounted, how the ancients who were called, who were named, Teochichimeca, Azteca, Mexitin, Chicomoztoca came, arrived, when they came to seek, when they came to take again possession of their land here" (León-Portilla and Shorris 2001, 192). This introduction identifies the narrative as being about exile and return ("they came to take again possession of their land here"). The narrative tells us that these people "brought along the image of their god, the idol that they worshipped" (193). This god, Huizilopotchli, speaks to his people just as Yahweh does.

The narrative goes on to explain how the Mexica people tried to settle in different places but were expelled. Fear of expulsion from their new home country is not the focus of Second Isaiah but is the focus of many *corridos* and also of *Crónica Mexicáyotl*. Near the end of *Crónica Mexicáyotl*, these nomadic people are told by a prophet-priest to look for a sign: an eagle perched on a cactus eating a serpent (or the heart of a defeated god). The Mexica people do find just such an eagle on a cactus, and the narrative announces a hopeful note: "O happy, blessed are we! We have beheld the city that shall be ours! Let us go, now, let us rest" (205).

If one looks at the *corridos* that Cuéllar has selected, none of them ever appeal to Second Isaiah to form their analogies. On the other hand, we find closer verbal parallels between *Crónica Mexicáyotl* and some of the *corridos* selected by Cuéllar. A line in one of Cuéllar's (2008, 132) selected *corridos* says, "We returned happily to the Mexican motherland." That is analogous to the lines in *Crónica Mexicáyotl* about returning precisely to the Mexican heartland: "O happy, blessed are we! We have beheld the city that shall be ours!" (León-Portilla and Shorris 2001, 205).

Sometimes Cuéllar has chosen *corridos* that serve his analogies while overlooking the diversity of other views in *corridos*. For example, Cuéllar (2008, 68) says that the "*corridos* ... also serve as expressions of

112   Hector Avalos†

oppositional culture." However, Los Tigres del Norte, a popular Mexican American musical group, wrote a 1997 *corrido* called "Mis Dos Patrias" ("My Two Fatherlands"), which affirms that Mexican immigrants can be equally devoted to both the United States and to Mexico. This *corrido* rejects an approach that views identity as part of an "oppositional culture" and encourages acceptance of both identities. Unlike Second Isaiah, which sees identity as a stark dichotomy (Jewish versus Babylonian), "Mis Dos Patrias" affirms a hybrid identity that Cuéllar never seems to view as legitimate. In other words, Cuéllar seems to be accepting the legitimacy of the stark ethno-religious dichotomy exemplified by Second Isaiah, even when some Mexican Americans themselves reject it in the very musical genre Cuéllar chooses for his illustrations.

On a rhetorical level, *Crónica Mexicáyotl* sometimes has better analogies as well. One line of "Mis Dos Patrias" reads, "But what does it matter if I am a new citizen; I continue to be as Mexican as the pulque [an alcoholic drink made from the maguey plant] and the cactus" ("pero que importa si soy nuevo ciudadano; sigo siendo mexicano como el pulque y el nopal"; Los Tigres del Norte n.d.). The cactus as a symbol of Mexican identity can be traced at least as far back as *Crónica Mexicáyotl*.

There are also some significant differences between the Mexican American immigrant experience and that of the Jews of Second Isaiah. Undocumented Mexican immigrants fear being forcibly removed from the United States, but forcible removal from Babylon is not much of an issue in Second Isaiah. Babylonians were not hunting down "illegal" Jews in order to return them to their Jewish homeland. It is the opposite in Second Isaiah, which addresses Jews who sometimes had grown too comfortable or felt too welcome in Babylon. Not all of these Jewish exiles wished to go back to Judea. That is why *Cronica Mexicáyotl* forms a more apt analogy to the plight of the undocumented Mexican immigrant in the United States. That indigenous narrative is permeated by episodes where the nomadic Mexica people were expelled from whatever new homeland initially accepted them.

As is the case with much of Christian scholarship, Cuéllar dismisses as inferior the religion of other Near Eastern cultures. Thus, Cuéllar (2008, 71) discusses how Second Isaiah rejects the attraction of Jewish exiles to "the pageantry and color and splendor of the empire's cult. In Isaiah 46:1–13, the prophet-singers allude to its tutelary god Marduk who is the legitimator of the Babylonian empire and its practices of domination." However, Marduk is no more of an imperialist than is Yahweh, whose goal is also total domination, as indicated in Isaiah 45:23: "To me every knee shall bow, every tongue shall swear." Moreover, Marduk is portrayed as a liberator of his favored people, who were subject to Assyria prior to gaining their freedom from that empire. Marduk himself experienced exile to Elam, and Nebuchadnezzar I (ca. 1125–1104 BCE) brought him back to Babylon (Abusch 1999, 543–49).

In fact, sometimes what is said about Marduk even sounds like Isaianic prophecies later interpreted to refer to Jesus. Consider the Mesopotamian incantation series known as Surpu, where one finds a list of blessings expected from Marduk: "To extirpate sin, to remove crime/to heal the sick/to lift up the fallen/to take the weak by the hand/to change fate" (Reiner 1958, 25). This sounds somewhat like Isaiah 61:1: "to bring good tidings to the afflicted; he has sent me to bind up the brokenhearted, to proclaim liberty to the captives, and the opening of the prison to those who are bound."

Accordingly, Cuéllar's entire project still centers on the same objectives found in Euro-American Christian biblical scholarship. Cuéllar uses experiential analogies in order to retain the relevance of the Bible in the lives of Mexican immigrants, just as Euroamerican missionaries use biblical experiential analogies to retain or recruit believers. That is why Cuéllar's work can be seen as part of Christian missiology, rather than as some historico-literary inquiry about how *corridos* actually use the Bible or Second Isaiah. Cuéllar is constructing the analogy rather than studying an analogy made by Mexican immigrants themselves.

Indeed, the effort to make the Bible the source of analogies does not really stem from below. It is not coming from the authors of *corridos* or from immigrants but from biblical scholars who are already part of the educated elite strata of society. Left to their own devices, the authors of *corridos* look mostly elsewhere for their experiential analogies. The popularity of their *corridos* confirms that those nonbiblical analogies are connecting with audiences without any need to introduce the ones from Second Isaiah.

Gale Yee

Yee finds an analogy between the character of Ruth and the way in which Asian Americans are thought to be model minorities and perpetual foreigners. By the latter, she means that Asians are always asked where they are from and that she is assumed to be nonnative, even though she was born in Ohio. For Yee (2009, 134), the story of Ruth can be seen as the story of an exploited immigrant, and an indictment "for those of us who live in the First World who exploit the cheap labor of developing countries." Yet, I am not sure I encounter anything in biblical immigrant stories that European authors cannot describe in their own experiences just as well.

One example comes from Thomas Mann (1875–1955), who won the Nobel Prize in Literature in 1929 and wrote his famous tetralogy *Joseph and His Brothers* between 1930 and 1943. Mann (1963, 638) observes, concerning Joseph, that "even at home he and his, the children of Abram, had always been gerim and guests long settled and well adapted." Joseph would always be viewed as a foreigner. Mann was a keen observer of what it was like to live between two cultures, Egyptian and Hebrew, even if he was not an immigrant himself. Similarly, Max Müller (1823–1900), who is often described as an Orientalist and philologist, was an immigrant. Although born and raised in Germany, he spent much of his academic career in England. His autobiography includes references to how his immigrant status related to his work on Hinduism. He also could find analogies between his immigrant status and Hindu literature (Müller 1901).

Themes of being the outcast and living in exile permeate American literature. Martin Shockley's study of Christian symbolism in John Steinbeck's 1939 *The Grapes of Wrath* illustrates how Euro-American literary critics, who were not biblical scholars, were already exploring the analogies between biblical themes and Euro-American experiences of exile decades before minoritized criticism became prominent by that name. *The Grapes of Wrath* features the flight of the impoverished Joad family from Oklahoma to California during the Dust Bowl years. Shockley (1956, 87) observes: "Like the Israelites, the Joads are a homeless persecuted people. They too flee from oppression, wander through the wilderness of hardships seeking their own Promised Land. Unlike the Israelites, however, the Joads never find it."

Therefore, I see at least some of what passes for minoritized criticism as already being practiced by Europeans who are immigrants and minorities (e.g., Müller the German in England) in respect to other cultures. I also see so-called minoritized criticism among some Europeans who, like Mann, did not have to be immigrants or minorities to see the issues that immigrants or minorities would have with a majority culture. Nonbiblical literary critics such as Shockley had long been observing analogies between biblical experiences and those of Americans who were also oppressed and exploited without being ethnic minorities.

It is not that such biblical analogies to modern immigrant or minority experiences are themselves bad or useless. My objection is to the idea that the Bible has something different or unique to offer minorities in terms of experiential analogies. I object to the idea that the Bible is a superior manual for minorities, immigrant or not. The truth is that one can find similar analogies with any other ancient collection of literature. Immigrant stories are found in many other cultures. So, minority scholars are still not explaining why the Bible deserves to be the main or only source for analogies that can apply to modern immigrants.

Consider the story of Sinuhe from Egypt. Sinuhe was an Egyptian official of the Middle Kingdom (ca. 2000–1700 BCE) who migrated to the land of Retenu in what is now Lebanon or Syria. Sinuhe was received very well, and he was assured that he would "hear the speech of Egypt" to make him feel more welcome (Pritchard 2011, 7). The king of that land married his eldest daughter to Sinuhe and allowed Sinuhe to choose where he wanted to live. The king made him ruler of a tribe. Sinuhe was very happy and raised children there. But he still missed Egypt and wanted to return to his land.

The story of Sinuhe has many parallels with the story of Joseph, who was also given the daughter of an official and became second in command to Pharaoh (Gen 41:40–46). One can find an illustration in Sinuhe to the idea of exile and return, as is argued for Second Isaiah and Mexican Americans in Cuéllar's (2008) *Voices of Marginality*. One could find analogies today to immigrants who are happy in America but still long for their country of birth. One could praise the land of Retenu for treating immigrants well and giving them an opportunity to rise. There seems to be no ethnic prejudice, as judged by the willingness of the ruler to marry his daughter to Sinuhe. The ruler of Retenu seems sensitive to the needs of immigrants to hear their own language and feel comfortable.

Yes, we can find many stories that would match anything in the Bible and could give comfort to immigrants today. However, minoritized scholars do not normally choose those nonbiblical stories. In so doing, biblical scholars are showing again a religiocentric and ethnocentric orientation that continually steers them only to the Bible, the text of their own religion or culture. It may be true that biblical stories are chosen because they are the most familiar to modern audiences, but this overlooks that it is biblical scholars and their clerical predecessors who have established biblical texts as authoritative for their audience (Avalos 2007, 2010). A more liberatory approach would actively inform audiences that the Bible is only one part of a vast body of texts from ancient times that can also provide experiential

116 Hector Avalos†

analogies. An egalitarian approach would include the ancient Near Eastern literary canon and not perpetuate the restricted biblical canon.

Representativism and Bibliolatry

Minority scholarship engages in a standard practice found in European scholarship. I call it representativism, and it affirms that a particular view in the Bible is representative, while others—usually bad ones, such as slavery, religious intolerance, and genocide—are unrepresentative. Representativism is found frequently in minoritized scholarship addressing immigration. Many of the scholars doing minority criticism realize that the Bible can be seen as predominantly patriarchal and religiously intolerant at times toward immigrants. Therefore, some minoritized scholarship, much like some European biblical scholarship, frequently selects supposedly immigrant-friendly biblical passages (e.g., Lev 19:18) and/or tries to defend passages that are not (e.g., Smith-Christopher 1996, 2007; Avalos 2016).

For example, the idea that foreigners and natives were treated in an egalitarian fashion in ancient Israel is supposedly espoused by Lev 24:22: "You shall have one law for the sojourner and for the native; for I am the LORD your God" (RSV). M. Daniel Carroll R., who identifies as Latino, includes that passage alongside those containing the phrase "whether he is a native-born Israelite or an alien." Carroll R. (2008, 106) concludes, "This expresses in another way their equal standing before the law." However, any modern notion of equality for aliens in ancient Hebrew law is misleading. For the most part, aliens had to surrender their culture and religion to be accepted. Thus, Ruth had to surrender her Moabite religion and culture to be accepted in a Yahwistic culture (Donaldson 1999). Immigrants in ancient Israel were subject to the same or similar penalties if they violated the laws of Moses (e.g., Num 15:20–29). Immigrants who valued their own religion might be put to death for not following the religion of the host culture. This equality of treatment would be no different under the understanding of Islamic law by ISIS, known also as the Islamic State. Foreigners who blaspheme, for example, are treated the same as Muslims who blaspheme. One should also not overlook that Leviticus makes a stark difference between enslavement of fellow Hebrews, which has term limits, and enslavement of foreigners, which does not (Lev 25:44–46).

Ethno-theology as Colonialism

The works produced by minoritized scholarship are overwhelmingly by scholars with Christian affiliations. Many of them explicitly offer theological answers to issues. In *Christians at the Border*, Carroll R. attempts to argue for a more liberal and merciful policy toward undocumented immigrants. After informing readers that he is "an Old Testament scholar by training," he adds that he is also "committed to the mission of the Christian church" (Carroll 2008, 19). Although Carroll R. (19) attempts to address exegetical issues pertaining to texts that speak of immigrants, he tells us that "among Christians, my experience has been that there is little awareness of what might be a divine viewpoint on immigration."

I am open to hearing sound legal or humanitarian arguments for being more liberal toward undocumented workers. I am open to hearing what biblical authors thought was a divine viewpoint about immigrants. However, I do not know how to go about researching "what might be a divine viewpoint on immigration." I cannot verify what a divine viewpoint might be. Unless one shares the main theological presuppositions held by Carroll R., then all claims about divine viewpoints are circular. They reduce to "I believe x is the divine viewpoint because I believe x is the divine viewpoint." This would not be held to be a valid rationale in any other area of the humanities that we can name in modern academia.

Another sort of theologizing presumes a monolithic, sectarian view of an ethnic group. For example, in the widely praised *A Galilean Journey*, Virgilio Elizondo routinely assumes that all Mexican Americans have a devotion to the Virgin of Guadalupe. Elizondo (2000, 123) states, "As the universal church celebrates its foundational experience on pentecost, so the Mexican American Christian community celebrates its foundational experience as a local church on the feast of our Lady of Guadalupe." This conflation of a Catholic and a Mexican American identity is followed by Andrés Guerrero (1987) in his *A Chicano Theology*. Elizondo (1983, 123) adds, "In the celebration of Our Lady of Guadalupe, we Mexican Americans celebrate the common mother of all the inhabitants of the Americas." This statement overlooks that a sizable portion of Latinos are now Protestant. It is sociologically inaccurate to conflate a Mexican American identity with a Catholic identity if a sizable portion of Mexican Americans are Protestant.

Elizondo's view of the Virgin of Guadalupe is historically questionable as well. Stafford Poole, himself a Catholic priest and an academic histo-

118 Hector Avalos†

rian, has done extensive work on the sources of the Guadalupe tradition. Poole concludes that the story of the supposed apparitions of the Virgin of Guadalupe to a peasant Indian named Juan Diego in 1531 were largely invented in the 1600s by privileged criollos (white Spaniards born and raised in Mexico). Far from being a story meant to empower indigenous people, Poole (1995, 2) observes: "Criollo preachers took up the new development with enthusiasm, with a resulting wealth of published sermons in the period from 1660 to 1800. All these celebrated the criollo nature of the devotion to the detriment of the Indian message.... The criollos were the new chosen people; no other people had a picture of the Virgin that she had personally painted."

Otherwise, much of Marian devotion itself is not a radical departure surging from the bottom strata of society. Marian devotion, as is the case with these criollo accounts of the Virgin of Guadalupe, is simply part of European Christian traditions imposed from the top in the Americas (Poole 1995, 2; see Pelikan 1996). Therefore, Elizondo exemplifies how minoritized biblical scholarship is used to further sectarian, ethno-theological assumptions. Elizondo's assumption that all Mexicans have or should have a common devotion to the Virgin of Guadalupe reveals itself to be part of yet another colonialist perspective, which views Christianity, or at least Catholic Christianity, as the religion all Mexicans do share or should share.

Interpretive Flexibility as Apologetics

The interpretive flexibility of biblical texts is another common emphasis in minoritized scholarship. It is claimed that the Bible is special because it offers the flexibility needed to adapt to different cultures and historical contexts in which believers live. It is further claimed that this is part of the genius or even divine feature of the Bible. One example of this sort of approach is found in Daniel Schipani's essay "Transformation in Intercultural Bible Reading: A View from Practical Theology," in the anthology *Bible and Transformation* (De Wit and Dyk 2015).

Schipani (2015, 99) begins his essay by informing readers that "the connection between reading a sacred text and experiencing human transformation is an assumption inherent in the very value assigned by religious communities to certain texts deemed sacred."

Schipani (99) adopts Walter Wink's notion of the "bankruptcy of the biblical critical paradigm." Schipani (100) also agrees with Wink's idea

Minoritized Biblical Scholarship as Christian Missiology and Imperialism 119

that the goal of Bible study is "the conscious transformation of persons … centered on commitment to the will of God.… Our interest is … in finding that subtle intersection between the text and our own life where … we encounter the living God addressing us at the point of our and the world's need." Aside from utilizing a wholly theological claim that humans can "encounter the living God," interpretive flexibility is being touted as a unique virtue of biblical texts. Schipani (103) remarks: "The sacred text of the Bible has great disclosive potential and inexhaustible meaning. Throughout the centuries, readers have assumed, implicitly and explicitly, that the Bible has an enduring potential to offer manifold meaning that can actually guide, instruct, teach, challenge, convict, sustain, inspire, and empower the faithful."

Schipani (101) aims to provide concrete empirical evidence for the applicability of this interpretive flexibility by having eighteen groups from Colombia, Perú, El Salvador, and Guatemala engage "in an intercultural reading process focused on the text of Luke 18:1–8," which relates the parable of a widow's plea for justice from a judge. One result of this experiment was that "many readers do not necessarily refer to the Holy Spirit or the Spirit of God as such, but speak of experiencing the very presence of God in their lives, especially as they practice communal and intercultural reading of the Bible with a partner group" (115).

Actually, Schipani (115) goes further in claiming that a more specific theological understanding results: "They offer testimonies of a deeply felt, immanent reality that illustrates the Pauline understanding that the presence of the Spirit is the reality of God's personal presence in the midst of the people." The problem with this claim is that the Bible's interpretive flexibility is not any greater than what we can find in any artificially constructed anthology, sacred or not. If one were to construct any anthology of texts with a wide range of dates, historical contexts, and genres from any ancient Near Eastern culture, one could achieve similarly manifold interpretive results. In fact, one could argue that this type of emphasis on the manifold ways in which one can interpret Scripture is not some radical or transformative departure from tradition but rather a further affirmation of very traditional Christian hermeneutics. Indeed, the manifold senses of Scripture were recognized already in the Hebrew Bible and in early Christian literature (Fishbane 1985; Kugel and Greer 1986).

More recently, it can be argued that interpretive flexibility represents a variant of European hermeneutical approaches exemplified in Hans Georg Gadamer's (1989) classic *Truth and Method*. Note Gadamer's (119)

120   Hector Avalos†

observation, which he applies to all literature, not just sacred literature: "In a certain sense interpretation probably is re-creation, but this is a re-creation not of the creative act but of the created work, which has to be brought to representation in accord with the meaning the interpreter finds in it." Schipani's exercise in gathering interpreters from different backgrounds is reminiscent of what Gadamer calls the "fusion of horizons" (*Horizontverschmelzung*), which entails dialogue and mediation (see also Thiselton 1980).

In other words, this sort of minoritized approach, which focuses on the virtues of manifold senses of Scripture, is not really new or transformative. It is part and parcel of ancient and modern Jewish, Christian, and secular European thought about the nature of interpretation. Furthermore, the emphasis on the interpretive flexibility of the Bible to explain its success overlooks the role of imperialism in establishing the dominance of the Bible in the world. The popularity of the Bible was not a process emanating from below but a top-to-bottom process all through Christian history (Avalos 2010). Indeed, it was not indigenous, conquered people who first expressed some need or want for a set of scriptures that they could then interpret to make their lives better. Rather, missionaries and Christian conquerors came and imposed these texts on indigenous people or tried to convince indigenous people that they needed these texts to be civilized and lead better lives.

In general, Schipani overlooks the imperialistic nature of how this text became sacred to so many people who then descended from the conquered people. Instead of seeing a reader's interest in the Bible as an artifact of conquest, Schipani sees it as part of some need emerging from below. Therefore, Schipani does not really offer some radical, transformative, or postcolonial approach but another variant of Christian textual imperialism.

Conclusion

Minoritized biblical scholarship is predominantly a continuation and expansion of Eurocentric Christian biblical scholarship. It is Eurocentric because it follows a program, first fully developed by Protestants in Europe, to bring biblical literacy to the world (Avalos 2010). Most of minoritized biblical scholarship is a Christian missiological enterprise, insofar as it seeks to recruit minorities and non-Europeans to the position that the Bible is still relevant to them. The main strategies for maintaining the supremacy and relevance of the Bible center on finding or inventing experiential analogies for minorities, choosing what are deemed to be good texts as representative of the Bible, assuming or promoting ethno-theological Christian identities, and extolling the interpretive flexibility of the Bible as a unique or superior textual advantage.

Empirically, I am not sure that minoritized biblical criticism has so far generated conclusions that are radically different, in terms of religionism and bibliolatry, from those of Euro-American scholars. One does some-times see allusions to "Desacralizing the Text" (Bailey, Liew, and Segovia 2009b, 30). Yet, most minoritized biblical scholarship actually ends up privileging biblical texts even when they are desacralized. I see as much diversity about what it even means to do Latino hermeneutics in the volume, to which I recently contributed, as I see in any volume about what it means to do Christian hermeneutics produced by scholars of purely European ancestry (Lozada and Segovia 2014; Avalos 2014). I have not witnessed any single conclusion that could not have been made or has not been made by someone not using an explicitly minoritized approach, as I illustrated with Mann, Müller, and Shockley.

My idea of minoritized criticism is quite different. The minorities are not so much the modern elite biblical scholars, who are themselves part of an ecclesial-academic complex and who have far more power and privilege than most other segments of society. The minorities to be empowered are all of the ancient cultures that have been marginalized by biblical scholars.

I have long contended that bibliolatry and Christian religiocentrism have effectively silenced the texts of many ancient Near Eastern cultures, which could also be praised as innovative or as ethically advanced if they had the army of modern apologists that Christianity does. The silencing of those texts is itself part of Christian textual imperialism. My goal is for scholars to give voice to the texts in the ancient Near East that have been marginalized by our guild itself. A truly egalitarian and altruis-tic approach is for Christian biblical scholars to realize that they must now share a smaller portion of the global textual pie in order to allow other marginalized texts to be heard and read again. If there is to be a minoritized criticism, then it should center on spotlighting more texts and cultural artifacts from Mesoamerica, Ugarit, Mesopotamia, Egypt, and other places that have been devalued and marginalized by biblical scholars themselves.

122   Hector Avalos†

Works Cited

Abusch, Tzvi. 1999. "Marduk." Pages 543–49 in *DDD*.

Ashcroft, Bill, Gareth Griffiths, and Helen Tiffin, eds. 1989. *The Empire Writes Back: Theory and Practice in Postcolonial Literatures*. London: Routledge.

Avalos, Hector, ed. 2004. *Introduction to the U.S. Latina and Latino Religious Experience*. Boston: Brill.

———. 2005. *Strangers in Our Own Land: Religion in U.S. Latina/o Literature*. Nashville: Abingdon.

———. 2007. *The End of Biblical Studies*. Amherst, NY: Prometheus.

———. 2010. "In Praise of Biblical Illiteracy." The Bible and Interpretation. https://tinyurl.com/SBL06106i.

———. 2014. "Rethinking Latino Hermeneutics: An Atheist Perspective." Pages 59–72 in *Latino/a Biblical Hermeneutics: Problematics, Objectives, Strategies*. Edited by Francisco Lozada Jr. and Fernando F. Segovia. SemeiaSt 68. Atlanta: SBL Press.

———. 2015. *The Bad Jesus: The Ethics of New Testament Ethics*. Sheffield: Sheffield Phoenix.

———. 2016. "Diasporas 'R' Us: Attitudes toward Immigrants in the Bible." Pages 33–46 in *The Bible in Political Debate: What Does It Really Say?* Edited by Frances Flannery and Rodney A. Werline. London: Bloomsbury T&T Clark.

Bailey, Randall, Tat-siong Benny Liew, and Fernando F. Segovia. 2009a. "Preface." Pages ix–x in *They Were All Together in One Place? Toward Minority Biblical Criticism*. Edited by Randall Bailey, Tat-siong Benny Liew, and Fernando F. Segovia. SemeiaSt 57. Atlanta: Society of Biblical Literature.

———. 2009b. "Toward Minority Biblical Criticism: Framework, Contours, Dynamics." Pages 1–43 in *They Were All Together in One Place? Toward Minority Biblical Criticism*. Edited by Randall Bailey, Tat-siong Benny Liew, and Fernando F. Segovia. SemeiaSt 57. Atlanta: Society of Biblical Literature.

Carroll R., M. Daniel. 2008. *Christians at the Border: Immigration, the Church, and the Bible*. Grand Rapids: Baker Academic.

Cuéllar, Gregory Lee. 2008. *Voices of Marginality: Exile and Return in Second Isaiah 40–55 and the Mexican Immigrant Experience*. New York: Lang.

De Wit, Hans, and Janet Dyk, eds. 2015. *Bible and Transformation: The Promise of Intercultural Bible Reading.* SemeiaSt 81. Atlanta: SBL Press.

Donaldson, Laura E. 1999. "The Sign of Orpah: Reading Ruth through Native Eyes." Pages 130–44 in *Ruth and Esther: A Feminist Companion to the Bible.* Edited by Athalya Brenner. Sheffield: Sheffield Academic.

Elizondo, Virgilio. 1983. *Galilean Journey: The Mexican American Promise.* Maryknoll, NY: Orbis Books.

Fishbane, Michael. 1985. *Biblical Interpretation in Ancient Israel.* New York: Oxford University Press.

Fuller Theological Seminary. N.d. "THM in Intercultural Studies." https://tinyurl.com/SBL06106j.

Gadamer, Hans-Georg. 1989. *Truth and Method.* 2nd rev. ed. Translated by Joel Weinsheimer and Donald G. Marshall. New York: Crossroad.

Guerrero, Andrés G. 1987. *A Chicano Theology.* Maryknoll, NY: Orbis Books.

Kugel, James L., and Rowan A. Greer. 1986. *Early Biblical Interpretation.* Philadelphia: Westminster.

León-Portilla, Miguel, and Earl Shorris, eds. 2001. *In the Language of Kings: An Anthology of Mesoamerican Literature; Pre-Columbian to the Present.* New York: Norton.

Los Tigres del Norte. "Mis Dos Patrias." N.d. Immigration *Corridos.* https://tinyurl.com/SBL06106k.

Lozada, Francisco, Jr., and Fernando F. Segovia, eds. 2014. *Latino/a Biblical Hermeneutics: Problematics, Objectives, Strategies.* SemeiaSt 68. Atlanta: SBL Press.

Mann, Thomas. 1963. *Joseph and His Brothers.* Translated by Helen T. Lowe-Porter. New York: Knopf.

Middleton, Stephen, David R. Roediger, and Donald M. Shaffer. 2016. *The Construction of Whiteness: An Interdisciplinary Analysis of Race Formation and the Meaning of White Identity.* Jackson: University Press of Mississippi.

Müller, Max. 1901. *My Autobiography.* New York: Scribner's Sons.

Muñoz-Larrondo, Rubén. 2014. "Toward a Latino/a Vision/Optic for Biblical Hermeneutics." Pages 203–29 in *Latino/a Biblical Hermeneutics: Problematics, Objectives, Strategies.* Edited by Francisco Lozada Jr. and Fernando F. Segovia. SemeiaSt 68. Atlanta: SBL Press.

Pelikan, Jaroslav. 1996. *Mary through the Centuries: Her Place in the History of Culture.* New Haven: Yale University Press.

Poole, Stafford. 1995. *Our Lady of Guadalupe: The Origins and Sources of a Mexican National Symbol, 1531–1797*. Tucson: University of Arizona Press.

Pritchard, James B. 2011. *The Ancient Near East: An Anthology of Texts and Pictures*. Princeton: Princeton University Press.

Reiner, Erica. 1958. *Surpu: A Collection of Sumerian and Akkadian Incantations*. Graz: Selbstverlage des Herausgebers.

Ruiz, Jean-Pierre. 2011. *Readings from the Edges: The Bible and People on the Move*. Maryknoll, NY: Orbis Books.

Schipani, Daniel S. 2015. "Transformation in Intercultural Bible Reading: A View from Practical Theology." Pages 99–116 in *Bible and Transformation: The Promise of Intercultural Bible Reading*. Edited by Hans de Wit and Janet Dyk. SemeiaSt 81. Atlanta: SBL Press.

Shockley, Martin. 1956. "Christian Symbolism in *The Grapes of Wrath*." *CollEng* 18:87–90.

Smith-Christopher, Daniel L. 1996. "Between Ezra and Nehemiah: Exclusion, Transformation, and Inclusion of the Foreigner in Post-exilic Biblical Theology." Pages 117–42 in *Ethnicity and the Bible*. Edited by Mark G. Brett. Leiden: Brill.

———. 2007. *Jonah, Jesus, and Other Good Coyotes: Speaking Peace to Power in the Bible*. Nashville: Abingdon.

Thiselton, Anthony C. 1980. *The Two Horizons: New Testament Hermeneutics and Philosophical Description with Special Reference to Heidegger, Bultmann, Gadamer, and Wittgenstein*. Carlisle: Paternoster.

Tilley, Helen, with Robert J. Gordon, eds. 2007. *Ordering Africa: Anthropology, European Imperialism, and the Politics of Knowledge*. Studies in Imperialism. Manchester: Manchester University Press.

Yee, Gale. 2009. "'She Stood in Tears amid the Alien Corn': Ruth, the Perpetual Foreigner and Model Minority." Pages 119–40 in *They Were All Together in One Place? Toward Minority Biblical Criticism*. Edited by Randall Bailey, Tat-siong Benny Liew, and Fernando F. Segovia. SemeiaSt. Atlanta: Society of Biblical Literature.

Bordered Hospitality and "the Least of These": The Bible as a Tool of Citizenship Excess in the Contemporary US Immigration Crisis

Jacqueline M. Hidalgo

The unending pandemics of recent years have exacerbated preexisting inequities and globalized violence around global migration.[1] Many receiving nations, such as the United States, employed the COVID-19 pandemic to further refuse migrants, terrorize them, and imprison them. As a scholar living in the United States, I also return to this essay, which I began in the fall of 2014, in the midst of a right-wing rhetorical effervescence of cruelty as the grounds of citizenship sown throughout the presidential campaign and presidential term of office of Donald J. Trump, though not sown strictly by him and not restricted to the United States.[2] What Trump signifies is a national political foregrounding of the discourse and agenda of citizenship excess.

By the summer of 2016, Trump's campaign won a popular plurality in Republican primaries because of his appeal to xenophobic US nationalism. He launched his campaign by lambasting unauthorized migrants in general and ethnically Mexican migrants in particular, while promising to build a wall on the US-Mexico border (Trump 2015). He also stressed a policy of total deportation of unauthorized migrants, while suggesting he might prevent any further Muslim migration to the United States if he were elected president (LoBianco 2015).[3] Late that summer, he backed

---

1. In this essay, because of my critique of logics of the nation-state that construct citizenship excess, I do not attend to whether migrants are necessarily "foreign" or "domestic." Hence, I use the term *migrant* rather than *immigrant* or *emigrant*, which are terms that emphasize national differentiation.

2. See in particular the description of "cruelty as citizenship" in Beltrán 2020.

3. With regard to deportation, in 2015, candidate Trump's campaign website called "for a 'shutdown' of Muslim immigration." In January 2017, then-President

down some on his pledge of mass deportation while maintaining a comparatively anti-immigrant stance (Bierman and Mehta 2016). His running mate, Mike Pence, furthered that line of Christian-supremacist xenophobia by suggesting that legal routes of immigration would be refused to migrants coming from countries with active "terrorist" networks. This position he articulated during a 15 July 2016 appearance on *Hannity* on Fox News Channel (Schliefer and Beavers 2016). In fall 2016, Trump's election, along with many of his subsequent actions and his rhetoric, underscored the enduring appeal of citizenship excess to certain members of the population.

Although Trump's vehemently antimigrant rhetoric may inflect the frustrations of the neoliberal economic order, he has given voice to those frustrations through rhetorics of racialized and Christian supremacist discrimination. His critiques of free trade more often proceeded through the frames of xenophobia and isolationism than through a robust critique of neoliberalism. He has reaffirmed the prototype of the US citizen as of European descent, cisgendered male, heterosexual, and Christian. Even more than that, he has underscored the desire to tightly circumscribe and recentralize the concept of US *citizen* in an era when it is partially the excesses of citizenship that bring turmoil to the lives of millions of people living in the United States, and even of more migrants globally.

I understand Trump's interlocking feats of race-baiting, Christianist, antimigrant xenophobia as the fallout of what Hector Amaya, a media studies scholar, terms "citizenship excess." Amaya (2013, loc. 114 of 6129) "theorizes that citizenship is inherently a process of uneven political capital accumulation," one in which political capital accumulates among those who already have a surplus of citizenship capital to play with. Political hierarchies are established within citizenship, but the surplus of citizenship itself works to "discriminat[e]" (to "push down") and to "balkanize[e]" (to "push away") minoritized populations through projects of differential inclusion and exclusion in relationship to processes of accumulation of

---

Trump issued an executive order blocking immigration from seven majority-Muslim nations. Popularly called "the Muslim ban," this executive order went through various iterations in the face of court litigation. Likely in order to mask the overt religious discrimination of this executive order, Trump's original campaign platform was removed from his website. For further discussion of the campaign statement on Muslim immigration and its disappearance from the campaign website in early 2017, see Vega, Siegel, and Mallin 2017.

Bordered Hospitality and "the Least of These"   127

political capital (loc. 143 of 6129). The United States, along with several other nations, has spent decades militarizing one of its borders and has increasingly militarized its border patrol forces (Dunn 1996). Such militarization affects those who live in the borderlands most significantly, but the logics of citizenship excess weave themselves throughout the broader United States.

The strategies of citizenship excess are often most apparent within right-wing rhetorics and politics, even when antimigrant thought does not emphasize the Christian Bible. Rather, as with Trump, the assumption is that the Bible is still rightfully the province of the right wing, whether they actually quote it or not. However, as a minoritized critic, what intrigues me more is how citizenship excess can affect the way that minoritized elites turn to and engage the Christian Bible in order, ostensibly, to defend the rights of unauthorized migrants.

Citizenship Excess and Biblical Liberals

For this analysis, I take as point of departure a press conference, held on Friday, 18 July 2014, by Deval Patrick, then the governor of the state of Massachusetts. This press conference centered on his decision to allow the federal government into the commonwealth in order to manage temporary housing for children detained attempting to cross the border between Mexico and the United States over the course of the summer. My concern here is not that his readings of the biblical texts are especially bad; indeed, they are certainly preferable to right-wing readings. My concern, rather, is that his interpretive approach remains consistent with a broader US practice of reading the Christian Bible with and through citizenship excess.

A media storm had already been circulating around the influx of Central American migrants, especially children, and significant media attention had already fallen on massive anti-immigration protests in Murrieta, California. This story had been broadly reported on the national news (on CNN's coverage, see, for instance, Martinez and Yan 2014). In the light of other work of mine, I could not help but attend to the irony of such protests in a town bearing the name of a Basque migrant, a surname that is the same as that of a famous, mythic nineteenth-century Mexican rebel against US rule. While some media and public figures were protesting the rather inhumane incarceration of children, who might have been better treated as refugees, the antimigrant sentiment of the Murrieta protesters was also raging in the Commonwealth of Massachusetts. For example, Mayor Judith Flanagan Kennedy of Lynn, Massachusetts, had led a charge against migrants in her city. She claimed that migrants put too much financial pressure on the public school and health care systems (see, for instance, the local coverage from MyFoxBoston 2014). The discourses of Mayor Kennedy, the Murrieta protesters, and the larger English-language media framed the arriving migrants as inherently illegal and as a drain on the resources of a United States in desperate financial times.

In that summer of 2014, Governor Patrick seemed like quite the compassionate hero. Patrick had been contacted by the federal government about providing space for the children in Massachusetts, and he agreed to do so, though he was quick to emphasize that the federal government would pay for and manage the space assigned to these children. Patrick then named what were, for him, two commingling inspirations that required him to act to provide such space in Massachusetts for these children. First, he named historical precedents in the United States. He mentioned the rescuing of Irish, Haitian, Russian, Ukrainian, Cambodian, and Sudanese children during times of crisis. He also lifted up the failure of the United States to accept Jewish refugees in 1939. Second, beyond naming his patriotic reasons, he also claimed that he wished to aid migrant children because of the teachings of his religion, especially as found in the Jewish and Christian Bibles. He declared,

> The other reason I have offered our help is more personal, less about patriotism and more about faith. I believe that we will one day have to answer for our actions—and our inactions. My faith teaches that "if a stranger dwells with you in your land, you shall not mistreat him," but rather "love him as yourself; for you were strangers in the land of Egypt" (Lev 19:33–34). We are admonished to take in the stranger, for "inasmuch as you did it to one of the least of these," Christ tells us, "you did it to Me" (Matt 25:43, 45). Every major faith tradition on earth charges its followers to treat others as we ourselves wish to be treated.[4]

Unpacking this quotation further will be the focus of this essay. Despite—or perhaps even because of—the seeming hospitality of Patrick's biblical hermeneutics, Patrick wields the Bible as a tool of citizenship excess, whereby the associated privileges and powers of citizenship accumulate

---

4. For YouTube clips of the news conference, see WBUR 2014; Patrick 2014.

Bordered Hospitality and "the Least of These" 129

and become weaponized for the perpetuation of those privileges. Strikingly, the example of Patrick reveals how the Bible persists as a locus of citizenship excess: its power, its accumulation, its marginalization of others—even when deployed in seemingly progressive rhetorics.

In the broader US discursive context, Patrick staked out the liberal—and seemingly compassionate—position. The protesters quickly showed up in Boston demanding that the governor retract his decision, and the media often interviewed protesters claiming that there were underserved children already in the United States in need of resources (Sison 2014). Such antimigrant discourses are familiar within a framework of citizenship excess. They overtly patrol the boundaries of national belonging, proclaiming a clear sense of who deserves national care. Even though citizenship excess was most clearly and stridently on display in the rhetoric of antimigrant protesters, Governor Patrick also participated in its deployment by drawing on his "love of country" and the teachings of his faith, specifically as laid out in a couple of key biblical passages.

Governor Patrick notably performed staged solidarity across minoritized communities and marshaled interfaith religious leadership to his side at the press conference. When citing the litany of refugee children that the United States has welcomed in the past, he chose countries from every continent. Further, he cited two prominent biblical passages from both the Hebrew Bible and the New Testament, and he seemingly evoked the ethic that M. Daniel Carroll R. (2008) outlines in his volume *Christians at the Border: Immigration, the Church, and the Bible*. Carroll argues that the Bible can orient Christians around a practice of compassion toward the foreigner, the stranger, the other. He calls for a "soft embrace" of the other (139–40). Seemingly inspired rhetorically by this ethic, Patrick contends that his "faith teaches that 'if a stranger dwells with you in your land, you shall not mistreat him,' but rather 'love him as yourself; for you were strangers in the land of Egypt' (Lev 19:33–34)."

Yet I wonder whether Carroll would view Patrick's actions as truly embracing and compassionate. Patrick's version of hospitality was to offer two military bases, the Westover Air Reserve Base in Chicopee and the Joint Base in Cape Cod, as the locations in which to incarcerate migrant children. While these sites were identified in his speech, they may have been identified as much as a month earlier (Patrick 2014; Shoenberg 2014). Isolated on these military bases, the children were hardly being welcomed into the broader commonwealth. The United States had

130 Jacqueline M. Hidalgo

incarcerated migrant children before and did so again many times in the years that followed.

Most famously, in the previous decade (2006), the United States began using the T. Don Hutto Detention Center in Taylor, Texas, to detain families and children. Hutto marked the first mass incarceration of children "without criminal charges" since the Japanese American concentration camps of World War II (Amaya 2013, loc. 1841 of 6129). Even before Hutto, the Immigration and Naturalization Service had detained unauthorized migrant families in the Berks Facility in Leesport, Pennsylvania, in 2001 in the wake of 9/11. As Patrick emphasized in his remarks, Massachusetts would not be welcoming children into local homes and neighborhoods. Although he clarified that migrant children would have access to education and space to play, media examinations of Hutto showed that the spaces for the incarcerated children, who are juridically termed "inmates," were prison-like, with minimal time for classes, which were generally taught in English.

How can one claim that such incarceration is the hospitable, compassionate choice? According to Amaya (2013, loc. 2040 of 6129), citizenship excess actually requires such a construal, because it relies on "an assumption that undocumented people do not have the rights that we typically associate with citizenship." For Amaya, the very framework of citizenship that grants rights based on some other sort of belonging besides shared humanity within a given territory is the fundamental conundrum of the modern framework of "citizen." Drawing the lines of citizenship as a set of privileges that can and must be unevenly distributed leads to an excess of citizenship capital accumulating among some, while others are marginalized and dehumanized.[5] Within this logic, just agreeing to incarcerate children rather than immediately deporting them becomes the liberal, compassionate action. What in citizenship excess prevents us from demanding that migrants hold a broader base of rights? Why cannot we imagine that migrant children have a right to free play and settlement rather than incarceration?

---

5. Amaya's arguments about citizenship excess resonate with Sylvester A. Johnson's (2015, 399–400) critique of modern democracies—and specifically the US's democracy—as resting on "a racial constitution" where "they endow the people with ruling power but not everyone gets to be 'the people.' ... By this account, democracy is not an innocent, virtuous political order. It is, rather, the product of the colonial relation of power."

Bordered Hospitality and "the Least of These" 131

Biblical Identification and Authorization as the
Hermeneutic of Citizenship Excess

Governor Patrick's smooth use of a seemingly compassionate biblical reading as a tool of citizenship excess relies further on a logic of identification with certain actors in the biblical narrative, an identification whereby he presumes himself to be with and among the privileged elite of the narrative. When he reads the Bible, he readily sees himself in the position of the Israelites, rather than the stranger; likewise, he sees himself among the sheep that were compassionate to "the least of these." Both correlative readings require the assumptions of citizenship excess, for instance, that compassion toward the stranger is Patrick's to offer as the appropriate citizen.[6]

Even more intriguingly, the use of the story from Matthew is quite striking within one of the most important tropes of citizenship excess, what Amaya (2013, loc. 1451 of 6129) terms "the pastoral"—the tendency to imagine the nation as sheep that must be protected and segregated from forces of potential harm. Indeed, a brief survey of biblical scholarship on both passages reveals a consistent anxiety over the tensions of identification and belonging, of who counts as a stranger and who is the "these" in the "least of these." Most importantly, so many interpreters presume that they read from and with the authorized position of power, as the nation of Israel in Leviticus or as the chosen sheep of God in Matthew. Thus, they wonder about the identity of those whom they deem to be other and query the limits of the compassion they deserve.

More fundamentally, examining some facets of biblical scholarship with respect to these two passages reveals something about how scriptures function. Even historical-critical interpreters tend to take a side in this text, to place themselves within it as the person who is not "the stranger" or the person who is not the "least of these." This presumed starting positionality as being more on the side of power and belonging plays right into citizenship excess.

---

6. Moreover, citizenship excess in the US should be contextualized in relationship to histories of settler colonialism and enslavement (see Beltrán 2020). In the context of settler colonial states such as the US, often rhetorics of hospitality reflect an assertion of territorial control on the part of the so-called host, an assertion deeply bound up with colonial dynamics of power (see Medina 2022).

132 Jacqueline M. Hidalgo

Identifying as Biblical Israel in Leviticus

Given the history of US rhetorics, which deeply connect the United States as a nation to biblical Israel, and the histories of settler colonial and imperial violence that have accompanied such rhetorics, a minoritized critic would likely be suspicious of readings that connect a US interpreter too easily to Israel. Indeed, many scholarly texts in North American biblical and religious studies have examined how Jewish biblical traditions have been appropriated (often in supersessionist manner) by dominantized Euro-US Christians as part of a narrative of divine right to land and power in the Western hemisphere (Cherry 1998; Shalev 2013). Further, Robert Allan Warrior (1997) shows how both the United States and the liberationist deployments of the exodus narrative generally presume that the reader identifies with Israel. Yet, this persistent identification haunts certain biblical interpretations, sometimes at overt levels, even when those interpreters are trying to be critical of facile identification with the biblical material.

Joel S. Kaminsky's reading of Leviticus is a case in point. Kaminsky helpfully challenges the weight that has been placed on Lev 19:18 and the command to "love thy neighbor as thyself." He underscores how ancient rabbis already recognized that problematic limits could restrict the good of this command; indeed, would it not be better to love the neighbor more than oneself (Kaminsky 2008, 132)? However, in trying to make the case for the insightful political realism embedded in the Levitical code, Kaminsky's argument also specifically addresses concerns of citizenship that directly connect the United States to biblical Israel. Kaminsky (123) interprets the term used in Lev 19:18 for "neighbor" (root רעה) as "fellow citizen." The word certainly can connote a more intimate sense of "friend" or "fellow citizen," but this choice of rhetorical emphasis in translating Lev 19:18 should be related to the translation of Lev 19:33–34. The contrast between "fellow citizen" and "resident alien" (in Kaminsky's translation) underscores the import of political categories of belonging in reading a biblical mandate.

Kaminsky directly situates his interpretation in relationship to US concerns with citizenship and national belonging, even while he helpfully tries to recognize the otherness of the ancient biblical material and the discomfort that we as readers likely have with its cultural norms. Thus, he observes, "Contemporary readers are often upset by the ways in which Israel's theology created distinctions between Israelites and non-Israelites" (124). He further argues that, while these distinctions may seem problematic to our modern notions, Israel's conception of itself

Bordered Hospitality and "the Least of These" 133

as a holy nation may also enable a whole people to feel responsible for making a better world rather than placing that responsibility only on the shoulders of certain citizens (127). Kaminsky would disagree with Governor Patrick's translation and interpretation of Lev 19:33–34, because for him "resident aliens" (root גור, shared with the verb "sojourn") does not include all "strangers." Rather, these "strangers" should be understood as "resident aliens" living in Israel with Israelites, and "resident aliens obey certain cultic regulations" (124).

Kaminsky (124) then draws a parallel to the United States and argues that participation in the United States comprises a similar observance of rights and responsibilities, including "having to adjust to American cultural norms." Certainly, the Torah describes legal and linguistic expectations of sojourners in Israel, but connecting those expectations too quickly to US melting-pot notions of assimilation may only serve to perpetuate the citizenship excess that pervades so much US biblical engagement (Carroll 2008, 105–7). Although the connection to the United States is simply meant as a helpful analogy, the US–biblical Israel identification persists, even when an interpreter is otherwise circumspect about the historical distance between the present and the context of the text's origins.

Here Carroll's approach is, of course, markedly different, given his concerns. He emphasizes rather the translation of "sojourner" (not "stranger" or "resident alien"), which helps to underscore the sense of migration—of movement—that may also lie behind the term. Thus, he emphasizes the "potentially precarious situation" that a sojourner may face (Carroll 2008, 103). Providing a more liberative reading that underscores God's continuing intervention on the side of the "helpless," Carroll's (104–5) reading also emphasizes the fuller text here of Lev 19:33–34, which reinscribes Israelites as former sojourners themselves, who must be kinder to sojourners than Egypt had been to them.

Are We the Sheep? Who Are the Least of the These?

All such interest in identification reveals the embeddedness of thinking with and through the Bible as and about the nation. In part, such thinking may be the consequence of the frequent but often difficult to parse language of "nations" within biblical texts. Scholarly interpretations of the second passage that Governor Patrick quotes, the judgment of the sheep and the goats in Matthew, likewise point to anxieties of identification in interpretation that hinge specifically on questions of national belonging.

134 Jacqueline M. Hidalgo

Matthew 25:31–40 has a long history of interpretive ambiguity, even with regard to identifying genre, let alone identifying its multiple characters. It is a unique set of verses, not paralleled in the other gospels, and it has a couple of unique words, which, intriguingly, are associated with "cursed" and "eternal punishment" (Cortés-Fuentes 2003, 103–4). Although it is generally but ambiguously classed as an apocalyptic or eschatological discursive space with the tendencies of a parable, scholars often use genre to make a case about the proper identification of the sheep and the goats.

Thus, for instance, Dan O. Via (1987) makes the case for classifying it as a work of apocalyptic imagination, but he makes that case in part because he thinks understanding Matt 25 as apocalyptic imagination sheds light on who the "nations" are. According to his argument, the text is consequently an ethical demand placed on everyone: "All people, in or out of the church, are responsible for all people, in or out of the church" (93). By contrast, while arriving at a similar ethical reading, David A. deSilva (1991) classifies the text "as a 'future more vivid' parable. The story appears without the usual parabolic incipits, but parabolic elements are woven into the story to move the hearers' focus away from the futureness of the events to the present ethical realities of the kingdom" (172). He would still argue that the use of eschatological imagination underscores the ethical drive, but it is this future temporality, and not the parabolic genre, that DeSilva relies on in determining the identity of the nations being judged. He argues that the futurity of the parable means that the gospel has gone to all nations, and thus all people are being held accountable.

Coming late in the gospel, this story immediately precedes Jesus's announcement to his disciples that Passover is coming in two days and that the Son of Man will be betrayed to crucifixion (Matt 26:1–2). Thus, a tale of the Son of Man sitting in future glory and passing judgment precedes the announcement of the Son of Man's earthly judgment (Carter 2014, 167). In the tale, the Son of Man is in glory and judges all the nations (πάντα τὰ ἔθνη), separating out sheep to his right and goats to his left (Matt 25:31–32). Based on ancient Mediterranean approaches to the right and the left hands, it is generally assumed that this arrangement signifies that sheep are good and goats are bad (Via 1987, 96).

The Son of Man in 25:31 is called the king/emperor (Βασιλεὺς) in Matt 25:34, and he proceeds to pass judgment. First, he informs the sheep at his right that they "inherit the kingdom/empire" because they cared for him when he was hungry, thirsty, a stranger (ξένος), naked, sick, and in prison. The sheep, now dubbed the "just/righteous" (οἱ δίκαοι; Matt 25:37), ask

Bordered Hospitality and "the Least of These"

when it was that they did these things. The king/emperor replies, and here I offer an overly literal translation to make clear some of the strain of ambiguity, "just as you did to one of these who is my brothers/siblings who is the least, you did to me" (τούτων τῶν ἀδελφῶν μου τῶν ἐλαχίστων; 25:40). Then, he sends the goats to the devil for not having done "to the least of these" as the sheep had (25:45).

Scholars query the identities of the sheep and the goats by wondering who is included in "all the nations." Frequently, the conclusion is that this phrase is used to refer to gentiles in other places and hence must do so here as well. Still, critics such as deSilva (1991, 174) argue that the eschatological orientation of the text, along with the Great Commission in Matthew, means that distinctions between Jews and gentiles should be considered irrelevant here. Interpretive choices about the sheep and goats may also be relevant in determining "the least of these my siblings." Governor Patrick presumed that his faith placed him among the pious sheep and that "the least of these" referred to everyone in need. However, that is not necessarily the only interpretation possible.

Scholars such as David Cortés-Fuentes challenge the universality of either "the nations" or "the least of these." Arguing that gentiles alone are being judged, Cortés-Fuentes posits that "the least of these" refers specifically to followers of Jesus. He points out that the word for "brothers/siblings" generally refers to nonbiological siblings only when referring to Christians and that perhaps the use of the "least" is connected to a phrase for "these little ones" (ἕνα τῶν μικρῶν τούτων) in 10:42 and 18:6, 10, 14, which would mean that the phrase refers specifically to believers (Cortés-Fuentes 2003, 107). Thus, the sheep are not the characters with whom the intended audience would identify; instead, Cortés-Fuentes posits that early Christian audiences, and contemporary Latinx ones, identify with "the least of these." For Cortés-Fuentes (109), the passage could then just as likely be a form of narrow, nationalistic self-promotion as it is an ethic of solidarity; that may also be why Jesus is to be found in and among "the least of these."

Even though my instincts and desires draw me more to Governor Patrick's interpretation, I cannot help but wonder whether that reveals my own embeddedness within discourses of US citizenship and its excesses.[7] Perhaps the framework of the nationalist pastoral draws citi-

---

7. Carroll (2008, 171) responds even more harshly to Cortés-Fuentes, claim-

136   Jacqueline M. Hidalgo

zens to the sheep. Rather than identifying with the sheep as Patrick does (or I might wish to do), rather than identifying with the chosen who are beneficent to others, who have the privilege to offer others crumbs or incarceration, Cortés-Fuentes focuses on the implications of taking "the least of these" as the proper subjects and audience of address in this passage. He reads Latinx contexts as being more tied to the least, who do not and cannot expect "others to extend their helping hand.... For our communities to survive, as that of Matthew's church, we need to take care of our own people" (Cortés-Fuentes 2003, 109). His reading of "the least of these" in relationship to Latinx contexts suggests that this eschatological discourse/parable cannot be an easily universalized ethical demand on the sheep, because this text is not really about the sheep and what they are asked to do. Rather, the text was written for and is about the least of these and the imaginative world they cultivate to survive.

Cortés-Fuentes's reading teeters on the edge of a hermeneutics of "correlation and correspondence," which can flatten the contexts of the ancient world and the multivocality of biblical texts as well as the contemporary world to which a correspondence is drawn (Ruiz 2011, loc. 342 of 5170). Yet, such readings can also shock us into querying who claims to have privileged access and privileged identification with biblical texts. Given that the Christian gospels, including Matthew,[8] were produced, circulated, and made Scripture by communities living in the diaspora, a reading with and through migration would seem like a more natural starting point in interpreting these texts. If one presumes migrants and diasporic subjects as the intended audience and originating communities of these texts, then such a stance should transform the characters that people read for and

---

ing "that he has missed the potential application of the passage and the thrust of the Bible in general." While I understand, especially in the framework of Carroll's argument, why Cortés-Fuentes's reading does not work, I do not write from a position that sees the Christian Bible as a univocal text with one orientation. Further, I cannot help but wonder whether a quest for univocality in biblical texts is connected to citizenship excess, and specifically to those practices of authorization that wield the Christian Bible as the appropriate property of the reader and a tool of citizenship excess.

8. Given the references to the temple's destruction, Matthew was likely written after 70 CE, for a community experiencing various forms of displacement. The appearance of Syria in Matt 4:24 and its citation in early Christian sources in Syria make it likely that this is a text circulating in diasporic Jewish and "Christian" communities responding to experiences of displacement (Carter 2014, 127–28).

identify with in these texts.[9] Yet such readings might produce, as Cortés-Fuentes wonders with regard to Matt 25, results that are narrowly nationalistic and self-interested.

Beyond Identification and Its Excesses of Authorization

Even if it is true that ancient communities were thinking within ancient nationalistic terms in producing these texts, it does not have to hold that we read them so. Sylvester A. Johnson's examination of the biblical "myth of Ham" in nineteenth-century African American discourses provokes an important question about the liberative limits of even oppressed groups trying to identify themselves in biblical narrative, especially when they seek to understand themselves as the "people of God." He argues that such an identification too often lends itself to "the persistent refusal of modern peoples to denounce violence when it is divine" (Johnson 2004, 133). His work points to why and how the Bible may so often be mobilized as a tool of citizenship excess: the Bible has been engaged through a practice of authorization that ultimately legitimizes violence as part of separating the people of God who belong to the text and those who belong outside the mercy of the text.

I do not think it coincidence that reading with authorization and treating unauthorized migrants as less deserving of equal rights both trade on words with *authority* at their root. What would happen if we all read from the position of "illegitimate folk," those "unauthorized by a dazzling deity" instead (133)? Although Johnson writes from a different context, I think that starting with the assumption that we—especially US citizens, including minoritized ones—are "unauthorized" in our reading of biblical narrative might be an important corrective to citizenship excess. Rather than globally casting unauthorized migration as a terrifying crisis, such reading would focus on concern for the human rights of everyone, with no one cast as the more legitimate sheep inheriting the kingdom.

Even as I am troubled by how Governor Patrick uses the Bible to envelop migrants in a soft embrace of incarceration, I also wonder whether there

---

9. Margaret Aymer outlines some of the different migrant and diasporic strategies that clarify some of the narrative and communal tensions found in early Christian texts. For Aymer (2014, 57), Matthew evidences "a migrant strategy of separation" that seeks to recruit the world only to the home culture; such a reading resonates with Cortés-Fuentes's approach.

138   Jacqueline M. Hidalgo

might be more playful blurring possible, even within his remarks. Might there be another sort of Bible or at least biblical reading practice possible? If the Bible does not get used as a tool of and for the circumscription of citizens, even those who beneficently detain strangers, embracing biblical textual ambiguities and phrasing might help us destabilize the boundaries of citizenship. Are Israelites necessarily natives in Lev 19? They are migrating from Egypt, where they were foreigners, and this memory of being migrants is activated such that the line between natives and strangers might be unclear. Although in a different vein, Matt 25 also blurs identities, since the least of these is somehow also Jesus, and since scholars never seem to agree about to whom "the least of these" actually refers.

Governor Patrick himself pushes these borders in his last comment: "Every major faith tradition on earth charges its followers to treat others as we ourselves wish to be treated." While troublingly universalizing all religions, he alters the normal phrasing of the golden rule, and his phrasing may try to blur the boundary between "others" and "ourselves." Could such a blurring between others and ourselves portend a future without boundaries between citizens and migrants? What if biblical readers refuse to identify strictly as the Israelites? What if they think of themselves as biblical strangers rather than natives? Would the collection of texts still be the Bible if it were divorced from the discourses of citizenship and its excesses?

Works Cited

Amaya, Hector. 2013. *Citizenship Excess: Latino/as, Media and the Nation.* New York: New York University Press. Kindle.

Aymer, Margaret. 2014. "Rootlessness and Community in Contexts of Diaspora." Pages 47–62 in *Fortress Commentary on the Bible: The New Testament.* Edited by Margaret Aymer, Cynthia Briggs Kittredge, and David A. Sánchez. Minneapolis: Fortress.

Beltrán, Cristina. 2020. *Cruelty as Citizenship: How Migrant Suffering Sustains White Democracy.* Minneapolis: University of Minnesota Press.

Bierman, Noah, and Seema Mehta. 2016. "Trump Backs Away from Full Mass Deportation, but His Speech Packs a Slew of Hard-Line Proposals." *Los Angeles Times*, 31 August. https://tinyurl.com/SBL06106l.

Carroll R., M. Daniel. 2008. *Christians at the Border: Immigration, the Church, and the Bible.* Grand Rapids: Baker Academic.

Carter, Warren. 2014. "Matthew." Pages 127–42 in *Fortress Commentary on the Bible: The New Testament*. Edited by Margaret Aymer, Cynthia Briggs Kittredge, and David A. Sánchez. Minneapolis: Fortress.

Cherry, Conrad, ed. 1998. *God's New Israel: Religious Interpretations of American Destiny*. Rev. and updated ed. Chapel Hill: University of North Carolina Press.

Cortés-Fuentes, David. 2003. "The Least of These My Brothers: Matthew 25: 31–46." *Apuntes* 23.3:100–109.

deSilva, David A. 1991. "Renewing the Ethics of the Eschatological Community: The Vision of Judgment in Matthew 25." *Koinonia* 3:168–94.

Dunn, Timothy J. 1996. *The Militarization of the U.S.-Mexico Border, 1978–1992*. Austin: University of Texas Press.

Johnson, Sylvester A. 2004. *The Myth of Ham in Nineteenth-Century American Christianity: Race, Heathens, and the People of God*. New York: Palgrave Macmillan.

———. 2015. *African American Religions, 1500–2000: Colonialism, Democracy, and Freedom*. New York: Cambridge University Press.

Kaminsky, Joel S. 2008. "Loving One's (Israelite) Neighbor: Election and Commandment in Leviticus 19." *Int* 62.2:123–32.

LoBianco, Tom. 2015. "Donald Trump Promises 'Deportation' Force to Remove 11 Million." CNN, 12 November. https://tinyurl.com/SBL06106m.

Martinez, Michael, and Holly Yan. 2014. "Showdown: California Town Turns Away Buses of Detained Immigrants." CNN, updated 3 July. https://tinyurl.com/SBL06106n.

Medina, Néstor. 2022. "Reconsiderar la hospitalidad en relación con la migración." *CRIT* 398:117–30.

MyFoxBoston.com. 2014. "Lynn Officials: Illegal Immigrant Children Are Stressing City Services." Fox 25 WFXT, updated 14 July. https://tinyurl.com/SBL06106o.

Patrick, Deval. 2014. "Sheltering of Unaccompanied Children Press Conference 7/18." YouTube, 18 July, 18:14. https://tinyurl.com/SBL06106bi.

Ruiz, Jean-Pierre. 2011. *Readings from the Edges: The Bible and the People on the Move*. Maryknoll, NY: Orbis Books. Kindle.

Schliefer, Theodore, and Olivia Beavers. 2016. "Pence 'Very Supportive' of Latest Version of Trump Muslim Ban." CNN.com, 16 July. https://tinyurl.com/SBL06106p.

Shalev, Eran. 2013. *American Zion: The Old Testament as a Political Text from the Revolution to the Civil War*. New Haven: Yale University Press.

Shoenberg, Shira. 2014. "Federal Government Told Massachusetts Officials in June That Housing for Illegal Immigrant Children Was Overwhelmed." MassLive.com, 5 August. https://tinyurl.com/SBL06106q.

Sison, Bree. 2014. "Protesters Rally against Mass. Plan to House Immigrant Children." CBS WBZ4, 26 July. https://tinyurl.com/SBL06106r.

Trump, Donald J. 2015. "Presidential Announcement Speech." *Time*, 16 June. https://tinyurl.com/SBL06106s.

Vega, Cecilia, Benjamin Siegel, and Alexander Mallin. 2017. "Original Muslim Ban Erased from Trump Campaign Website." ABC News, 8 May. https://tinyurl.com/SBL06106t.

Via, Dan O. 1987. "Ethical Responsibility and Human Wholeness in Matthew 25:31–46." *HTR* 80:79–100.

Warrior, Robert Allen. 1997. "A Native American Perspective: Canaanites, Cowboys, and Indians." Pages 277–85 in *Voices from the Margin: Interpreting the Bible in the Third World*. New ed. Edited by R. S. Sugirtharajah. Maryknoll, NY: Orbis Books.

WBUR. 2014. "Gov. Deval Speaks On Sheltering Child Migrants - State House News Service." YouTube, 18 July, 7:27. https://tinyurl.com/SBL06106bh.

Passed On and Passing On:
Reading John's Affective Transfer

Tat-siong Benny Liew

The Latin root for *grief* is *gravis*, which is etymologically also related to the words *grave* and *engrave*. The link between *grave* and *engraving* is clear once we consider the words that are often etched on tombstones. The etymological connections between these words point to the thought that painful experiences of death and destruction can become textualized. They are written down because someone does not want the experiences to be forgotten. Instead, writing functions here not only to register the wounds and the sorrow but also to enable them to be passed on to readers despite the fact that the experiences themselves might have passed.

Reading African American women writers such as Toni Morrison and bell hooks, Elise Miller (2016, 464) suggests that writing and reading can be understood as "a re-imagining and re-construction of the past … rooted in processes of mourning." They "can provide a space within which what is forgotten, lost, or erased can be recalled and memorialized" (477). Taking mourning, grieving, writing, and reading as related activities or processes, I will turn to John's Gospel to illustrate what I think will be important for minoritized biblical interpretation in these times of death and dread: a rhetoric and politics of mourning in a temporal boomerang.

Affective Transfer through Scars and Wounds of Jesus

In her book titled *Passed On,* Karla FC Holloway (2003) discusses how African American mourning and burial practices in response to Black

---

An earlier version of this essay appeared as "Good Grief: Mourning as Remembrance and Protest," in *Doing Theology in the New Normal: Global Perspectives,* ed. Jione Havea (London: SCM, 2021), 279–96. Used with permission.

-141-

142   Tat-siong Benny Liew

people's vulnerability to untimely deaths in the United States play a crucial part in the construction of Black identities. In that sense, those who have passed on may still have insights to pass on to those who are alive. Similarly, the gospel writer was passing on a story of (a resurrected) Jesus to readers (including us now) after Jesus had already passed on by Roman execution. John's Gospel can therefore be read as a form of recalcitrant memory or even a "militant refusal to allow certain objects to disappear into oblivion" by a colonized people (Eng and Han 2000, 695). The description of loss and remains in a politics of mourning as "register[ing] a tension between loss and survival, absence and presence" seem to be perfectly applicable to John's Gospel about Jesus (Winters 2016, 50).

Let's face it: John's Gospel portrays a world that is far from rosy. Grief is a story, and John's Gospel is in many ways a story of grief. Its protagonist, Jesus, is presented as the slaughtered Passover lamb (1:29, 36; 19:13–42). In other words, he is not only killed but also animalized (see Moore 2017, 107–26). This association between Jesus and a lamb in John's Gospel is all the more troubling if one keeps in mind the Roman gladiatorial combats, in which captured criminals were sent out to entertain a bloodthirsty audience by battling fierce animals, often with neither arms nor armor and dying like feeble lambs (Liew 2016, 136–37).

Despite his claim that his nourishment comes from doing God's will (John 4:31–34) and that humans should not worry about physical sustenance (6:25–27, 35), John's Jesus feeds people with fish and bread not once but twice (6:1–14, 21:9–14). He also compares people who consumed "bread from heaven" in the past with those who will eat his flesh as "the living bread" (6:22–59). We clearly see from this that human lives depend on animals and plants. That John's Jesus dies as a slaughtered lamb to give life to his followers (3:14–16, 6:47–58, 10:11–18) exposes how the Romans routinely treated their colonial subjects as less than human to nourish their own lives.

In this light, the words of John's Jesus regarding being "hated" and being "persecuted" by "the world" (15:18–21, 16:33, 17:14–16) take on a whole different layer of meaning. The outlook seems even more ominous when John's Jesus matter-of-factly declares that his followers will not fare any better than he does (13:16, 15:20),[1] so his followers must also be will-

---

1. See, at the same time, 14:12, where John's Jesus also says that his followers will do "greater works" than what he has done.

Passed On and Passing On 143

ing to die (12:23–26). He proceeds to clarify that their prospect of being killed is not a matter of if but when (16:1–2). Although John's Jesus repeatedly tells Peter to "feed" and "tend" his lambs and sheep (21:15–17), his flock seems to be fed and led only to be slaughtered.

All those references to Jesus's hour in John (2:4; 7:30; 8:20; 12:23, 27; 13:1; 16:21, 25, 32; 17:1) only imply his "vulnerability to premature death"; as his interlocutors point out, he is "not yet fifty years old" (Gilmore 2007, 28; John 8:57).[2] Given John's talk of a world above and a world below (3:7, 12–13, 31; 6:38, 41, 51, 60–62; 8:23; 19:11), the departure or return of John's Jesus to his Father (7:33–34; 13:1–3; 16:5–11, 28; 17:11–13; 20:16–17)—a departure that he also promises to his followers (14:1–7)—comes across to me as something similar to the "flying African" traditions about which Morrison and others write and discuss, even or especially in a realized eschatological framework.

Gay Wilentz (1992, 63) writes, "Legends abound throughout the New World about Africans who either flew or jumped off slave ships as well as those who saw the horrors of slavery when they landed in the Americas and 'in their anguish sought to fly back to Africa.'" These flying legends have been read metaphorically as either suicides or escapes, or as reflecting "not only a wishful claim to power, but also a worldview, a broad-based 'cultural system' of human flight" (Young 2017, 52). What Joseph R. Winters (2016, 72) says about the agency depicted by a character named John in W. E. B. Du Bois's (1907, 228–49) *Souls of Black Folk* is transferrable to what we find in John's Gospel: it is an agency "defined by self-loss, death, and vulnerability." Painting a world full of hatred and death, John's narrative haunts us with its memory or its story of a dead-but-resurrected and present-yet-absent Jesus (Liew 2016).

John's Jesus makes several ghostly appearances after his crucifixion and resurrection. After appearing to Mary Magdalene (20:11–18), he appears to his disciples in two consecutive weeks (20:19–29). Thanks to the "doubting Thomas" tradition (20:24–29), the better-known episode between these two weekly appearances by John's resurrected Jesus is undoubtedly the second one. John's Jesus comes across in these episodes like a phantom, as he can obviously go through closed doors or solid walls (20:19, 26). Then we learn, because of Thomas's expressed desire or need to verify Jesus's identity by checking out his wounds (20:24–25), that this

---

2. Unless otherwise noted, Scripture quotations follow the NRSV.

144   Tat-siong Benny Liew

resurrected Jesus in John's narrative is actually a specter with substance—or he has suddenly shifted from magical to material. Besides telling and allowing Thomas to touch and feel the wounds in both his hands and his side, John's Jesus, likely in response to Thomas's "I will not believe" declaration ahead of Jesus's apparitional arrival (20:25), emphasizes the importance of faith both before and after Thomas's verbal response to Jesus's invitation to touch and feel him (20:27–29).

Because of these repeated references to faith and the explicit contrast with doubt made by John's Jesus—"Do not doubt but believe" (20:27)—the problem of doubt becomes for some the dominant meaning of these verses, with poor Thomas becoming the symbol of skepticism (Most 2005). Regardless of how one may want to read Thomas, there is much more to think about besides the question of doubt. Notice that John's Jesus himself, without anyone asking, *volunteers* to show his hands and his side to his disciples when he appears to them a week earlier (20:20). In other words, he shows his other disciples basically what he shows Thomas. It is not only because of Thomas's doubt that he shows his hands and his side.

In a chapter within her recent book, Candida Moss (2019, 22–40) focuses on this Johannine episode and observes that there has not been adequate scholarly attention given to the resurrected body of John's Jesus. Citing sources such as Homer, Plato, Virgil, Galen, and Christian readers from late antiquity, Moss argues that it makes more sense to read the hands and side of John's resurrected Jesus as referring to his crucifixion scars rather than his crucifixion wounds, especially if we assume that John's Jesus is showing his hands and side to authenticate that he is indeed their crucified master and/or to confirm that he is not an apparition. This is so for Moss because (1) scars were often used in the Greco-Roman world to identify people, and (2) scars should have developed on the *physical* body of John's Jesus more than a week after his crucifixion if he was not a ghost. Having said that, Moss herself admits that the wound that John's Jesus suffered on his side might have taken longer to heal, and that there is an existing and influential tradition that reads Jesus's hands as covered with scars but his side as an open wound. Given the ambiguity of the Greek, which Moss (28–29) also acknowledges, I tend to think that we can go with either "scars" or "wounds," or both, especially since they bring different nuance to these back-to-back appearances by John's Jesus.[3]

---

3. I need and want to acknowledge that Moss's (2019, 25) preference to read

Affective Transfers through Scars

In making her argument, Moss (29) cites Philo's use of the Greek word τύποι "to describe the impressions left by old wounds." Interestingly, Sara Ahmed (2014, 6, 11, 15, 70, emphasis original) reminds her readers that we need to *"remember the press in an impression"* as she discusses how emotion or affect "sticks" or "leaves its mark or trace" on "objects of emotion" with which we come into contact and, in the process, presses on these objects to form or "intensify" surface and boundary by potentially "align[ing] bodily and social space."[4] Concerned with state narratives about "moving on," Ahmed (201–2, emphasis original) shares Moss's hesitation regarding rushing to healing and asks us to "rethink our relation to scars, including emotional and physical scars," because their "lumpy" covering *"always exposes the injury"* of the past in the present. Scars can remind us that "recovering from injustice cannot be about covering over the injuries" and that "justice involves feelings" (202).

We know the injuries that John's Jesus suffers are physical. Not only is he physically abused and crucified, but his dead body is also jabbed and gashed by a spear (18:22; 19:1, 3, 16–18, 34). However, we should not lose sight that his injuries are also emotional. He was derided before his

---

"scars" comes from her important consideration of disability studies, especially in light of a long and strong tradition that is in many ways connected with a triumphal temporality of linear and teleological progress: namely, reading resurrection as a promise of future "perfection."

4. Emotions operate "to 'make' and 'shape' bodies as forms of action, which also involves orientations towards others" (Ahmed 2014, 4, 6). In other words, the "press" in impression can lead to detachment or alignment. The emphasis on "impression" also allows Ahmed (2014, 6) to "avoid making analytical distinctions between bodily sensation, emotion and thought as if they could be 'experienced' as distinct realms of human 'experience.'" Ahmed's "sociality of emotions" is also meant to correct the conventional understanding that emotions either go from "inside-out" or from "outside-in." Instead, Ahmed (10) argues that "emotions create the very effect of the surfaces and boundaries that allow us to distinguish an inside and an outside in the first place … [because] the 'I' and the 'we' are shaped by, and even take the shape of, contact with others." Referring to Ahmed's (12) work here is in a sense reading Ahmed against the grain, since she is primarily interested in how social norms and hence particular forms of subordination "stick," but I am interested in how feelings of grief can also stick for a politics of resistance. If emotion is "a form of cultural politics or world making," then theoretically it can also serve a different politics to make a different world, as Ahmed's (12, 145–90) chapters on "queer feelings" and "feminist attachments" indicate.

crucifixion (19:2–3), and he worries about his mother and his disciples when he is hanging on the cross, so he asks them to care for each other (20:26–27). We also sense his emotional struggles when he, anticipating his arrest and his "hour," openly tells his disciples that his "soul is troubled" (12:27). His farewell discourse (chs. 14–17) is also full of anguish, as he tries to comfort, warn, and teach his disciples as well as pray to his Father all at the same time. He talks about his disciples being troubled (14:1) and filled with sorrow (16:6), and how they will weep, mourn, and have pain (16:20–22).

John's Gospel also makes it clear that the physical and emotional scars on the body of John's Jesus, if we choose to side with Moss's preference, are results of injustice. Caiaphas is willing to sacrifice John's Jesus to prevent a military attack by the Romans (11:45–53, 18:14). While Annas and his police have no response when John's Jesus challenges them to name his transgression (18:19–24), Pilate plainly and openly admits that he does not have a case against John's Jesus (18:38).

When the creases of Jesus's scars and his disciples' flesh press against each other in John's Gospel, the generated impression involves what Ahmed calls "the cultural politics of emotion" (Ahmed 2014, title): people circulate and negotiate affective energy among one another in their inter-subjective relating and relationship.[5] This Johannine episode illustrates in a graphic way how the disciples' formation carries the pain and injustice suffered by John's Jesus (see Singleton 2015, 1, 55). When John's text is pressed on its readers, it may also impress on them how colonized identity is connected with buried memory and history.

Affective Transfers through Wounds

If I can read scars as a conduit of affective remains, what about reading the hands and side of John's Jesus as open wounds?[6]

---

5. Cathy Park Hong (2020, 157) in her book on "minor feelings" talks about how people in her minoritized culture are aware that emotions can "infect others," hence the tendency to keep pain and trauma secret. However, scholars of memory studies have pointed out that silence can just be an "audible void" through which affect transmits and transfers (cited in Kim 2019, 85).

6. My reading here is greatly indebted to and inspired by Lily Chiu's reading of the writings of Linda Lê, a French-Vietnamese writer, even though neither Chiu nor Lê discusses John's Gospel. See Chiu 2009.

In his piece about mourning and melancholia, which has been so important for thinking about a politics of mourning, Sigmund Freud (1953–1974, 14:247) suggests that one of the "traits" of a melancholic is "an insistent communicativeness which finds satisfaction in self-exposure." I have commented elsewhere that John's Jesus seems to suffer from "a form of logorrhea": not only does he talk a lot, but he also talks a lot about himself (Liew 2009, 260). Moreover, Freud (1953–1974, 14:248) writes explicitly about wounds and states, "The melancholic are not ashamed and do not hide themselves, since everything derogatory they say about themselves is at bottom said about somebody else."

Homi K. Bhabha (1991, 102) refers to this point by Freud, connects it with the work of Frantz Fanon, and writes,

> This inversion of meaning and address in the melancholic discourse—when it "incorporates" the loss or lack in its own body, displaying its own weeping wounds—is also an act of "disincorporating" the authority of the Master. Fanon ... says something similar when he suggests that the native wears his psychic wounds on the surface of his skin like an open sore—an eyesore to the colonizer.

Since John's Gospel is clear that the Romans were the only ones with the power to kill (18:31) and that the wounds of John's Jesus came from the hands of the colonizing Romans, reading his wounds through Bhabha's reading of colonial wounds through Freud and Fanon can also add nuance to the gospel.[7]

John's Jesus in this reading is returning as a colonized victim who bears and bares his wounds not only to protest against the colonizers but also to transfer the feeling *of* the cross to his disciples, including Thomas (20:20, 27). He performs a show-and-tell that is similar to Emmett Till's

---

7. As many scholars have pointed out, Freud's so-called science was partly or even primarily his strategies to detach himself from the stigma of being Jewish. The end of the nineteenth century—with colonialism at its height, the so-called science of race gaining ground, and industrialization accelerating—was a time when Jews were the easy scapegoat for many in a rapidly changing world (e.g., Gilman 1993). Freud was basically colonized internally within Europe, and antiquity—including literary texts from Greco-Roman antiquity—became his compulsion and deflection to address his racial/ethnic stigmatization (Armstrong 2005). Colonial dynamics may well be a point of connection between one's reading of John's Gospel and Freud's work on mourning and melancholia, if one reads both specifically within a colonial framework.

148 Tat-siong Benny Liew

mother deciding to have an open casket during her son's funeral "so that the world could see what they had done to [her] child" and to "pass on" the "cultural haunting" of being African American (Holloway 2003, 25, 136; see 130). This makes sense especially because his disciples, with the exception of the Beloved Disciple, may not have been present to witness the death of John's Jesus.

Besides the fact that none of them is said to be present during the crucifixion scene in John (19:25), John's Jesus has also announced that his disciples would scatter and abandon him during his "hour" (16:32). Furthermore, the greeting of "peace" that John's Jesus gives his disciples in both of his back-to-back appearances through closed doors (20:19, 26) should remind a careful reader of the disciples' desertion and hence absence from the foot of the cross. This is so because John's Jesus assured them immediately after his announcement about their scattering at his "hour" that they should still have "peace," since his "Father" would keep him company (16:32–33). More than just authenticating his identity as their crucified, dead, and now risen *and living* Lord, John's Jesus makes a point to flaunt his wounds to his disciples so they will, like the beloved disciple, feel him, feel with him, and identify with him.

John's narrative is not shy about a "transcorporeal and transformative" relation between Jesus and his disciples (6:53–57; see Buell 2014, 71, 79–80). John is also clear that this relation involves affective transfer. We see this when John's Jesus is so moved by Mary's loss of her brother, Lazarus, that John's Jesus ends up weeping (11:28–36), even or especially when he knows that he can awaken Lazarus from his death (11:1–6, 11–15). Similarly, by showing his wounds to his disciples and to Thomas, John's Jesus enables them to feel, know, and remember that colonial loss and trauma are both personal and collective. In this reading, the open wounds of John's Jesus become infectious. By showing and opening up his crucified body to his disciples, John's Jesus opens them to see and feel the deep traumas of the colonial world under Rome.[8] As Ahmed (2014, 4) suggests, what we feel and what we do are "shaped by the contact we have with others."

---

8. Besides his initiative to show his disciples and Thomas his open wounds, John's Jesus also mentions peace in both of these accounts in John 20. In his Farewell Discourse, John's Jesus talks about giving his peace to his disciples and about God's sending of the Holy Spirit as the advocate, so they would not be fearful in his absence (14:15–31). In his first postresurrection visit to his disciples, John's Jesus fulfills this promise with the words, "Receive the Holy Spirit" (20:22). The Holy Spirit is the promised Advocate that John's Jesus will send after his own departure (14:16) to teach his

Referring to Freud's work on melancholia, loss, and grief, Judith Butler (1997, 145) wonders about gender performance being done and "understood as 'acting out.'" The Buddhist monks and nuns in Vietnam who performed public suicides by fire (or by disembowelment) in Vietnam in the 1960s were clearly, to use Butler's words, "acting out."[9] Not only were these acts done in public, but a tip was also sent to an American news correspondent the night before the first of such suicides to ensure that the act would be captured and circulated worldwide (Yang 2011, 1, 5–7). They were "clearly theater[s] staged by the Buddhist monks to achieve a certain political end" (Browne 2003, 101).

Media in the United States tended to be divided in framing these incidents either as protests against President Ngo Dinh Diem's pro-Catholic and anti-Buddhist policies or as acts of communist sympathizers working with the Viet Cong to destabilize the Republic of Vietnam (Skow and Dionisopoulos 1997). One must remember that the Diem regime of South Vietnam was initially backed by the United States and its Catholic President (John F. Kennedy) in order to contain and combat the spread of communism. The so-called Buddhist crisis of 1963 in Vietnam can be read as a protest against both domestic oppression *and* colonial domination (whether through religious or state intervention or both). These public performances of suicide, these open and haunting displays of wounds and deaths, should therefore be read as a staging of national and colonial grief;

---

followers "everything, and remind [them] of all that" he has said to them (14:26) and to testify on his behalf alongside the disciples (15:26–27; see 16:12–15). Given the function of the Holy Spirit to remind his followers—and readers of John's Gospel—what John's Jesus has said before, what will we find if we go back and see what John's Jesus has said about the two subjects that he brings up in these two visits with his disciples: namely, sins and the need to believe?

John's Jesus has been very clear that sins have to do with two things: not believing in him (15:21–25, 16:5–11) and hence death (8:23–24). He is also clear that believing in him is linked to matters of life and death (11:25–26). Although not spoken by John's Jesus himself, the narrator in John's narrative also connects people believing in Jesus with not only Roman oppression but also Jesus's own death (11:45–53). The message that John's Jesus shares with his disciples in these two closed-door visits, therefore, has much to do with death.

9. On the tradition of self-immolation for religious and/or political purposes, see King 2000 and Yang 2011, 8–9. In dealing with past losses, there is a problematic tendency to recommend "working through" them to bring about some kind of healing and rush to the future but pathologize those who "act out" (Cvetkovich 2003).

150 Tat-siong Benny Liew

it is a staging that repeatedly demands "something to be done" (Gordon 1997, 139, 168, 183, 194, 202; 2011, 1–3).

One suicide, therefore, led to another and another, as more and more Buddhist clergy and ordinary citizens in Vietnam were exposed and awakened to their colonial pain and grief by what Bhabha calls an open sore and eyesore. After Thich Quang Duc killed himself by self-immolation on 11 June 1963, four more monks and a nun set themselves ablaze before a military coup. These suicides helped bring about the end of Diem's regime on 1 November 1963. Even after that, monks continued to commit suicide by self-immolation to protest the increasing presence of United States in Vietnam under President Lyndon Johnson. In fact, a citizen of the United States, Norman Morrison, also burned himself to death in front of the Pentagon on 2 November 1965 to protest the Vietnam War, or what Vietnamese call "the American War" (see Patler 2015). While Morrison's self-immolation is arguably best known, his was not the only one that took place in the United States during this war (King 2000, 128).[10]

The way these acts of self-immolation continued not only in Vietnam but also across the Pacific is simply striking. Without denying the important difference that these people took their own lives and were not killed by others, as John's Jesus was,[11] I want to point to what they share: namely, an emphasis on performativity and on affective transfers. By showing his pierced hands and side not once but twice (20:20, 27), John's Jesus literally engages in a performance, or what Richard Schechner (1985, 35–36, 150 n. 1) calls "twice-behaved behavior." Since John's Jesus shows but makes neither *overt* nor *specific* comments about his wounds, one may also read this scene in light of Benjamin's "choreographic panto-

---

10. Michelle Murray Yang (2011, 4) writes, "From 1965 to approximately 1970, at least eight Americans self-immolated to protest the war in Vietnam. These individuals included Alice Herz, an elderly widow, Celene Jankowski, a young wife and homemaker from Indiana, Roger LaPorte, a member of the Catholic Worker movement, Florence Beaumont, a homemaker from a suburb of Los Angeles, Norman Morris, a Quaker who self-immolated outside the window of Robert McNamara's Pentagon office, and George Winne, a college student at the University of California at San Diego."

11. Although John's Jesus does claim that he lays down his life on his own initiative (10:11–18), it is clear that he is referring to his willingness to face dangers, including plots to kill him (7:14–27, 8:39–40, 11:7–10, 18:1–9, 19:8–11; see 12:27), rather than run away to save his life. The thought by some that John's Jesus may be contemplating suicide is also shown to be a misunderstanding (8:21–27).

Passed On and Passing On

mime" that registers loss by "bringing bodies to the foreground" (Butler 2003, 470; see Benjamin 1998).

Trauma, Mourning, and Solidarity

With scars and/or open wounds, the resurrected body of John's Jesus carries and exhibits the colonial violence covered up by Pax Romana. That the resurrected body of John's Jesus continues to bear scars and/or open wounds might also explain why Mary Magdalene and the other disciples have difficulty recognizing the resurrected Jesus (20:11–16, 21:4–8). People who have gone through traumas do change; they literally look different because their bodies now are stamped with particular scars and/or wounds, especially if the trauma involves something like crucifixion. With John's Jesus volunteering to show his scars and/or open wounds in these two postresurrection appearances, the Fourth Gospel, like the picture of a burning Duc, provides its readers with a frozen-in-time image of Rome's imperial terror and brutality by perpetuating the trauma experienced by John's Jesus as a literary spectacle (see Yang 2011, 2–3). Thomas, as a result, personally and emphatically identifies (with) John's Jesus as "*my* Lord and *my* God" (John 20:28, emphasis added). These words of identification may take on additional meaning if they are read as an allusion to Ps 35:23, given that psalm's imprecatory plea for God to defeat and destroy the enemies of God's own people (see deClaissé-Walford 2011).

John Ashton (1991, 514; cited in Moss 2019, 135 n. 5, emphasis added), despite his lack of interest in the body and the physical injuries of John's resurrected Jesus in this scene, writes, "If John invented this story, as there is every reason to believe, it was not surely, to stimulate his readers to reflect upon the tangibility of risen bodies, but to *impress* upon them the need for faith." This is indeed an impressive scene in Ahmed's sense of the word, because of Thomas's rather astonishing and aggressive demand, especially if one understands the text as referring to open wounds rather than scars: he wants to put his finger *in* the nail holes on the hands of John's Jesus, and then his (whole?) hand *into* the spear wound on the torso of John's Jesus (20:25). Talk about an affective relation that "mark[s] the passages of intensities … in body-to-body … mutual imbrication" (Seigworth and Gregg 2010, 13)! As if the Gospel writer is afraid that readers may miss the picture, the narrative has John's Jesus basically repeating Thomas's words to Thomas when he appears to him (20:27). These words should bring up for a reader "visceral sensations of revulsion and disgust" (Most 2005, 49).

152   Tat-siong Benny Liew

Moreover, these repeated words may remind readers that there are human hands behind the nail and spear wounds borne by John's Jesus (19:13–18, 23, 31–34). The passage functions, then, to align the feelings of the gospel's readers *with* the pain of John's Jesus and *against* the aggression or bloodlust of his assailants. Since these with-and-against feelings are associated with Roman crucifixion in particular and imperial violence in general, they should provoke also feelings of dread and perhaps even terror about the future.[12] As Ahmed (2014, 47) writes, "A ghost-like figure ... [can give] us nightmares about the future, as an anticipation of future injury."

The impression one gets from this scene becomes even heavier because of these anticipated nightmares of the future. What we basically have are two more scenes through which John's Gospel impresses on its characters and its readers the reality of dread and death for their future. First, John's Jesus tells Peter that he will lose his freedom, with the narrator quickly clarifying that John's Jesus is actually referring to his death (21:18–19). As I have mentioned above, even the call to "feed" or "tend" the sheep of John's Jesus (21:15–17) may not be positive, given not only the fate of Peter but also the death of John's Jesus as the Passover lamb. Second, through a conversation between Peter and John's Jesus, the narrator seems to explain for the text's readers or help them make sense of the death of the Beloved Disciple (21:20–23). The resurrection of John's Jesus only ends with frustrated expectations and more references to existing scars/wounds and future death; there is no real resolution or reconciliation to wrap up John's Gospel. If anything, the ghostly appearances of John's Jesus, the "foretelling" of Peter's demise, and the mention of the Beloved Disciple's death may cause its readers to think about "what comes after loss for the survivors" (Kim 2019, 55).

That John's narrative specifies Thomas and then Peter in these scenes about scars/wounds, death, and affective transfer is also curious or perhaps even crucial to consider. Both of them have expressed their respective readiness to die with John's Jesus (11:16, 13:37); both also asked John's Jesus, when he tried to teach his disciples about his imminent departure, where he would be going (13:36, 14:5). By showing his scars and/or wounds to his disciples and then to Thomas, John's Jesus is "acting out" a performance that "makes visible (for an instant, live, now) that which is always

---

12. Glenn W. Most (2005, 56) also discusses Thomas's feelings of dread in this passage, but the dread for Most has to do with Thomas's realization of John's Jesus as "a sublime religious *mysterium*."

Passed On and Passing On 153

already there: the ghosts, the tropes, the scenarios that structure over individual and collective life" (Taylor 2003, 143). These messages of death, one after another after another, bring up the larger picture of—and "structure of feeling" for—people who needed to be remembered, recognized, and mourned after their deaths under Roman colonization (Williams 1975).

John's Gospel testifies in a sense to its community's vulnerability to colonial carnage, as Caiaphas's comment (11:45–53) clearly shows.[13] These closing episodes in John 20–21 give us a Jesus who, despite his repeated references to his imminent departure (7:33–34; 8:21; 12:35–36; 13:33, 36; 14:1–4, 12, 18–19, 25–28; 16:5–11, 16–19, 28; 20:17), actually refuses to disappear and continues to spectralize without any definite closure. By giving us two conclusions (20:30–31, 21:24–25), John seems to struggle with his "minor feelings [that] are ongoing," and so he has difficulties closing his gospel (Hong 2020, 57). In addition, these chapters may serve as a way for John's readers to *also* feel the suffering and death of John's Jesus through what I am calling affective transfers. "Those who have not seen and yet have come to believe" (20:29) may hence be referring to those whom John's Jesus calls "those who will believe in me through [his disciples'] word" (17:20).

With the term *postmemory*, Marianne Hirsch (2001, 10, emphasis original; see Hirsch 2012) proposes that later populations who have not experienced the Holocaust directly may nevertheless, through a process of *"retrospective witnessing by adoption,"* have the capacity of "adopting the traumatic experiences—and thus also the memories of others—as experiences one might oneself have had." These chapters, if I may borrow Jermaine Singleton's (2015, 51) words about a play by August Wilson, show how grief "is transferred ... as a result of and in resistance to an enduring struggle with ... oppression." John's Gospel ends, then, by passing on an ongoing grief to its readers. Readers are now supposed to carry on the memory of Jesus by, in John's language, "testifying" (1:7–9, 15, 32–34; 3:11, 26, 32–33; 4:39; 5:31–33, 36–37, 39; 8:14, 17–18; 10:25; 12:17; 15:26–27; 18:37; 19:35; 21:24).

---

13. As the story of Lazarus also shows, even resurrection can provide only a temporary respite from the threat and power of death, since the chief priests plan to kill him again (John 11:1–44). One must not forget, however, that the plots to kill Lazarus and Jesus, as the Fourth Gospel makes clear, have to do with the people's fear of the Romans (11:45–53). The deaths and resurrections of Lazarus and of Jesus are, after all, closely connected in John's Gospel. See Liew 2016, 141–49, 154–55.

Thinking about his own experience among slaves, Frederick Douglass (2000, 289–90) writes:

> They would sing, as a chorus, to words which to many would seem unmeaning jargon, but which, nevertheless, were full of meaning to themselves. I have sometimes thought that the mere hearing of those songs could do more to impress some minds with the horrible character of slavery, than the reading of whole volumes of philosophy on the subject could do. I did not, when a slave, understand the deep meaning of those rude and incoherent songs. I was myself within the circle; so that I neither saw nor heard as those without might see and hear. They told a tale of woe which was altogether beyond my feeble comprehension; they were tones loud, long, and deep; they breathed the prayer and complaint of souls boiling over with the bitterest anguish. Every tone was a testimony against slavery, and a prayer to God for deliverance from chains. The hearing of those wild notes depressed my spirit, and filled me with ineffable sadness. I have frequently found myself in tears while hearing them. The mere recurrence of those songs, even now, afflicts me; and while I am writing these lines, an expression of feeling has found its way down my cheek. To those songs, I trace my first glimmering conception of the dehumanizing character of slavery. I can never get rid of that conception. Those songs will follow me, to deepen my hatred of slavery, and quicken my sympathies for my brethren in bonds. If any one wishes to be impressed by the soul-killing effects of slavery, let him go to Colonel Lloyd's plantation, and, on allowance-day, place himself in the deep pine woods, and there let him, in silence, analyze the sounds that shall pass through the chambers of his soul,—and if he is not thus impressed, it will only be because "there is no flesh in his obdurate heart."

Using the word *impress* three times in this passage, Douglass underscores Ahmed's point about how feelings can be impressed on "objects of emotion." The horror of slavery left an impression on Douglass when he was in the circle of slaves singing their sorrow songs, and the feelings and emotions he felt, though messy and leaving him bewildered at first, eventually became knowledge for Douglass. These slave songs unsettled and provoked Douglass, moving him to become more sympathetic with those who suffered and to render harsher judgment against the system of slavery (Winters 2016, 43–44).

In addition, these affects further turned into a hope for the future. Believing that his memory—and the emotions associated with it—can be contagious, Douglass invites his readers to visit a plantation (Nguyen

2016, 25–26). Having the experience of being among the slaves and moved by their songs would, in his view, *almost* certainly "impress" his readers enough to cause them to stand in solidarity with the enslaved, though his ending clauses do show that one cannot guarantee that affective transfer will take place in exactly the way he hopes.

When Douglass was but a young boy, his aunt Hester got into trouble for speaking with a male slave after dark. As a punishment, their master, not knowing that Douglass (2000, 285) was hiding in a closet, tied her up in the kitchen, stripped her to her waist, and whipped her, "and soon the warm, red blood (amid heart-rending shrieks from her, and horrid oaths from him) came dripping to the floor." Having witnessed the entire ordeal, Douglass (285) writes, "I was so terrified and horror-stricken at the sight … I expected it would be my turn next." What happened to his aunt traumatized Douglass; her experience became in his mind practically his own, and the only difference was when the trauma was and would be experienced.

If affect can be transferred to Douglass when he witnessed by himself a scene of pain and horror, what may it be like to witness such a scene together with someone else? The agony of crucifixion suffered by John's Jesus ends up facilitating a transfer of familial relations (19:26–27). At the words of John's Jesus from the cross, the Beloved Disciple takes the place of John's Jesus, takes the mother of John's Jesus home, and takes care of her as her fictive but filial son. The Beloved Disciple, therefore, shares more than the pain and vulnerability of John's Jesus; he shares the responsibility and ancestry of John's Jesus as well as the grief and loss of Jesus's mother.

According to Ahmed (2014, 54), "How we feel about others is what aligns us with a collective, which paradoxically 'takes shape' only as an effect of such alignments. It is through how others impress upon us that the skin of the collective begins to take shape." Mourning for injuries, death, and loss of John's Jesus—and the transfers of affect and emotion that mourning entails—can result in a political alliance not only among many Johannine characters but also among readers of the gospel. The appearances of John's resurrected but unhealed Jesus, with his scarred and/or wounded body, haunt us and give us hope at the same time.

Twisting Time in Twisted Times

A politics of mourning keeps alive and passes on losses of the past to disrupt a plot of unified and linear progress. It unsettles us with memories

156 Tat-siong Benny Liew

that we prefer to forget and that others do not want us to remember. It demands a reckoning by refusing to forget past losses.

Through a careful reading of the works of Du Bois, Ralph Ellison, and Toni Morrison, Winters (2016, subtitle) argues in his book about "race, melancholy, and the agony of progress" that these African American writers present to us a different sense of time, as they tell and retell stories of wreckage brought about by racial capitalism, especially their shared refusal to let go of the past and leave it completely in oblivion. He shows how Du Bois (1907) goes *back* to the sorrow or slave songs and uses that tradition to function as a trope throughout *The Souls of Black Folks* to cry out for justice and to undermine narratives of unified and linear progress (Winters 2016, 31–83; see Zamir 1995). Moreover, he presents "a jazz-informed temporality and style" in Ellison's and Morrison's grief-filled writings (Winters 2016, 89–90). Not only do they write episodes that go back and forth in time, as if they were doing the swing in jazz, but Ellison and Morrison also employ several of jazz's signature repertoires—including using repetition, playing with dissonance, and emphasizing improvisation—so that their writings may come across to readers as being out of joint, to underscore a disjointed time that is far from linear (25, 86–135).

It is well known among Johannine scholars that there is much emphasis on time in John's narrative. Beginning with a prologue that is before the time of creation (1:1–18), John begins with, one may say, a time *before* time and covers that (timeless?) duration in eighteen verses. With references to three different Passovers (2:13, 6:4, 11:55/12:1), John's narrative slows down drastically by spending approximately four chapters on one year (chs. 2–5) and then six chapters on another year (chs. 6–11). The narrative time slows even more when John spends the last nine chapters on the last week of Jesus's life (chs. 12–20). In addition to those references to the Passovers, John's narrative is full of other temporal markers. These include: "hour(s)" (4:21, 23, 52–53; 5:25, 28; 11:9; 16:2, 4; 19:27), "day(s)" (1:29, 35, 39, 43; 2:1, 12, 19–20; 4:40, 43; 5:9; 6:22; 7:37; 11:6, 17, 39, 53; 12:1, 7, 12; 14:20; 16:23, 26; 19:14; 20:19), "week" (20:1, 19, 26), "months" (4:35, 6:7), "year(s)" (2:20; 5:5; 8:57; 11:49, 51; 18:13), and "time" (5:6; 7:6, 8, 33; 12:35; 14:9).[14] There are specific mentions of Sabbaths (5:9, 10, 16,

---

14. There are also in John's Gospel specific references to "my hour" by John's Jesus (2:4; 7:30; 8:20; 12:23, 27; 13:1; 16: 21, 25, 32; 17:1). There are more general uses of the term *day* to refer to daytime (9:4, 11:9), "the last day" (6:39, 40, 44, 54; 11:24; 12:48), or

Passed On and Passing On 157

18; 7:22, 23; 9:14, 16; 19:31) and other Jewish festivals besides the Passover (5:1, 7:2, 10:22; see Yee 1988).

John's Gospel is also known for its aporias. With several rather problematic literary seams, the Fourth Gospel is not exactly straightforward. Instead, it appears at times out of joint and out of time. For instance, the prosaic John the Baptizer appears suddenly and awkwardly a couple of times in the cosmic and poetic prologue (1:6–8, 15). John's Jesus accuses his disciples of not being concerned with where he would be going (16:5), even though that concern has been raised by Peter and possibly also by Thomas (13:36, 14:5). In ways similar to how John's Jesus continues his Farewell Discourse (chs. 14–17) for several more chapters *after* telling his disciples that he will not say much more and that they should all get up and leave (14:30–31), John's Gospel will go on for another chapter (ch. 21) even *after* what reads like a conclusion to the gospel in 20:30–31.

While scholars committed to historicism and the historical-critical methods have explained these aporias in terms of John's inability to weave materials from different sources seamlessly into a single narrative (e.g., Bultmann 1971; Smith 1965; Fortna 1970; Brodie 1993), I wonder whether we cannot read them as John adopting a different temporality to challenge a narrative of linear progress known as Pax Romana. After all, John is also known for espousing a "realized eschatology" (e.g., Dodd 1953; Culpepper 2008; see Williams and Rowland 2013). Just as the end in or of the future is already realized now (John 3:17–19, 5:24; see also 5:28–29), another Advocate who is yet to come in the future will help the disciples remember and understand what John's Jesus told them in the past (14:16, 26; 16:1–4). Time is simply not linear in John's Gospel. The Advocate's role clearly shows that the past will remain relevant despite the passing of time. The Fourth Gospel also tells us that the disciples have to wait until after Jesus's death and resurrection to remember what Jesus said about raising up the temple three days after it was destroyed (2:13–22). The disciples also lack understanding when John's Jesus is with them, such as the symbolic entry that he makes into Jerusalem (12:12–16) or his act of washing his disciples' feet (13:1–7).[15] Many episodes in the life of John's Jesus—such as what he

---

the period of Jesus's lifetime (8:56). In addition, there are mentions of "morning" (8:2, 18:28), "noon" (4:16, 19:14), "night" (3:2, 9:4, 11:10, 13:30, 19:39, 21:3), and even one specific reference to "four o'clock in the afternoon" (1:39). For studies of John's Gospel and time, see Culpepper 1983, 51–75; Estes 2008.

15. For more examples, see also John 14:25–31, 16:1–4, 20:1–10.

158 Tat-siong Benny Liew

says about his death (12:31–33, 18:28–32), about the implications of his death (11:45–53), or about the Holy Spirit (7:37–39)—will make sense to the gospel's characters (and readers) only after the death of John's Jesus. John's Gospel can be understood as a cultural "rememory" that recalls and rewrites the story of Jesus (Morrison 2004, 43, 112, 116, 189, 222, 226, 238, 254; Rody 1995, 101–2; Tabone 2019, 193).

Besides the past boomeranging back to the present and the future, the future also intrudes into the present of John's narrative. The two asides about John the Baptizer in the prologue (1:6–8, 15) are a good example, especially since they anticipate what the Baptizer will do—namely, testify on behalf of John's Jesus—in 1:19–37 and again in 3:25–30. The prologue, as cosmic and as infinite as it sounds, also gives a clear indication of the resistance that John's Jesus will face and nevertheless overcome (1:5, 10–13) even before any mention of him coming into the world in flesh (1:14). Similarly, a temporal leap is present in the Baptizer's testimony for John's Jesus. By referring to John's Jesus as "the lamb of God" (1:29, 36), the Baptizer's words basically foretell the death of John's Jesus as the Passover lamb on "the day of Preparation" for the Passover (19:14, 31–33, 42).

Johannine scholars have explained these temporal twists in John's narrative in terms of analepses and prolepses (Culpepper 1983, 51–75). Once we take issues of power and context (both cultural and sociopolitical) into serious consideration in our reading of John, however, we may no longer read these temporal disjunctions or aporias as merely manifestations of John's "literary design," but, like swinging back and forth in jazz, as representations of a "non-synchronous temporality" that is part and parcel of a politics of mourning and grief (Culpepper 1983, subtitle; Mohanty 1987, 42). With its disruption of a linear temporality, this politics is neither fully triumphant nor redemptive. Traumatic experiences and memories can trigger feelings of dread about the future as well as being triggered in moments of flashback (Cho 2008, 19–20).[16] As a result, the Holy Spirit will speak to the disciples about what is to come (John 16:12–13) as well as remind them of what they have been told by John's Jesus (14:25–26). Given how John's narrative world is full of death and dread, especially the dread of death, this Gospel's repeated emphasis on giving its readers (eternal) life (3:14–16, 35–36; 4:13–14; 5:21, 24–29, 39–40; 6:26–27, 32–40, 47–69;

---

16. Cho credits the phrase "dreading forward" to Lyndsey Stonebridge (1998, 29 n. 9), who, in turn, suggests that the phrase came from Henry Green/Henry Yorke.

8:12; 10:9–10, 25–28; 11:24–26; 12:23–25, 47–50; 17:1–3; 20:30–31) actually comes across as an anxious overcompensation.

Conclusion

The importance of grief and mourning in John's Gospel can be seen in the scenes with Mary Magdalene at the empty tomb (20:1–18). Although Peter and the Beloved Disciple accompany Mary to the empty tomb and enter the empty tomb without her, they are visited by neither the angels nor John's Jesus. Glenn W. Most (2005, 35–36) makes an important suggestion that it is Mary weeping that leads to the appearance of both the angels in the empty tomb and the resurrected Jesus in the garden.[17] Note how John's narrative refers to Mary's weeping repeatedly (20:11, twice), and has both the angels and John's Jesus asking her about the reason for her weeping (20:13, 15). Mary's response to them further shows that her tears have to do with the missing body of John's Jesus (20:13, 15). She is weeping for her inability to mourn her loss of John's Jesus properly without his body, the absence of which "brings home to her in an especially distressing way her irrevocable loss" (Most 2005, 36). Contrary to Peter and the Beloved Disciple (20:10), Mary Magdalene simply refuses to leave the tomb even though it is empty and she is there alone again, just as she went to the tomb all by herself in the early morning supposedly to mourn the passing of John's Jesus. It is *her grief*—her desire and her determination to mourn properly—that brings about not only the first actual appearance of angels in John's Gospel but also the resurrected appearance of John's Jesus after his death and burial.

I have argued that the resurrection of John's Jesus has more to do with transmitting colonial trauma and colonial grief. It is more a form of protest against colonialism through a demonstration of injuries (scars and/or wounds) than a process, a promise, or a possibility of healing. With John's realized eschatology, there is little indication that John's resurrected Jesus is coming back to set things right. Instead of a teleological resolution or a crowning closure, we have to be attentive to see what possibilities may develop in time, over time, and back through time.

---

17. However, I do not agree with Most (2005, 36–37) when he suggests that Mary's weeping causes her failure to recognize John's Jesus and that she is grieving "for the wrong reason."

160   Tat-siong Benny Liew

Most readers would agree, I think, that we "live in disturbing times, mixed-up times, troubling and turbid times," with widespread feelings of death and dread (Haraway 2016, 1). Regarding reading the Bible in these times, I have proposed reading John as a piece of colonized and minoritized writing for and as a politics of grief and mourning. Using John's Gospel as an illustration and John's Jesus as an exemplary reminder and remainder of colonial oppression and death, I highlighted how such a politics can (1) protest against narratives and practices that bury people and events that have passed on to boast about progress into the future and (2) facilitate a passing on of affect that may help build social alliances and collective resistance. Such a reading makes a political claim and carries the potential, through the transmission of affect, to foster the building of a group identity.

This is not a politics of passivity and resignation but one that may motivate readers by confronting them persistently with previously unacknowledged or underrecognized losses suffered by colonized and minoritized subjects who have been made minor, insignificant, precarious, and/or disposable. It emphasizes that "not only white supremacy, with its attendant processes of exclusion, subjugation, and bodily and territorial expropriation, but its continuing national disavowal are both constituent elements of nation-building in the United States" (Kaplan 2007, 514). It attests to how our narratives—biblical, national, or otherwise—are broken and full of brokenness.[18] (Re)Telling these stories of brokenness is itself a proof that we may actually have a say in how these stories develop. How we remember and what we envision are related.

Since Ahmed's (2014, 2, 8, 13, 63, 66, 220) "sociality of emotion" emphasizes that affects are socially mediated and learned, it has much to do with "past histories of association" and hence entails a temporal

---

18. As such, a minoritized reading of the Bible for and as mourning does not necessarily uphold biblical authority or supremacy. John's Gospel, for instance, is broken in terms of gender. Moss (2019, 32), for example, wonders why John's Jesus seems to have no problem with Thomas touching his resurrected body but did not allow Mary Magdalene to do so. We see this gender difference even earlier, when Mary Magdalene, upon discovering that the stone has been removed from the tomb, has to find Peter and the Beloved Disciple to accompany her back to the tomb site, thus implying that "matters have gotten beyond her own competence and that she needs male help" and that the witness of two males is needed for something to be believable (Most 2005, 30). On the gender troubles of John's Gospel in general, see Fehribach 1998. Related to this and to its emphasis on death, there are moments within the Fourth Gospel that also seems to devalue what is fleshly and material. See Buell 2014, 71–72.

Passed On and Passing On   161

aspect. Generations of affective effects rely on history because "the process of *recognition* (of this feeling, or that feeling) is bound up with what we *already know*" or, I would add, not know (25; see 101–21). In addition, past histories often stay with us through emotions, which Ahmed (202) calls "the very 'flesh' of time." Our emotions are therefore both informed by history and infused with history. Perhaps that is partly why one finds a consistent practice of referring to Hebrew Scripture in the Fourth Gospel (e.g., 2:13–17; 5:39–40; 6:30–31, 41–51; 7:37–39; 8:12–17; 10:31–38; 12:37–41; 13:12–20; 15:22–25; 17:12; 19:23–25, 28–37; see Myers and Schuchard 2015; Daise 2020). If we recognize that "the persistence of the past in the present" is often expressed through emotions, then astute readers of affect in these times must also read in ways that go beyond these times (Ahmed 2014, 187). One explanation that Michel Foucault (1998, 369; see Guilmette 2014) himself gives for his genealogy project is a commitment to "record ... what we tend to feel is without history."

There are three caveats that I need to make clear, however. First, I am offering this rhetoric and politics of mourning as an option for minoritized biblical interpretation in these times without making any claim for its priority, primacy, or superiority. Second, affective transfer, as Douglass's invitation for his readers to visit a plantation acknowledges, is a potential and not a guarantee. Ahmed's (2104, 39) emphasis on the circulation of "objects of emotion" rather than that of emotion itself is her way to underscore that emotion does not transfer easily, so proximity or contacts among people do not necessarily mean that they will all share the same emotion.[19] Going back to what Ahmed says about affect being informed and infused by history, readers' affective connection with or response to John's Gospel is largely dependent on what they have learned about and thought of the Bible. The feeling of grief and mourning that I have identified may or may not transfer with different readers.[20]

Third, to suggest that an ancient document such as John's Gospel keeps alive the past is not necessarily saying that John's Gospel contains *pure* history. After all, grief "fractures representation" even as "loss pre-

---

19. As a result, Ahmed (2014, 10–11, 218) hesitates to talk about "transmission" or "contagion" of emotions that circulate, even though she also has "no doubt that affects can and do pass between bodies."

20. Moore (2019, 189–95) raises the provocative question whether biblical interpretation that focuses on affect will not be effectually a form of "reader emotional-response criticism."

cipitates its own modes of expression" (Butler 2003, 467). I am only saying that text and history do not exist as binary oppositions in any absolute way, especially when an ancient text, as John's Gospel does (21:24), explicitly claims to (re)collect and pass on a testimony (LaCapra 2016; Pieters 2005; see Ahmed 2014, 216–17; Caruth 2016, 11–25).[21] The way testimonies or claims to history are passed on or rooted out is highly political. Readers of John's Gospel are also now in a position to give their own testimonies to the Gospel's testimony. Like performance and as a performance, a testimony suggests "simultaneously ... a process, a praxis, an episteme, a mode of transmission, an accomplishment, and a means of intervening in the world" (Taylor 2003, 15). It demands that others should at least listen (Ahmed 2014, 200).

In different ways, my last two caveats raise the question of accessibility. Emotion and affect can be transferred, but they can seldom if ever be transferred completely. "I know how it feels" may be a common and well-meaning expression, but feelings are so personal that transferring feelings is akin to translation: some nuance is generally lost in the process, not to mention that mourning is about loss and hence is always already about *partial* presence (Winters 2016, 49). This is particularly important to acknowledge when we are talking about loss and grief in an oppressive political context, so we must be careful not to fall into a kind of sentimentality that ends up trivializing a traumatic past or present (Hartman 1996, 10). Similarly, John's Gospel does not hide that it is a mediated product. While claiming to pass on the testimony of the Beloved Disciple, John's narrative is also clear that an editorial process was in play to decide what would be included in or excluded from the text (21:24–25; see 20:30–31). John's emphasis that the Beloved Disciple's testimony is "true" (21:24; see 19:35) also brings up the question of one's legitimacy as a witness, since most of us know that the testimonies of minoritized persons and of women are not necessarily recognized as trustworthy (Oliver 2001, 94–100).

Rather than seeing this affective and textual opacity as a hindrance, perhaps we can see this opacity as a need to listen with greater care and

---

21. Regardless of how one may feel about John's Gospel, what one may decide about the nature of the Beloved Disciple's testimony, or how one sees the relationship between John's narrative and the Beloved Disciple's testimony, one cannot deny that the Fourth Gospel was written by a follower of a colonized Jew in the context of the Roman Empire. It is therefore a witness to how someone thought and felt about life at that time and place.

humility to see whether we may become more attuned to joining others in their pain and grief, especially those who are less protected, made more vulnerable, or less satisfied with the status quo (Taylor 2003, 15; Butler 2009, 25–26; Winters 2016, 50). It is undeniable that "at the core of the historical thinking of Fanon, Bhabha, and Said, among many others, is still the ethically responsible witnessing of that trauma of empire, the story of which must be told and retold, so that it can be fully understood—and then acted upon positively and productively" (Hutcheon 2003, 24). As director Rithy Panh says toward the end of his documentary about the atrocities of Cambodia's Khmer Rouge, "There are many things that man [*sic*] should not see or know.... But should any of us see or know these things, then we must live to tell of them.... I make this picture ... I now hand over to you, so that it never ceases to seek us out" (cited in Nguyen 2016, 99).[22] This, along with the reminder that mourning can keep alive "what-could-have-been" alternatives and "what now" questions, would be my unhopeful hope in passing on the haunting pasts (Gordon 1997, 2011; Yang 2011, 16).

Reading the Bible as a minoritized critic in these troubled and troubling times, I am hoping against hope that my response to the Bible with a focus on grief and mourning will not only reanimate these stories but also move readers to remember, respond, remonstrate, and reimagine, even or especially in these times of "neoliberal politics of abandonment and state authoritarianism" (Kim 2020, 86).[23] Perhaps this ancient library of books called the New Testament can still help us remember and reimagine, with its mourning of a ghostly Jesus figure in these times when various places of the world seem to be taking a repressive turn.

Works Cited

Ahmed, Sara. 2014. *The Cultural Politics of Emotion.* 2nd ed. Edinburgh: Edinburgh University Press.

---

22. Referring to Emmanuel Levinas's thought on insomnia as a wakefulness because of a disturbance, Kelly Oliver (2001, 134) suggests a similar understanding for witnessing as a kind of response-ability to the demand of an-other.

23. The importance of emotions, affects, and desires for politics has actually been shown arguably most clearly in the so-called populist movement of Donald Trump. See, e.g., Schrock et al. 2017; Skonieczny 2018; Phoenix 2019; Yates 2019. On the role of emotion in racism, see Ioanide 2015.

Armstrong, Richard H. 2005. *A Compulsion for Antiquity: Freud and the Ancient World*. Ithaca, NY: Cornell University Press.

Ashton, John. 1991. *Understanding the Fourth Gospel*. Oxford: Oxford University Press.

Benjamin, Walter. 1998. *The Origin of German Tragic Drama*. Translated by John Osborne. New York: Verso.

Bhabha, Homi K. 1991. "A Question of Survival: Nations and Psychic States." Pages 89–103 in *Psychoanalysis and Cultural Theory: Thresholds*. Edited by James Donald. New York: St. Martin's.

Brodie, Thomas L. 1993. *The Quest for the Origin of John's Gospel: A Source-Oriented Approach*. New York: Oxford University Press.

Browne, Malcolm W. 2003. "Malcolm W. Browne: Vietnam, Persian Gulf." Pages 91–110 in *Reporting America at War: An Oral History*. Compiled by Michelle Ferrari with commentary by James Tobin. New York: Hyperion.

Buell, Denise Kimber. 2014. "The Microbes and Pneuma That Therefore I Am." Pages 63–87 in *Divinanimality: Animal Theory, Creaturely Theology*. Edited by Stephen D. Moore. New York: Fordham University Press.

Bultmann, Rudolf. 1971. *The Gospel of John*. Translated by George R. Beasley-Murray. Philadelphia: Westminster.

Butler, Judith. 1997. *The Psychic Life of Power: Theories in Subjection*. Stanford, CA: Stanford University Press.

———. 2003. "Afterword: After Loss, What Then?" Pages 467–73 in *Loss: The Politics of Mourning*. Edited by David L. Eng and David Kazanjian. Berkeley: University of California Press.

———. 2009. *Frames of War: When Is Life Grievable?* Brooklyn: Verso.

Caruth, Cathy. 2016. *Unclaimed Experience: Trauma, Narrative, and History*. Twentieth anniversary ed. Baltimore: Johns Hopkins University Press.

Chiu, Lily V. 2009. "'An Open Wound on a Smooth Skin': (Post)Colonialism and the Melancholic Performance of Trauma in the Works of Linda Lê." *IGSAP* 21. https://tinyurl.com/SBL06106u.

Cho, Grace M. 2008. *Haunting the Korean Diaspora: Shame, Secrecy, and the Forgotten War*. Minneapolis: University of Minnesota Press.

Culpepper, R. Alan. 1983. *Anatomy of the Fourth Gospel: A Study in Literary Design*. Philadelphia: Fortress.

———. 2008. "Realized Eschatology in the Experience of the Johannine Community." Pages 253–76 in *The Resurrection of Jesus in the Gospel of John*. Edited by Craig R. Koester and Reimund Bieringer. Tübingen: Mohr Siebeck.

Cvetkovich, Ann. 2003. *An Archive of Feelings: Trauma, Sexuality, and Lesbian Public Cultures*. Durham, NC: Duke University Press.

Daise, Michael A. 2020. *Quotations in John: Studies on Jewish Scripture in the Fourth Gospel*. New York: T&T Clark.

deClaissé-Walford, Nancy L. 2011. "The Theology of the Imprecatory Psalms." Pages 77–92 in *Soundings in the Theology of the Psalms: Perspectives and Methods in Contemporary Scholarship*. Edited by Rolf A. Jacobson. Minneapolis: Fortress.

Dodd, Charles H. 1953. *The Interpretation of the Fourth Gospel*. New York: Cambridge University Press.

Douglass, Frederick. 2000. *Slave Narratives*. Edited by William L. Andrews and Henry Louis Gates Jr. New York: Library of America.

Du Bois, W. E. B. 1907. *The Souls of Black Folk: Essays and Sketches*. Chicago: McClurg.

Eng, David L., and Shinhee Han. 2000. "A Dialogue on Racial Melancholia." *PsychDial* 10:667–700.

Estes, Douglas. 2008. *The Temporal Mechanics of the Fourth Gospel: A Theory of Hermeneutical Relativity in the Gospel of John*. Leiden: Brill.

Fehribach, Adeline. 1998. *The Women in the Life of the Bridegroom: A Feminist Literary-Historical Analysis of the Female Characters in the Fourth Gospel*. Collegeville, MN: Liturgical.

Fortna, Robert T. 1970. *The Gospel of Signs: A Reconstruction of the Narrative Source Underlying the Fourth Gospel*. Cambridge: Cambridge University Press.

Foucault, Michel. 1998. "Nietzsche, Genealogy, History." Pages 369–91 in *Essential Works of Foucault, 1954–1984*. Vol. 2, *Aesthetics, Method, and Epistemology*. Edited by James D. Faubion. Translated by Robert Hurley et al. New York: New Press.

Freud, Sigmund. 1953–1974. *Standard Edition of the Complete Psychological Works of Sigmund Freud*. Edited and translated by James Strachey. 24 vols. London: Hogarth.

Gilman, Sander. 1993. *Freud, Race, and Gender*. Princeton: Princeton University Press.

Gilmore, Ruth Wilson. 2007. *Golden Gulag: Prisons, Surplus, Crisis, and Opposition in Globalizing California*. Berkeley: University of California Press.

Gordon, Avery F. 1997. *Ghostly Matters: Haunting and Sociological Imagination.* Minneapolis: University of Minnesota Press.

———. 2011. "Some Thoughts on Haunting and Futurity." *borderlands* 10.2:1–21.

Guilmette, Lauren. 2014. "In What We Tend to Feel Is without History: Foucault, Affect, and the Ethics of Curiosity." *JSpecPhil* 28:284–94.

Haraway, Donna J. 2016. *Staying with the Trouble: Making Kin in the Chthulucene.* Durham, NC: Duke University Press.

Hartman, Geoffrey H. 1996. *The Longest Shadow: In the Aftermath of the Holocaust.* Bloomington: Indiana University Press.

Hirsch, Marianne. 2001. "Surviving Images: Holocaust Photographs and the Work of Postmemory." *YJC* 14:5–37.

———. 2012. *The Generation of Postmemory: Writing and Visual Culture after the Holocaust.* New York: Columbia University Press.

Holloway, Karla FC. 2003. *Passed On: African American Mourning Stories.* Durham, NC: Duke University Press.

Hong, Cathy Park. 2020. *Minor Feelings: An Asian American Reckoning.* New York: One World.

Hutcheon, Linda. 2003. "Postcolonial Witnessing—and Beyond: Rethinking Literary History Today." *Neohelicon* 30:13–30.

Ioanide, Paula. 2015. *The Emotional Politics of Racism: How Feelings Trump Facts in an Era of Colorblindness.* Stanford, CA: Stanford University Press.

Kaplan, Sara Clarke. 2007. "Souls at the Crossroads, Africans on the Water: The Politics of Diasporic Melancholia." *Callaloo* 30:511–26.

Kim, Jinah. 2019. *Postcolonial Grief: The Afterlives of the Pacific Wars in America.* Durham, NC: Duke University Press.

———. 2020. "The Insurgency of Mourning: *Sewol* across the Transpacific." *AmerJ* 46:84–100.

King, Sallie B. 2000. "They Who Burned Themselves for Peace: Quaker and Buddhist Self-Immolators during the Vietnam War." *BCS* 20:127–50.

LaCapra, Dominick. 2016. "Trauma, History, Memory, Identity: What Remains?" *HistTheor* 55:375–400.

Liew, Tat-siong Benny. 2009. "Queering Closets and Perverting Desires: Cross-Examining John's Engendering and Transgendering Word across Different Worlds." Pages 251–88 in *They Were All Together in One Place? Toward Minority Biblical Criticism.* Edited by Randall C. Bailey, Tat-siong Benny Liew, and Fernando F. Segovia. SemeiaSt 57. Atlanta: Society of Biblical Literature.

———. 2016. "The Gospel of Bare Life: Reading Death, Dream, and Desire through John's Jesus." Pages 129–70 in *Psychoanalytic Mediations between Marxist and Postcolonial Readings of the Bible*. Edited by Tatsiong Benny Liew and Erin Runions. Atlanta: SBL Press.

Miller, Elise. 2016. "Mourning and Melancholy: Literary Criticism by African American Women." *TSWL* 35:463–89.

Mohanty, Chandra Talpade. 1987. "Feminist Encounters: Locating the Politics of Experience." *Copyright* 1:30–44.

Moore, Stephen D. 2017. *Gospel Jesuses and Other Nonhumans: Biblical Criticism Post-poststructuralism*. SemeiaSt 89. Atlanta: SBL Press.

———. 2019. "The Rage for Method and the Joy of Anachronism: When Biblical Scholars Do Affect Theory." Pages 187–211 in *Reading with Feeling: Affect Theory and the Bible*. Edited by Fiona C. Black and Jennifer Koosed. SemeiaSt 95. Atlanta: SBL Press.

Morrison, Toni. 2004. *Beloved*. New York: Vintage.

Moss, Candida. 2019. *Divine Bodies: Resurrecting Perfection in the New Testament and Early Christianity*. New Haven: Yale University Press.

Most, Glenn W. 2005. *Doubting Thomas*. Cambridge: Harvard University Press.

Myers, Alicia D., and Bruce G. Schuchard, eds. 2015. *Abiding Words: The Use of Scripture in the Gospel of John*. RBS 81. Atlanta: SBL Press.

Nguyen, Viet Thanh. 2016. *Nothing Ever Dies: Vietnam and the Memory of War*. Cambridge: Harvard University Press.

Oliver, Kelly. 2001. *Witnessing: Beyond Recognition*. Minneapolis: University of Minnesota Press.

Patler, Nicholas. 2015. "Norman's Triumph: The Transcendent Language of Self-Immolation." *QH* 104.2:18–39.

Phoenix, Davin L. 2019. *The Anger Gap: How Race Shapes Emotion in Politics*. New York: Cambridge University Press.

Pieters, Jürgen. 2005. *Speaking with the Dead: Explorations in Literature and History*. Edinburgh: Edinburgh University Press.

Rody, Caroline. 1995. "Toni Morrison's *Beloved*: History, 'Rememory,' and a 'Clamor for a Kiss.'" *ALH* 7:92–119.

Schechner, Richard. 1985. *Between Theater and Anthropology*. Philadelphia: University of Pennsylvania Press.

Schrock, Douglas, Benjamin Dowd-Arrow, Kristen Erichsen, Haley Gentile, and Pierce Dignam 2017. "The Emotional Politics of Making America Great Again: Trump's Working Class Appeals." *JWCS* 2:5–22.

Seigworth, Gregory J., and Melissa Gregg. 2010. "An Inventory of Shimmers." Pages 1–25 in *The Affect Theory Reader*. Edited by Melissa Gregg and Gregory J. Seigworth. Durham, NC: Duke University Press.

Singleton, Jermaine. 2015. *Cultural Melancholy: Readings of Race, Impossible Mourning, and African American Ritual*. Urbana: University of Illinois Press.

Skonieczny, Amy. 2018. "Emotion and Political Narratives: Populism, Trump, and Trade." *P&G* 6.4:62–72.

Skow, Lisa M., and George N. Dionisopoulos. 1997. "A Struggle to Contextualize Photographic Images: American Print Media and the 'Burning Monk.'" *CommQuart* 45:393–409.

Smith, D. Moody. 1965. *Composition and Order of the Fourth Gospel: Bultmann's Literary Theory*. New Haven: Yale University Press.

Stonebridge, Lyndsey. 1998. "Bombs and Roses: The Writing of Anxiety in Henry Green's 'Caught.'" *Diacritics* 28.4:25–43.

Tabone, Mark A. 2019. "Multidirectinal Rememory: Slavery and the Holocaust in John A. Williams's *Clifford's Blues*." *TCL* 65.3:191–216.

Taylor, Diana. 2003. *The Archive and the Repertoire: Performing Cultural Memory in the Americas*. Durham, NC: Duke University Press.

Wilentz, Gay. 1992. "Civilizations Underneath: African Heritage as Cultural Discourse in Toni Morrison's *Song of Solomon*." *AfrAmRev* 26:61–76.

Williams, Catrin H., and Christopher Rowland, eds. 2013. *John's Gospel and Intimations of Apocalyptic*. London: T&T Clark.

Williams, Raymond. 1975. *The Long Revolution*. Westport, CT: Greenwood.

Winters, Joseph R. 2016. *Hope Draped in Black: Race, Melancholy, and the Agony of Progress*. Durham, NC: Duke University Press.

Yang, Michelle Murray. 2011. "Still Burning: Self-Immolation as Photographic Protest." *QJS* 97:1–25.

Yates, Heather E. 2019. *The Politics of Spectacle and Emotion in the 2016 Presidential Campaign*. Cham: Palgrave MacMillan.

Yee, Gale A. 1988. *Jewish Feasts and the Gospel of John*. Wilmington, DE: Glazier.

Young, Jason R. 2017. "All God's Children Had Wings: The Flying African in History, Literature, and Lore." *JAR* 5:50–70.

Zamir, Shamoon. 1995. *Dark Voices: W. E. B. Du Bois and American Thought, 1888–1903*. Chicago: University of Chicago Press.

Of Escoffier, *Gastronomie*, Craft, and Canon

Yii-Jan Lin

Introduction

The mark of a minoritized hermeneutic is its attendant discussions of parameters, authenticity, identifications, and counteridentifications. This is not due to a lack of focus or self-absorbed navel-gazing but is rather the inevitable result of *being marked*. Those methodologies categorized as special interest, marginal, or simply not *Wissenschaftliche* must continually define and justify their presence in the field of biblical studies. *Un*marked methodologies, understood as unquestionably central and essential, need make no such justifications. The presumptive bread and butter of hermeneutics can do its thing, unbothered and unfettered by existential questions of the first order. Meanwhile, those pushed to the margins, deemed charity cases and/or diversity acquisitions, return to perennial questions of self-definition.

Just as overarching scholarly volumes on apocalypses inevitably begin with a discussion of genre, so works explicitly identified as minoritized—African, Latinx, Asian American, womanist, postcolonial, and so on—regularly open with difference and *différance*. Jin Young Choi's (2015, 2) postcolonial, feminist reading of Mark, for example, begins by marking its distance from the hermeneutics of the epistemological certainty of the post-Enlightenment West: "My Asian context is one in where the religious dispositions and practices of the Korean people—based on spiritual experience, embodiment, and relationality—have been fused into the Christian faith, as believers have cried out under colonial and patriarchal oppressions." Mitzi J. Smith (2015, 4) likewise introduces the womanist reader *I Found God in Me* with difference—in particular, difference in the face of opposition: "This project takes for granted the legitimacy and viability of womanist biblical interpretation as a discipline, even as some reject it

-169-

as normative biblical studies, and disingenuously regard it even as racist that we audaciously start with and concern ourselves with the lives of black women and our communities." These statements of legitimation and opposition within the field are what majoritized readings mostly exclude, with the unconscious assumption that no such apologia and contextualization are needed since they are a given.

Statements of difference turn to *différance*, especially in definitive volumes of minoritized readings, where parameters and identities must contend with issues of representation, intention, and authenticity. Tatsiong Benny Liew's (2008, 5) answer to the titular question *What Is Asian American Biblical Hermeneutics?*, for example, brilliantly acknowledges:

> If the "Asian American" in Asian American biblical hermeneutics becomes solely a matter of "who" and/or "what," it will end up assuming and/or accentuating a referentiality that supposedly yields identity, authenticity, and legibility. It will then become problematic, not only because of its exclusionary and ethnographical or colonial implication, but also because of its essentialist (mis)understanding of a racial/ethnic identity.

Rather than offering any programmatic conclusion to the questions of "who" and "what," Liew (7) suggest a deferral of definitions through a "tradition of citation"—that is, repeated reference to work of Asian Americans, without too much worry over "who," through a "reference without referentiality."

Fernando Segovia (2014, 2, emphasis added) likewise rejects a stable referentiality in the introduction to *Latino/a Biblical Hermeneutics: Problematics, Objectives, Strategies*: "In terms of rationale, the project seeks to ascertain how such critics approach their vocation as critics in the light of their identity as members of the Latino/a experience and reality—*howsoever they define the social-cultural situation of the group and their own affiliation within it.*"

Once again, difference pairs with *différance* as Segovia significantly and instructively sidesteps the question of "who" and therefore "what" through a collective that defies neat categories and definitions.

Nevertheless, certain issues of identity and intention seem like hard boundaries. Many identities can produce works that can be categorized as ethnic/racially minoritized, but, almost without exception, white identities cannot. This general understanding derives from a long history of white appropriation and from the understanding that the work comes from per-

Of Escoffier, *Gastronomie*, Craft, and Canon 171

sonal context, history, and experience. This is apparent, for example, in both the explicit definition and implicit cultural contours of Alice Walker's (1983, xi) definition of *womanist*, which begins: "Womanist 1. From womanish. (Opp. Of 'girlish,' i.e., frivolous, irresponsible, not serious) A black feminist or feminist of color." Womanist blogger Trudy (2013) of *Gradient Lair* answers "Who can be a womanist?" rather more bluntly:

> [White women] needing to co-opt or be appropriative of the identifier "womanist" despite Black women's history (and present) of dealing with their exploitative cultural appropriation and dehumanization makes me feel as if they are more concerned with controlling and centering themselves, *again* (as if they aren't already centered as women, globally) than dismantling oppression.... White women should focus on how to actually be feminists ... instead of trying to dominate the space of Black women and other women of colour.

Similar statements might be made of white persons wishing to write (non-descriptive) scholarship explicitly labeled as Latinx, Asian, and so on biblical criticism.[1] That such should ever be the case might seem a great improbability, but the controversy of Rachel Dolezal's out-ing as a white woman in 2015 and the following defense of so-called transracialism make this hard boundary necessary (Tuvel 2017).

That only minoritized persons can write minoritized criticism does not mean that the inverse is also true. Not all work by minoritized persons counts as minoritized criticism—although this principle seems to violate the spirit of indefinability. For some scholars in the field, intention and commitment must mark a work for it to fall under this categorization. This became clear in a recent online forum regarding which books belong under the title "Asian and Asian American Interpretation." While perusing the handful of books already listed by collaborative contribution, almost all monographs of biblical scholarship, I dragged out the perennial question: What scholarship belongs? I asked the question motivated by intellectual and personal curiosity:

> But I write from self-interest, of course: my work has primarily been a critique of the field, not an interpretation of text, and it has been most

---

1. The lines of identity and legitimacy are a bit more blurred in other minoritized fields outside strictly racial categories, e.g., postcolonial, LGBTQIA, and disability studies.

172   Yii-Jan Lin

> discussed among philologists and those usually understood as "a-contextual"—but I most certainly bring up and name white supremacy and racial theory in it.[2] Where my book has not been discussed has been in the circles of postcoloniality, minoritized hermeneutics, etc. So I find myself (as usual) belonging neither here-nor-there. (comment on Choi 2017)

The reply by the author of the original post clearly highlights explicit self-identification and commitment to scholarly activism as essential to the definition:

> I don't think that any work done by an ethnic Asian American is necessarily Asian American interpretation. [Another commenter] already mentioned consciousness, community, and construction of reality. I would add one more—commitment, as I understand this kind of work as a form of activism…. But when the author doesn't explicitly claim that her work is [Asian American], I don't assume that she wants to get it boxed in. (Choi 2017)

By considering self-naming in publication, Choi respects an author's agency and choice. But this also opens new avenues of consideration.

The following is a more whimsical meditation on such considerations through the world of cuisine. The points of comparison between two seemingly incongruous spheres will quickly become clear, and my aim, as in all productive comparative studies, is to startle into being answers—or new compelling questions—for the field of minoritized biblical criticism.

Gastronomie and Academy

George Auguste Escoffier was born in 1846 in France near Nice.[3] At the age of thirteen, he began his apprenticeship at his uncle's restaurant, Le Restaurant Français, and thus began the culinary career of arguably the most revered man in Western culinary history. The main reason for this fame and reverence is not Escoffier's cooking per se—although he served as head chef in many legendary restaurants, such as the Savoy in London and, ultimately, the Paris Ritz in 1898. The most significant contribution Escoffier (2009) made to gastronomy is his codification of French cuisine—what is now known as classical cuisine—so that his book, *Le guide*

---

2. I refer here to Lin 2016, a work discussing the history of textual criticism.

3. For the definitive biography of Auguste Escoffier in English, see James 2002.

culinaire, is the holy writ of chefs everywhere. He crystallized and articulated the principles underlying French cuisine and declared and classified what are called the five mother sauces, some of which are well-known by name to restaurant-goers everywhere: béchamel, Espagnole, velouté, hollandaise, and tomate.

But what does Escoffier have to do with minoritized biblical hermeneutics? Or, to paraphrase Tertullian, what does *gastronomie* have to do with academy? I bring up the subject of cuisine and cookery to conduct a comparison of guilds in which culture and craft are intermingled and inseparable. When I teach the seminar Race, Ethnicity, and the New Testament, I begin by posing this set of questions to my students: If I cook a dish and set it before you, is it Chinese food, because I am ethnically Chinese? And if I sit down for a meal and consume it, is it Chinese food because I eat it? Does my *regular* consumption of such food make it Chinese food? What are the parameters of the culture of a cuisine? Are there essential elements or principles like the five mother sauces?

This comparison between gastronomy and academy can be fruitful because we most generally think of food and types of cuisine as a matter of course—our assumptions about food and to which culture they belong are usually unquestioned. When we *do* question cultural labels of cuisines, it is usually in the case of chain restaurants, such as Panda Express and Taco Bell. Are these really Chinese and Mexican restaurants? Many westernized dishes, such as General Tso's chicken, may also seem far from authentic—but the general's chicken actually has roots in Chinese exile and immigration to the United States (Dunlop 2007). To label a dish—or even the chain restaurants that market such dishes—as "fake" oversimplifies histories of immigration, assimilation, and, yes, appropriation. Through these questions of authenticity, we begin to see how cuisine and minoritized studies overlap. But generally we accept that there is a thing called "Chinese cuisine" (or we may quibble and say "Cantonese" or "Shanghainese"). But these questions of gastronomy and academy involve many of the same issues, those of craft, production, consumption, and canon.

The first aspect of this comparative exercise is that of identity and expectation. In my own experience, my appearance and my full, formal name, Yii-Jan Lin, carry along with it the expectation of a certain product that I will create as a scholar. Let us, for the moment, set aside the generally true principle that my background *does* drive my interests and writing toward a certain direction. When my name appears on an application or lecture announcement, a general expectation is that I will or do address

Asian American hermeneutics, issues of immigration, perhaps postcolonial theory, and critical race theory. This is not an incorrect assumption, and it is mostly true. But what if I engage none of these issues? What if I write "pure" historical-critical scholarship without a discussion of social location and contextual issues? Will there be a general negative judgment of my work by those outside historical-critical studies? How does the burden of representation shift from methodology to methodology as I write?

Fusion

There exist no absolute answers to these questions, and certain expectations are completely understandable and reasonable. But let us turn to cuisine for a moment to think about this differently. The great celebrity chefs who cook for television shows and write cookbooks and sell their products in supermarkets—Emeril Lagasse, Wolfgang Puck, Gordon Ramsay—cook more or less from classical cuisine. A higher echelon of chefs—at least in some minds—is composed of head chefs at Michelin-starred restaurants, including Thomas Keller, Ferran Adrià, and Daniel Boulud. These chefs all use classical French cuisine as a basis for their food. You will of course notice that the top chefs are all white men.

But consider David Chang for a moment. He is the chef and creator of Momofuku Ko, along with several other restaurants around the world. Momofuku Ko (2023) has repeatedly been awarded two Michelin stars, and Chang's other, less formal restaurants (e.g., Ssäm, Noodle Bar, Nishi) attract foodies in droves. Whence came this prolific genius? Chang's mother and father came to the United States from North and South Korea, respectively, in the 1960s. Like many Koreans, the Changs were Presbyterians highly involved at church—something Chang rebelled against as a teenager. This ironically (or naturally) sparked his interest in religion, which he majored in while at Trinity College (MacFarquar 2008). Chang did not go on to produce Asian American theology or biblical criticism. Instead, he went on to produce beautiful food. But what kind of food? Chang's restaurants—as you can tell from their names—combine what we consider Asian with Western cuisines. But where did Chang study? At the French Culinary Institute in New York City. Yet his product is sometimes understood as fusion cuisine and most definitely as Asian (see Kasper 2013). I cannot think of any prominent Asian American or Asian chef who is *not* associated with Asian or fusion cuisine (e.g., both Roy Choi and Erik Bruno-Yang create fusion cuisine).

Of Escoffier, *Gastronomie*, Craft, and Canon 175

The great Thomas Keller had no formal culinary education but learned as he worked in kitchens, beginning in West Palm Beach in rather humble origins (Ruhlman 2001, 263–71). Now he heads two famous restaurants, Per Se in New York and the French Laundry in Yountville, California, both of which are perpetually booked full. On the menu of the French Laundry, certain items appear perennially, expressing Keller's love of nostalgic Americana. These include courses named "grilled cheese and tomato soup" or "PB&J," which feature elements of these dishes taken to the heights of haute cuisine—for example, using sliced brioche, farmhouse cheddar, and tomato essence water, or fruit gelée and peanut butter truffles (Ruhlman 2001, 304–5). But no one writes or reviews Keller—ever—as a fusion chef, even though no one in their right minds would first consider PB&J, a decidedly American dish, part of French classical cuisine (McWilliams 2012, 166). This haute cuisine performance of high-low contrasts has become a signature of Keller's oeuvre. One listing of the pantheon of chefs runs as follows:

> Alice Waters and Chez Panisse may have started the locavore movement. Jean-Georges Vongerichten perfected high-end fusion cooking, and Wolfgang Puck invented the celebrity chef. But Keller, with his emphasis of tiny courses, his application of rigorous classical French technique to both high and low cuisine, created a new style of fine American dining. (Kelly 2010)

My questions here are many: When we say "fusion," what does that mean? The fusion of *what*, exactly? The author identifies chef Vongerichten here with "fusion cooking," but not Keller. What separates the two? That Vongerichten pairs classical training with "the exotic and aromatic flavors of the East" (Jean-Georges 2017). Colonial Orientalism continues to drive the categorization of cuisines, and fusion cooking most typically signifies East-meets-West, a romanticized European trope. I would venture to say that pairing Euro-American (read: white) cuisines with cuisines of any peoples of color typifies fusion, for example, Mexi-Cali and French–North African cooking.

Keller can thus cook his unique dishes unmarked, but David Chang cannot, although both work with pairing American cuisines (Korean and white nostalgia American) and French classical. Furthermore, it seems assumed that one's heritage and ethnic identity infuses one's food. Consider Chang's restaurant Má Pêche. Chang collaborated with chef Tien

Ho in the concept of the restaurant, which served French-Vietnamese food. Ho is of Vietnamese descent—but he came to the United States at the age of nine in 1982, and he apprenticed and worked in classical cuisine, including Café Boulud (Moskin 2009). Yet, despite his training, we glimpse a struggle with authenticity, identity, and the pressure of ethnic representation in chef Ho's various interviews.

Of French cuisine he says, "I don't know how to do true, beautiful, 'authentic' French cuisine. So everything is an interpretation. Everything has its own unique spin and touch to it because it's who I am" (Raposo 2013). All cooking is arguably interpretation, but while Ho seems to have a touch of imposter syndrome on the one hand, he bears the burden of his identity on the other: "Well, I think that a lot of people expect me to do an Asian thing again, or in general. But I wanted to do what I first learned how to do, which is classic French cuisine" (Ulla 2012). But Ho also thinks his Asian interpretation is an inevitability: "Vietnamese flavors may pop up, because I am Vietnamese" (2012).

The crossover between these chefs and biblical scholars, cuisines and hermeneutics, should be obvious. Biblical scholars of color still train in so-called classical methodology and experience the double expectation of classical rigor and ethnic authenticity—or exotic interpretation. No one would deny that our social location somehow drives our output as scholars and craftspeople of a guild. But do certain methodologies inevitably come from certain social locations? How do fraught concepts such as authenticity and essentialism play in these associations? Again, I ask: When I cook food, is it Chinese food? When I write as a biblical scholar, am I an Asian American biblical scholar? Or am I a scholar who is Asian American? Could I ever be an unmarked scholar, like the majority of those in the field of biblical studies?

Cuisines and Essence

This brings us to the next aspect of comparison to consider, that of essence and principles. Are there essential elements to certain minoritized hermeneutics? Can we proclaim that African American hermeneutics necessarily deal with the history of slavery, or Asian American with immigration, or Latinx with liberation theology? Are there borders to what we consider to be legitimate scholarship of any one of these hermeneutics? And can anyone write them? If we balk at the thought of a white scholar writing African American scholarship, is this due more to issues of history, power, or authenticity?

Of Escoffier, *Gastronomie*, Craft, and Canon   177

The question of essentialism in cuisine is similar: Are there boundaries to what can be labeled Afro-Caribbean cuisine or Ecuadorian? Perhaps these exist as ever shifting constellations of elements that cease to be meaningful the moment we insist on clearly defined boundaries. The very definition of cuisine changes depending on which scholar of history, food, and anthropology one asks. The late great Sidney Mintz (1996, 96) defines *cuisine* (as differentiated from "national" or "haute" cuisine) as regional in character—evocative of a *place*—and essentially social:

> I think a cuisine requires a population that eats that cuisine with sufficient frequency to consider themselves experts on it. They all believe, and *care* that they believe, that they know what it consists of, how it is made, and how it should taste. In short, a genuine cuisine has common social roots; it is the food of a community—albeit often a very large community.

Here Mintz touches on something akin to what Choi calls "consciousness" and "commitment" in minoritized criticism, that is, the *caring* for the cooking craft of a region, derived from its local social and historical roots.

National cuisines (which are not cuisines at all, according to Mintz 1996, 94–97) form with nations and national identities, constructed with the aid of political and military expansion. National cuisines play a part in nationalistic pride and international relations (and colonialism) through exhibiting supposedly representative values and cultural flavor through a collective of representative dishes from disparate regions (see Trubek 2000, 67). Traveling and immigrating cooks (and now tourism bureaus) publish these abroad in various forms (see Mintz 1996, 97). In the end, then, national cuisines showcase a representative—and somewhat caricatured—profile of certain regional dishes, which is separated from the localized, daily lives of individuals and their immediate communities.

In parallel, conscious and committed minoritized scholars who write from their own experience and personal background produce something akin to cuisine in the regional sense, that is, cuisine that is tied to geography, community, and local experience and memory. One profound example of this is Manuel Villalobos's (2011, 207) recounting of his first memory of being labeled as queer:

> This incident took place during a Good Friday in a remote village of Mexico, where Jesus' body was displayed for veneration. All the "boys" and "girls" were lined up in order to kiss Jesus as a sign of respect and compassion. When I approached Jesus' body, without hesitation I kissed

178 — Yii-Jan Lin

> him on the mouth. The priest, irritated, "situated" me in my "place" by saying, "What are you doing" Are you *del otro lado*/are you *from the other side*?" Immediately, by instinct, I knew that being *del otro lado* was something that I should fear and avoid.

This story presents local ingredients of ritual, language, festival, and colonial history mixed with piercing personal memory, sensations, and realization. In writing this locally produced story, Villalobos (207) refuses to present his work as representative—as national cuisine, so to speak: "I do not pretend to talk about or represent the experience of other GLBT Latinos/as who are out there struggling with the 'mark of the beast,' as Anzaldúa calls it. My coming out through my writings is for the purpose of coping with my own struggles of living in the borderland, as a *nepantlero* and as a *Mexicano del otro lado*."

Nevertheless, elements of his story and larger article can be read as dominant themes of Latinx hermeneutics, for example borderlands, crossings, indigeneity, postcoloniality, and exile. But the instant "Latinx hermeneutics" is reified as a category treating these specific themes, that is, when it is profiled as a national cuisine, the regional, individual story fades. In Villalobos's case, were I to describe this work as "part of Latinx hermeneutics, which treats issues of borders, exile, and indigeneity," I would efface his local narrative and, with it, the unique intersectionality of his experience. The category of "Latinx" swallows up the remote Mexican village, the kissing of Jesus on the lips, and Villalobos's story as a *nepantlero*. The family dish of regional ingredients, passed down from the abuelas, becomes "Mexican food."

Obviously, "Mexican food" may be said to have certain dominant themes, but understanding this essentially versus consequentially makes the difference between caricature and portrait. In other words, it is not that "Mexican food" must and essentially comprises x, y, and z but that these came naturally from regional agriculture, tastes, and histories. In between the regional and national cuisine, many dishes and narratives are filtered out and unrepresented.

The same can be said of minoritized criticism as a category in general: it tends to include certain elements—for example, the autobiographical criticism found in Villalobos's article. But this should not be part of a litmus test or list of requirements for what properly belongs in such a category, since the category itself should dissolve into personal and communal histories and concerns. Otherwise, these labels have

Of Escoffier, *Gastronomie*, Craft, and Canon 179

value only as collectors' items, rounding out must-have lists with the "diversity" they provide.

Classical Cuisine

But whose collectors' items would these criticisms be? Whose gaze and judgment are at work here? After all, "minoritized" implies a minoritizer. "Mexican food" implies a consumer audience ignorant of and/or outside regional communities. Who are they? There is, of course, no simple or singular answer to this, and some answers may seem contradictory—there are, for example, people of Chinese descent who occasionally enjoy "junk" Chinese food (myself included). But regardless of different judgments and complex perspectives, there exists both in the culinary world and biblical scholarship a standard of product and execution powered by codification within institutions that certify, hire, and publicize.

This brings us back to Escoffier. How is it that this man, with his declaration that there are five mother sauces, still haunts every chef who hopes to achieve meaningful certification in the culinary world? The exam to become a Certified Master Chef, as administered by the American Culinary Federation (2006), still relies on classical cuisine as articulated by Escoffier as its watermark of professional competency. The objective listed under the classical cuisine exam states:

> The candidate must demonstrate the ability to understand, interpret and execute the philosophy of Auguste Escoffier and classical cuisine as prescribed in *Le Guide Culinaire*. The candidate will demonstrate a thorough knowledge of the foundations of classical cuisine and preparation throughout the presented menu. The mastery of classical techniques and presentation will be strictly adhered to according to *Le Guide Culinaire*. (13)

More than a century after its publication in 1903, *Le guide* (its imposing nickname) continues its dominance in the world of professionalized cooking. Of course, concessions have been made for cooking outside French haute cuisine—"global cuisine" forms *one* component of the master chef exam, with the following objective:

> The candidate must demonstrate knowledge of several global cuisines. The practical component of this discipline will be demonstrated by the preparation of three main dishes from three different regions of

180   Yii-Jan Lin

the world. It is expected that the candidate demonstrates a knowledge *representative* of the traditions, philosophies, and methodology that is indicative of each cuisine. (15, emphasis added)

Et voilà, there are the collector's items: three global cuisines that add "diversity" to an exam and course of study that assumes French classical cuisine to be the foundation of all cookery.[4] This assumption exists almost everywhere chefs are trained and certified. Even in culinary schools outside Europe and America, students and professionals don a toque, learn to brunoise, julienne, clarify stock, and maintain a *mise en place*.

How did French haute cuisine climb to such prominence and attain the title of classical? That history takes too many twists and turns, from the medieval period to the modern, to recount here (see Trubek 2000). In brief, however, we can identify several key elements: the formation of haute cuisine in French royal courts and aristocratic houses, the translation of this cuisine for the bourgeoisie in the nineteenth century, the rise of restaurants in the twentieth century, and the codification and promotion of French haute cuisine by dominant figures such as Escoffier, who insisted on the preeminence of French methods and connected them with social standing (128–29).

Like national cuisine, haute cuisine has evolved several steps away from any particular regional cooking. Rather than deriving from a local community, haute cuisine "need not have geographical roots; its social character is based on class" (Mintz 1996, 101). Its concern does not focus on the practical matter of feeding families with readily available ingredients but on quite the opposite. Haute cuisine developed in royal courts and houses through sumptuous feasting "as a means of asserting social rank and power" (Mennell 1985, 58). It therefore glories in elaborate presentation, rare spices, and complicated methods. It may have been born from local cooks and ingredients once upon a time, but its origins are difficult to make out after the intervening years of elaboration and refinement.

French haute cuisine, after accumulating a repertoire of methodologies and a reputation among the social elite of Europe, achieved the status

---

4. Although candidates face only one exam component explicitly titled "classical," clearly all components outside the "global cuisine" portion of the exam are grounded in French classical cuisine. Throughout the other portions of the test, students are asked to tend to a *garde manger*, clarify stock, produce terrines, and bake *vol au vent* or *bouchée* (American Culinary Federation 2006).

Of Escoffier, *Gastronomie*, Craft, and Canon   181

of professional standard through the establishment of culinary schools (e.g., L'Ecole Professionnelle de Cuisine) and trade publications (e.g., *L'art culinaire*; Trubek 2000, 90–91). Escoffier completed the process by gathering what he felt was quintessential and publishing it all under the iconic and instructive title *Le guide*—"The Guide," that is, the necessary volume for achieving culinary mastery.

Any scholar of the history of biblical criticism has already been drawing parallels while reading through the last few paragraphs. The professionalization of biblical studies, from the seventeenth century to the present, follows the same trajectory. Granted, scholarship has never boasted the same economic opulence as the feasts of royal courts, but the intricacy of its theological debates, philological minutiae, and historical reconstructions present a type of luxury as well. Modern biblical criticism also has a broad locale of origin, Germany rather than France, but it also now stands removed from the local elements that fed its beginnings. We may know of Bengel's German Pietism, but that is no longer associated with the methods he passed on, which have come to be understood as historical (or, paradoxically, ahistorical) rather than contextual, for example, as described in the standard history textbook of New Testament studies: "Although colored by *strange concepts*, the mass of [Bengel's] work was dedicated to a *historical* understanding of the NT" (Baird 1992, 80, emphasis added).

The classical standard of biblical studies, historical criticism, thus grew in specialization among the intelligentsia of Europe, who then codified its methods and published their superiority. Certification of scholars came first through intellectual genealogies of *Doktorvaters* and then through the schools, both institutional and intellectual, that surrounded them. As the standard modus of its field, historical criticism need not mark itself but presides as the classical method that is assumed in certifying exams, coursework, and editorial boards. The rest are relegated to global cuisines, so to speak. At no point does historical criticism need to regionalize itself as European hermeneutics.

But some may argue that historical criticism is not regional or contextual because, rather than presenting reading from a particular location or experience, its methods are the foundation of biblical scholarship, the fundamentals of the craft itself. The same could be argued for classical cooking: though its origins may be historically French, it presents basic techniques for cooking in any cuisine. Surely all chefs must have knife skills and knowledge of braising, reducing, and caramelizing foods?

If, however, an integral part of French classical cuisine and historical criticism is simply fundamental techniques of a craft, then these techniques are not quintessentially French or historical-critical but foundational for all cuisines and methods. The basic reaction of fat and acid over heat may be utilized in making hollandaise, but it is simply an essential chemical reaction used in countless cuisines, such as in Indian Madras curry.

Likewise, undergirding the very foundation of biblical studies are the ability of literacy and a basic *paideia* required for reading different types of texts.[5] Competency in ancient languages, knowledge of the historical contexts of the primary texts, and a rudimentary working knowledge of textual criticism might constitute a second order of fundamental skills. These might be compared to knife skills, which absolutely every chef must possess, but not every chef uses in each creative endeavor, whether in one service of an evening or one phase of a career. We might relegate these to the duties of the sous chef and the philologist—and, indeed, philology has been called lower criticism, as the support for higher criticism. But this ignores the interpretive work of translators and textual critics (see Lin 2016, 1–20). Even knife skills and basic kitchen prep demonstrate interpretation in the fileting of a fish and the chiffonade of parsley. Nevertheless, head chefs and biblical interpreters generally concentrate their focus on the composition of their final interpretation, accepting the preparatory interpretive work of others.

Beyond these first and second orders of knowledge, required of all biblical scholars, lies the realm of hermeneutics, in which historical criticism reigns as the standard. Its methodology may seem naturally dominant because of its foregrounding of fundamentals—ancient contexts and philology—but in actuality, historical criticism, as much as minoritized hermeneutics, relies on theoretical premises of epistemology and semiotics. The problematic issue is not, then, its method, but the assumption that its theoretical premises are nonexistent or commonsensical, rendering other methods as inessential in comparison. Its majoritized status forms, in short, a hierarchy of craft like that of cuisine, as outlined by American chef Mark Miller:

> At [a leading culinary school], French food in its technique and recipes is seen as superior: dominant is the given and superior is the assumption.

---

5. I bracket out of this discussion what might constitute this type of education, for the sake of brevity.

Of Escoffier, *Gastronomie*, Craft, and Canon 183

> For example, when students make a curry, they spend three days making
> the veal stock, and then they pull the box of curry powder off the shelf....
> They don't understand the multitude of expressions curry can have.
> [The students] have a Eurocentric palate. But we don't have a Eurocentric
> world anymore. [There is] an unconscious re-affirmation of the Euro-
> centric model.... A culinary caste system is being set up, and it is being
> reaffirmed all the way along: symbolically, linguistically, technically, and
> taste wise. (quoted in Trubek 2000, 130–31)

In the example mentioned above, the box of curry (as versus the carefully
crafted veal stock) compresses numerous histories, cultures, and their spices
into one convenient and quick package for easy use. It satisfies as a gesture
toward diversity without sacrificing time needed for classical cuisine. As a
postcolonial object, it collects, domesticates, and commodifies the exotic.

Postcolonial studies in the academy, no less in biblical studies, has emphasized violent histories of colonialism in discussions of power, identity, and
language. But a facile understanding of postcolonial theory quickly carica-
tures its methodologies. Like grabbing a box of curry, a scholar can mention
Homi Bhabha, find a few analogues that work for hybridity and mimicry in
an ancient text, and be done. This generally passes for competency in the
guild and allows the field's arbiters—those who deem historical criticism as
quintessential and central—to feel they have understood the theory, out of
polite obligation, but continue to believe that nothing compares to the "real"
work of philology and history. What they fail to grasp is critical theory—but
theory is difficult, while memorizing terminology is not, and the latter has
become a stand-in caricature of what comprises minoritized criticism

Eating and Dining

But as much as the box of curry serves as an easy target of scorn as a
symbol of consumer Orientalism, its broad usage indicates a story more
complicated than simply culinary hierarchy and exoticization. This pack-
aged curry might be thoughtlessly used by classically trained chefs, but it
is also used by Asian chefs and cooks, professionally and in homes. As a
postcolonial *objet*, the box of curry does not easily demarcate colonizers
and colonized by its consumption. Instead, its function reveals cultural
appropriation in multiple directions and sticky webs of global marketing,
shipping routes, and economies. Through these last phenomena, the box
of curry has become, above all, accessible and available.

184 Yii-Jan Lin

For those cooking at home for families, the process of selecting, grinding, and mixing spices, clarifying butter, or pounding lemongrass is mostly impossible, regardless of the ethnic identity of the cook. Creating haute cuisine occupies the world of elite chefs, with the privilege of time and wealth. But food is everyone's necessity, whether in forms pedestrian or sublime—not everyone may dine, but everybody eats. The box of curry, or the can of SPAM[6] or the pot of stew, meets the everyday need of hunger efficiently and inexpensively.

Not everyone may read ancient Greek—but millions of Christians and interested people read the Bible. Thousands of individuals and communities consume—metaphorically and literally, in ritual—the word of God. What role does the haute cuisine of scholarship play in their reading and interpretation? For the privileged, Sunday school or Bible classes, or the occasional course at a seminary, may be an option. But for many, the bedside Bible and the preaching on Sunday serve as their daily bread. Do we, as scholars of minoritized biblical criticism, deny the need of hungry folk through our very scholarship? What is our responsibility to make our work accessible and nourishing to those outside the guild? How is this possible when, in the pressure of publication-driven careers, review committees, deans, and provosts may discount accessible work as *un-Wissenschaftlich*? And does the penalty of relevancy need always to fall on the backs of scholars of color, who already bear a double burden as diversity hires and lone spots of black and brown for their schools?

At the same time, how does the nourishing food of those outside the obsessions of the guild outshine our scholarship? Street-vendor cooks will not have trained at the Culinary Institute of America—but that does not mean they are not cooking beautiful food. A trained chef can appreciate this food—Anthony Bourdain, the champion of street food, immediately comes to mind—but not every chef cares or has a professional obligation to explore outside restaurant walls. Some minoritized criticisms—womanist, *mujerista*, and minjung, for example—arose from experiences outside and excluded from the academy. How do these continue the conversation between the guild and those outside, and how do others begin that conversation from a point of privilege? When does the dialogue become exploitative, and when is it mutually beneficial?

---

6. SPAM is another complicated food product, with a military and colonial history. See Matejowsky 2012.

Of Escoffier, *Gastronomie*, Craft, and Canon 185

Working in the Guild

Last, any discussion of accessibility and the academy must also consider the accessibility of a living wage in the academic job market. Whatever our training or background, the reality is that, as more academics go unemployed or underemployed, the ratio of jobs to applicants makes it very difficult for young scholars—or any scholars—to find stable, tenure-track faculty positions. Higher education, as we all know, is changing. How is our mentoring and guidance of scholars changing to reflect this? Is it conscionable for schools to admit the same number of doctoral students each year when only a handful of jobs are available each season? Are the realities and likelihoods made clear to each prospective student? Our desire may be to see more and more students of color and those marginalized in other modes participate in the field and the academy—but at what cost to their possible futures?

To enter culinary school and believe that you will become a celebrity chef—or even a head chef at a notable restaurant—is incredibly naive. More likely, you can work as a line cook, or perhaps you could design and consult for a prepackaged food company, or perhaps you can teach nutrition.[7] Those are the stark realities of entering the culinary profession. It is hard, physical labor, with long hours and burned hands and aching backs. It is not so different with scholarship. The cost is great and the outcome very uncertain. What is the responsibility of those working to empower the minoritized who also wish to empower students entering the field?

This meditation, a prolonged analogy, poses a battery of questions, venturing few answers, if any at all. My hope is that this comparative musing, if not immediately offering resolution, provides a clarifying distance from which to view the enterprise of minoritized biblical criticism. The multitude of questions, however, signals the possibility for new creativity and conceptualizations of our field and the structures of the guild.

The way people eat and cook in their own homes and in restaurants changes with each era, with the very concept of a public restaurant and classical cuisine coming to existence only a couple of centuries ago. The

---

7. According to the US Department of Labor, culinary jobs are growing at a rate slightly above average. But these are hardly plum head-chef positions: the median annual pay for head chefs and cooks is $43,180, still lower than the $57,857 paid on average to assistant professors in theology positions. See United States Department of Labor 2018 and Higher Ed Jobs 2013.

similar newness of biblical criticism, in comparison to millennia of biblical interpretation, should not be forgotten. The normative way things are is simply another phase and construction. As this construction creaks and groans during massive changes in education—and especially in theological and religious education—the dynamic questions asked within minoritized criticism should lead the way forward.

Works Cited

American Culinary Federation. 2006. *Certified Master Chef Examination Manual.* St. Augustine, FL: American Culinary Federation. https://tinyurl.com/SBL06106c3.

Baird, William. 1992. *From Deism to Tübingen.* Vol. 1 of *History of New Testament Research.* Minneapolis: Fortress.

Choi, Jin Young. 2015. *Postcolonial Discipleship of Embodiment: An Asian and Asian American Feminist Reading of the Gospel of Mark.* New York: Palgrave Macmillan.

———. 2017. "Asian and Asian American Interpretation." Facebook, 3 November. Private link. Content used with permission.

Dunlop, Fuschia. 2007. "The Strange Tale of General Tso's Chicken." National Public Radio, 28 February. https://tinyurl.com/SBL06106v.

Escoffier, Auguste. 2009. *Le Guide Culinaire: Aide-mémoire de cuisine practique.* Paris: Flammarion.

Higher Ed Jobs. N.d. "Tenured/Tenure-Track Faculty Salaries (Results of 2012–13 Faculty in Higher Education Salary Survey by Discipline, Rank and Tenure Status in Four-Year Colleges and Universities)." https://tinyurl.com/SBL06106w.

James, Kenneth. 2002. *Escoffier: The King of Chefs.* London: Hambledon & London.

Jean-Georges. N.d. "About Jean-Georges Vongerichten." https://tinyurl.com/SBL06106c4.

Kasper, Lynn Rossetto. 2013. "How Momofuku's David Chang Learned to Embrace the Word 'Fusion.'" The Splendid Table, 16 August. https://tinyurl.com/SBL06106x.

Kelly, Raina. 2010. "How Thomas Keller Transformed American Dining." *Newsweek,* 14 September. https://tinyurl.com/SBL06106y.

Liew, Tat-siong Benny. 2008. *What Is Asian American Biblical Hermeneutics?* Honolulu: University of Hawai'i Press.

Lin, Yii-Jan. 2016. *The Erotic Life of Manuscripts: New Testament Textual Criticism and the Biological Sciences*. New York: Oxford University Press.

MacFarquar, Larissa. 2008. "Chef on the Edge: David Chang's Search for the Perfect Restaurant." *The New Yorker*, 24 March. https://tinyurl.com/SBL06106z.

Matejowsky, Ty. 2012. "SPAM and Fast-food 'Glocalization' in the Philippines." Pages 369–92 in *Taking Food Public: Redefining Foodways in a Changing World*. Edited by Psyche Williams-Forson and Carole Counihan. New York: Routledge.

McWilliams, Mark. 2012. *The Story behind the Dish: Classic American Foods*. Santa Barbara, CA: Greenwood.

Mennell, Stephen. 1985. *All Manners of Food: Eating and Taste in England and France from Middle Age to the Present*. New York: Blackwell.

Mintz, Sidney W. 1996. *Tasting Food, Tasting Freedom*. Boston: Beacon.

Momofuku. 2023. "About Us + Team." https://momofuku.com/our-company/team.

Moskin, Julia. 2009. "Momofuku, Take 5." *New York Times*, 1 September. https://tinyurl.com/SBL06106aa.

Raposo, Jacqueline. 2013. "We Chat with Chef Tien Ho of Montmartre." *Serious Eats*, 23 April. https://tinyurl.com/SBL06106c8.

Ruhlman, Michael. 2001. *The Soul of a Chef: The Journey toward Perfection*. New York: Penguin.

Segovia, Fernando F. 2014. "Introduction: Approaching Latino/a Biblical Criticism: A Trajectory of Visions and Missions." Pages 1–44 in *Latino/a Biblical Hermeneutics: Problematics, Objectives, Strategies*. Edited by Francisco Lozada Jr. and Fernando F. Segovia. SemeiaSt 68. Atlanta: SBL Press.

Smith, Mitzi J. 2015. "Introduction." Pages 1–16 in *I Found God in Me: A Womanist Biblical Hermeneutics Reader*. Edited by Mitzi J. Smith. Eugene, OR: Cascade Books.

Trubek, Amy B. 2000. *Haute Cuisine: How the French Invented the Culinary Profession*. Philadelphia: University of Pennsylvania Press.

Trudy. 2013. "Who Can Be a Womanist?" *Gradient Lair* (blog), 29 September. https://tinyurl.com/SBL06106c9.

Tuvel, Rebecca. 2017. "In Defense of Transracialism." *Hypatia* 32.2:263–78.

Ulla, Gabe. 2012. "Tien Ho on Struggles, Ownership, and French Cooking." Eater: New York, 26 October. https://tinyurl.com/SBL06106ac.

United States Department of Labor. 2018. "Occupational Outlook Handbook: Chefs and Head Cooks." Last modified 30 January. https://tinyurl.com/SBL06106ab.

Villalobos, Manual. 2011. "Bodies *Del Otro Lado* Finding Life and Hope in the Borderland: Gloria Anzaldùa, the Ethiopian Eunuch of Acts 8:26–40, *y Yo*." Pages 191–221 in *Bible Trouble: Queer Reading at the Boundaries of Biblical Scholarship*. Edited by Teresa Hornsby and Ken Stone. SemeiaSt 67. Atlanta: Society of Biblical Literature.

Walker, Alice. *In Search of Our Mother's Gardens: Womanist Prose*. New York: Houghton Mifflin Harcourt, 1983.

Confronting Christian Identity, Chosenness, and Violence in a Predominantly African American Graduate Theological Center

Vanessa Lovelace

> Here is what I would like for you to know: In America, it is traditional to destroy the black body—it is heritage.
>
> —Ta-Nehisi Coates, *Between the World and Me*

> Southern trees bear a strange fruit,
> Blood on the leaves and blood at the root,
> Black bodies swinging in the southern breeze
> Strange fruit hanging from the poplar trees
> —Lewis Allan, "Strange Fruit"

The recurrent deaths of young Black people in America by white vigilantes and law enforcement officers have reignited the debate regarding the disdain with which white America views Black bodies.[1] However, it is not only the deaths of young Blacks that call our attention to the disregard with which some white Americans hold Black bodies. Black

---

Abel Meeropol wrote the poem "Strange Fruit" under the pseudonym Lewis Allan in 1937. Jazz singer Billie Holiday's 1939 recording of the poem turned it into a famous protest song against the brutality of the lynching taking place mostly in southern US towns.

1. Initial media accounts reported that George Zimmerman, a white Sanford, Florida, Neighborhood Watch captain, killed Black male teen Trayvon Martin, who was visiting his father in the gated community where Zimmerman lived. Zimmerman's father, who is white, complicated Zimmerman's ethnic identity by claiming that, since George's mother is Hispanic, so is his son (Stutzman 2012). Other high-profile deaths of Blacks at the hands of law enforcement officials have included Tamir Rice; Michael Brown; Elijah McClain; George Floyd; Breonna Taylor; and Ahmaud Arbery.

-189-

190   Vanessa Lovelace

women's bodies in particular draw derision from the white gaze (for a thorough treatment of this subject, see Yancy 2008). For example, tennis star Serena Williams and principal ballerina Misty Copeland—the Hottentot Venuses of our day—have been treated as freaks of nature on public display, scorned for succeeding with muscular body types and large breasts in a world where the norm is white females with tall and thin body types.[2]

In this essay I interrogate the intersection of race, gender, and sexuality in certain biblical narratives. I will discuss what I believe, as a minoritized biblical critic of African descent teaching in a predominantly African American graduate theological center, is an important subject in theological education: how white America's violence against symbolic and physical Blackness in America has been justified, to a large degree, by the selective use of biblical narratives. In particular, narratives such as the story of Israel's chosenness by G-d have been appropriated by white Americans, since the nation was founded to foster anti-Black attitudes.

The Legacy of the Biblical Curses of Cain and Canaan

Ever since the first Africans arrived in America, Black bodies have been despised, abused, and exploited to maintain white power over Blacks. The #BlackLivesMatter movement and other social movements are the latest to promote awareness of violence and discrimination against Blacks.[3] However, in much of the media coverage, what has gone largely unspoken is how the Bible has been used to justify violence against Black people.

Although it is not a direct link to violence against Blacks, the interpretation of Gen 4:11 by some over the centuries has laid the

---

2. Sarah (or Saartjie) Baartman, also known as the Hottentot Venus, was a South African woman exhibited in freak shows throughout Europe in the nineteenth century for her enormous buttocks and genitalia. See, for example, Litchfield (2018) on taunts on Williams for her skin color and physical appearance.

3. In 2013 Alicia Garza, Patrisse Cullors, and Opal Tameti organized the #Black-LivesMatter movement in response to the acquittal of George Zimmerman in the murder of Trayvon Martin. Although not specified by name, the FBI's Counterterrorism Division's (2017) Intelligence Assessment titled "Black Identity Extremists Likely Motivated to Target Law Enforcement Officers" predicts that movements such as #BlackLivesMatter will justify future acts of violence toward law enforcement based on real or perceived unfair treatment of African Americans by law enforcement.

Confronting Christian Identity, Chosenness, and Violence 191

groundwork. The story of Cain and Abel is the story of the first murder in the Bible. Cain and Abel were brothers who brought offerings to Israel's deity. The deity looked favorably on Abel's offering of the first-born of his flock but rejected Cain's firstfruits from the ground. Cain became angry and killed Abel. In response, the deity cursed Cain to wander the earth, but he protested that his life would be threatened. The deity marked Cain so that no one who encountered him would kill him. The mark in question is unidentified in the text. However, this did not prevent some interpreters from supposing that the mark was Blackness and that, therefore, Blackness must be a curse: "[The Black's skin color] originated with Cain, the murderer of his brother, whose family were destined to have the black colour as a punishment" (Goldenberg 2003, 179). Following from this story of crime and punishment, some further argued that the devil copulated with Eve to produce Cain, the father of Blacks (Quinones 1991, 53).

Closer to the mark (pun intended) in associating Blackness with being cursed is the curse of Canaan (also referred to by the misnomer "the curse of Ham"), based on the story of Noah and his sons. Noah's son Ham found his father naked and in a drunken stupor in his tent (Gen 9:22). Instead of covering his father's nakedness, he went and told his brothers Shem and Japheth. They took a garment and walked backwards into the tent to cover their father without seeing him naked. When Noah awoke and learned what Ham had done, he cursed Ham's son Canaan instead of Ham: "Cursed be Canaan; lowest of slaves shall he be to his brothers" (Gen 9:25 NRSV).

Apologists for the curse of Ham are quick to explain not only that it was Noah and not Israel's deity who cursed Canaan but also that he cursed only Canaan and not his descendants. Nevertheless, interpreters over the centuries have used the curse of Canaan to defend the heredi-tary enslavement of people of African descent. According to their interpretation, the Table of Nations (Gen 10) lists the descendants of Shem and Japheth as the lighter-skinned people of Asia and Europe, respectively, and the descendants of Ham, besides Canaan, as the darker-skinned people of northern Africa (Cush, Egypt, and Put). As in the case of Cain, there is no relationship between Canaan and black skin color in the text. Still, interpreters who associated Ham's descen-dants with being cursed defended the enslavement of black-skinned people on the basis that they were descended from Canaan. Eventu-ally, the enslavement of black-skinned peoples was also imputed to the

192   Vanessa Lovelace

mark of Cain, by making Ham a descendant of Cain through marriage (Goldenberg 2003, 178).[4]

Scholars continue to debate when the association between the curse of Ham or Canaan and anti-Blackness originated.[5] Nevertheless, the idea that Black people were descended from the Canaanites is evident in early modern European literature. An example comes from seventeenth-century English explorer Richard Jobson, who wrote of his travels to Ethiopia and the Gambia River. He reported that the king's numerous wives and concubines as well as his large penis were the result of being a descendant of Ham. He writes, "For undoubtedly these people originally sprung from the race of *Canaan*, the sonne of *Ham*, who discovered his father *Noahs* secrets, for which *Noah* awakeing cursed Canaan as our holy Scripture testifieth … are furnisht with such members as are after a sort burthensome unto them" (Jobson 1623, 65–66). Since biblical writers attributed sexual deviance and idolatry to the Canaanites (Lev 18:2–30, Deut 7:4), whose destruction, the Deuteronomic writer insists, is required by Israel's deity to maintain Israel's religious autonomy, violence against Black bodies is likewise justified because the status of modern-day Canaanites has been transferred to them.

It should be noted that Native Americans and African Americans are not the only people who have been associated with the biblical Canaanites. The appropriation by the Christian West of the curse of Canaan to exclude the indigenous Other was a frequent practice during the colonization process. For example, Kaled bin Walid, an Aboriginal convert to Islam, explained that his decision to embrace Islam despite his Christian upbringing was largely influenced by the racism in Australia. He recalled that, at the age of thirteen, his white foster parent explained that because he was "a descendent of Ham," he and "other blacks were cursed to be servants of the white race" (Boer and Abraham 2009, 470). However, in contrast to the biblical mandate to annihilate the indigenous Canaanites, or by comparison the indigenous Aborigines in Australia, as part of

---

4. Ricardo Quinones explains that the association between Cain and Blackness is the result of the conflation of Cain with Ham. Since both errant sons were cursed and banished, some believed that Ham had been banished to the Nile, thus "Ham traditionally came to be associated with the continent of Africa, and hence with blacks" (Quinones 1991, 53).

5. Stacy Davis (2008) disputes the often-repeated claim that anti-African sentiments originated with rabbinic interpretations of Gen 9:18–27.

Western colonization, white America has needed Black people for white identity construction.

White Identity Construction and Violence against Black Bodies

Whiteness involves a delicate interplay between familiarity with and distancing from "racial others." White racialization begins in early childhood "through a contrastive dynamic, a dynamic that expose[s] [white children] early on to the color line that [comes] replete with racist value-codes of exclusion and inclusion," and that grants power and authority to whiteness over Blackness (Yancy 2008, 48).

The white identity construction was not only realized by means of "negating, disliking, and hating the dark other" (49) but also through the objectification of and violence against the Black body. Particularly in the Jim Crow South, the construction and maintenance of white supremacy required the ritualized yet brutal enforcement of racial and gender roles and boundaries. A particularly effective method of enforcement was the spectacle lynching of Black bodies by white mobs. The noose hanging from the tree, bridge, or telephone pole was a symbolic form of intimidation warning Blacks what awaited them if they dared to transgress white space and social codes that only whites were aware had been broken.

The violence perpetrated against Black bodies during these acts regularly included mutilation. An eyewitness to the lynching of Luther Holbert, a black Mississippi sharecropper, and Holbert's wife reported the following:

> The two Negros ... were tied to trees and while the funeral pyres were being prepared, they were forced to hold out their hands while one finger at a time was chopped off.... Some of the mob used a large corkscrew to bore into the flesh of the man and woman. It was applied to their arms, legs and body, then pulled out, the spirals tearing out big pieces of ... flesh every time it was withdrawn. (Holden-Smith 1995, 32)

The lynched bodies were often mutilated for their parts for preservation as keepsakes. Participants and spectators would collect remains at the site—body parts, tree limbs, blades of grass, anything having proximity to the event—as a remembrance of having been witness to the ritual performance. The lynching souvenir also fixed the victim within a historical moment, transforming it "into a captive object to be owned, displayed, and quite possibly, traded" (Young 2005, 646).

194   Vanessa Lovelace

Several scholars have chronicled the way that many of the participants in acts of violence against Blacks, particularly lynchings, were engaging not only in "celebratory acts of racial control and domination" but also in "religious act[s], laden with Christian symbolism and significance" (Wood 2009, 48). According to Amy Wood (48), the ritual aspect "psychically restored a sense of communal purity and social order" that Black people unsettled. For Wood (4–5), the act of "witnessing," which referred both to public testimonial of faith and to the one witnessing the lynching spectacle as public ritual, connected the spectator to a larger community of witnesses and conferred a sense of white solidarity and superiority. Each of these accounts is an attestation to lynchings as public affairs attended by hundreds, sometimes thousands, of community members, among them men, women, and children. Those in attendance also included leading citizens of the community, such as business owners and elected officials (Holden-Smith 1995, 37).

Much of the literature on lynching as spectacle has noted the resonance between prolynching rhetoric and white evangelical Christians' concerns for morality, racial purity, and Black criminality. For example, scholars such as Kristina DuRocher (2011, 114) show how defenders of lynching used the same language as evangelical Protestants regarding the need to protect the moral and racial purity of white women and children from depraved Black males.[6] While the alleged motivation for mob gatherings was usually the accusation that a Black male had raped a white female, statistics compiled by the National Association for the Advancement of Colored People (NAACP) show this to be inaccurate. The NAACP documented that less than 30 percent of Black males lynched between 1889 and 1918 had actually been accused of sexually assaulting a white woman. Instead, the majority of lynchings were motivated by white vengeance for the alleged murder of a white person by a Black person (Holden-Smith 1995, 38). Nevertheless, the perception of the Black male bogeyman threatening the racial purity

---

6. Prior to the early twentieth century, white lynching victims outnumbered Blacks, primarily in the West, where religious and ethnic outsiders were largely targeted (see Holden-Smith 1995). The almost exclusive lynching of southern Blacks by southern whites began in the early twentieth century (1900–1946). Interestingly, this period was referred to as the progressive era. Although the majority of the victims were Black males, women were also lynched. Civic groups first introduced legislation in the United States Congress in 1900 and for decades after to make lynching a federal crime, but their efforts failed until President Joseph Biden signed H.R. 55, "The Emmett Till Antilynching Act" in 2022. For a history of efforts to pass antilynching legislation in Congress, see Sitkoff 2008.

Confronting Christian Identity, Chosenness, and Violence   195

of the white community not only justified racial violence against Blacks but also was granted divine sanction by white religious institutions in the postbellum South. A theological perspective rooted in white supremacy buttressed the efforts of southern religious groups to maintain a racial hierarchy in the United States (Bailey and Snedker 2011).

The Task of the Minoritized Biblical Critic

Despite the documented relationship between religion, sexuality, and violence against Blacks and other racial/ethnic minorities by whites in the United States, in both the predominately white and predominately Black settings where I have taught biblical studies, my students have seldom heard of the curse of Cain or the curse of Ham/Canaan. They are not aware that passages in the Bible have been used to justify violence against Native American or First Nation peoples and African-descended peoples, as the stand-ins for modern-day descendants of Canaan, or to defend white supremacy and segregation. Therefore, in my opinion, too many students at US graduate theological schools are ill-equipped to challenge racial bigotry clothed in biblical language.

I taught at a consortium of five historically Black seminaries in the US South. It is the case that the Bible "remains for a significant number of African American women and men the primary (though not exclusive) conduit of the community's understanding of God" (Martin 1999, 656). Consequently, as a minoritized biblical critic preparing Christian men and women for leadership in local and global communities, I believe that I have a responsibility to engage them in conversations around what it means to identify with the chosen people, the Israelites in the Bible, while simultaneously being historically subjected to enslavement, segregation, and acts of violence against them due to the supposed divinely sanctioned curse of Blackness.

Talking Biblical Chosenness in the Classroom

Some time ago, I had the opportunity to discuss the biblical concept of chosenness with students in an online exegesis course I taught on Joshua. The Hebrew term בהר, for "chosen," is most fully developed in the book of Deuteronomy.[7] The writer describes Israel as having been set apart from the other nations as G-d's chosen people:

---

7. Although there is no specific language of chosenness in the book of Genesis,

196 Vanessa Lovelace

> For you are a people holy to the LORD your God. The LORD your God has chosen you to be a people for his treasured possession, out of all the peoples who are on the face of the earth.... Know therefore that the LORD your God is God, the faithful God who maintains covenant loyalty with those who love him and keep his commandments, to a thousand generations. (Deut 7:6, 9 ESV; see 14:2)

Israel's status as YHWH's chosen was contingent on separating themselves from the indigenous peoples in the land that they were about to enter and on maintaining their relationship to their deity. The way that they demonstrated their fidelity was to show covenantal loyalty by keeping the statutes and commandments. One of those statutes was to devote to חרם, to "utterly destroy," the indigenous peoples in the land and to remove any trace of their cultural and religious heritage.

The Former Prophets in the Hebrew Bible (Joshua to Kings) portray contrasting views of the people's faithfulness to this edict.[8] As we discussed in the course, according to Joshua 10:40, the Israelites did as they were commanded and "utterly defeated all that breathed." In contrast, Judges 2 chastises the people for their failure to carry out this mandate. The Former Prophets depict Israel's downward spiral and decline as a nation as YHWH's judgment of Israel for disobeying this covenant decree:

> So the anger of the LORD was kindled against Israel; and he said, "Because this people have transgressed my covenant that I commanded their ancestors, and have not obeyed my voice, I will no longer drive out before them any of the nations that Joshua left when he died" [NRSV]. In order to test Israel, whether or not they would take care to walk in the way of the LORD as their ancestors did, the LORD had left those nations, not driving them out at once, and had not handed them over to Joshua. (Judg 2:20–23)

Israel's disobedience (usually interpreted by the class as religious apostasy) and the deity's subsequent judgment were a frequent subject of dialogue

---

interpreters often read G-d's call of Abram in Gen 12:2–3 in this way. They see the call to leave land and kin for a land that G-d would give him—a promise of land that belonged to the Canaanites, Hittites, Amorites, and others (Gen 15:18, 21; Exod 3:17)—as God's choice of Israel over all nations (Lohr 2009,10).

8. These books are referred to as the historical books in the Protestant Old Testament (Joshua, Judges, Ruth, 1 and 2 Samuel, 1 and 2 Kings). Biblical scholars also refer to this corpus as the Deuteronomistic History or narratives because the author(s) composed these books from the theological perspective of the book of Deuteronomy.

Confronting Christian Identity, Chosenness, and Violence 197

in the forum board discussions. Prior to this course, the extent of most of my students' knowledge of the book of Joshua could be condensed into one scriptural passage:

> Now therefore revere the LORD, and serve him in sincerity and in faithfulness; put away the gods that your ancestors served beyond the River and in Egypt, and serve the LORD. Now if you are unwilling to serve the LORD, choose this day whom you will serve, whether the gods your ancestors served in the region beyond the River or the gods of the Amorites in whose land you are living; *but as for me and my household, we will serve the Lord.* (Josh 24:14–15, emphasis added)

Therefore, the prevailing response in the online forum discussions regarding the Israelites' shortcomings was disbelief that the chosen people of G-d could fail so miserably at keeping G-d's covenant stipulation to destroy the indigenous peoples of the land. A few of the students questioned the fairness of a deity choosing one group from among the others as special. Yet, the idea of the ancient Israelites as the chosen people is taken for granted in the US Black Christian tradition. Thus, the students in my online class consistently referred to the Israelites as "G-d's chosen people" or the "children of Israel." Moreover, Black Christians see themselves as heirs of the promise to Abraham through Jesus Christ: "Just as Abraham 'believed God, and it was reckoned to him as righteousness,' so, you see, those who believe are the descendants of Abraham" (Gal 3:6–7). Take, for example, this quote by a student in one of the online forum discussions:

> As we embark upon our study of the book of Joshua I think it is important that we remember the Abramic [*sic*] covenant in Genesis 12 and 15. God told Abram that He was going to bless him personally, nationally and universally. Because of the faith and obedience of Abram/Abraham Israel is bestowed with the identity of being chosen by God.... Israel was God's chosen generation by election and we are His chosen generation by adoption.

As indicated, for this student and others, chosenness meant obedience. Therefore, they believed that since G-d had promised Abraham the land occupied by the Canaanites (Gen 12:4–7, 15:18–21), the Israelites were obligated to take possession of the land by force even if it meant killing its inhabitants. Moreover, despite their discomfort with the killing of innocent men, women, and children, they justified it by arguing that the

198 Vanessa Lovelace

immorality and idolatry practiced by the Canaanites (claims not textually supported) had to be eliminated or the Israelites would be tempted to follow in their ways.

In fact, the students repeatedly stated that the Israelites were acting according to G-d's command and that, likewise, obedience to G-d was expected of Christians. Many of them expressed the opinion that disobedience to G-d had caused the decline of America, just as covenant disobedience led to the invasion and destruction of Judah and Jerusalem and the Babylonian exile. If the nation would repent and return to G-d, they argued, then it would become prosperous again. Now, the students did not specify what they considered as the American deterioration. However, as they were mostly evangelical Christians, I suspect that this decline was understood as laws imposed by the courts, such as the ban on state-sanctioned school prayer, the legalization of abortion, and same-sex marriage.

By now it should come as no surprise that, since the students saw themselves as Abraham's heirs, they unanimously identified with the Israelites. The required course readings were intended to help them think critically about how the interpretation of the text depended on whose point of view they interpreted it from. The readings came from a diverse set of authors: Randall C. Bailey, Walter Brueggemann, Laura Donaldson, and Robert Warrior.

Bailey's (1998) article, "The Danger of Ignoring One's Own Cultural Bias in Interpreting the Text," analyzes the various functions of Afrocentric biblical interpretation from the nineteenth century to the present. He shows how, on one hand, nineteenth-century Afrocentric biblical criticism freely critiqued and modified biblical interpretation to promote the liberation of Black people. On the other hand, he argues that contemporary African American interpretation seems to have forgotten this interpretive strategy and adopted an alien culture's reading. He encourages African Americans to embrace their own cultural biases in interpreting biblical texts for the benefit of their health and well-being. Bailey's article helped the students to reflect on whether they were reading the text from their own cultural bias or had appropriated the worldview of those interpreters whose interests opposed theirs.

Brueggemann's (2013) "The God of Joshua: An Ambivalent Field of Negotiation" got them to contemplate the notion that chosenness consists in the negation of the Other. Brueggemann explains that the exclusion of the Other from the covenant's promises justified the violence commanded by the deity against those outside the covenant. Brueggemann raised questions

Confronting Christian Identity, Chosenness, and Violence   199

for the class regarding the lack of dissent from Israel or the deity against violence. He comments, "YHWH is here totally committed to the enterprise, passionate for the exclusiveness of the chosen, and zealous to deliver on the land promise that goes with chosenness" (19). The students had to consider Brueggemann's question as to whether Israel's deity would have relented against violence if the chosen had voiced dissent.

Donaldson's (2011) article, "Joshua in America: On Cowboys, Canaanites and Indians," begins with the story of the massacre of Native Americans in Conestoga, Pennsylvania, in 1763 by the Paxtung Rangers or "Paxton Boys." The men, "Scotch-Irish Presbyterians," justified their slaughter of the Indians on the basis that the book of Joshua had commanded the destruction of the "heathen" "red Canaanites" (274). Donaldson, who also is Native American, examines the relationship between biblical interpretation and the North American eugenics movement. Donaldson's article was beneficial for students to begin to make the connection between the biblical command to destroy the Canaanites and the real-life occupation of Native American land and the forced removal, relocation, and decimation of Native Americans.

The article that most helped them to regard the Canaanites through a different lens was "A Native American Perspective: Canaanites, Cowboys and Indians," by Warrior (1989). Warrior argues that appropriation of the exodus story by theologies of liberation often ignores the fact that the exodus is not a suitable model of liberation for indigenous peoples. The students saw clearly for the first time the conquest from the perspective of the Canaanites. They realized for the first time that G-d the Liberator embraced by Black liberation theology could be G-d the Conqueror for Native Americans.

Despite the argument around whether the biblical account of the conquest of Canaan happened as recorded, the students were accepting of the fact that a number of Puritans saw Native Americans as the Canaanites to be destroyed if they did not convert to Christianity or cooperate with American expansionism. On the one hand, the students were beginning to see the annihilation of the indigenous peoples through Canaanite eyes. On the other hand, it was still difficult for them to question the underlying theological and ethical problems of occupying the promised land, when the theology of Black liberation drew largely on the exodus narrative of freedom from slavery. Yet, this article was a clear example for the students of how those interpreting the Bible can interpret the text with a cultural bias that can be harmful to others.

200 Vanessa Lovelace

These students are not alone in identifying either with the ancient Israelites or *as* the biblical Israelites. From the apostle Paul to Protestant Christians in England, the Israelites became a typology for the persecution of Christians—the former by the Romans, the latter by the English royalists. Puritans in England replaced Israel with Britain as G-d's chosen nation. They viewed themselves as the conscience of the nation of England, which they believed needed to be purged of the Babylonian/Catholic influences that were contaminating the Church of England, lest it come under G-d's judgment as the Jewish people had by rejecting Christ (Guibbory 2005, 203–24).

The Puritan emigrants to New England revised this interpretation to depict the king of England as Pharaoh and themselves as the new Israel fleeing persecution for the promised land, where G-d would use them for a new purpose (Barkun 1997, 5). By contrast, Africans taken as captives to the Americas appropriated the exodus story to fit their struggle for freedom. In this interpretation, "God would send Deliverance to the Negroes, from the power of their Masters, as he freed the Children of Israel from Egyptian bondage" (Frey 1991, 62). Nevertheless, once Blacks were granted freedom and citizenship, they too largely accepted the idea of American exceptionalism because they were now included.

Yet since its founding, the ideal of America as G-d's chosen nation has had a direct impact on US foreign policy, which operates within the framework that America's mission as G-d's elect is to redeem the world from the forces of evil (Judis 2005, 2). I have pointed out to the students that, at a minimum, accepting one group as divinely chosen over another group has the "potential to devalue the outsider, perhaps viewed as nothing more than the object of mission (i.e., to be made an insider)" (Lohr 2009, 2). This makes it easier to commit physical violence against the Other, such as Donaldson demonstrated above.

Christian Identity and Racial Hatred

This brings us back to Bailey's point about Afrocentric biblical interpreters reading and appropriating biblical texts without the benefit of acknowledging their own cultural biases. I pointed out to the students that, while most of them read the story of Joshua through the lens of obedience to the deity, their ancestors read Joshua and other biblical texts with an eye toward freedom and equality. For example, the former slave Denmark Vesey, inspired by Joshua 6:21, believed that God had called him to devote

Confronting Christian Identity, Chosenness, and Violence   201

to destruction the slave owners of Charleston, South Carolina, in retribution for their treatment of Africans held in bondage. Vesey, along with members of Emanuel African Methodist Episcopal, plotted a failed slave revolt in 1822. Vesey's interpretation of Joshua was just one instance of African Americans reading the Bible through a liberative lens.[9]

The mass murder of church members at Emanuel, also known as "Mother Emanuel," on 17 June 2015 stunned the nation and the world. The murders took place at a Wednesday night Bible study meeting at the church. A young white man who had joined the group that evening opened fire on the worshipers, killing nine and injuring others. This event took place just weeks after my Joshua class had concluded. Therefore, we did not have an opportunity to make the connections between biblical interpretation and this contemporary event. We would have discussed, for example, the reluctance of law enforcement officials to accept that the shooter acted with racial malice. Despite the fact that the shooter was white and the victims were Black, when Charleston's police chief was asked whether he believed that the shooting was motivated by hate, he replied, "I do not believe this was a hate crime" (Kaplan 2015).

Once Charleston's law enforcement officials had identified and captured Dylann Roof, the alleged shooter, one of the troubling details reported was that he had been inspired to commit such a heinous act by the white supremacist Christian Identity movement. Historians have traced the roots of the Christian Identity movement in the United States to the post–World War II era.[10] White supremacist groups such as the Ku Klux Klan, Aryan Nation, and Phineas Priesthood, which claim Christian inspiration for their philosophy of violence against nonwhites, are affiliated with the movement.[11] These groups promote racial segregation and strife in America.

---

9. Cheryl Kirk-Duggan (2010) also takes on chosenness in her critique of the exodus motif in Scripture as a model for liberation.

10. Christian Identity's antecedent is the marginal British social movement known as the British-Israel movement or British-Israelism. Its supporters maintained that the British are the lineal offspring of the lost "ten tribes of Israel," whose identity had previously been hidden (Barkun 1997, 6).

11. Phineas Priesthood is not a formally organized group or institution but rather the concept that any individual can be a "Phineas priest" by committing an act that pays homage to the priest Phineas, whom G-d rewarded for taking a sword and killing an Israelite man and his Midianite wife for defiling Israel (Num 25:6–8; Southern Poverty Law Center, n.d.).

202 Vanessa Lovelace

Christian Identity espouses a doctrine that the white race is descended from Adam, that Jewish people are the progeny of Satan's copulation with Eve in the garden of Eden, and that non-Jewish, nonwhite people are the "mud races" or "mud peoples" sprung from subhuman ancestors. Moreover, Christian Identity claims that it is whites, not the Jews, who are G-d's chosen people:

> WE BELIEVE the White, Anglo-Saxon, Germanic and kindred people to be God's true, literal Children of Israel. Only this race fulfills every detail of Biblical Prophecy and World History concerning Israel and continues in these latter days to be heirs and possessors of the Covenants, Prophecies, Promises and Blessings YHVH God made to Israel. This chosen seedline making up the "Christian Nations" (Gen. 35:11; Isa. 62:2; Acts 11:26) of the earth stands far superior to all other peoples in their call as God's servant race (Isa. 41:8, 44:21; Luke 1:54). (as quoted in Buck 2009, 110)

According to this creedal statement, the superiority enjoyed by whites is the result of having been endowed with a spirit of intellect by G-d that makes all other races inferior. It does not take much for one to conclude that Christian Identity followers abhor miscegenation. As mentioned above, such groups also believe that violence is warranted to maintain racial purity.

Christian Identity adherents also envision a Christian Aryan homeland in America. Their eschatological expectation of a white America as the site of G-d's kingdom on earth requires either the expulsion ("repatriation") or elimination of nonwhites. The most benign of these options is the repatriation of Jews and nonwhites to specific regions in the United States. The more menacing belief is Christian Identity's vision of a racial apocalypse, where the white race, led by Christ, will rule the earth (Buck 2009, 116). As such, Christian Identity groups have been stockpiling arms in anticipation of Christ's return to initiate the race war. In some versions, white vigilantes will initiate the "Racial Holy War" against Jews and nonwhites. Christian Identity's missionary outreach is to recruit followers who share their racial agenda. For many Christian Identity group members, the animosity between white and Black separatists is seen as the fuel to ignite the flame that will instigate a war between the races (Rowan 1996).

Stuart Wexler wrote in a *Newsweek* magazine article that Roof shot the worshipers in the hope that he could be the one to ignite a race war. In a line of previous white vigilantes who had committed acts of racial

Confronting Christian Identity, Chosenness, and Violence 203

violence, Roof saw himself as the lone, self-appointed loyalist who would awaken Black rage to wage a war against whites in response to his actions. Shooting survivors described a somewhat conflicted Roof, who, after being warmly welcomed into the Bible study group, nonetheless stood an hour later and shouted, "You are raping our women and taking over our country" (Wexler 2015).

Roof's pronouncement was indicative of Christian Identity's accusation that Jews and nonwhites have contaminated the Christian purity of white womanhood through rape, robbed white Christians of their identity and history, and imposed an alien morality on the nation. They have stood and proclaimed that they want their country back (Rowan 1996). These extremists largely oppose law enforcement and believe that much of the local, state, and federal laws are not aligned with G-d's law. Therefore, in their minds, the laws do not apply to them, and they can resist these evil laws with force when they deem it necessary.

Reading the Bible in these Times

Only the Jewish people can claim the status of G-d's chosen people as designated in the Hebrew Bible. Chosenness in the context of biblical Israel attests to the nation's special relationship to G-d. So then, what does it mean to assert one's Christian identity based on chosenness or election when both white racists and antiracists alike lay claim to such a title? Members of the Christian Identity movement believe that they are G-d's true chosen people and African-descended peoples are cursed with Blackness. Therefore, based on the curse of Ham, Blacks are inferior to whites, and white supremacists condone violence to keep Blacks and other nonwhites segregated from whites. Black Christians also claim that they are the heirs of Abraham and therefore enjoy the status of chosenness.

Nevertheless, we see, on one hand, the danger of appropriating a biblical interpretation based on a cultural bias that is detrimental to a group's health and well-being. On the other hand, Christian racial and ethnic minorities embrace a doctrine of election that is exclusionary, on the ideal that it somehow excludes them from the discrimination experienced by the nonelect (despite evidence to the contrary). Too often in this instance the oppressed become the oppressors.

As a minoritized biblical critic, I believe that it is important that Christians of all racial/ethnic categories admit that the church's doctrine of election has been used to exclude. Letty Russell (2009, 41), paraphrasing

Renita Weems, contends that election in the hands of Christians is a "primary theological source" for those with power to discriminate against those who differ along categories of race/ethnicity, gender, sexuality, and class, while "determining who is fit and unfit, who is worthy and unworthy."

We can begin to confront this legacy by teaching our students what Rosemary Radford Ruether (2007, 251) refers to as dismantling the "theology of American Empire" by unmasking the false notion of America as heirs of biblical Israel, G-d's chosen nation with power and privilege over other peoples and nations, and moving toward a "U.S. theology of liberation and letting go." This requires, in her words, an "explicit theological critique of those ideological themes that have been exploited by the theology of 'America' as elect nation, chosen by God to dominate and redeem the world" (251).

Works Cited

Bailey, Amy Kate, and Karen A. Snedker. 2011. "Practicing What They Preach? Lynching and Religion in the American South, 1890–1929." *AJS* 117:884–87.

Bailey, Randall C. 1998. "The Danger of Ignoring One's Own Cultural Bias in Interpreting the Text." Pages 66–90 in *The Postcolonial Bible*. Edited by Rasiah S. Sugirtharajah. Sheffield: Bloomsbury T&T Clark.

Barkun, Michael. 1997. *Religion and the Racist Right: The Origins of the Christian Identity Movement*. Chapel Hill: University of North Carolina Press.

Boer, Roland, and Ibrahim Abraham. 2009. "Noah's Nakedness: Islam, Race, and the Fantasy of the Christian West." Pages 461–74 in *Sacred Tropes: Tanakh, New Testament, and Qur'an as Literature and Culture*. Edited by Roberta Sterman Sabbath. Leiden: Brill.

Brueggemann, Walter. 2013. "The God of Joshua: An Ambivalent Field of Negotiation." Pages 13–25 in *Joshua and Judges*. T@C. Minneapolis: Fortress.

Buck, Christopher. 2009. *Religious Myths and Visions of America: How Minority Faiths Redefined America's World Role*. Santa Barbara, CA: ABC-CLIO.

Davis, Stacy. 2008. *This Strange Story: Jewish and Christian Interpretation of the Curse of Canaan from Antiquity to 1865*. Lanham, MD: University Press of America.

Donaldson, Laura E. 2011. "Joshua in America: On Cowboys, Canaanites and Indians." Pages 273–90 in *The Calling of the Nations: Exegesis, Ethnography, and Empire in Biblical-Historical Perspective.* Edited by Mark Vessey, Sharon V. Betcher, Robert A. Daum, and Harry O. Maier. Toronto: University of Toronto Press.

DuRocher, Kristina. 2011. *Raising Racists: The Socialization of White Children in the Jim Crow South.* Lexington: University of Kentucky Press.

FBI, Counterterrorism Divison. 2017. "Black Identity Extremists Likely Motivated to Target Law Enforcement Officers." 3 August. https://tinyurl.com/SBL06106bj.

Frey, Sylvia R. 1991. *Water from the Rock: Black Resistance in a Revolutionary Age.* Princeton: Princeton University Press.

Goldenberg, David M. 2003. *The Curse of Cain: Race and Slavery in Early Judaism, Christianity, and Islam.* Princeton: Princeton University Press.

Guibbory, Achsah. 2005. "'The Jewish Question' and 'The Woman Question' in Samson Agonistes: Gender, Religion, and Nation." Pages 184–204 in *Milton and Gender.* Edited by Catharine Gimelli Martin. Cambridge: Cambridge University Press.

Holden-Smith, Barbara. 1995. "Lynching, Federalism, and the Intersection of Race and Gender in the Progressive Era." *YJLF* 8:31–78.

Jobson, Richard. 1623. *The Golden Trade: Or, a Discovery of the River Gambra and the Golden Trade of the Aethiopians.* London: Okes.

Judis, John B. 2005. "The Chosen Nation: The Influence of Religion on U.S. Foreign Policy." *PB* 37 (March). https://tinyurl.com/SBL06106ae.

Kaplan, Sarah. 2015. "For Charleston's Emanuel AME Church Shooting Is Another Painful Chapters in Rich History." *Washington Post,* 18 June. https://tinyurl.com/SBL06106af.

Kirk-Duggan, Cheryl. 2010. "How Liberating Is the Exodus and for Whom? Deconstructing Exodus Motifs in Scripture, Literature and Life." Pages 3–28 in *Genesis.* T@C. Minneapolis: Augsburg Fortress.

Litchfield, Chelsea, Emma Kavanaugh, Jaquelyn Osborne, and Ian Jones. 2018. "Social Media and the Politics of Gender, Race and Identity: The Case of Serena Williams." *European Journal for Sport and Society* 15:2. https://tinyurl.com/SBLPress06106c3.

Lohr, Joel N. 2009. *Chosen and Unchosen: Conceptions of Election in the Pentateuch and Jewish-Christian Interpretation.* Winona Lake, IN: Eisenbrauns.

Martin, Clarice. 1999. "Womanist Biblical Interpretation." Pages 655–58 in vol. 2 of *Dictionary of Biblical Interpretation*. Edited by John H. Hayes. 2 vols. Nashville: Abingdon.

Quinones, Ricardo. 1991. *The Changes of Cain: Violence and the Lost Brother in Cain and Abel Literature*. Princeton: Princeton University Press.

Rowan, Carl T. 1996. "America's Violent Decline." *Washington Post*. https://tinyurl.com/SBL06106ag.

Ruether, Rosemary Radford. 2007. *America, Amerikkka: Elect Nation and Imperial Violence*. Oakville, CT: Equinox.

Russell, Letty M. 2009. *Just Hospitality: God's Welcome in a World of Difference*. Louisville: Westminster John Knox.

Sitkoff, Harvard. 2008. *A New Deal for Blacks: The Emergence of Civil Rights as a National Issue; The Depression Decade*. New York: Oxford University Press.

Southern Poverty Law Center. N.d. "Phineas Priesthood." Ideologies. https://tinyurl.com/SBL06106ah.

Stutzman, Rene. 2012. "George Zimmerman's Father: My Son Is Not Racist, Did Not Confront Trayvon Martin." *Orlando Sentinel*, 15 March. https://tinyurl.com/SBL06106ai.

Warrior, Robert Allen. 1989. "Canaanites, Cowboys, and Indians: Deliverance, Conquest, and Liberation Theology Today." *C&C* 49.12:261–65.

Wexler, Stuart. 2015. "Beyond Dylann Roof: Why White Supremacists Want a Race War." *Newsweek*, 26 June. https://tinyurl.com/SBL06106aj.

Wood, Amy Louise. 2009. *Lynching and Spectacle: Witnessing Racial Violence in America, 1890–1940*. Chapel Hill: University of North Carolina Press.

Yancy, George. 2008. *Black Bodies, White Gazes: The Continuing Significance of Race*. Lanham, MD: Rowman & Littlefield.

Young, Harvey. 2005. "The Black Body as Souvenir in American Lynching." *TheatJ* 57:639–57.

Whose Recognition?
Latino/a Studies and the Need to Belong

Francisco Lozada Jr.

In a recent review of the volume *Latino/a Biblical Hermeneutics*, edited by Fernando F. Segovia and myself, Tat-siong Benny Liew (2015) astutely raises a question related to the audience (or community/ies) of the volume: "Whose recognition may Latino biblical criticism be seeking?" This is how I interpret Liew's question: Have the coeditors (and contributors) given any thought regarding the identity of the community from which they are seeking recognition? More specifically, do the authors have a readership in mind when they are conceiving and doing Latino/a biblical interpretation?[1] Is it the academy (howsoever defined), Latino/a scholars, or other scholars, to name a few? This question is what I aim to address in this critical reflection on the question of whose recognition. It is a modest attempt to begin a conversation among ethnic/racial minoritized biblical interpreters around the question of recognition.

---

1. The nomenclature *Latino/a* aims to be inclusive of both women and men as well as to signify the problematics of gender and sexuality formations along a binary system. Recently, the nomenclature *Latinx* has been employed in discourse and writings aimed at capturing all of the above problematics, thus signifying a gender-neutral label for Latinas/os. For this essay, the term *Latino/a* will be used, a similar descriptor employed by the studies referenced below, unless they are making reference to a community's identity based on their country of origin (e.g., Mexicans, Mexican Americans, or Puerto Ricans). Knowing full well that no one term can capture the wide diversity of individuals who self-identify as Latina/o/x, it is important to acknowledge the importance of inclusivity among all. For an excellent essay on the development of the term *Latinx*, see Salinas and Lozano 2017.

To be fair to the contributors, the question of recognition did not directly guide the impetus for *Latino/a Biblical Hermeneutics*. Rather, the volume, a collection of essays, was motivated by the question, What is Latino/a biblical interpretation? In Liew's final comment on the volume, he briefly directs his attention to several authors' references and motivations for doing Latino/a biblical interpretation. What he brings to the surface in his assessment is the question of recognition. In other words, is recognition a desire that Latino/a biblical critics are seeking when they conceive of and practice Latino/a biblical interpretation? I understand his use of *recognition* to be along the lines of identification and epistemology. To recognize someone is to acknowledge that their existence and epistemology are equal to all others. In other words, the way that they (Latinos/as) conceive and do Latino/a biblical interpretation is one and the same as the way other communities conceive and do biblical interpretation. For this reason, I seek recognition in Latino/a biblical interpretation from a broad readership, with the aim to include my reading within the tradition, much as is done in the field of Latino/a studies, as I will show below.

A word on the question of recognition is first necessary. The question of recognition, in the tradition of identity politics, focuses on those minoritized identities and cultural expressions that are marginalized, devalued, or despised based on their race/ethnicity, gender, sexuality, religion, or disability—to name a few social marginalized identities in the United States (see Hughes and Blaxter 2007, 115; Fraser and Honneth 2003). The politics of recognition aims to render these minoritized identities equal with all other identities in a particular society, but also to bring about that their epistemologies result in outcomes such as academic respect and relevance of their work. In other words, the aim is to establish that their construction of knowledge and their insights are equal to other ("dominant") work in the scope of the discipline of biblical interpretation. In responding to Liew's question, I aim to clarify from whom I am seeking recognition and why.

To do so, I have chosen to focus on three studies in the field of Latino/a studies. Why Latino/a studies? First, the field is quite similar in content. Both fields, Latino/a biblical interpretation and Latino/a studies, focus on some aspect of the Latino/a condition and/or how the Latino/a identity contributes to both the production and reception of knowledge. Second, both fields are similar in approach. In other words, both are interdisciplinary by way of working with other fields, combining various fields, and intersecting with other fields. (For a sharp and theoretical delineation of ethnic/racial minoritized ways of doing biblical interpretation, see Segovia 2009.) Third, both fields have similar aims. That is, both seek recognition from their respective academic disciplines as well as from other ethnic/racial academic disciplines.

It follows, then, that with regard to subject matter, approach, and aim, both Latino/a biblical interpretation and Latino/a studies have a desire to be recognized as legitimate and valuable sources of epistemology. Often, in my opinion, Latinos/as and other minoritized readers are seen and/or treated as visiting the discipline of interpretation rather than recognized as belonging to the discipline. Both fields are part of their own respective disciplines, whether the history of biblical hermeneutics or the history of US studies, or howsoever Latino/a studies scholars define their academic identity.

Consequently, I intend to examine three works in Latino/a studies to seek insight into how these authors seek recognition through their works. My overall aim is twofold: first, to help bring clarity to what it means to be a Latino/a biblical critic; and second, to encourage other Latino/a and minoritized biblical critics to continue this reflection on whose recognition *we* are seeking in doing what *we* do with texts. These studies all look to reconstruct the past in a way that keeps in dialogue with related Latino/a issues in the present, such as immigration, the sense of belonging, and colonialism. All of the studies are published by university presses, suggesting an academic audience/community, and thus are written in the genre of academic language, while introducing the problematic of identity and representation of Latinos/as. These three elements point to the reality that the authors are seeking recognition primarily from the academic community.

As a way to go deeper into addressing the question of recognition, I intend to examine these studies' subject matter, approach, and aims. These elements are loosely examined in a linear procedural fashion—subject first, approach next, and then aim. However, these elements are not mutually exclusive; they may be and often are combined. These three elements will lead, hopefully, to help me clarify the question of recognition for myself and to inspire others to think about the question as well. I will conclude with a critical reflection on what these three examinations of works in Latino/a studies contribute to the question of recognition and how this question influences my own work in Latino/a biblical interpretation. I will give close attention to the introductions of each volume, with some attention to the other parts of the volumes when apropos.

210   Francisco Lozada Jr.

Natalia Molina, *How Race Is Made in America*

Natalia Molina's (2014) *How Race Is Made in America* explores how immigration policies between 1924 and 1965 influenced the construction of Latino/a race, and subsequently other races, in relation to citizenship in the United States. The volume opens up to readers the dynamics of how the enactment of immigration policies, by government institutions (national and local) and with the support of agribusiness and other industries, prohibited the flow of migration in general and from Mexico in particular. This slowing down of migration led these institutions to construct race not just for Mexican Americans (and other Latinos/as in general) but also for eastern and southern Europeans, Asian Americans, Native Americans, and African Americans. In other words, this study shows that the marking of racialization on one community affects the marking of racialization on another, including the construction of white identity. This study, in keeping with Latino/a and minoritized biblical hermeneutics, illustrates the focus on the representation of Otherness. This focus suggests that Molina is seeking recognition for those scholars in the field of ethnic/racial studies and/ or American studies,[2] among others, who are engaged with the problematic of race/ethnicity and the representation of minoritized communities.

I would also contend that she is interested in the larger (all-inclusive) academic field of history. Her work at the same time aims to break through any notion of "minoritized" and "dominantized" dichotomies in order to offer an alternative vision of US history (Segovia 2009, 285). It is an attempt not to be universalizing but to be universal out of its particularity. In other words, she seeks recognition from the academic community in general that the identification, epistemology, and representation of Latinos/as are seen as equal and apart as subjects to be studied and understood.

A guiding question driving this volume is a discussion or explanation of how "Mexican Americans remain, in the perception of many in the United States, as less than full citizens, as well as why they are often associated with illegality" (Molina 2014, 1). This theme of belonging is found throughout all three studies. Molina is interested in how immigration regimes—government officials; agribusiness; local, state, and national policing—contributed

---

2. Some areas of both Latino/a studies and ethnic/racial studies are housed under the nomenclature of American studies or various other departments. The question of why is beyond the scope of this reflection. However, to learn about the history of Latino cultural studies, see Aparicio 2003.

to the perception of Mexican Americans in the United States as less than full citizens and, frequently, as undocumented immigrants. The immigration regime was successful in remaking the identity of Mexican Americans because it employed racial categories that influenced the way *we* (as Molina [2] argues) understand race, thus influencing how race is understood by society and, consequently, how those with Mexican heritage are constructed.

The scope of Molina's inquiry focuses on the period between 1924 and 1965. This she sees as a period in US history that strongly influenced the construction of race through the channels of immigration policy. Molina marks the beginning of this particular historical period with the passing of the 1924 Johnson-Reed Immigration Act. Molina (20) reminds readers that from 1917 to 1924 immigration into the United States was reduced by 85 percent through a number of legislative acts, suggesting a climate of suppressing immigration due to nativists' linking of immigrants to unions that were linked with communists or with socialists supportive of unions.

The Johnson-Reed Act of 1924 was significant because it initiated the process of defining the ethnic and racial identities of new immigrants. First, the act reduced the number of southern and eastern Europeans, mainly Jews, entering the United States. These Europeans were considered an inferior "breed." At the same time, as a result of the act, those Europeans (northern and Western) who were permitted to enter were defined as white, since race was defined along Black/white lines. Second, the act also deemed the Chinese, the Japanese, and other Asian groups as inferior. As a result, it denied them naturalization in the United States. Third, the act cast Mexicans crossing the southern border as "illegal." Consequently, it criminalized Mexicans who entered into the United States without approval; indeed, the Border Patrol came into existence in 1924 in order to stop the flow of migration from Mexico.

Overall, the 1924 Johnson-Reed Act was the first comprehensive immigration law that established quotas. Molina (49) states, "The Immigration Act of 1924 limited the annual number of immigrants from a specific country to two percent of the number of people from that country who were already living in the United States, based on the 1890 census data." In other words, by establishing this preferential quota, the act dictated that only 2 percent of southern and eastern Europeans could enter the United States, thus creating a white (Anglo-Saxon) America. One was now either "white" or "Black." At the same time, the act did not cease immigration from the Western Hemisphere, to the dismay of nativists, who lobbied for blockage but could not override the agribusinesses that needed cheap labor. Thus, immigration from Mexico did not cease; however, Mexican Americans, who were categorized as "white" since they were not "Black," were still treated as illegal.

As Molina suggests, the reason the act did not affect the Western Hemisphere was capitalism—the lure of cheap labor, particularly along the border states of Texas, New Mexico, Arizona, and California. It was not until 1965, through the Hart-Cellar Act or Immigration Act of 1965, that the quota system was abolished. The 1965 act not only ended the national quota system; it also initiated a new immigration regime, which, according to Molina (2014; see her epilogue, "Making Race in the Twenty-First Century," 139–52), continues today. The 1965 act set an annual ceiling of 170,000 immigrants from the Eastern Hemisphere and 120,000 from the Western Hemisphere. Following the 1965 Hart-Cellar Act, immigration into the United States increased, mainly because in 1952 the McCarran-Walter Act had already given preference to those immigrants who had family present in the United States and to those with professional and technical skills deemed useful to the US market (140).

All of this is to say that Molina's focus on the category of identity and the debates centering on race is similar to the work that Latino/a biblical interpretation is engaged in these days. The period 1924–1965 is an important one for the construction of the Latino/a identity in the United States, one with lasting effects in today's cultural and political arenas on how Latinos/as are received by dominant and powerful groups as well as by our respective academic disciplines. This surfaces in Molina's understanding of how immigration regimes have contributed to the construction of race in the United States and, more specifically, of the effects of this construction on Mexican Americans in relation to other groups. Her focus is not on what caused migration or what the journey was like for Mexicans entering the United States, but on their reception—on how society received them when they arrived as well as how society treated those who had always been in the United States as if they were visiting. Her subject matter centers on the problematic of identity and representation, a central concern for those in the academic community who are addressing this question through the act of the production and reception of knowledge.

The approach Molina takes to reconstruct a cultural history of Latinos/as in tandem with immigration history is quite interdisciplinary.[3] As

---

3. Interestingly, the publishers have placed on the back cover three disciplinary areas that they see this volume falling under: US history, ethnic studies, and immigration. Thus, publishers play a role in the recognition of a volume/author.

Whose Recognition? Latino/a Studies and the Need to Belong 213

is readily visible thus far, several disciplinary areas inform this volume. The primary area is Latino/a studies, as a subarea of ethnic/racial studies or American studies. The main focus is on Latino/a identity, but this does not mean that such identity does not influence the problematic of identity among other ethnic/racial minoritized communities in the United States. This field, Latino/a studies, is then projected on the area of immigration and immigration policies and laws. Such interdisciplinary moves highlight how Latinos/as, and subsequently other minoritized groups, are perceived and treated by powerful immigration regimes—those institutions seeing all immigrants as inferior. Key to seeing how these immigration regimes function is understanding how they participate in the racialization of Latinos/as and others by proposing and lobbying political powers to pass legislation stating that they (Mexican Americans) do not belong. Therefore, underlying Molina's unraveling of this strategy is her understanding of race.

Molina works with a relational understanding of race as opposed to a comparative approach to race that focuses on looking at minoritized groups separately. Her thinking is informed by the theoretical work on race by Michael Omi and Howard Winant (1986) in the volume titled *Racial Formation in the United States from the 1960s to the 1980s*. This work sees race as a socially constructed concept that gets its signification within certain historical moments—such as between 1924 and 1965. These different moments in history, which Omi and Winant call racial projects, are embedded in the social structures and cultural representations of racialized groups—such as in the laws and policies of immigration as well as in stereotypes or assumptions about Mexican Americans.

Informed by this understanding of race, and in Molina's case by this understanding of *Mexican*, she aims to study the various racial projects taking place between 1924 and 1965. As mentioned, for Molina, Mexican race cannot be understood apart from other racialized groups. When one group is racialized, such racialization affects other groups. Traditionally, a comparative approach has been used to understand the identity of Mexican Americans, taking a compare/contrast approach to other groups and treating each independently.

For instance, when northern and western Europeans were categorized as "white," this had a bearing on Mexican identity as either white or Black—the dominant binary construction of race at the time. In 1848, at the end of the US war with Mexico, the Treaty of Guadalupe categorized Mexicans in the newly acquired territory of the United States as "white" and thus

214   Francisco Lozada Jr.

"extended eligibility" of citizenship to them (Molina 2014, 5). The question was not legally settled until 1897. That year, Ricardo Rodriguez took his application for citizenship to the US District Court for the Western District of Texas for naturalization approval (re Rodriguez 81F.337), since he had been born in Mexico. The question in front of the court was whether Rodriguez was white or Black, since only whites could be naturalized at the time. Rodriguez was ruled white and thus eligible for naturalized citizenship; as a result, those Mexicans living in the United States would be eligible to become naturalized citizens (Molina 2014, 5, 45).

Despite this ruling, in 1930, during the period of the economic Depression, the US Census (i.e., part of the immigration regime) classified the race of Mexican Americans not as white but rather as "Mexican" (5). This ruling and classification, according to Molina, also affected how Blacks, Native Americans, Asians, and whites were understood and represented. By revealing how Mexican Americans were racialized as "Mexican," the ruling not only fixed the meaning of *Mexican*; it also fixed the identity of other racialized groups. Such was the case, for example, with Asians, who could not be placed within the binary of Black and white and were thus made ineligible for naturalized citizenship in 1924. Such was the case as well with Blacks, who were treated as not belonging in the United States, even though they were citizens. Meanwhile, Native Americans were granted (or had imposed on them) citizenship through the Citizenship Act in 1924 (52). Molina's main point is that the way in which one group is defined by immigration regimes affects other groups. According to Molina, Blacks were seen as second-class citizens, similarly to Native Americans, who were not considered white. Asian Americans' identity and citizenship status were based on how other groups such as Latinos/as were identified. If ethnic/racial groups could be deemed nonwhite or non-Black, immigration regimes could deport them.

All of this is to say that, for Molina, race needs to be seen relationally in order to better understand why Mexicans living in the United States as well as Mexican Americans were classified using various racialized identities by immigration regimes. One cannot understand US history without understanding how other groups have been classified in terms of ethnicity and race and the resultant effects that such classification has had on all groups. It follows, then, that, with her focus on race as relational, Molina is seeking recognition from a broader academic community in history, ethnic/racial studies, American studies, and immigration history. Such an approach is interdisciplinary and thus looks both inside and outside the

Whose Recognition? Latino/a Studies and the Need to Belong   215

Mexican American (and Latino/a) community to highlight new insights and angles in the construction of Latino/a identity.

In other words, Molina weaves in and out of the Latino/a community, drawing attention to a broader construction of race and Mexican American identity. The volume's aim—to understand the construction of race through policies, laws, and organizations as well as the impact of this construction on the identity of Mexican Americans—is an issue not only for all Latinos/as but also for every other identity group in the United States As Molina (2014, 2) suggests, the study "provides a way for scholars to discursively map the elusive historical construction of race and account for its material consequences in policy, law, and everyday life." Thus, her work not only recognizes and valorizes Mexican American identities; it also deconstructs any binary notion of white-Black that remained during this past—and, I would add, that remains today in the racialized discourses used in many political and cultural conversations in the United States.

In examining these discourses, Molina attempts to discuss how various racialized groups are connected with one another by employing a concept called "racial scripts." To clarify what she means by racial scripts, Molina (6–11) explains that they function in three ways.

First, racial scripts provide a heightened sense of attention to how attitudes, policies, laws, customs, and practices construct the racialized identities of groups. Racial scripts emanate from ordinary citizens as well as from institutions. For instance, in chapter 3 ("Birthright Citizenship beyond Black and White"), Molina discusses how, even though Mexicans were granted the right to naturalize based on the Treaty of Guadalupe in 1848, legislation attempted to take their citizenship away in the 1920s and 1930s. In the 1930s, racial scripts existed by way of various proposed legislations that attempted to limit the number of Mexicans entering the United States as well as to repeal any birthright citizenship—namely, the idea that, if one was born in the United States, one is granted citizenship.[4]

These racial scripts emerged, as I mentioned already, due to the economic downturn in the 1930s (the Depression), which sparked a push to repeal any birthright citizenship to Mexicans. Proponents of this legisla-

---

4. The Civil Rights Act of 1866 gave citizenship to both whites and Blacks *born* in the US, with the exception of Native Americans (Molina 2014, 72). The Fourteenth Amendment codified this act in the US Constitution in 1868. In effect, it overturned an earlier ruling by the Supreme Court (*Dred Scott v. Sandford* in 1857), which declared Blacks ineligible to become citizens (Molina 2014, 69).

tion attempted to stop Mexican immigration, because they did not want Mexicans lured by cheap labor, or Mexican Americans born in the United States, to receive or retain citizenship, out of fear that they would take jobs from "whites." The attempts of immigration regime proponents failed because of previous interpretation of the Fourteenth Amendment in 1868, which granted birthright citizenship to those, like African Americans, who were born (or naturalized) in the United States.

Another case connected to this ruling, *United States v. Wong Kim Ark*, came before the Supreme Court in 1898. Ark, who was born to Chinese parents in the United States, traveled to China and upon his return was denied entry, because officials defined his citizenship based on his parents' nationality (*jus sanguinis*, "right of blood"). Ark won his case. The point here is that legislation that emerged in the 1930s aimed at ceasing Mexican American citizenship was related to previous racial scripts aimed at ceasing citizenship for Asians. By 1898, citizenship had been granted to three nonwhite groups born in the United States (*jus solis*, "right of soil")— Mexican Americans, Asian Americans, and African Americans. Yet, all three racialized groups' citizenship was questioned, using various racial scripts, throughout the twentieth century—and, I would add, continues to be questioned even today.

A second function of racial scripts is to see connections among racialized groups as well as the structures involved in writing these scripts. For instance, in chapter 2 ("What Is a White Man"), Molina describes how eugenics organizations participated in trying to stem Mexican immigration in the 1920s and 1930s. In doing so, they made the argument that southern and eastern Europeans were of an inferior "breed" of people. Such inferiority, they argued, would ruin Americans' ("white") racial stock. They applied this understanding of racial science to Mexican immigrants, who carried American Indian blood, thus contaminating the blood of the "descendants of the colonists and early settlers" (Molina 2014, 57); consequently, they influenced the passing of the 1924 Immigration Act. This act established quotas for immigration but was not as successful at limiting immigration from the Western Hemisphere as that from the Eastern Hemisphere. The attempts of structures such as the American Eugenics Society to bring forth a test case against Mexican immigration were unsuccessful, yet, as mentioned already, led to the creation of the Border Patrol in 1924.

Finally, racial scripts function to put forth *counterscripts*, which challenge those dominating racial scripts and suggest alternative proposals.

Whose Recognition? Latino/a Studies and the Need to Belong   217

In chapter 5 ("Deportation in the Urban Landscape"), Molina discusses the summer of 1954 in Los Angeles, when the Immigration Naturalization Service enacted a militarized campaign to deport Mexicans. This government campaign was called Operation Wetback. It racialized and criminalized all those of Mexican identity, particularly those in Los Angeles—even, I would add, all Latinos/as. Molina describes the roundup of Mexicans at the Elysian Park detention center in Los Angeles, which was conducted with the help of local police, citizens, Border Patrol agents, and even doctors who reported on those patients they suspected were "illegal." In so doing, Molina also quotes various African Americans who proposed counterscripts to the oppressive racial scripts that saw detained Mexican Americans (and Mexicans living in the United States for whatever reason) as not belonging in the United States. One such counterscript said: "This Country was originally theirs. Wonder if those immigration cops realize how it makes us Negro people feel when they start kicking the Mexicans around" (Molina 2014, 125). Such counterscripts point to the injustice imposed on Mexican Americans (and Mexicans living in the US) and indicate that Mexican Americans, similarly to African Americans, are simply another vulnerable group.

Racial scripts thus not only show the connections among racialized groups; they also pull back the curtain to show how structures or institutions participate in creating racial scripts. What is more, racial scripts produce counterscripts that provide alternative narratives and challenge dominating racial scripts. Overall, Molina's use of racial scripts to understand the history of Mexican Americans and other racialized groups shows how these groups are all linked in one way or another to the racialization of Mexican Americans, and vice versa, through immigration laws, policies, and practices, to name a few such strategies.

To conclude, the subject matter, approach, and aim of Molina's volume clearly indicate that she is seeking the recognition of those in the academy within various interdisciplinary fields (US history, ethnic/ racial studies or American studies, and immigration history). It is obvious that she seeks to recognize the contributions of both Mexican Americans and Mexicans residing in the United States as well as their dignity, along with the contributions and dignity of other minoritized communities. By problematizing this Latino/a (Mexican American) identity and aiming to reconstruct a history of immigration that shows new angles of its participation in racialization, she is seeking to include this history in the larger narrative of US history. The desired result, I

218   Francisco Lozada Jr.

am assuming, is that if one could see how immigration regimes participated in the act of exclusion, particularly the exclusion of those ethnic/
racialized persons born or naturalized in the United States, one might
attain a sense of belonging.

Inés Casillas, *Sounds of Belonging*

Inés Casillas's (2014) *Sounds of Belonging* continues the broader theme
of community from *How Race Is Made in America*, namely, identity as
belonging. The aim of the volume is a close reading of Spanish-language radio or broadcasting in the twentieth century on immigration
and its role in calling attention to various issues related to immigration.
These stations function as public advocates, as the subtitle suggests, in
that they provide information, ranging from the heightened sense of
deportation raids to changes in the immigration laws. Basically, this
volume covers the variety of issues related to Latino/a immigration
in the United States as well as along the border states of the United
States and the northern states of Mexico. The volume also calls attention to the issue of sexual innuendos, sexist language, and sexuality of
the male voice that many stations rely on in their major broadcasting.
By recognizing Latino/a specificity vis-à-vis radio and deconstructing
the notion that Latinos/as do not belong in the United States, Casillas
demonstrates that radio, for the Spanish-language audience, is just as
important as other technology in understanding the identity and representation of the Latino/a community.

For instance, Casillas mentions how, in announcing that he was running for president (21 May 2007), Governor Bill Richardson used the
radio station La Raza (97.9 FM) out of Los Angeles, specifically a nation-
ally syndicated broadcast hosted by El Cucuy ("The Bogeyman"), to
inform the Spanish-language listening audience of three million people
that he was putting his name in the race. Such instances show readers
of this critical volume not only that radio is strongly understudied in
the field of cultural studies but also that radio is the primary means of
conveying information to the Latino/a Spanish-language listenership
(Casillas 2014, 1–2). This event sparked the momentum for other radio
stations to host other politicians, such as President Bill Clinton and Sen-
ator Edward Kennedy, as well as Senators Hillary Clinton and Barack
Obama, who were then running for president. These politicians also
appeared on the radio station hosted by El Cucuy's rival, El Piolín ("The

Whose Recognition? Latino/a Studies and the Need to Belong   219

Tweety Bird") from Radio Nueva (101.9 FM), also out of Los Angeles with national coverage.[5]

Both instances point to the importance of radio and radio hosts, who function as translators and interpreters (English to Spanish) to reach the Latino/a community across the United States as well as to capture the Latino/a vote. What is more interesting, as Casillas (3) points out, is that these activities show how Latino/a communities, including immigrant communities, are excluded from English-language political conversations, not just on the radio but across other media. Casillas's subject matter, Spanish-language radio, thus focuses once again on the problematic of identity, but more specifically on the theme of belonging. Therefore, she is seeking recognition from those in the academic community, or more specifically those in media studies, as the back cover of her volume specifies. She is also aiming to break through the dichotomy of Spanish-language radio/English-language radio, with the former as inferior and the latter as superior, toward a study of Spanish-language radio as equal to and apart from English-language radio.

Hence, the volume takes an interdisciplinary approach, bringing together media studies and Latino/a studies (or at a broader level, ethnic/ racial studies or American studies) with feminist critique of the language employed by these Spanish-language radio hosts and discussion of how they operate. For example, not only do these radio programs typically function during early morning programming, when many working-class Latinos/ are immersed in the service and construction industries are listening to the radio, but they also serve as a resource center for the Latino/a immigrant community on the question of citizenship and immigration reform (Casillas 2014, 3–4). Such an experience of radio leads the listenership to a sense of cultural citizenship, as informed by Renato Rosaldo's (1994) notion, where the hearers are provided a sense of sanctuary, that they belong in the United States. For Latinos/as, who experience disenfranchisement on many fronts, these radio programs leave listeners with a sense of being full members in a society or cultural citizenship (4). In other words, the listenership receives a message that someone in the United States is looking out for them.

As Casillas mentions, much of the political and social programming occurs in the morning hours, but throughout the day many radio stations

---

5. Other examples include New York and Miami's El Vacilón ("The Jokester") and Chicago's El Chokolate ("The Chocolate") and El Pistolero ("The Shooter").

220

follow the same rotation. To begin with, the morning hours are hosted by "rambunctious male radio hosts" who interact with the audience on many political and social issues. Then, the noon and midafternoon hours typically host professional health care and/or psychological folks with a question-and-answer call-in format. Last, the evening hours conclude with sentimental or nostalgic music, reminding listeners of their homeland. All of these programs help to navigate the Latino/a community and the new immigrant community through the disparities of economic and racialized status in the United States, both publicly and personally.

These programs, according to Casillas, are also marked by the "accent" or "word choice" that the hosts use in Spanish. The Spanish spoken can point to the hosts' nations of origins. The hosts also employ a Spanish that is distinct from that used outside Latin America. Class as well as racialization are also marked by a particular use of Spanish language, dialect, and idioms. Most of these indicators are missed by English-only listeners. These programs do not avoid the blunt discursive jabs from those arguing for English-only laws, for whom all spoken Spanish is the same. As a result, Spanish spoken in the United States —including Spanish-language programs existing on US airwaves—leads to the perception of Latinos/as in a negative way. Ironically, however, Spanish spoken outside the United States and listened to by English-only listeners leads to the perception of Latin Americans as belonging to a different national body, according to Casillas (2014, 6).

The Spanish language, along with race and citizenship, is often marginalized from the English-language media outlets, because it may offend English-only listeners. Therefore, Spanish-language radio stations are vital for the many identities within the Latino/a community. They not only help them learn how to negotiate between two worlds; they also serve as sites of critical discussion of immigration policies and other issues directly affecting the Latino/a condition (health and wellness), which cut across the lives of many of their listeners.

The approach Casillas takes in this volume engages in a horizontal analysis of Spanish-language radio programs as well in a vertical analysis unearthing the history of these programs. For instance, Casillas studies the popularity of Spanish-language radio in the present and describes how this popularity led her to study the radio industry in general. The explosive growth of radio programming that emerged dramatically in the 2000s has its roots as far back as the early part of the twentieth century in the United States, particularly in locales with larger Spanish-speaking or -hearing folks. Some have correlated this to the increase in the Latino/a population in the latter half of the century, and the data confirms this with numbers that show that Latino/a listeners (Spanish or not) listen to the radio on average three hours per week more than the average US radio listener (Casillas 2014, 7). Thus, in 2009, in the major markets for Spanish-language radio (such as Los Angeles, Houston, Miami, and New York City), Spanish-language radio had more listeners than their English-language counterparts. Even the nontraditional markets (such as Salt Lake City, North Carolina, and Nebraska) have experienced the growth of Spanish-language radio.

For all of these reasons, Casillas believes that, to understand this expansion of Spanish-language radio, it is vital to focus on its role in identity construction within the Latino/a community. Such an explosion is a reflection of globalization, where communities function as "counterpublics." Informed by Nancy Fraser's (1993) notion of counterpublic, Casillas (2014, 8–9) sees these radio stations as sites where Latinos/as communicate with one another to challenge oppressive discourses and practices, but also as places where they can regroup to reaffirm their identities.

However, as Casillas points out, not all Latinos/as have the same listening habits. Even though Latinos/as make up 17 percent of the population in the United States, only 5.5 percent of radio programs are in Spanish (Casillas 2014, 10). At the same time, 55 percent of Spanish-radio listeners make less than $25,000 annually, which means that the other almost-half earn more. What she is suggesting here is that, while Latinos/as are very much a bilingual community with a diverse class identity, they are not typically imagined this way by the larger media industry. Latinos/as listen to both Spanish- and English-language radio, and in many cases those Latinos/as who are English-dominant (second and third generations, for example) choose Spanish- over English-language radio or television, according to a Pew Research Center survey (Casillas 2014, 10).

Even though Latinos/as are listening to radio programming in both languages, Casillas's focus is on the expanding Spanish-language radio programming emanating out of the West Coast, which reaches well beyond this region in the United States. Her focus is on the Mexican-dominant and growing Central American listenership on the West Coast (specifically Los Angeles), recognizing that the Latino/a community is not monolithic. Each Latino/a region in the United States has its particular listenership. On the East Coast and the Midwest, where one finds a larger Caribbean population of Latinos/as as opposed to the West Coast,

222 Francisco Lozada Jr.

stations might provide a weather report of the warmer Caribbean temperatures (Casillas 2014, 12). Casillas—informed by Pat Zavela's notion of "peripheral vision"—says that all of these stations maintain a binational perspective, keeping an eye on what is going on in their host country while also keeping in touch with their sending country. Thus, the stations hone in on listeners' sense of unsettlement as a result of living in two countries, one physically and the other mentally (12; Zavella 2011). Some stations have also contributed to the "Mexicanization" of other Latinos/as living in a dominant Mexican US city, such as Puerto Ricans, by way of ideals, language, and customs.

All of this illustrates Casillas's aim of showing the importance of studying Spanish-language radio and its construction of Latino/a identity across space and time. Her study also shows that the focus is on the present as opposed to the past. In other words, she believes that in studying Spanish-language radio, the focus is on "what is happening" as opposed to "what has happened." Such focus on the present highlights that cultural histories are not only read about; they are also heard and felt through the radio (Casillas 2014, 12). By focusing on radio programming from 1922 to the present, Casillas aims to recover a construction of the history of Spanish-language radio. She does so by studying audio archives and secondary literature, despite both being difficult to retrieve, as well as by studying print culture and industry journals.

In a sense, she is engaged in an interdisciplinary media ethnographical investigation, using focus groups and taped radio programming that she self-compiled. Casillas aims to build a picture of Spanish-language radio to understand the social structure behind and in front of the picture. Such an interdisciplinary, multimethodological investigation, as she calls it, implodes a Black/white dichotomy in the study of US culture, as well as in those previous studies that focus on English-language radio alone. When studying radio in the United States, Casillas demonstrates, Spanish-language radio must be included in the analysis in order to understand Latinos/as along the lines of race, gender, and citizenship. For the voice of the radio becomes "the stand-in for the physical body of listeners," according to Casillas (2014, 13).

Spanish-language radio also becomes the stand-in for the male voice, which Casillas investigates as the problematic of patriarchal language. For instance, in chapter 3 ("Sounds of Surveillance: U.S. Spanish-Language Radio Patrols La Migra"), Casillas shows how much of the radio programming, especially in the morning hours, has also functioned to patrol the whereabouts of immigration officials or *La Migra*. This served for listeners to tune into various radio programs that not only informed them subtly of possible immigration raids but also allowed them to learn about the updated immigration laws. Sometimes, this information regarding immigration was framed around a more-playful chatter time in the morning (still heard today, I might add) hosted by male voices, but with problematic performances of gender and sexuality. This playfulness reified gendered and sexual inequity among the Latino and Latina communities. It also questioned the sincerity and inclusiveness of their roles as public advocates, says Casillas.

For instance, in chapter 4 ("Pun Intended: Listening to Gendered Politics on the Morning Shows"), Casillas focuses on the popularity of El Cucuy. El Cucuy holds celebrity status among his audience. Coming from Central America, he is known for his philanthropy throughout the Latino/a community as well as throughout Latin America (Casillas 2014, 120). However, El Cucuy employs a number of linguistic puns that portray women in an inferior status. His masculine expressions are those that function transnationally, which validate the importance of the male voice. Rarely do women come on the show, and, when they do, their intelligence is often questioned as well as mocked. His popularity as an advocate for the working-class immigrant covers over his gendering and sexualizing of women in the community. In other words, because these voices are female or because someone is perceived as having feminine or gay characteristics through voice inflections, they are perceived as nonauthoritative or made fun of.

Casillas's deconstructive work in this chapter underscores the importance of not romanticizing the discourse and the popularity of these male voices in the morning across the country. Many of them, like their Anglo partners (I would add), employ a certain language that exists among many (not all) of the working-class male audience, a language that marginalizes women in both sound and perception and that refrains from the problematics of gender and sexuality. Thus, these hosts reinscribe hypermasculinity and degrade women, sexually marginalizing them within the Latino/a community (Casillas 2014, 119).

By focusing on Spanish-language radio programming in an interdisciplinary fashion, Casillas aims to remind her academic readership that radio is an excellent site to study the diversity of Latino/a identity. On the positive side, radio provides the Latino/a community a sense of belonging; on the negative side, it fixes Latina female identity as inferior. For sure,

224 Francisco Lozada Jr.

Casillas is seeking the recognition of the academic community within her respective fields: media studies and Latino/a studies—and, broadly, I would argue, ethnic/racial studies and American studies. However, I would also argue that she is aiming to persuade those in media studies to dismantle the old borders and mark new ones in the field (Segovia 2009, 294). Such studies, like the above, also aim for recognition, for inclusion in the US history of radio. It is not only derivative of the tradition; it is the tradition. Moreover, as described above, such knowledge of history is important for a sense of belonging among US Latinos/as.

Eileen J. Suárez Findlay, *We Are Left without a Father Here*

The final study I wish to discuss is Eileen J. Suárez Findlay's (2014) *We Are Left without a Father Here.* Suárez Findlay carries a theme that was introduced in the previous study but that was not developed as much as it is in this volume, namely, masculinity. Suárez Findlay is interested in how the scripted understandings of manhood and family influenced the persuasion of many in Puerto Rico to migrate to the United States, particularly to the sugar beet fields of east-central Michigan in the summer of 1950. She was led to this study by the discovery of letters in the Archivo General de Puerto Rico from numerous agricultural Puerto Rican migrants who traveled to Michigan with the encouragement of the Puerto Rican government. In these letters they plead or request that the (populist) government assist Puerto Rican migrants and their families (who remained behind) with food and housing (both in Michigan and on the island). These Puerto Rican migrants went to the sugar beet fields of Michigan to lift themselves out of poverty and to find income, since the island was going from an agricultural economy to an industrial one, led by the populist government and the elite classes as well as by US industry.

Suárez Findlay's study illustrates that not all migration went through New York; at times, some immigrants also migrated to other parts of the country—such as Chicago; Michigan; Lorain, Ohio (and, I would add, Cleveland); Texas; Arizona; Hawaii; and many other places. New York was surely the place to which the majority migrated, but, to understand the Puerto Rican diaspora, Suárez Findlay shows that it is also important to understand their presence in other, nontraditional diasporic locales.

What Suárez Findlay discovered through many of the letters was the exploitation that they (five thousand Puerto Rican migrants in Michigan during the summer of 1950) experienced upon arrival—a contrary experience for which they were not prepared by their own government in their negotiation with the Michigan agribusiness owners. What these letters also showed was the historical production of manhood after World War II. In other words, the discourse by Puerto Rico's populist government employed masculinity to encourage migration, rather than challenge US colonialism on the island through industrialization (Suárez Findlay 2014, 4). The government espoused a rhetoric that said it was the responsibility of the father to provide for the family, as Suárez Findlay suggests in chapter 1 ("Family and Fatherhood in 'A New Era for All': Populist Politics and Reformed Colonialism"). She provides a translation of Muñoz Marín's words:

> The cry "Believe in your manhood!" punctuated early PPD [the populist government] discourse. Muñoz Marín defended Puerto Ricans' masculine dignity in language that resonated on many possible levels: freedom from colonial indignities, freedom from the chattel slavery that lurked in many Puerto Ricans' past, freedom from the current misery of poverty, freedom to both protect and control one's family and dependents. (41)

Suárez Findlay suggests that this rhetoric was used both on the island and abroad in places where many Puerto Ricans migrated, such as Michigan. Puerto Rican fathers needed jobs to buy homes and to provide for families, needed homes to rule over, so the populist government, led by Muñoz Marín, encouraged agricultural migration to the United States.

Such rhetoric, interestingly, also disguised racial concerns in public political discussions (6). How so? These discussions intertwined gendered discussions with racial discussions. They linked the memory of slavery not only to those who were the victims of slavery (Black Puerto Ricans) but also to all Puerto Ricans, no matter what they signified in terms of race, as signified by the male (European, impoverished) image of el jíbaro (derogatively understood as a "hillbilly" in English; 7, 37, 67).[6] Such deracialization and declassing of the history of slavery was part of the discourse of both the elite and the popular male individuals who promoted Puerto Rican modernity and economic development on the island. To do so would solve the dire economic situation (low wages and unemployment) in Puerto Rico. From

---

6. For instance, the popular populist image of el jíbaro surely displays features of Europe as opposed to Africa. Some might even suggest that indigenous features are also absent in the picture of el jíbaro.

226   Francisco Lozada Jr.

the government's point of view, the rhetoric of masculinity and domesticity subsequently would promote migration to remedy this economic situation.

Migration to the Midwest came with encounters with Mexicans and Mexican Americans, who had already been working the sugar beet fields for many years. These Mexican Americans and individuals of Mexican descent had migrated in family groups from Texas and were well-established in this rural setting. When these Puerto Rican men came to Michigan, the encounters created some solidarity as well as some differences between the two communities. On the one hand, Puerto Ricans had been US citizens dating back to 1917. As US citizens, they were taken aback (as if they were better because of their US status) because, first, they were subjected to the same miserable accommodations and lack of sustenance as others, and, second, because they were not paid weekly, as promised by the companies (e.g., Michigan Field Crops, Monitor Sugar, Michigan Sugar, Green Giant) that had contracted them there. On the other hand, many Mexican Americans served as resources for, in addition to standing in solidarity with, these Puerto Rican men who demanded justice from both the companies and their government, as Suárez Findlay discusses in chapter 4 ("Arriving in Michigan: The Collapse of the Dream").

Their experience of injustice in Michigan emanates from the political leadership in Puerto Rico. Suárez Findlay's approach in reconstructing this past is also interdisciplinary, combining historical studies, feminist studies, and Latin American studies—all specialized areas calling for a specialized readership housed in various academic circles. The volume is not seeking recognition from popular communities but rather from those who work academically with the problematic of identity (Latin American, Latino/a, and gender identities).

Suárez Findlay's historical reconstruction begins with a revisiting of Puerto Rico's political history. She reminds readers that Luis Muñoz Marín led the populist movement in Puerto Rico in the 1930s through the 1950s, as part of a reformist political party, the Partido Popular Democrático, established in 1938 from a combination of liberal reformers, New Deal technocrats, and veteran union activists. In 1940, Muñoz Marín led the Partido Popular Democrático as the then-leader of the Senate. He later, in 1948, become the first governor elected by the people of Puerto Rico (rather than by the US government).

Many of the men who migrated to Michigan in the 1950s were strong supporters of the Partido Popular Democrático. The Partido Popular Democrático was interested in transforming the island from an agricul-

Whose Recognition? Latino/a Studies and the Need to Belong   227

tural to an industrial society. As part of this transformation, many rural folks moved to the urban centers of the island. However, there were not enough jobs available for them, so the government began a campaign to encourage migration to the United States. This push for a "reformed colonialism," as Suárez Findlay (2014, 25) calls it in chapter 1 ("Family and Fatherhood in 'a New Era for All'"), lived by the motto "Bread, Land, and Freedom." The campaign aimed for "just wages, land reform, and independence of political expression and affiliation" (35). The Partido Popular Democrático's aim was to reform colonialism—modernity intertwined with US colonialism (29). It aimed to mimic the ideals and standards of the United States, no matter how imperfect some of these ideals and standards were, so that all Puerto Ricans would aspire to them on the island as well (30).

For many Puerto Ricans, Muñoz Marín represented hope amid the dire economic situation in which they found themselves as a result of the island's political and economic transformations. He was the embodiment of these proposed changes. He employed gender-inclusive language as well as religious language to appeal to the populace. Suárez Findlay (38) provides examples of such language in translation. Thus, "You are not children who must always be spoken to sweetly. You are men and women with responsibilities of men and women who deserve to be told the truth. All of you are part of this democratic work which we are making all together." Similarly, "Believe in yourselves! Don't think of yourselves as tiny or weak or inferior! The light of God is in the nature of all those men and women whom God has created in this world. Believe in yourselves! Have faith in your own strength and power to make justice and ensure your own fixtures."

At the same time as he used inclusive language, Muñoz Marín also presented himself in patriarchal ways. These translated words clearly express a tone of paternalism and contain a theological assumption to the effect that Muñoz Marín was a demigod. If the people believed in him, they would be OK. For Suárez Findlay (2014, 40), this tone of paternalism was Muñoz Marín "positing an ideal masculinity" to both women and men. What is more, he employed religious language as a way to convince the populace that God was on his side. Along with this benevolent colonial rhetoric, according to Suárez Findlay, Muñoz Marín often employed the word *bregar* in order to persuade the populace to emigrate. Suárez Findlay (11), drawing on Arcadio Díaz-Quiñones's (2000) work *El arte de bregar*, translates and interprets *bregar* as "Negotiation, slipping from one

228   Francisco Lozada Jr.

position to another to 'achieve a difficult balance between conflictual elements.' *Bregar* maintains dignity in the face of adversity. It entails struggle without frontal clash, implying a pact or a dialogue between parties.... *Bregar*, needless to say, is often a weapon of the less powerful."

Muñoz Marín used *bregar* in his speeches as a way to establish an agreement with the United States to assist Puerto Ricans in migrating. In other words, Muñoz Marín utilized *bregar* on behalf of the people of Puerto Rico to establish an arrangement with members of the US agricultural industry, such as sugar beet owners in Michigan, promising the migrants that they would be able to work and earn a just wage so that they could provide for their families. At the same time, the workers would employ *bregar* as a way to survive in Michigan and as a way to open new possibilities with Mexican Americans as well as with the Catholic Church in Detroit,[7] which supported not just the Puerto Rican men but also the Mexican Americans through the abuses they received from the agricultural industry. In chapter 5 ("The Brega Expands"), Suárez Findlay reports that even the women would employ *bregar*—in a reverse way—to call the Partido Popular Democrático and Muñoz Marín's attention to the exploitation that their husbands and family members were experiencing in Michigan and to ask how they were going to remedy the situation. Suárez Findlay's approach brings a new angle to understanding Puerto Rican diaspora and colonialism, one in which gender (masculinity) as a colonial tool is addressed more directly.

The aims of this volume are multiple. Suárez Findlay is interested in showing how the notion of masculinity is intertwined in the discourses of political men, thus having dire effects for women, who are perceived only in the role of domesticity. These discourses are also intertwined with colonialism. Suárez Findlay's volume exposes US colonialism and its supporters (the Partido Popular Democrático), who exploited the Puerto Rican people by encouraging migration to the United States, where they faced abusive conditions.

Puerto Rican men migrated because they were experiencing poverty, lack of housing and jobs, and a mass transition from rural society to urban community with no possibility of employing their existing skills. Puerto

---

7. The Saginaw Diocese where many of these sugar beet fields were located did not openly denounce the abuses of the working and living conditions (Suárez Findlay 2014, 131). The support came from Detroit, from Father Clement Kern of Holy Trinity Catholic parish (148).

Ricans likened these dire conditions in Michigan to the *barracones*, where slaves on the island were forced to live at one time. In addition, they were not paid hourly and biweekly as promised, but were paid by some companies, such as Michigan Field Crop, at the end of the harvest season, which meant that the men had no cash to survive on and no guarantees that they would be paid. They had heard what happened to Mexican Americans who were not paid at the end of a season. Some companies paid *por ajuste* (by the quantity picked), which had not been agreed on in their (the Puerto Ricans') negotiations. The Puerto Rican men wanted to be paid as agreed on—weekly or every two weeks.

As a result of these dire working and living conditions, the men protested. When they did so, Suárez Findlay (2014, 139) records, they were told that "only Americans were paid by the hour." Such comments, consistent with the themes of other volumes described in this essay, indicate the lack of belonging that Puerto Ricans experienced, not just physically but also as members of the US nation. Eventually, about three thousand men returned to Puerto Rico at the end of the period. Some left much earlier, if they were capable of so doing; others dispersed throughout the country, with many remaining in the Midwest (Detroit; Chicago; Lorain, Ohio) and some reaching New York. Muñoz Marín spoke to some of these men and their families when they returned and tried to establish, through *bregar*, new agreements that would be just; by that time, however, the men did not trust the rhetoric of Muñoz Marín or the Partido Popular Democrático.

What this study shows, through the letters Suárez Findlay discovered, is a political discourse covered with a sense of manhood that influenced many poor on the island to migrate to places such as Michigan. They were told, more or less, that if they could not provide for their family, they would not be in control of the home and thus contain women in the home. Such paternalism and patriarchy were also employed, in a way, to *bregar* (negotiate) with US industry, to establish a relationship with these migrant men. Thus, the men felt it was necessary to leave Michigan. In the end, however, the protests expressed through the letters indicate that the Partido Popular Democrático exploited these men and their families. The Partido Popular Democrático did respond to these complaints for fear that the crisis in Michigan would stop their intention of a new colonial or reformed-colonial situation, but their image among these men was not as popular as it had been before they had migrated to the United States.

Hence, this study, like the previous two analyzed, weaves in and out of the Latino/a community, by way of studying Puerto Rican migra-

230   Francisco Lozada Jr.

tion to and from the United States. Methodologically, it combines both feminist and gendered studies in disclosing the paternalistic and sexist language employed in Partido Popular Democrático discourses. These discourses served as a way to domesticate Puerto Rican women in the home and to promote migration as remedy for some of the ills, such as poverty, that existed on the island, as it became an industrial nation. It follows, then, that such a focus on subject, approach, and aim surely is seeking recognition from the academic community, particularly from those immersed in US history, gender studies, and Latin American and Latino/a studies. In similar fashion to the studies above, Suárez Findlay aims to implode the dichotomy separating the Puerto Rican diaspora from US history. The diaspora is to be seen as equal to other migratory movements, and a part of history to be studied. What is more, colonialism is not absent from the problematic of gender. Intertwined with the diaspora is a patriarchal and paternalistic rhetoric that reinscribes hypermasculinity and subdued domesticity.

Concluding Reflections

What do these three evaluations of works in Latino/a studies contribute to the question, Whose recognition is sought in doing Latino/a studies or, in my case, Latino/a biblical interpretation? I will discuss three contributions to the question at hand, each associated with a particular study but each also reflected in the other two studies.

First, in *How Race Is Made in America*, Molina sees the construction of race as relational. In other words, how Latinos/as are constructed through immigration laws and policies, and how citizenship is extended based on whether someone is perceived and named as "white," influences how other groups, including whites, are constructed in US history. This emphasis on seeing the construction of race as relational disrupts any one way of categorizing race.

When parts of Mexico became part of the United States in 1850, Mexicans living in the United States were made citizens and deemed "white." Their indigenous identity was overlooked until a later time, when folks tried to limit their citizenship by placing them alongside Native Americans. Such attempts not only affected Mexicans living in the United States but also reified the notion that since Native Americans were not "white," they did not belong, although, as history testifies, they were in what came to be known as the United States centuries before Europeans. The way in which groups such as the Chinese, Japanese, and other Asians were constructed in terms of race, and whether they were deemed assimilable, led to a number of laws using race to keep these groups out of the United States, despite the fact that many of them had been born in the United States. Even gender played a role: women (citizens) who married noncitizens would lose their citizenship, although this was overturned in 1922 through the Cable Act.

Thus, Molina's engagement in seeing race as relational tells me that she is interested in seeking recognition from other ethnic/racial minoritized academic groups. Like Molina, in doing Latino/a biblical interpretation, I also seek recognition from those working in the field of ethnic/racial minoritized readings of the text.

Second, in *Sounds of Belonging*, Casillas, among many other aims, places her recovery of the history of Latino/a radio within the tradition of media studies. Such a move, as I see it, shows that Casillas is seeking the recognition of her peers in media studies, particularly those engaged in its history and cultural production. One cannot understand radio without understanding how Latino/a radio emerged, and why, and what it aimed to do. By placing her research within the history of radio, Casillas opens a space for other minoritized studies to contribute. At the same time, she provides space for a broad range of related fields—such as ethnic/racial studies, feminist studies, and gender studies, to name a few—to continue furthering their work. All of this is to say that Casillas's work appears to seek recognition from within and from without (traditionally speaking), in order to provide, in many ways, a different, alternative vision of the field.

In thinking of my own work in Latino/a biblical interpretation, I also see my work as joining the chorus of the history of interpretation that is often excluded within the history of biblical hermeneutics, as well as studies from other scholars interested in the history of interpretation. Dominant biblical interpretation does not own the tradition of the history of interpretation, and Latino/a biblical interpretation is not simply visiting the history of interpretation. It is part of the tradition; it belongs. Thus, my own approach to Latino/a biblical interpretation is seeking the recognition of the field of biblical hermeneutics or interpretation.

Third, the volume *We Are Left without A Father Here* by Suárez Findlay really pushes the interdisciplinary boundaries with regard to approach. In other words, she is in dialogue with traditional ways of recovery (e.g., excavating the archives and observation/listening to the

232   Francisco Lozada Jr.

patterns that surface) but also moves beyond the borders of studying topics such as the Puerto Rican diaspora. Thus, I see her work as seeking recognition from the academy in general. I see her study combining different fields of study such as colonial history and masculinity studies.

The impact of such interdisciplinary work on how recovery has been traditionally conceived challenges readers to see, for example, how the Puerto Rican diaspora was not monolithic, nor isolated from the construction of gender, both female and male. Suárez Findlay's recourse to this perspective suggests to me that her work is seeking the recognition of everyone in the academy, including women scholars. She also aims to bring along those male scholars who see gender construction as relational. How the male is constructed relates to how the female is constructed, and vice versa.

In a similar vein, in Latino/a biblical interpretation, I also aim to seek recognition from those who see gender as a construction as well as from those who see the effects of colonial discourse or benevolent colonial discourse as having an impact on how gender is represented.

These studies demonstrate that seeking recognition is a challenge to distinguish. At the same time, as Liew suggests, such a question is important in understanding what Latino/a biblical interpretation is. What it does is to visit the question, Who is the audience from whom we are seeking recognition? As all of these studies have also illustrated, they are seeking a different angle of vision on the subjects they are researching. With a different vision comes a sense of belonging, which is a theme found in all of the studies, including, I would add, in the history of Latino/a biblical interpretation.

One last item, which I cannot deal with at this time, is the issue of desire. In any form of communication, there is a sender and a receiver. Why was I attracted to these works? The receiver of such works must have a desire to consider a different point of view on a topic. Without a desire to read something familiar but surely something different, one gives up a bit of oneself for the possibility of change. In general, Latino/a biblical interpretation is not just for Latinos/as; it is for everyone, I would argue. Just as Friedrich Schleiermacher is not just for Germans, nor is the new National African American Museum of History and Culture for African Americans only, so is Latino/a biblical interpretation not just for Latinos/as. By reading Wallace Stevens, William Shakespeare, or Emily Dickinson, to name a few authors, I have a desire to experience a different reality from a different period and point of view. If I can learn from

European and Anglo-American writers, why cannot they learn from Latinos/as? Thus, this topic of desire is something to explore further in the near future, within Latino/a biblical interpretation as well as within the question of recognition.

Works Cited

Aparicio, Frances R. 2003. "Latino Cultural Studies." Interview by Juan Zevallos Aguilar. Translated by Dascha Inciarte and Carolyn Sedway. Pages 3–31 in *Critical Latin American and Latino Studies*. Edited by Juan Poblete. CSA 12. Minneapolis: University of Minnesota Press.

Casillas, Dolores Inés. 2014. *Sounds of Belonging: U.S. Spanish Language Radio and Public Advocacy*. New York: New York University Press.

Díaz-Quiñones, Arcadio. 2000. *El arte de bregar. Ensayos*. San Juan: Calculated Industries.

Fraser, Nancy. 1993. "Rethinking the Public Sphere: A Contribution to the Critique of Actually Existing Democracy." Pages 109–42 in *Habermas and the Public Sphere*. Edited by Craig Calhoun. Boston: MIT Press.

Fraser, Nancy, and Axel Honneth, eds. 2003. *Redistribution or Recognition? A Political-Philosophical Exchange*. London: Verso Books.

Hughes, Christina, and Loraine Blaxter. 2007. "Feminist Appropriations of Bourdieu: The Case of Social Capital." Pages 103–25 in *(Mis)recognition, Social Inequality and Social Justice: Nancy Fraser and Pierre Bourdieu*. Edited by Terry Lovell. New York: Routledge.

Liew, Tat-siong Benny. 2015. Review of Francisco Lozada Jr. and Fernando F. Segovia, eds., *Latino/a Biblical Hermeneutics: Problematics, Objectives, Strategies*. *Review of Biblical Literature*. https://www.sblcentral.org/home/bookDetails/10076.

Molina, Natalia. 2014. *How Race Is Made in America: Immigration, Citizenship, and the Historical Power of Racial Scripts*. Berkeley: University of California Press.

Omi, Michael, and Howard Winant. 1986. *Racial Formation in the United States: From the 1960s to the 1990s*. New York: Routledge.

Rosaldo, Renato. 1994. "Cultural Citizenship and Educational Democracy." *CultAnthr* 9:402–11.

Salinas, Cristobal, Jr., and Adele Lozano. 2017. "Mapping and Recontextualizing the Evolution of the Term *Latinx*: An Environmental Scanning in Higher Education." *JLE* 18.4: 302–13. doi:10.1080/15348431.2017.1390464

Segovia, Fernando F. 2009. "Poetics of Minority Biblical Criticism: Identification and Theorization." Pages 279–311 in *Prejudice and Christian Beginnings: Investigating Race, Gender, and Ethnicity in Early Christian Studies*. Edited by Laura Nasrallah and Elisabeth Schüssler Fiorenza. Minneapolis: Fortress.

Suárez Findlay, Eileen J. 2014. *We Are Left without a Father Here: Masculinity, Domesticity, and Migration in Postwar Puerto Rico*. Durham, NC: Duke University Press.

Zavella, Pat. 2011. *I'm Neither Here nor There: Mexicans' Quotidian Struggles with Migration*. Durham, NC: Duke University Press.

Unsettled Homecomings:
A Repatriate Reading of Ezra-Nehemiah

Roger S. Nam

The apropos call for biblical scholars to reflect on the task of reading in these times carries significance beyond our academic field. I received the generous invitation to contribute to this discussion while on a year-long sabbatical as a visiting professor at Sogang University in Seoul, Korea. The importance of the question playfully emerged in an interaction with my then-six-year-old son, just a few weeks into his own journey as a third-generation child returning to Korea. After playing at the apartment playground with other neighborhood kids, he returned home and asked, "Am I Korean, or am I American?" Even a six-year-old had the sense to know that there was something different about his identity from the other children, despite having a common ethnic origin. How does one respond to a child, knowing that his own perceived identity is a totalizing aspect of his personhood and his perceived places of access?

In many ways, this simple conversation with a child signifies a wider societal phenomenon. The unparalleled ethnic heterogeneity of these times forces new understandings of identity with concomitant power struggles

---

I am grateful to the faculty of the Sogang University Graduate School of Theology for hosting me for a sabbatical and providing an initial forum to share my ideas of repatriation as a reading lens. My return to Korea in 2014 marked forty-seven years since my mother and father first left their country in 1967, following the passage of the Immigration-Nationality Act of 1965. Serendipitously, the passage of forty-seven years also spans the purported exile (586 BCE) and return under Persian rule (539 BCE). An earlier version of this essay appeared as "Reading the Bible Repatriately: Ezra-Nehemiah, A Case Study," in *Samuel, Kings, Chronicles, Ezra-Nehemiah, Volume 2*, ed. Athalya Brenner-Idan and Gale A. Yee, Texts@Contexts 8 (London: T&T Clark, 2021), 203–20. Reproduced by permission.

236   Roger S. Nam

and marginalization. Accordingly, minoritized critics must form reading
strategies that align to this reality. In this paper, I present a brief chronological review of the biblical studies guild in relation to the prospects of
minoritized criticism. I contend that perceptions of minoritized biblical
criticism have threatened traditional historical-critical approaches. However, in the present moment, the ethnic diversity of these times gives more
legitimacy for minoritized readings. Drawing on the seminal addresses
of Vincent Wimbush (2011) and Fernando Segovia (2015), as the first
two people of color to have occupied the Society of Biblical Literature's
presidential position, I propose broad constructs for moving forward in
minoritized readings.

I advocate for repatriation as an effective prefigurative reading strategy
alongside the many rich expressions of minoritized approaches. What does
this signify? Drawing on Sharon K. Hahn, Tat-siong Benny Liew (2008,
2) distinguishes the terms of *prefigurative* and *prescriptive*: the prefigurative approach does not claim exclusivity but rather intends to function as
a complementary option. A repatriate reading, therefore, takes seriously
the multivalent cultural expressions within North America and has direct
repercussions on present issues that we must face as biblical critics. The
final section will present some of the themes that emerge from a repatriate
reading of Ezra-Nehemiah as a second-generation Korean American.

Where We Have Been

Minoritized biblical scholars stand as members of an academic guild with
roots in the Enlightenment and the alleged autonomy of the historian.
(For a review of the historical-critical method in the context of intellectual
history, see Legaspi 2010.)

From the turn of the eighteenth century, biblical scholarship has relied
heavily on historical-critical methods, an umbrella term that covers a variety of diachronic exegetical approaches, such as source criticism, form
criticism, redaction criticism, and so forth. These approaches emerged and
reached relative prominence at different points in the last two centuries.
All of these different critical methods share an emphasis on reconstruction of historical contexts and textual developments in the spirit of Julius
Wellhausen's source criticism of the Pentateuch.

Throughout this period of historical-critical scholarship, biblical
scholars pursued truth on terms that were considered objective and scientific. The aim of scholarship was to recapture "original" meanings through

skilled philology and reconstruction of ancient contexts. The historical studies or biblical contexts were the center of interpretation, via the principle of analogy. The context of the interpreter was not merely secondary; it was rarely even acknowledged. Rather, scholars pursued scientific reconstructions, assigning dates and strata to textual units with the vigor of an archaeologist excavating a tell. Theoretically, proper application of historical critical methods assured reliable results.

The fruits of these historical critical pursuits were quite remarkable, as critical studies opened up an enormous amount of data to illuminate biblical texts and correct previous erroneous interpretations. Textual discoveries, such as Ras Shamra and the Dead Sea Scrolls, as well as the maturing field of Assyriology, brought forth an abundant data set for biblical scholars. New genres were acknowledged. Ancient Near Eastern religions gave a broader context for Israelite religion and muddied the uniqueness of biblical texts. The nature of historiography shifted, from the perceived von Rankean approach of objectivity to one that recognized the politicized nature of ancient Near Eastern scribal cultures. Textual studies underwent a lengthy shift from the pursuit of an assumed scientific reconstruction of the *Urtext*, replete with emendations, to a gradual acknowledgment of the multiple textual traditions of antiquity that represented biblical texts. Most significantly, historical-critical studies demonstrated the composite nature of biblical texts and the multiple accretions over different phases of ancient Israel. Two centuries of historical-critical study resulted in a more sophisticated understanding of the nature of the biblical text.

Yet under the very principle of criticism as articulated by Ernst Troeltsch (1991), historical criticism requires continued review and revision of new data and new conclusions. (For a summation on the influence of Ernst Troeltsch on historical criticism, see Drescher 1993.) Inevitably, historical-critical scholarship questioned the allure of reader objectivity as the limitations of diachronic methods opened the door for synchronic approaches. The 1980s saw the beginnings of the decline of Wellhausen's JEDP paradigm after a century of its axiomatic dominance. On a broader scale, the intellectual climate of postmodernity had cut into some of the bravado of the idea of the objective interpretation.

John Collins (2005) argues that postmodernity's critique of a unilateral reading was actually an inevitable result of the historical-critical enterprise. The historical focus freed the text from so-called objective approaches and allowed the fluidity of the text to emerge. This fluidity was already a phenomenon during the actual textualization of the Bible based

238   Roger S. Nam

on the pattern of appropriating traditions for present contexts, such as the
Pauline usage of Hab 2:4 or the Chronicler's retelling of the history of the
Davidic monarchy. Historical-critical methods explained that new social
contexts, whether the Persian Empire or the nascent Christian church,
warranted new interpretations of received traditions. However, the natural progression of this line of thought opened the door for more explicit
reference to the modern reader's social context. Texts have meaning only
with readers, and said readers have assumptions and political agendas that
influence interpretations.

Alongside the attack of history and the newly emerging recognition of
the importance of reader context, the demography of the biblical studies
field began to shift. Up to the 1980s, the field of biblical studies largely con-
sisted of white, male, Protestant scholars. However, recent times have seen
the addition of more ethnic minorities. (In addition, the field of biblical
studies saw increased numbers of Catholic, Jewish, and atheist scholars as
well as more diversity in gender and sexuality.) The growing recognition of
the importance of multiple perspectives has led to an improvement in nurturing the voice of ethnic minorities, whether through monograph series
for minoritized readings or dedicated sessions for minoritized scholars in
the annual meetings of the Society of Biblical Literature. Higher-education
accrediting bodies and nonprofit groups, such as the Forum for Theological Exploration, pressure theological institutions to embrace greater ethnic
diversity in scholarship. More recently, the financial crises in theological
education have created more expansive recruiting efforts toward a more
diverse pool of applicants. As a result, institutions are more conscientious
about hiring people of color.[1] More than ever before, minoritized biblical
critics may find themselves in tenured or tenure-track spaces, which afford
a privilege more elusive to the minoritized critics of earlier generations.

Despite these positive movements, the spaces for minoritized criticism still do not commensurately reflect the diverse realities of North
America. Regardless, I hope that minoritized critics can appreciate an
unprecedented opportunity to define ways in which we read biblical texts
for the academy and the broader society. Despite advances in the work
of minoritized criticism, Segovia (2009) notices the lack of explicit theoretical foundation. Although the concept of minoritized criticism is still

---

1. For a snapshot, the Association of Theological Schools (n.d.) states that in
1991 the nonwhite faculty was slightly less than 10 percent, growing to about 19
percent by 2012.

theoretically nascent, our unique voices can potentially reverse marginalizing approaches and open new vistas of biblical interpretation. In the next section, I argue that contextualized approaches need not be ahistorical but that historical-critical tradition and contextualized synchronic approaches are deeply complementary, particularly in reading the Bible in a fruitful way for both our minoritized communities and the broader society in which we dwell.

Where We Can Go

Before suggesting a path for the future of minoritized biblical studies, I must explain my own social location. Academically, I am formally trained in traditional historical-critical methods of the Hebrew Bible. I attended a doctoral program in Near Eastern Languages and Cultures with emphases on traditional fields such as Semitics and archaeology. My graduate reading lists contained authors such as William Albright and Frank Moore Cross, with little from authors such as Homi Bhabha and Jacques Derrida. Ethnically, I am a second-generation Korean American, but, of course, that answer is distressingly simplistic. I have lived in Korea for a total of five years during adulthood, including a recent sabbatical year. Much of my life in America has been in communities with strong Korean American populations (San Francisco, Los Angeles), but I have raised my young family in a significantly less-diverse suburb near Portland, Oregon. I was raised in a Protestant household, and my interest in biblical texts was initially nurtured within faith contexts. To date, almost exclusively, my scholarship has drawn on ideas extrinsically distinct from my own persona. At the same time, I am aware that I have my biases, assumptions, and agendas, like every other scholar.

With that said, it will come as no surprise that I largely object to the bifurcation between historical-critical and minoritized approaches. Many of the scholars who work exclusively in the historical-critical tradition perceive that minoritized readers have little interest in ancient contexts. Here the assumptions of John Barton's (1998) passionate defense of historical criticism are particularly to the point. This assumption is false and does a tremendous disservice to those working along the lines of minoritized approaches. Since the beginning stage of post-critical scholarship, many traditional scholars considered the notion of reader bias as an attack on their own rigorous training in languages and exegetical methods. Several of these scholars rejected notions of reader-centered interpretations, decrying them as a free fall into relativism. However, many minoritized critics, in fact, are well-trained in historical methods, apply them, and even come to similar results as historical-critical approaches. Historical criticism and minoritized approaches need not be adversarial. In fact, the intersection of historical context and reader context can preserve an ideal theoretical platform for minoritized criticism.

Furthermore, the very concept of a clear divide between original and reader contexts is problematic. Historical criticism clearly teaches that biblical texts are composite, as the result of continuous redaction of received traditions. For example, 1 and 2 Chronicles take earlier traditions from Samuel and Kings and rework and supplement the material to match the concerns of the Persian period. Yet, in actuality, such editorial activity essentially replicates the actual work of Samuel and Kings, the rest of the Deuteronomistic History, the Torah, and so on. Each of these sections of the Hebrew Bible underwent formation and reformation during preexilic, exilic, and postexilic periods before crystallization into the Hebrew Bible. These biblical narratives were written down precisely because they were presumed to have value for future generations who received and adapted those traditions. Consequently, biblical scholars must reconsider the supposed bifurcation between text and readers.

To this problem, Brennan Breed (2012) proposes that this fuzzy boundary between text and reader can actually provide a way forward through the concept of a nomadic text.[2] Because of the lack of any singular context, Breed (2015) suggests an avoidance of any direct questions regarding a purported original but rather encourages the alternate question of "What can this text do?" He argues that this question can still account for contextual origins but can more productively examine the function of texts within communities across spatial and temporal boundaries. Breed states that intentional attention to the life of the text will catalyze new dialectic approaches in scholarship, ultimately widening the possibilities for biblical theology. For Breed (2015), these spaces include "learning across those borders, from other communities, about their versions and meanings and contexts for sacred scripture." Breed argues that historical contexts can offer a starting point in the discussion of texts, but that the social locations

---

2. See the expanded theoretical basis in Breed's (2014) monograph. Also see a concise summary with insightful responses by Nyasha Junior, Jeremy Schipper, and William Brown on At This Point (Breed 2015).

Unsettled Homecomings: A Repatriate Reading of Ezra-Nehemiah   241

of readers can then extend these discussions in directions most meaningful for those particular locations.

A lot of questions remain as to how to regulate dialectical work that takes these three worlds in place. How do readings coexist with paradoxical, even contrarian readings? Of course, the tendencies to prioritize certain readings, without some methodological control, may merely result to reinforce interpretive hegemonies that have been plaguing biblical studies since its inception. For minoritized critics, questions of textual authority are particularly significant, as assimilation is an immigration strategy. Thus, readings of biblical texts are often tied to our own communities of faith, and when such readings subvert traditional notions of authority, minoritized critics find themselves excluded from their own social group.

It is in response to this question that I draw on two landmark Society of Biblical Literature presidential addresses: those by Wimbush, the first person of color to hold the position, and by Segovia, the first from the Global South. The Society of Biblical Literature presidential office traces to 1880; Wimbush occupied the position in 2010 and Segovia in 2014. Each address gives a distinct contribution to the place of minoritized criticism. Both presidential addresses have different perspectives and unique callings to the biblical studies guild. Yet areas of convergence arise, and these convergences may serve to guide us in claiming our own place as minoritized critics.

First, minoritized criticism must claim relevance beyond the academy. Wimbush confronts the painful racial history of the Society of Biblical Literature, particularly in the absence of intentional spaces for minoritized critics, citing the late 1980s as a key moment of change with the publication of *Stony the Road We Trod* at the initiative of Thomas Hoyt Jr. and John W. Waters (Felder 1991). Wimbush uses the categories of enslaving, enslaved, and runagates from Frederick Douglass's (1845) *Narrative of the Life of Frederick Douglass, an American, Slave, Written by Himself*. For Wimbush, the key figure was the runagate as a runaway in both body and consciousness. As an analogy of the Society of Biblical Literature, Wimbush (2011, 20) was arguing that the critical interpreter "must seek to escape, must run, must be oriented 'outside the circle.'" The circle stands for traditional historical-critical studies, which had erroneously connected the ancient Near Eastern world to the modern white world (12). Yet the double consciousness of the runagate led to a certain clairvoyance in interpretation. The call for a runagate is not restricted to Black interpreters but is for all who can recognize ways in which biblical texts have been harnessed and used as an instrument of oppression. For Wimbush, the experiences of the minoritized critic can potentially occupy a unique vantage point in biblical readings to affect broader society.

Similarly, Segovia draws on earlier Society of Biblical Literature presidential addresses to argue that, historically, the biblical studies guild has not called for societal impact during critical times. The place of intellectualism as a positive force on a wider society is neither assumed nor self-evident. Segovia (2015, 26) builds on Edward Said (1996) and argues for a formative place of intellectual spaces to influence and challenge trends in the general populace. He describes the present age as a period with multiple crises. Biblical readings must "bring the field to bear upon the major crises of our post–Cold War times, in both individual and converging fashion" (26). Segovia calls for a biblical criticism that will bridge these worlds of text, interpretations, and interpreters. This relevance seems magnified for those biblical scholars who find themselves primarily in positions of relative privilege as professors and administrators at institutions of higher education. Segovia then argues that an impactful political discourse can address three primary issues of importance for these times: global economics, climatological problems, and worldwide migration.

Second, minoritized criticism must be dialectical in order to achieve societal relevance. A dialectical approach can allow for greater access to speak and represent multiple readings of a biblical text. Such scholarship must create methodological entry points for sharing concerns and readings. Of course, the danger of emphasizing the interpreter's context may result in forms of relativism or chaos. Because readings of the Bible often tie to faith communities, a methodological frame must guide the readings. Herein lies a critical way forward and crucial task for minoritized scholars. In accord with our given space in academic circles, we must strive to engage in dialogues not just among other minoritized biblical scholars but among all those who engage with the thematic elements within biblical texts. For example, Breed's question, "What can the text do?" can extend dialogue beyond scholars to broader reading communities.[3] Accordingly, minoritized scholars must read the Bible in a way that empowers moral

---

3. One must be aware of the tensions present in the issues of inclusion and exclusion under the rubric of "biblical scholars." Jeremy Schipper argues that the dialectic must cross the disciplinary silos and engage those outside academic fields, broadening access to the dialogue (Breed 2015).

and ethical directives for our world. Our readings should connect communities and help people come to a better understanding of the religious dimensions of our texts.

Third, minoritized criticism must be interdisciplinary. Because minoritized critics represent such a broad swath of humanity, diverse theoretical approaches must frame the dialogue. Social models often set delimiters in categories such as ethnicity, gender, and class; thus, these models can incorporate perspectives outside the traditional majority readers and connect overarching themes across different minoritized groups. Since the onset of sociological approaches in the 1980s, biblical scholars have been better equipped to apply such models judiciously (for a recent review of social scientific approaches, see Chalcraft, Uhlenbruch, and Watson 2014). Nowadays, we are more aware of the dangers of anachronism or the temptation to let social models straitjacket readings of texts. Instead, we recognize that the best sociological readings catalyze our imaginations and help us understand new ways of reading.[4] These interdisciplinary approaches allow for input from those not trained in the historical-critical field; one can think of the impact in biblical studies of literary scholar Robert Alter or anthropologist Mary Douglas. Such interdisciplinary dialogue must be nurtured further, as the current modus operandi is actually more fractionalization and insular work.

Thankfully, many of the approaches toward minoritized biblical criticism already seek to be broadly impactful, dialogical, and interdisciplinary. With the loosened hegemony of historical-critical methods, a minoritized criticism in this spirit may contribute to reinvigorate biblical scholarship. For much of modern critical study, biblical criticism has been sterile, with formulaic approaches such as text criticism to source criticism to redactional criticism and so on. I wish to present repatriation as a reading strategy for minoritized criticism. In line with previous musings on minoritized criticism, repatriation readings need not serve as prescriptive but may be seen, rather, as prefigurative (Liew 2008, 2).

---

4. In my own specialty of ancient economies, economic anthropological theories have helped biblical scholars think of noncapitalist settings without modern equivalents of money, inflation, unemployment. More than give us new terms, sociological models allow us to enter ancient Near Eastern contexts so different from our natural intrinsic modes of life. Such economic paradigms place high value on social relations, kinship, and land, values associated with Asia and Africa more than North America (see Nam 2012).

244 Roger S. Nam

This reading strategy makes no claim to interpretive exclusivity. Rather, this particular lens is intended to open up complementary visions of the text and how it can richly articulate the minoritized contexts of today's readers in line with the ancient contexts of the repatriate Judeans of the Persian Empire.

Repatriation as a Reading Strategy

In the early twentieth century, the social sciences established immigration studies as an academic field, in response to the massive influx of Europeans to the United States and the accompanying controversies resulting from this demographic shift. (For a broad review of the intellectual history of the field, see Foner, Rumbaut, and Gold 2003.) Immigration research was extraordinarily interdisciplinary in its approach, with contributions from history, sociology, anthropology, linguistics, even archaeology. Yet despite the relative longevity of immigration studies as a field of research, it is only recently that repatriate studies has emerged as a distinct subdiscipline. Indeed, the first focused study on the phenomenon of repatriation developed from a working group in the American Anthropological Association under Robert Rhodes (1979). The subdiscipline still remains in its very nascent stages (Rumbaut 2003).

Scholars often assumed that returning home was a relatively straightforward phenomenon. To complicate matters, countries typically did not collect data on repatriation, as they did not consider their own returning citizens as immigrants (Khoser 2000). However, with the rapidity of globalization, along with the sheer number of migrants, scholars have appropriately realized the unique experience of return to a country of origin. Repatriation pervades all geographic and temporal boundaries. One recognizes repatriation during every period of recorded history. Presently, the study of repatriation has become both humanistic and humanitarian. It is humanistic in that repatriation concerns itself with the real struggle regarding identity issues of displaced peoples. It is humanitarian in that political freedom and economic survival often motivates the repatriation.

With repatriation studies as a relatively new field, scholars have yet to find consensus on a singular definition of repatriation, though most adopt George Gmelc's (1980, 136) definition of it as "any movement of emigrants back to their homeland to resettle." The publication of this article by Gmelc on repatriation, it should be noted, marked the legitimization of repatriation as a subdiscipline within immigration studies. The reasons

Unsettled Homecomings: A Repatriate Reading of Ezra-Nehemiah   245

for initial emigration are varied: long-term study abroad, political and religious refugees, mail-order brides, long-term migrant workers, forcibly abducted slaves, and so forth. With respect to repatriation, various classifications are advanced. Thus, Gabriel Scheffer (2006) distinguishes between a repatriation that he declares as "forced" and more neutral and voluntary movements back to the homeland due to pragmatic economic and social pressures. Similarly, Francesco Cerase (1974) identifies four types of repatriates: retirement, failure, conservatism (never intended to integrate), or innovation (returns with innovation). Further, Michael Piore (1979) simplifies Cerase's model into two main, self-explanatory types: success and failure, with parameters for judgment as primarily economic. Some even dispute the term *repatriation* itself, preferring instead *transnationalism*, to emphasize the liminality between two political and cultural identities, or even *circular migration*, emphasizing the temporal nature of multiple repatriations. The latter term is apt, since the return to a country of origin is often a single step from a continuous migration pattern (Bartram, Poros, and Monforte 2014, 121–24).

Despite the formidable role of the postexilic repatriation for the development of the Hebrew Bible, repatriate studies has not received much coverage in biblical studies. Admittedly, we have little reliable data on the Judean repatriation of the sixth and fifth centuries BCE. Though it contains historically dubious data, Ezra-Nehemiah does recount a rich report of a repatriate existence. In a way, this understanding of immigrant life follows Ezra-Nehemiah, particularly if read through the lens of social memory. As biblical scholars have demonstrated, it is often the memory of the event that is more informative than the actual historical event.[5] This social memory within Ezra-Nehemiah will help to consolidate into a portrayal of repatriate life in Yehud. This self-identity in narrative and labels provides a meaningful paradigm to understand the place of the remnant in the greater Persian world. To this end, a theology that encapsulates this complexity is long warranted.

---

5. As biblical scholars see the postexilic period as a defining vantage point for the Israel narrative, thus the recollection includes many of their own projections. Consequently, the usage of social memory in Hebrew Bible studies has exploded in recent years. Prominent examples include Phillip Davies (2008); Diana V. Edelman and Ehud Ben Zvi (2013, 2014); Yael Zerubavel (1995). Many of the present research draws on Jan Assmann's (1992) seminal work on cultural memory as a tool for forging identity for ancient Egypt.

246   Roger S. Nam

The Judean return as articulated in Ezra-Nehemiah offers an opportunity to reflect on modern Korean repatriation for two primary reasons. First, for Koreans, the historical construction of Korea is deeply tied to blood purity, almost obsessively so (Shin 2006). Ethnic purity reflecting national ideology often reaches official policy, such as in the declaration of President Park Chun Hee (1963–1979) to Koreanize the national language, thus temporarily eliminating Chinese characters from the writing systems. Nationality and ethnicity are synonymous. Japanese colonial policies of forced assimilation in the twentieth century ironically strengthened Korean nationalism. The end of Japanese colonization in 1945 did not slow down this emphasis on blood purity; rather, the Korean War and subsequent American military occupation continued to bring issues of purity and emphasis on racial homogeny to the forefront. These issues continue to manifest themselves in different ways: explicit parental distrust of marrying foreigners, resistance over adoption, negative attitudes toward mixed-race children, renaming of lexical items, insistence on domestic rice—all stemming from a sometimes-illogical commitment to nationalism and ethnic purity.

Second, Korean American repatriation comes after a much more long-term displacement. Fitting for discussion of a repatriate theology in Ezra-Nehemiah, some studies focus on the experience of second-generation peoples on return to their country of origin (Mandel 2008; Christou 2015; for a recent Korean American repatriation perspective, see Kim 2008). Not surprisingly, many of these repatriates have great hope at their return but often are shocked to find a very different place. Still others are disappointed that their homes remained static and did not change at all. Oftentimes, such returns result in conflict with original peoples. For others, repatriation does not close the migration loop, as further disenchantment leads to additional migration. Many second-generation repatriates arrive in Korea with cultural ties more tuned to America. Most have limited Korean language skills. Because of the long period of expatriation, Korea has changed dramatically since the family of origin's period. During the 1960s, when my parents emigrated from Korea to the United States, Korea had an economy comparable to poorer Asian and African countries. By 2014 it had become the world's thirteenth-largest economy, according to the 2014 Gross Domestic Product.

Associated with this long-term repatriation is the voluntary nature of the migration. Despite Cyrus's magnanimous edict, some of the diaspora Judeans freely chose to remain in their new countries. Similarly, the movement of Korean Americans back to Korea is almost always voluntary

Unsettled Homecomings: A Repatriate Reading of Ezra-Nehemiah   247

and not life dependent. These Korean Americans return with social capital from their roots and try to form their place in a very different land. There are many divergences between the Korean American and the Judean returnee, but these points of contact encourage a dialogical investigation of those repatriate journeys.

The Korean American repatriation is merely one example across the world. Yet within such diversity of repatriate experiences, it is striking to observe broad commonalities that all of these disparate experiences share. Whether the repatriation is in the East or the West, whether after forty-seven weeks or even forty-seven years, whether the repatriates are self-perceived as rich or poor, or whether coerced politically or voluntary, repatriates share a common experience. The period of expatriation changes both the migrant and the mother country, sometimes in extreme ways. If such commonality can expand across social scientific studies of repatriation, then I suggest that these modern repatriate experiences may integrate our experiences as minoritized critics in a way that centers on the repatriate experience in biblical texts.

A Repatriate Reading of Ezra-Nehemiah

A full repatriate reading of Ezra-Nehemiah cannot be done here and will be reserved for a future work. However, I will briefly offer how a repatriate lens can enhance an imaginative reading behind some of these texts. Of course, the Judean repatriation heavily influenced much of the Hebrew Bible, especially books such as Chronicles, Esther, Ruth, and Daniel. I wish to focus on four themes that emerge in Ezra-Nehemiah, as they explicitly focus on the return to and resettling in Judah. These themes are neither exclusive nor comprehensive of the theology within Ezra-Nehemiah, but they may capture the repatriate experience as contained in the biblical texts as well as parallel migrations of today. A repatriate theology can provide a framework to allow us to articulate the uniqueness of our repatriate experiences with one another and with the experience of the Judean returnees as portrayed in Ezra-Nehemiah. Such a dialogue can serve the stated mandate of minoritized criticism.

Trauma

Although the exile experience has driven much of the scholarship of trauma in biblical texts, social-displacement theories suggest that the repa-

248 Roger S. Nam

triation event was similarly traumatic. (On trauma studies, see Carr 2014; O'Connor 2001; Smith-Christopher 2002.) Repatriates often hold a utopian vision of a return. Yet, multigenerational returns to a homeland reveal the brokenness of such utopian visions. Instead of belonging and security, repatriates often face immediate crises, both pragmatic, such as economic hardship, and existential, such as questioned identity. Such confrontation between perception and lived reality generates trauma in the repatriation.

Cathy Caruth (1995, 151) describes trauma as an event and continuing memory, which "registers the force of an experience that is not yet fully owned." In this regard, Ezra-Nehemiah forms a type of trauma literature, as articulated by Caruth, which calls for both recognition and continued expression of the traumatic event. Whereas Chronicles and much of the prophetic literature present the return to Jerusalem as the triumphant restoration of Israel, in Ezra-Nehemiah the returnees meet immediate conflict, and their hopeful return quickly digresses into an unsettled homecoming.

Ezra shatters the optimism of the Cyrus edict (Ezra 1:1–4) with reports of verbal and political struggles with surrounding adversaries. In the Nehemiah memoir, the trauma of repatriation figures prominently at the outset, with the battered state of the city walls and gates (1:3) leading to Nehemiah's response of weeping, fasting, and penitential prayer (1:4–11). The rest of Ezra-Nehemiah follows a similar movement of crisis in the midst of the struggle to reestablish religious practices. This paradoxical movement of trauma throughout restoration is particularly evident in divergent responses to the completion of the temple, as most of the people respond with joyful praise, but the older ones "wept with a loud noise" (Ezra 3:12). This remembrance of the earlier temple stymies the celebration with overtones of nostalgic longing for the past glories of the monarchic era.

Power

Like all social displacements, repatriation necessitates adjustments to new positions of power. As a starting point, repatriation can use Hannah Arendt's (1969, 43) definition of power, which draws on classical Weberian notions of domination but also recognizes how the actions of a community can negotiate power in subversive ways. This understanding of power works well for Ezra-Nehemiah, as the community navigates power relations with both the local groups who stayed in the land and the Persian overlords. However, whereas Ezra-Nehemiah recognizes their subservience to the Persian overlords, the texts clearly present the muted yet pervasive power of God as ultimately authoritative, as evident from the opening verse in which the "LORD moves the heart of Cyrus, king of Persia" (Ezra 1:1). Throughout the narrative, Judeans subversively negotiate their place within the empire through local and imperial instruments of power, namely, taxation and textuality.

Ezra-Nehemiah generally gives a positive portrayal of taxation, in that it supports the temple and those who service its cultic practices (Ezra 6:3–10, 7:15–24; Neh 10:32–39, 13:10–14). By pledging continued tribute, the returnees demonstrate their loyalty to the Persian leaders, who replaced the defunct Davidic line. This loyalty empowers the returnees against their adversaries, resulting in the completion of the temple and the city walls, two tangible expressions of restoration.

In addition to taxation, Ezra-Nehemiah prominently features the role of textuality, another instrument of ancient Near Eastern power, which is adopted by the returnees to leverage their own authority. Written texts form the major blocks of Ezra-Nehemiah. The two nearly identical lists of returnees (Ezra 2:1–70; Neh 7:6–72) surround the activities of rebuilding the temple and the wall. Ezra-Nehemiah employs code switching to Imperial Aramaic in integrating the royal epistles to navigate the conflict between the returnees against the various adversaries. Ezra-Nehemiah presents written Torah as divinely authoritative even against imperial taxation in Neh 5:1–13 (see Frei 2006 and rebuttal by Ska 2006). The public reading of the text spurs reconstruction of the temple and repair of the wall. Even the physical scroll features prominently in the dedicatory ceremony (Neh 8:5). Although Ezra-Nehemiah accepts colonized status for the Judeans, the strategic adoption of taxation and textuality, along with their respective reformulation for the Judean interests, brings power to the *golah* against their adversaries.

Identity

The repatriate struggle within the Persian orbit of power propels new expressions of their identity, a crucial marker for Ezra-Nehemiah, as evidenced by the flurry of recent scholarship on Second Temple identity (notably Ahn 2011 uses migration studies; see also Becking 2011; Jonkers 2011; Knoppers and Ristau 2009). One foundational aspect of this repatriate self-understanding is terms that the repatriates use to refer to themselves. Richard Jenkins (2008, 4) provides a suitable understanding of identity as "ways in which groups and individuals define themselves and are defined by others on the basis of race, religion, ethnicity, language, and culture." This definition emphasizes differentiation, a crucial part of the identity negotiation in the repatriation of Ezra-Nehemiah.

Throughout interpretive history, non-Jewish communities have failed to recognize the repatriate context of identity in Ezra-Nehemiah, resulting in mischaracterizations of exclusionism and xenophobia. The Judeans, as a subjected group within the Persian Empire, face a real danger of ethnic extinction from assimilation. The wide diaspora from multiple exiles and contention with local groups make identity formation immensely crucial for the *golah*. Consequently, Ezra-Nehemiah constructs an identity based on the community's own chosen standing before God, sustained through the exile experience.

The shared exile forces a binary view of identity, isolating Judeans against all other local groups. The text primarily refers to the returnees as the "children of exile" (Ezra 4:1; 6:19; 8:35; 10:6, 16) or "the exile" (1:11; 9:4; 10:6, 8). Other exclusive labels are also used: the "holy seed" (9:2), the "remnant" (9:13–15; Neh 1:3), "assembly of the exile" (Ezra 10:8), "return-ees of exile" (Neh 7:6), and "assembly of God" (Neh 13:1). These terms of self-identity contrast against competing groups, such as the now-maligned "people of the land" (Ezra 4:4; 9:1, 2, 11; 10:11; Neh 9:10, 24, 10:30). Further-more, Ezra-Nehemiah omits any mention of the diaspora Judeans in Egypt (see Elephantine Papyri; Jer 44:26–27).

The multiple census lists rigidly define this strict identity by naming the returnees (Ezra 2; Neh 7), as well as the constructors of the wall (Neh 3:1–32), the signatories of the pact (10:1–28), resettlers (Neh 11), and priests and Levites (12:1–26). The Jerusalem wall has a similar function of identity demarcation, but the exclusivity is more pronounced, with a phys-ical barrier that separates the *golah* from the rest of the world (Oeming 2012). The Levitical prayer of Neh 9 shapes the internal character of this repatriate identity, moving beyond mere separation to Torah obedience and exclusive worship through a fiercely monotheistic view of YHWH.

Hope

Within the successive generations of repatriation, the *golah* communities face trauma, power struggle, and continued quests for identity. Despite these difficulties, the very movement of repatriation implies an under-lying hope, that a difficult journey will culminate in the fulfillment of a better existence. Ezra-Nehemiah expresses such hope in different forms

Unsettled Homecomings: A Repatriate Reading of Ezra-Nehemiah 251

throughout the narrative. At strategic points, hope comes in the form of the Persian rulers, who act favorably to the returnees (Ezra 1:1–14, 6:3–12). In other places, the object of hope moves to YHWH through penitential prayers (Ezra 9:6–15; Neh 1:5–11, 9:5–37), which unabashedly express struggle but end in confidence in divine restoration. The weaving themes of trauma, power, and identity necessitate dependence on God to bring hope to the *golah* in the midst of their repatriation struggles. The Nehemiah memoir closes in turmoil. In the midst of proclamations of joy, the last chapter of Ezra-Nehemiah speaks of the ongoing issues of mixed marriages, discord, the need for Levites to work, Sabbath violation, and continuous encroachment from foreigner. Yet, the book still closes with the hopeful plea to "Remember me, my God, for good" (Neh 13:31).

Conclusions: Still Far from Home

These themes of trauma, power, identity, and hope emerge in the rich repatriate experiences of both the Judean returnees and the Korean diaspora. The social reality creates an opportunity for those who find themselves in repatriate spaces to provide readings for the distinct community who returned to Judea under the Persian Empire. These readings emphasize the crucial aspect of negotiating identity across borders and emerging with new, complex understandings of self. As with my child, this understanding arises most explicitly when confronted with a new social context.

Is he Korean? Is he American? How do we address a child who is, at least for a moment, navigating his own identity? Perhaps the repatriation experience contributes to our parenting strategy. The question, raw and honest, from the voice of child was filled with complexity. The innocence of the child refracted a complex cultural experience of a Korean American child, born in Los Angeles, moved to Lake Oswego, Oregon, then repatriated back to Korea. Of course, his question was not simple to answer. As his parents, we turned back to the child as a fallback strategy, perhaps to mask our own lack of confidence in addressing the question:

"What do you think?"
He answered, "I think that I am both Korean *and* American" (emphasis exaggerated, as befitting a six-year-old child).
"You are absolutely right," I replied.

And he is.

Works Cited

Ahn, John. 2011. *Exile as Forced Migrations: A Sociological, Literary and Historical Approach on the Displacement and Resettlement of the Southern Kingdom of Judah*. BZAW 417. Berlin: de Gruyter.

Arendt, Hannah. 1969. *On Violence*. New York: Harcourt, Brace & World.

Assmann, Jan. 1992. *Das kulturelle Gedächtnis. Schrift, Erinnerung und politische Identität in frühen Hochkulturen*. Munich: Beck.

Association of Theological Schools. N.d. "Racial Ethnic Students Represent Largest Growth Area for Theological Schools." https://tinyurl.com/SBL06106c6.

Barton, John. 1998. "Historical-Critical Approaches." Pages 9–20 in *The Cambridge Companion to Biblical Interpretation*. Edited by John Barton. Cambridge: Cambridge University Press.

Bartram, David, Maritsa Poros, and Pierre Monforte. 2014. *Key Concepts in Migration*. London: Sage.

Becking, Bob. 2011. *Ezra, Nehemiah, and the Construction of Early Jewish Identity*. Tübingen: Mohr Siebeck.

Breed, Brennan. 2012. "Nomadology of the Bible: A Processual Approach to Biblical Reception History." *BibRec* 1:299–322.

———. 2014. *Nomadic Texts: A Theory of Biblical Reception History*. Bloomington: Indiana University Press.

———. 2015. "What Can Texts Do? A Proposal for Biblical Studies." At This Point. https://tinyurl.com/SBL06106c7.

Carr, David M. 2014. *Holy Resilience: The Bible's Traumatic Origins*. New Haven: Yale University Press.

Caruth, Cathy. 1995. *Trauma: Explorations in Memory*. Baltimore: Johns Hopkins University Press.

Cerase, Fernando. 1974. "Expectations and Reality: A Case Study of Return Migration from the United States to Southern Italy." *IMR* 8:245–62.

Chalcraft, David J., Frauke Uhlenbruch, and Rebecca Watson, eds. 2014. *Methods, Theories, Imagination: Social Scientific Approaches in Biblical Studies*. Sheffield: Sheffield Academic.

Christou, Anastasia. 2015. *Counter-diaspora: The Greek Second Generation Returns "Home."* Cambridge: Harvard University Press.

Collins, John. 2005. *The Bible after Babel: Historical Criticism in a Postmodern Age*. Grand Rapids: Eerdmans.

Davies, Phillip. 2008. *Memories of Ancient Israel: An Introduction to Biblical History*. Louisville: Westminster John Knox.

Douglass, Frederick. 1845. *Narrative of the Life of Frederick Douglass, an American Slave, Written by Himself.* Boston: Anti Slavery Office.

Drescher, Hans-Georg. 1993. *Ernst Troeltsch: His Life and Work.* Minneapolis: Fortress.

Edelman, Diana V., and Ehud Ben Zvi, eds. 2013. *Remembering Biblical Figures in the Late Persian and Early Hellenistic Period.* Oxford: Oxford University Press.

———. 2014. *Memory in the City in Ancient Israel.* Winona Lake, IN: Eisenbrauns.

Felder, Cain Hope, ed. 1991. *Stony the Road We Trod: African American Biblical Interpretation.* Minneapolis: Fortress.

Foner, Nancy, Ruben G. Rumbaut, and Steven J. Gold, eds. 2003. *Immigration and Immigration Research for a New Century: Multidisciplinary Perspectives.* New York: Russell Sage Foundation.

Frei, Peter. 2006. "Persian Imperial Authorization of the Pentateuch." Pages 4–50 in *Persia and Torah: The Theory of Imperial Organization of the Pentateuch.* Edited by James W. Watts. SymS 17. Atlanta: Society of Biblical Literature.

Gmelc, George. 1980. "Return Migration." *Annual Review of Anthropology* 9:135–59.

Jenkins, Richard. 2008. *Social Identity.* 3rd ed. London: Routledge.

Jonkers, Louis. 2011. *Texts, Contexts and Readings in Postexilic Literature Explorations into Historiography and Identity Negotiation in Hebrew Bible and Related Texts.* FAT 2/53. Tübingen: Mohr Siebeck.

Khoser, Khalid. 2000. "Return, Readmission and Reintegration: Changing Agendas, Policy Frameworks and Operational Programmes." Pages 57–99 in *Return Migration: Journey of Hope or Despair?* Edited by Bimal Ghosh. Geneva: International Organization for Migration.

Kim, Nadia Y. 2008. *Imperial Citizens: Koreans and Race from Seoul to LA.* Stanford, CA: Stanford University Press.

Knoppers, Gary, and Kenneth A. Ristau, eds. 2009. *Community Identity in Judean Historiography: Biblical and Comparative Perspectives.* Winona Lake, IN: Eisenbrauns.

Legaspi, Michael. 2010. *The Death of Scripture and the Rise of Biblical Studies.* Oxford: Oxford University Press.

Liew, Tat-siong Benny. 2008. *What Is Asian American Biblical Hermeneutics? Reading the New Testament.* Honolulu: University of Hawai'i Press.

Mandel, Ruth. 2008. *Cosmopolitan Anxieties: Turkish Challenges to Citizenship and Belonging in Germany*. Durham, NC: Duke University Press.

Nam, Roger. 2012. *Portrayals of Economic Exchange in the Book of Kings*. BibInt 112. Leiden: Brill.

O'Connor, Kathleen. 2011. *Jeremiah: Pain and Promise*. Minneapolis: Fortress.

Oeming, Manfred. 2012. "The Real History: Theological Ideal behind Nehemiah's Wall." Pages 131–50 in *New Perspectives on Ezra-Nehemiah: History, Historiography, Text, Literature, and Interpretation*. Edited by Isaac Kalimi. Winona Lake, IN: Eisenbrauns.

Piore, Michael J. 1979. *Birds of Passage: Migrant Labor and Industrial Societies*. Cambridge: Cambridge University Press.

Rhodes, Robert, ed. 1979. *The Anthropology of Return Migration*. Norman: University of Oklahoma Press.

Rumbaut, Ruben. 2003. "Immigration Research in the United States: Social Origins and Future Orientations." Pages 23–43 in *Immigration Research for a New Century: Multidisciplinary Perspectives*. Edited Nancy Foner, Ruben G. Rumbaut, and Steven J. Gold. New York: Russell Sage Foundation.

Said, Edward. 1996. *Representations of the Intellectual: The 1993 Roth Lectures*. Reprint, New York: Vintage Books.

Scheffer, Gabriel. 2006. *Diaspora Politics: At Home Abroad*. Cambridge: Cambridge University Press.

Segovia, Fernando. 2009. "Towards Minority Biblical Criticism: A Reflection on the Achievements and Lacunae." Pages 365–94 in *They Were All Together in One Place? Toward Minority Biblical Criticism*. Edited by Randall C. Bailey, Tat-siong Benny Liew, and Fernando F. Segovia. SemeiaSt 57. Atlanta: Society of Biblical Literature.

———. 2015. "Criticism in Critical Times: Reflections on Vision and Task." *JBL* 134:6–29.

Shin, Gi-Wook. 2006. *Ethnic Nationalism in Korea: Genealogy, Politics, and Legacy*. Stanford, CA: Stanford University Press.

Ska, Jean-Louise. 2006. "'Persian Imperial Authorization': Some Question Marks." Pages 161–82 in *Persia and Torah: The Theory of Imperial Organization of the Pentateuch*. Edited by James W. Watts. SymS 17. Atlanta: Society of Biblical Literature.

Smith-Christopher, Daniel. 2002. *A Biblical Theology of Exile*. Minneapolis: Fortress.

Troeltsch, Ernst. 1991. *Religion in History*. Translated by James Luther Adams and Walter F. Bense. Edinburgh: T&T Clark.

Wimbush, Vincent L. 2011. "Interpreters—Enslaving/Enslaved/Runagate." *JBL* 130:5–24.

Zerubavel, Yael. 1995. *Recovered Roots: Collective Memory and the Making of Israeli National Tradition*. Chicago: University of Chicago Press.

Négritude and Minoritized Criticism: A Senegalese Perspective

Aliou Cissé Niang

In what circumstances did Aimé Césaire and I launch the word negritude in the years 1933–35? Together with a few other black students, we were at the time in a panic-stricken despair. The horizon was blocked. No reform in sight and the colonizers were legitimizing our political and economic dependence by the theory of *tabula rasa*. They deemed we had invented nothing, created nothing, written, sculpted, painted and sung nothing.... To establish an effective revolution, *our* revolution, we first had to get rid of our borrowed attire—that of assimilation—and assert our being, namely our negritude. (Senghor 1959, 14)

Il faut le leur demander; il faut aller apprendre chez eux l'art de vaincre sans avoir raison [We must ask them; we must go to learn from them the art of conquering without being in the right]. (Kane 1962, 37)

For this project on minoritized critics, I will build on the ideas of one of the pioneers of the Négritude movement, Léopold Sédar Senghor. His influence has shaped me from my native country of Senegal, West Africa, to the United States, where I have lived for several decades and now live and teach as a Senegalese, transnational biblical scholar. In undergraduate through PhD studies, I was trained and fully immersed in the kind of interpretation of the Bible that has little to do with my Senegalese context, let alone my transnational status. I started to build on some dimensions of Négritude as a resident PhD candidate in 2000 while coteaching a Post-

---

Part of this essay appeared previously in my "Senghorian Negritude and Postcolonial Biblical Criticism" in *Life under the Baobab Tree*, ed. Kenneth N. Ngwa, Aliou Cissé Niang, and Arthur Pressley (New York: Fordham University Press, 2023), 126–69. I thank Fordham University Press for granting me the permission for reuse.

-257-

258   Aliou Cissé Niang

colonial Biblical Theology seminar with Professor Leo G. Perdue at Brite Divinity School, Texas Christian University. My presentations became my first published book-essay on the importance of geography and resistance in colonial Senegal (Niang 2005, 319–29).

Earlier in my education, in Senegal, I was always intrigued by how some of the Senegalese leaders managed to arise from the colonial shambles that had nearly obliterated Senegalese culture and faith traditions to lead the country to independence. Little that I knew, it was a daring, existential journey with deep spiritual, intellectual, political, and sociocultural dimensions. The above epigraphs illustrate aspects of this journey—a "strange dawn" and "panic-stricken despair." The former happened in Senegal to Samba Diallo (fictionalized Cheikh Hamidou Kane himself, as well as his Diallobé and Senegalese people), and the latter in metropolitan France (with Senegalese colonial antecedents) to Senghor and his fellow West Indian student immigrants.

The "strange dawn" of the French colonial occupation and Senegalese responses to it shaped the autobiography of Cheikh Hamidou Kane—a riveting story that tells of the dehumanizing effect of the French colonial occupation, chillingly framed not only as a Senegalese Diallobé experience but as an African one as well. Kane chronicles a chilling feeling of defeat tempered with hope on the part of conquered Senegalese people, which became the impetus for a quest for effective and liberating answers to the then-prevailing colonial occupation. This was led by *la Grande Royale*, "The Most Royal Lady," of the Diallobé, who, along with the main character, Samba Diallo, made a radical decision: "We must ask them; we must go to learn from them the art of conquering without being in the right," she states.

With these words she influences her community members to send one of their finest Muslim students of the Qur'an, Diallo, to learn this "art of conquering without being in the right" or "to join wood to wood." To learn this so-called art, one had to attend the "new school," the colonial school— the most potent tool for turning colonized Senegalese people into French (Kane 1962, 9). The decision to send Diallo to France stakes the survival and future of Senegal (and African) culture on immigrant(s), like Kane himself, and like others such as Senghor, the architect of the Négritude movement. The lived experiences of colonization associated with the process of learning this art gave rise to Négritude.

bell hooks (1990, 145–53) and Jung Young Lee (1995, 42–53) observe that marginalized persons can and often do succeed in negotiating and

Négritude and Minoritized Criticism 259

creatively engaging their socially assigned space (permeated by distasteful lived experiences of alienation) and resiliently reinventing it into a site of endless possibilities for socioeconomic, political, and religious freedom. This is the kind of delicate location or space Négritude created. It is from this lens that I am arguing that the concept of Négritude as articulated by Senghor is not just a trope for defending African culture but a poetics of postcolonial biblical criticism, born in the diaspora to reposition and humanize people displaced by French colonization.

To reposition is a two-dimensional task, to "liberate" and "rehabilitate," that is, to free the colonized from French cultural domination and to reclaim some African cultural values displaced by colonization (Senghor 1964a, 417). The expediency with which the colonized sought to learn from the colonizer's ways gave rise to Négritude as a trope that helped immigrant students reposition and free themselves. I begin with a concise statement about three immigrant theorists—Edward Said, Homi Bhabha, and Gayatri C. Spivak—who are often mentioned in postcolonial biblical studies, and then move to Senghorian Négritude as more than a repositioning trope, as a poetics of postcolonial biblical criticism—the art of conquering with being in the right.

Négritude and Postcolonial Theory

I begin with Said's influential contribution. Orientalism, he tells us, is a Western, hegemonic historiography—an ideological discourse that presents itself as an epistemologically powerful, superior, and normative center that frames the margins as weak and vanquished, inferior, voiceless, and uncivilized. He engages this domineering geopolitical discourse in order to create an alternative space for marginalized people to be free and creatively imagine and emancipate themselves (Said 1979, 4–8, 329–52). Taken up with the same cause, Bhabha (1990b, 209) states, "I try to place myself in that position of liminality, in that productive space of the construction of culture as difference, in the spirit of alterity or otherness." Here, too, I find Bhabha (1990a, 75) engaged in the construction of "space for a subject peoples." The liminal space of which he speaks is "a hybrid," "third space," or simply a space that "gives rise to something different, something new ... a new area of recognition of meaning and representation" (Bhabha 1990b, 211). That is, "the affective experience of social marginality," where the oppressed can speak (Bhabha 1994, 246). Spivak also finds the margins crucial. She asserts, "I find the demand on

260 Aliou Cissé Niang

me to be marginal always assuming.... I am tired of dining out on being an exile because that has been a long tradition and it is not one I want to identify myself with" (Spivak 1990, 40–41). This awareness empowered her "radical acceptance of vulnerability" in order to deconstruct and make marginality a space for inclusion. Said, Bhabha, and Spivak find liminality to be a dynamic space teeming with new possibilities for repositioning.

Senghorian Négritude, like that of Léon-Gontran Damas and Aimé Césaire, includes dimensions of his former immigrant status in France (see Rabaka 2010, 2015). The writings of novelists Cheikh Hamidou Kane and Ousmane Sembène are infused with autobiographical elements that hinged on their lived experiences, as they were among the first Senegalese people to immigrate to France to acquire an education (see Gadjigo 2007; Busch and Annas 2008; Kane 1962, 1997). In fact, most of them became leaders who played a significant role in pre- and postindependence Senegal and charted much of the country's future. Since the first time I set foot in the United States, I soon learned that Senghorian Négritude is virtually absent in biblical studies, except in English and French departments.

Senghorian Négritude and Minoritized Criticism

Senghor was born in 1906 to Basile Diogoye Senghor—an African traditionalist, a Christian, and a successful trader—in a Sérère village, Joal-Djilor/Dyiloôr, located in the then-protectorate about eight miles from Dakar, Senegal, West Africa (Vaillant 1990, 12).[1] There, Senghor was shaped by his Sérère culture and faith traditions—an experience that was altered as soon as he arrived and entered the French colonial school. He was among the first generation of converts to Christianity who attended the French school taught by Catholic missionaries in Joal, Ngasobil, and later by seminarians of Father Francis Libermann College in Dakar.

As a boy, Senghor questioned the missionaries' version of Christianity and began to work out a fusion between his inherited Sérère faith traditions with his newfound Christian faith. As a subject living in the protectorate instead of a citizen of the so-called Four Towns, Senghor had

---

1. The protectorate *indigénat* is the location where those considered subjects and uncivilized live as opposed to the so-called *évolués*, "civilized or evolved," those living in the Four Colonial Towns or *Quatres Communes*—Saint-Louis, Dakar, Gorée, and Rufisque. It was in these towns that French colonists introduced the assimilation policy from 1887–1960.

to prove himself by learning what Cheikh Hamidou Kane characterizes as the "art of conquering without being in the right."

Senghor's education took him all the way to Metropolitan France, where he excelled in the French language and became a teacher and poet, president of Senegal from 1960 to 1980, and inductee to the prestigious l'Académie Française from 1983–2001. The Passerelle Solférino was renamed in 2006 by the French government as "Passerelle Léopold Sédar Senghor."

Previously known as the Passerelle Solférino, this footbridge was renamed in 2006 in memory of Léopold Sédar Senghor for the crucial role he played as poet, co-founder of the Négritude Movement, politician, and president of Senegal from 1960 to 1980, when he voluntarily relinquished his presidency. The footbridge is over the Seine River and connects the Museum d'Orsay and the Tuileries Gardens. Courtesy of David Lee Balch.

To my knowledge, Senghor was the first African to earn his *agrégation*, a rigorous degree in grammar equivalent to a PhD, in 1935, which helped him research the languages of his native Senegal (Vaillant 1990, 88). He was respected by his colleagues, critics, and supporters alike for his faithful church attendance in France, his demeanor, and his firm commitment to his studies (70–71). To my surprise, in spite of the renewed interest in Césairian and Senghorian Négritude, little if anything is said about Senghor's work in current postcolonial biblical criticism (Diagne 2011; Wilder 2005, 2015). What one often reads about are critical objections to Senghorian Négritude in particular, which I will address later. When he is mentioned, it is often in fleeting, negative remarks to appropriate something about Césaire (1972, 86, 94) or, mostly, Frantz Fanon, whose work he influenced, to say the least.

The place of Senghor's work in postcolonial discourse began with his own words. He writes:

> In what circumstances did Aimé Césaire and I launch the word negritude in the years 1933–35? Together with a few other black students, we were at the time in a panic-stricken despair. The horizon was blocked. No reform in sight and the colonizers were legitimizing our political and economic dependence by the theory of *tabula rasa*. They deemed we had invented nothing, created nothing, written, sculpted, painted and sung nothing.... To establish an effective revolution, *our* revolution, we first had to get rid of our borrowed attire—that of assimilation—and assert our being, namely our negritude. Nevertheless, negritude, even when defined as "the total of black Africa's cultural values" could only offer us the beginning of a solution to our problem and not the solution itself. We could not go back to our former condition, to a negritude of the sources.... To be really ourselves, we had to embody Negro African culture in twentieth-century realities. To enable our negritude to be, instead of a museum piece, the efficient instrument of liberation, it was necessary to cleanse it of its dross and include it in the united movement of the contemporary world. (Senghor 1959, 14; see also Kesteloot 1963, 80; Bâ 1972, 12)

By saying "we had to divest ourselves of our borrowed attire—that of assimilation—and assert our being," Senghor means the conundrum of identity and ethics engendered by the policy of assimilation that gave rise to Négritude. This marked the inception of the self-decolonizing or deassimilating process that I term *repositioning*.

In the 1943 bulletin *L'Étudient de la France d'Outre-mer: Chronique des Foyers*, designed to help immigrant students who were yearning to relearn

Négritude and Minoritized Criticism   263

and reposition themselves back in the civilization they left too soon, an immigrant student characterized his lived experience in France as a person "in transition mentally a hybrid. Neither native, since his French education has made him so different from his ancestors, nor European, since he has been brought up elsewhere" (quoted in Vaillant 1990, 181).[2] Senghor, according to Vaillant (1990, 128, see also 128–46), found in this liminal space an opportunity

> to integrate in himself the best of both worlds and be comfortable in both. He understood that this would be impossible without the reevaluation and acceptance of the core values of the Africa of his childhood. This was part of his basic identity, the remnants of his childhood that must be preserved. It would require the creation of a new person with a new voice. The voice would be neither French nor African, for the man was neither French nor African. It would be that of a new historical personage, the French Negro.[3]

To characterize Senghor as a person who was "neither French nor African," as Vaillant does, is to overlook his stern warning to African leaders against the temptation to abandon their preindependence, traditional African values, which he believed were indispensable for national inspiration. He writes:

> What are the Negro people doing, what would they do, with their newfound freedom? It is evident that freedom without consciousness is worse than slavery. The slave at least is conscious of his own slavery. We too often forget that cultural imperialism is the most dangerous form of colonialism; it deadens consciousness. The most striking thing about the Negro peoples who have been promoted to autonomy or independence is precisely the *lack of consciousness* of most of their chiefs and their disparagement of Negro-African cultural values. They are proud of the political freedom of their people, but they do not realize that true

---

2. Prior to Bhabha's use of this term, the idea of hybridity had already been used by this anonymous author, who could have well been Senghor, Césaire, or Damas.

3. The language of "new person" echoes Harlem Renaissance voices of the "new Negro." In fact, many American leaders of the Harlem Renaissance were very much conversant with the pioneers of Négritude, and some participated in the first 1956 conference in Paris, which featured Richard Wright, Fanon, and Césaire. They spoke life through poems by evoking their distasteful lived experiences. On the Harlem renaissance, see Locke 1997.

264   Aliou Cissé Niang

freedom is not of the body but of the mind. And we see them importing
just as they stand the political and social institutions of Europe, and even
their cultural institutions. (Senghor 1959, 290)

The chilling condition the anonymous immigrant student described above
reflects the deep introspective journey the "three Mousquetaires"—as Senghor (1979, 11) called himself, Césaire, and Damas—started. They had to
deassimilate or *decolonize* their hybridized mind in order to reposition and
rehabilitate themselves (Thiong'O 1981). To me, this is what Kane (1962,
34) means by the necessity for the colonized to acquire "the art of conquering without being in the right."

Senghor was determined to reclaim the once-objectified "whole complex of civilized values—cultural, economic, social and political which
characterize the black peoples, or, more precisely, the negro-African
World" (1962, 54–55). At the same time, he also recognized that Négritude was a work of many hands, a "WE" and not an "I," symbolically
publicized in his *Anthologie de la Nouvelle Poèsie Nègre et Malgache de
Langue Française* (Senghor 1948). Jean-Paul Sartre (1948, ix) recognized
its collaborative weight and thought it worthy to share its content with his
compatriots:

> What were you hoping for when you removed the gag that was keeping
> these black mouths shut? That they would sing your praises? Did you
> think that when they raised themselves up again, you would read adoration in the eyes of these heads that our fathers had forced to bend down
> to the very ground? Here are black men standing, looking at us, and I
> hope that you, like me, will feel the shock of being seen. For three thousand years, the white man has enjoyed the privilege of seeing without
> being seen. It was seeing pure and uncomplicated; the light of his eyes
> drew all things from their primeval darkness. The whiteness of his skin
> was a further aspect of vision, a light condensed.... Today, these black
> men are looking at us, and our gaze comes back to our own eyes; in their
> turn, black torches light up the world and our white heads are no more
> than Chinese lanterns swinging in the wind....
>
> If we want to crack open this finitude which imprisons us, we can no
> longer rely on the privileges of our race, of our color, of our technics: we
> will not be able to become a part of the totality from which those black eyes
> exile us, unless we tear off our white tights in order to try simply to be men.

While Sartre (xiv) further reduced Négritude to a self-annihilating *antiracist racist* reaction, some critics characterized it as a mere cultural essentialism or simply an outdated trope (Mphahlele 1974, 67; Soyinka 1976, 134; Depestre 1980).[4] Reiland Rabaka (2010, 178) recently charged Senghor with having invented not an "African essence" but

> a roguish regurgitation of white supremacist colonial antiblack racism by another name: "Negritude" or "Africanity." Critical readers are quick to query: how does Senghor "invent" an "authentic" African essence? Quite simply, he inverts Eurocentric negative descriptions and explanations of Africa and Africans, reinscribes them, and then re-presents them as Afrocentric, positive evidence of an ontological difference in and for black-being-in-the-world. Senghor cannot comprehend that these descriptions are invariably situated within the contours of the Eurocentric prison house, which constantly conceptually incarcerates and (re) colonizes non-European cultures and civilizations, because European culture and civilization is always and ever the model and measure of "true" human culture and civilization.

All these critics failed to see that Négritude was the way in which Senghor and his West Indies friends repositioned themselves to reclaim their African culture, which was once objectified by imperial France. It was a journey to freedom—a space to reembrace Black culture as something good and worth celebrating.

Sartre's point may be clever, but it is problematic, not only to Fanon (1967, 135), who thought it was destructive to the "black zeal," but more so to Senghor (1964a, 316–17, my translation), who, in a speech delivered at the Sorbonne, responded (in a diplomatic tone and acumen, as was his practice):

> What then is this NEGRITUDE that scares the delicate, that was presented to you as a new racism? It is in French that it was first expressed, sung and danced. This alone should reassure you. How would you like us to become racist, we who have been for centuries, innocent victims, black hosts of racism? Jean-Paul Sartre was not quite right when, in "Black Orpheus," he defines negritude "racism antiracist"; he is surely right when he presents it as a certain emotional attitude to the world.

---

4. Said (1993, 275–79) surprisingly mischaracterizes Négritude as nativism, failing to take seriously both the humanism (discussed in detail in Senghor 1964a) and the persistent advocacy for *la civilization de l'universel*, "universal civilization," of Senghor (dealt with extensively in Senghor 1977).

What, then, does this have to do with minoritized criticism and biblical interpretation? To answer, I return to Kane's intriguing advice, "We must ask them; we must go to learn from them the art of conquering without being in the right." This is a quest that requires a journey—an exile to Metropolitan France to find answers to the overwhelming colonial occupation. To go is daring, because of the potential risk that the immigrant might forget their roots. To the chief, another pivotal character in Kane's (1962, 34) novel, sending their children is a double-edged sword, as they "would learn all the ways of joining wood to wood … they would also forget. What they forget is themselves, their bodies, and the futile dream which hardens with age and stifles the spirit. So what they learn is worth infinitely more than what they forget." Thirty-four years later, Kane's (1997, 48–49, 51–54; compare with Kane 1962, 34, 45–47) *Les gardiens du temple*, a sequel to *Ambiguous Adventure*, confirmed that learning Western ways may indeed lead to forgetting one's roots but does not preclude or inhibit one's capacity to relearn that which has been forgotten.

As I noted earlier, Senghor, Kane, and a handful of Senegalese intellectuals took that risk, especially Senghor and Kane, whose education confirms the words of the Most Royal Lady. To leave home for Metropolitan France after proving oneself in French education at home was quintessential (Kane 2011; Thomas 2007). Senghor and his peers were immigrants but were not transnationals in the real sense of the word. To be sure, transnationals are migrants who leave their native countries for a host of reasons, one of which might be the pursuit of an education to improve one's living conditions. Some migrants are forced by natural drought, famine, or war. Alexandro Portes (1999, 36–48) describes this way of being as the ability to "frequently maintain homes in two countries, [and to] pursue economic, political and cultural interests that require their presence in both." Speaking of Senegalese emigration to Italy and other parts of Europe, Fedora Gasparetti (2011, 217) writes, "Senegalese migrants provide an excellent example of transnational migration: these transmigrants shape new transnational spaces through their movement, maintaining connections, building institutions, conducting transactions and influencing local and national events in the countries from which they emigrated."

A crucial dimension of many Senegalese transnationals now living in the United States is ubiquity—that is, according to Ousmane Kane (2011, 244–45), the ability to be "'here and there' … to travel back and forth from one country to the other." Most African Americans, such as Richard Wright and Langston Hughes, and the pioneers of Négritude who migrated to Europe were said to have earned a reputation as "good Blacks" mainly because of their intellectual acumen, and thus made the French empire look good (see Fabre 1991, 1–8; Kane 2011, 237–44). In spite of Wright's supposed ambivalent and at times derogatory views toward Africans, which some critics noted, he joined some pan-African and Negritude intellectuals such as Senghor and Alioune Diop in the struggle for the just equity and freedom of continental and diaspora Africans (Fabre 1991, 190–93; M'Baye 2009, 29–42). The good reputation the pioneers of Négritude earned due to their intellectual contributions in no way precludes the objectifications and racism they faced—lived experiences that forced them to finally question the French policy of assimilation.

Senghor and his colleagues from the West Indies arrived in France as most prominent African American elite thinkers and artists were leaving Metropolitan France. Subsequent, less-educated immigrants to France faced worsening immigrant conditions. Ousmane Kane (2011, 245) pinpoints the transnational's ability to make frequent trips between two countries and contribute economically, culturally, and politically to both—a mode of life that requires legal papers and money. Most of the immigrants who crafted the Négritude movement used their education to shape the future of their countries of origin politically, religiously, and economically—an act of repositioning themselves abroad and at home. To me, this is what Senghor did, as a migrant, to use his Négritude to free, reposition, and rechart the future of his native Senegal.

What does this have to do with minority criticism? I will focus on two dimensions of Négritude that I believe to be relevant to my contribution to minoritized criticism and biblical interpretation: the repositioning of Senegalese people to reclaim their culture and to contextualize Scripture.

Négritude as Repositioning

First, in spite of the elementary education that they had received at home, Damas, Césaire, and Senghor were confronted with the shortcomings of assimilation and the ugly face of racism as they were being objectified in France. The contradictions and ambivalences critics find in Négritude were in fact intrinsic to colonial discourse, which promoted the policy of assimilation and presented French culture as normative for the colonized.

Senghor's understanding of this conundrum inspired him to single-handedly recraft Négritude into a multidimensional concept with which to recover some African cultural values once suppressed by the colonized, in order to survive the overwhelming effects of objectification (Diagne 2014).[5] This is why dismantling France's ideological discourse—presented as epistemologically superior and normative French culture for uncivilized others to adopt—and repositioning his people became an expedient task for Senghor (Vaillant 1990, 12). To my mind, the effectiveness of Négritude as a countercolonial and repositioning tool with which to pave the way for the daunting task of decolonizing many African countries that were once part of France overseas outweighs its limitations.

To effectively counter French geopolitical discourse, Senghor was determined to use his French education to create an alternative space for marginalized people to be free and to creatively reimagine and emancipate themselves. As contradictory as this may sound, French education was therefore an expedient quest for him, Kane, and many others. They were convinced that the fate of their objectified culture depended on how liberative an immersion into the French school would be. As an immigrant, Senghor (1964a, 246), in particular, read Greco-Roman thinkers and African anthropologists to make the case against the Western emphasis on the primacy of reason, insisting that "intuitive reason is alone capable of an understanding that goes beyond appearances, of taking in total reality."

Reason is relational and analytical, intuitive and participatory. A person exists and *knows* in relation to another person—*a life together*, which Senghor first experienced in his African village (Joal-Djilor), informed by his Sérère faith traditions. In this rural milieu, a person's identity is contingent on the corporate participation of community members. Each villager learns to appreciate, enjoy, and experience another villager, and to find their identity in connection to the "other"—that is, an *Ubuntu-like* vision of life together (Senghor 1964b, 73, 93–94; Ramose 1998, 270–80).[6] Relat-

---

5. Négritude has ontological, aesthetic, epistemological, and political dimensions. According to Diagne, Négritude is still relevant today as a tool to fight against racism, and it would be a serious mistake to dismiss it as irrelevant, especially when our twenty-first century experiences at home and in the diaspora still tell us that "Black lives matter" today more than ever.

6. Senghor reformulates the Cartesian dictum, "I think, therefore I am," into "I feel, I dance the other, I am"—a dictum similarly to that of John S. Mbiti (1969, 106),

Négritude and Minoritized Criticism 269

ing and knowing self and the other is an expression of "vital force" (*l'élan vital*) that is integral to rhythm (Diagne 2011). Rhythm is

> the architecture of being, the internal dynamism that gives it form, the system of waves it emanates toward the *Others*, the pure expression of vital force. Rhythm is the vibrating shock, the force that, through the senses, seizes us at the root of *being*. It expresses itself through the most material and sensual means: lines, surfaces, colors, and volumes in architecture, sculpture and painting; accents in poetry and music; movements in dance. But, in doing so, it organizes all this concreteness toward the light of the *Spirit*. For the Negro African, it is insofar as it is incarnate in sensuality that rhythm illuminates the Spirit. (Senghor quoted in Diagne 2014, emphasis original)

Senghor sees the many interrelated forces that make up the cosmos as being manifestations of the same vital force, emanating from God and personified in human existence as the *life-force*, thus establishing a mystical *divine-human-nature-cosmos* relationship. A strong devotion to his Christian faith made it impossible for him to accept the Marxist critique of religion but retained its dialectics. If myth and intuitive reason permeates Scripture, then how might a Senegalese Christian such as Senghor contextualize Scripture?

Négritude and the Sacred

In spite of the deafening silence of Senghorian Négritude in postcolonial biblical studies, I was stunned to read comments made on Senghor's book *On African Socialism* by Francis A. Schaeffer, an American evangelical Christian, theologian, philosopher, Presbyterian pastor, and prolific author. Of Senghor, he writes:

> As I read his speeches I was very moved. If a man stood up in any of the Western countries and delivered these as political speeches, very few Christians would understand their real significance. The fact that Senghor is an African underlines the need to train our oversees missionaries in a new way, for the problem of communication in our day extends beyond the Sorbonne, Oxford, Cambridge, Harvard or Massachusetts

---

who agrees that the African's self-understanding hinges on the corporate personality of the group: "I am because we are; and since we are, therefore I am."

270 Aliou Cissé Niang

Institute of Technology to those places which we have traditionally thought of as the mission-field. The problem of communication does not end at our own shores. (Schaeffer 1990, 44)

He saw in Senghor a head of state beyond his time, who understood that whether "de Chardin uses the word god and Marx does not makes no difference, for the word by itself is meaningless until given content" (45). He goes on to agree with Senghor's reading of Marx, Engels, and de Chardin to emphasize the dialectical lens for understanding "religious forms," a method Senghor applied to Scripture as a way of contextualizing its message to his country, Senegal (89).

Critics who think that Senghorian Négritude is antiracist racism or cultural essentialism miss the biblical and African traditional religious themes and images as well as the vision for a cultural symbiosis that permeate Senghor's poetry and other writings. He has always been grateful to Jesuit Father Pierre Teilhard de Chardin, whom he credits with restoring his faith—a lived experience that shaped his critical reading and contextualization of Scripture. Father de Chardin taught him that Christ was the goal and crown of the natural and supernatural worlds—a fact that reached back to the first divine creative act. It was in this way that Jesus Christ was inextricably connected to the cosmos that he coherently unified as the Alpha but also the Omega—drawing on τὸ ἄλφα καὶ τὸ ὦ, "the Alpha and the Omega," the language of Rev 1:8, 21:6, and 22:13 (de Chardin 1976). The resurrection of Jesus Christ, he argues,

assumed the dominating position of all-inclusive Center in which everything is gathered together.... As mankind emerges into consciousness of the movement that carries it along, it has a continually more urgent need of a Direction and a Solution ahead and above, to which it will at last be able to consecrate itself. Who then is this God, no longer the God of the old Cosmos but the God of the new cosmogenesis ... you, Jesus, who represent him and bring him to us? (56–57)

To Senghor, the divine revelation that de Chardin describes did not contradict what he knew about African ontology. God has always been, in the Negro-African ontology, the uncreated Creator, the Force from which creation proceeds and is sustained—a symbiosis that resists any dichotomy between the natural and supernatural order (Senghor 1964a, 252–68). For this, he rereads Scripture to emphasize how myth and intuitive reason, which permeate Old Testament biblical cosmology, are concretely realized

Négritude and Minoritized Criticism 271

in the New Testament, especially the Johannine prologue (John 1:1–14) and Paul (Gal 2:20)—a realized phenomenon inherent in African cosmology (Senghor 1964a, 419). Put differently, in biblical myths, divine speech created the world (Gen 1:3, 6, 9, 11, 14, 20, 24, 26, 29). God's Word (*logos*)[7] became human in John 1:1, 14—making the biblical creator accessible to humans in the person of Jesus, whose redemptive work on the cross saves those who believe (Gal 2:20; 3:1–5:13–15, 26–29; Rom 8:1–2; Senghor 1977, 61).

The Christophanic call of the apostle Paul on the Damascus road (Gal 1:15–16, 2:20; Acts 9:3–8, 22:6–9, 26:13–17) is clearly echoed in Senghor's (1991a, 200–206) *Elegy for Jean-Marie:*

> God has tested us and found our weight and faith weak.
> We did not understand, Oh, Your mercy, merciful but just,
> Imbeciles that we were, men truly of little substance.
> We did not fall to our knees in the dust of our quest
> Beneath Christ's flaming heart like Paul on the road to
> Damascus.

This poem expresses how divine revelation encounters humans to shape the divine-human relationship, which, in his estimation, is similar to how the African, namely, the Sérère, people experience the divine daily. Senghor exploits parallels between biblical and African faith traditions (especially Bambara, Dogon, and Sérère, but not limited to them; see Laburthe-Tolra 2008, 35–43).

Western civilization is taught in academic settings and accepted as a reality not to question. To speak of African civilization is preposterous to many, such as the former president of France, Nicolas Sarkozy (Ray 2008). To Senghor (1964a, 8–12, 381–93), precolonial Africa had a civilization with various contextual manifestations, a core civilization shared by many African groups of people long before the transatlantic slave trade and subsequent colonialism—a point he and Cheikh Anta Diop (1978) tirelessly made (see Nwel 2008, 29–33). This is what he means by saying that biblical cosmology, embedding as it does "intuitive reason" and "mythological thought," is close to African cosmology. This near-

---

7. The French Oceanic Translation of the Bible and the French Jerusalem Bible render the Greek word *logos* as "Verbe," in contrast to the French Louis Segond and the French New Geneva Edition, which translate it as "Parole."

272   Aliou Cissé Niang

ness, to him, is clearly expressed in Scripture, in the way the redemptive Word of God relates to humans.

Although it has colonial precedence, Senghor's rereading of Scripture through an African lens was very much shaped by his Négritude as an immigrant. His uneasiness with the missionary version of Christianity escalated into a near spiritual death when he arrived in France. He almost lost his Christian faith, like Kane's hero Diallo, whose symbolic death enshrines that of his Diallobé as well as Senegalese culture. Senghor's near spiritual death was rescued by the works of de Chardin. It was at that point that his resurrected faith, so to speak, empowered him to overcome his near-despair lived experience, with a resilient, new, hopeful, poetic voice of life that inspired his poetry with the freedom to pray for oppressed and oppressors alike, rather than in terms of hatred or revenge. He prays this way:

> Lord Jesus, at the end of this book, which I offer You
> As a ciborium of sufferings
> At the beginning of the Great Year, in the sunlight
> Of Your peace on the snowy roofs of Paris
> —Yet I know that my brothers' blood will once more redden
> The yellow Orient on the shores of the Pacific
> Ravaged by storms and hatred
> I know that this blood is the spring libation
> The Great Tax Collectors have used for seventy years
> To fatten the Empire's lands
> Lord, at the foot of this cross—and it is no longer You
> Tree of sorrow but, above the Old and New Worlds,
> Crucified Africa,
> And her right arm stretches over my land
> And her left side shades America
> …
> At the feet of my Africa, crucified for four hundred years
> And still breathing
> Let me recite to You, Lord, her prayer of peace and pardon.
> …
> Dragging out Ancestors and spirits by their peaceful beards.
> And they have turned their mystery into a Sunday
> entertainment
> For the sleepwalking bourgeois
> …
> For You must forgive those who hunted down my children

Like wild elephants. And they disciplined them
With whips and turned into black hands those whose hands
were white
...
Yes, Lord, forgive France, who hates occupying forces
And yet imposes such strict occupation on me
Who offers a hero's welcome to some, and treats
The Senegalese like mercenaries, the Empire's black
Watchdogs. (Senghor 1991b , 69–72)

These words reveal the heart of Senghorian Négritude and the significance of its biblical dimensions. There is no room for a violent decolonization, against Fanon (1963, 35, 63) and Amilcar Cabral (see also Serequeberhan 1994, 79, 55–85). His are not the words of a coward, a sellout, or an assimilated Black African; they are, rather, a subversive, resilient invitation for reconciliation, tempered with the transforming and healing power of forgiveness in a world prone to colonial violence. He believes in what I call *redemptive activism*—a way of being in the world with others that firmly denounces injustice and oppression of any kind, tempered with a reconciliatory vision. Against a war of words that stifles reconciliation and forgiveness, Senghor offers a revolutionary prayer that simultaneously denounces France for its crucifixion of Africans and daringly invites it to the cross of Jesus Christ (Luke 23:34).

Conquering by Being in the Right: A Tentative Conclusion

As Senghorian Négritude was being severely critiqued and undermined in university settings, its influence was shaping much of the political and religious life of many Africans thirty years before Vatican II in 1962. Priests of African descent concerned with the distorted image of African identity and Christianity and the nature of its liturgy found Négritude suitable for removing European cultural elements from Christianity in order to make it palpable to Africans (Kinkupu et al. 2006). Senghorian Négritude, as an immigrant countercolonial and repositioning trope, was instrumental in the contextualization of African Christianity—a fact now recognized by most francophone politicians and clergy alike.

In fact, on 15–16 January 2008, a year after President Sarkozy insulted Senegalese people for being primitives, Africans, cultural, and faith traditions leaders from francophone countries held an interreligious conference in Dakar, Senegal, titled "Rencontre des traditions religieuses de l'Afrique

274   Aliou Cissé Niang

avec le Christianisme, L'Islam et la laicité: A Partir des écrits de Léopold Sédar Senghor" (De Paris 2008). In effect, the conference drew on Senghorian Négritude to chart a peaceable future for African countries, in response to spiking religiously based conflicts in the continent and beyond.

From its inception and subsequent development, Senghorian Négritude, as opposed to that of Césaire and Fanon, rested on prayer, forgiveness, reconciliation, and negotiation. Senghor knew that the sustainability of a peaceable future of humanity hinged on an intentional exercise of cultural and religious symbiosis—*a cultural symbiosis in which Black lives and contributions to civilization matter.* This *Ubuntu*-like call to life together that Senghor (Senghor 1964b, 73; see Ramose 1998, 270–80) emphasized in *On African Socialism* was the core argument that Senghor (1956, 1959)—along with some Blacks of the American and West Indian diaspora—boldly made during the First and Second International Congresses of Negro Writers and Artists in Paris and Rome, respectively. This argument, I believe, if reimagined for our times, might serve the current call of "Black Lives Matter" in America and beyond as well.

The church in African and non-European countries should mirror elements of their own cultures, such as language and rituals, instead of European ones. Imposing European Christianity on Africans ignores the multivalency and adaptability of Scripture as echoed in Pauline traditions and the book of Acts. Rereading Scripture in conversation with African cosmology introduces the kind of symbiosis that the institutionalized Christianity of Senghor's time did not tolerate but labeled as syncretism. Senghor rejects syncretism and concubinage for inculturation but prefers symbiosis, which, to him, allows for his Christian faith and Sérère faith traditions to inform each other (N'Dong 1997; see also Diop 2010, 53–85).

Senghor's Jesus must not be confused with the Jesus of institutionalized Christianity, or that of some of the French Catholics in France, or that of the missionaries he first encountered in Ngazobil, West Africa. Senghorian Négritude is the product of migrants who were forced to do something about their objectification, enabling them to create a home away from home, reposition themselves and their compatriots back into history, and decolonize missionary objectifications of African faith traditions and Christianity as syncretism by reframing them into symbioses. Senghorian Négritude is relevant to current postcolonial discourses not just as a theory or movement but as a poetics of postcolonial biblical criticism that may help both immigrants and transnationals alike to relearn and reposition themselves, should they forget.

Négritude and Minoritized Criticism 275

Senghorian Négritude has become the lens with which I, as a diaspora Senegalese and transnational biblical scholar, read biblical texts in America. I invite minoritized critics and leaders of the Black Lives Matter movement to revisit Senghorian Négritude (which shared similar concerns with the Harlem Renaissance leaders) as a poetics of postcolonial biblical criticism. It enshrines a hopeful vision of life against the odds, a vision that overcomes despair and repositions objectified people to live and proclaim liberty.

Works Cited

Bâ, Sylvia. 1972. *The Concept of Négritude in the Poetry of Léopold Sédar Senghor*. Princeton: Princeton University Press.

Bhabha, Homi. 1990a. "The Other Question: Difference, Discrimination and the Discourse of Colonialism." Pages 71–88 in *Out There: Marginalization and Contemporary Cultures*. Edited by Russell Ferguson, Martha Gever, Trinh T. Minh-ha, and Cornel West. New York: New Museum of Contemporary Art.

———. 1990b. "The Third Space: Interview with Homi Bhabha." Pages 207–21 in *Identity, Community, Culture, Difference*. Edited by Jonathan Rutherford. London: Lawrence & Wishart.

———. 1994. *The Location of Culture*. New York: Routledge.

Busch, Annett and Max Annas, eds. 2008. *Ousmane Sembène: Interviews*. Jackson: University Press of Mississippi.

Césaire, Aimé. 1972. *Discourse on Colonialism*. Translated by Joan Pinkham. New York: Monthly Review.

Chardin, Pierre Teilhard de. 1976. *The Heart of the Matter*. Translated by René Hague. New York: Harcourt Brace.

De Paris, Mairie, ed. 2008. *Rencontre des traditions religieuses de l'Afrique avec le Christianisme, L'Islam et la laicité: A Partir des écrits de Léopold Sédar Senghor*. Paris: UNESCO.

Depestre, René. 1980. *Bonjour et adieu à la négritude*. Paris: Éditions Laffont.

Diagne, Souleymane Bachir. 2011. *African Art as Philosophy: Senghor, Bergson and the Idea of Negritude*. Translated by Chike Jeffers. New York: Seagull Books.

———. 2014. "Négritude." In *Stanford Encyclopedia of Philosophy*. Last modified 24 February. https://tinyurl.com/SBL06106ak.

276 Aliou Cissé Niang

Diop, Cheikh Anta. 1978. *The Cultural Unity of Black Africa*. Chicago: Third World.

Diop, Mamadou. 2010. *La multivalence du sacré dans l'oeuvre de Léopold Sédar Senghor: Négritude, universalité, géopoétique*. Saarbrücken: Édition Universitaires.

Fabre, Michel. 1991. *From Harlem to Paris*. Chicago: University of Chicago Press.

Fanon, Frantz. 1963. *The Wretched of the Earth*. Translated by Constance Farrington. New York: Grove.

———. 1967. *Black Skin, White Masks*. Translated by Charles Lam Markmann. New York: Grove.

Gadjigo, Samba. 2007. *Ousmane Sembène: The Making of a Militant Artist*. Bloomington: Indiana University Press.

Gasparetti, Fedora. 2011. "Relying on Teranga: Senegalese Migrants to Italy and Their Children Left Behind." *Autrepart* 1:215–32.

hooks, bell. 1990. *Yearning: Race, Gender and Politics*. Boston: South End.

Kane, Cheikh Hamidou. 1962. *Ambiguous Adventure*. Translated by Katherine Woods. Portsmouth, NH: Heinemann.

———. 1997. *Les Gardiens du Temple*. Abidjan: Nouvelles Éditions Ivoiriennes.

Kane, Ousmane Oumar. 2011. *The Homeland Is the Arena: Religion, Transnationalism, and the Integration of Senegalese Immigrants in America*. New York: Oxford University Press.

Kesteloot, Lylian. 1963. *Les écrivains noirs de langue Française: Naissance d'une littérature*. Brussels: Institut de la Sociologie de l'Université Libre de Bruxelles.

Kinkupu, Leonard Santedi, Gerard Bissanthe, and Meinrad Hebga, eds. 2006. *Des prêtres noirs s'interrogent: Cinquante ans après*. Paris: Karthala / Présence Africaine.

Laburthe-Tolra, Philippe. 2008. "Le mysticisme dans l'oeuvre de Léopold Sédar Senghor." Pages 35–103 in *Journées de réflexion sur la "Rencontre des traditions religieuse de l'Afrique avec le Christianisme, l'Islam et la laïcité" à partir d'écrits de Léopold Sédar Senghor*. Paris: UNESCO.

Lee, Jung Young. 1995. *Marginality: The Key to Multicultural Theology*. Minneapolis: Fortress.

Locke, Alain. 1997. *The New Negro: Voices of the Harlem Renaissance*. New York: Simon & Schuster.

M'Baye, Babacar. 2009. "Richard Wright and African Francophone Intellectuals: A Reassessment of the 1956 Congress of Black Writers in Paris." *ABDIJ* 2 (January): 29–42.

Mbiti, John S. 1969. *African Religions and Philosophy*. 2nd ed. Oxford: Heinemann Educational.

Mphahlele, Ezekiel. 1974. *The African Image*. London: Faber & Faber.

N'Dong, Henri Biram. 1997. "Inculturation et non sycrétisme." *Éthiopiques* 59.

Niang, Aliou Cissé. 2005. "Postcolonial Biblical Theology in Geographical Settings: The Case of Senegal." Pages 319–29 in *Reconstructing Old Testament Theology: After the Collapse of History*. Edited by Leo G. Perdue. Minneapolis: Fortress.

Nwel, Pierre Titi. 2008. "La Négritude en acts plus qu'en paroles." Pages 29–33 in *Journées de réflexion sur la "Rencontre des traditions religieuse de l'Afrique avec le Christianisme, l'Islam et la laïcité" à partir d'écrits de Léopold Sédar Senghor*. Paris: UNESCO.

Portes, Alexandro. 1999. "Immigration Theory for a New Century: Some Problems and Opportunities." Pages 21–33 in *The Handbook of International Migration*. Edited by Charles Hirschman, Philip Kasinitz, and Joshua DeWind. New York: Russell Sage Foundation.

Rabaka, Reiland. 2010. *Forms of Fanonism: Frantz Fanon's Critical Theory and the Dialectics of Decolonization*. New York: Lexington Books.

———. 2015. *The Négritude Movement: W. E. B. Du Bois, Leon Damas, Aimé Césaire, Léopold Sédar Senghor, Frantz Fanon, and the Evolution of an Insurgent Idea*. New York: Lexington Books.

Ramose, Mogobe B. 1998. "The Philosophy of *Ubuntu* and *Ubuntu* as a Philosophy." Pages 270–80 in *The African Philosophy Reader*. Edited by Pieter H. Coetzee and Abraham P. J. Roux. New York: Routledge.

Ray, Philippe. 2008. . Paris: Éditions Philippe Rey.

Said, Edward. 1979. *Orientalism*. New York: Vintage.

———. 1993. *Culture and Imperialism*. New York: Knopf.

Sartre, Jean-Paul. 1948. "Orphée noir." Pages ix–xliv in *Anthologie de la nouvelle poésie nègre et malgache de langue française*. Edited by Léopold Sédar Senghor. Paris: Presses Universitaires Française.

Schaeffer, Francis A. 1990. *The Francis Schaeffer Trilogy: The Three Essential Books in One*. Wheaton, IL: Crossway.

Senghor, Léopold Sédar, ed. 1948. *Anthologie de la nouvelle poésie nègre et malgache de langue française*. Paris: Presses Universitaires de France.

———. 1956. "The Spirit of Civilisation or the Laws of African Negro Culture." *PresAfric* 1:51–64.

———. 1959. "Constructive Elements of a Civilization of African Negro Inspiration." *PresAfric* 2:262–95.

———. 1964a. *Liberté 1: Négritude et humanisme.* Paris: Éditions du Seuil.

———. 1964b. *On African Socialism.* Translated by Mercer Cook. New York: Praeger.

———. 1977. *Liberté 3: Négritude et civilisation de l'universel.* Paris: Éditions du Seuil.

———. 1979. "La mort de Léon-Gontran Damas." Pages 10–11 in *Hommage posthume à Léon-Gontran Damas (1912–1978).* Compiled by Présence Africaine, Société Africaine de Culture. Paris: Présence Africaine.

———. 1991a. "Elegy for Jean-Marie." Pages 200–206 in *Léopold Sédar Senghor: The Collected Poetry.* Translated by Melvin Dixon. Charlottesville: University of Virginia Press.

———. 1991b. "Prayer for Peace." Pages 69–72 in *Léopold Sédar Senghor: The Collected Poetry.* Translated by Melvin Dixon. Charlottesville: University of Virginia Press.

Serequeberhan, Tsenay. 1994. *The Hermeneutics of African Philosophy: Horizon and Discourse.* New York: Routledge.

Soyinka, Wole. 1976. *Myth, Literature and the African World.* Cambridge: Cambridge University Press.

Spivak, Gayatri Chakravorty. 1990. "Strategy, Identity, Writing." Pages 35–49 in *The Post-colonial Critic: Interviews, Strategies, Dialogue.* Edited by Sarah Harasym. New York: Routledge.

Thiong'O, Ngũgĩ wa. 1981. *Decolonizing the Mind: The Politics of Language in African Literature.* Portsmouth, NH: Heinemann.

Thomas, Dominic. 2007. *Black France: Colonialism, Immigration, and Transnationalism.* Bloomington: Indiana University Press.

Vaillant, Janet. 1990. *Black, French, and African: A Life of Léopold Sédar Senghor.* Cambridge: Harvard University Press.

Wilder, Gary. 2005. *The French Imperial Nation-State: Négritude and Colonial Humanism between the Two World Wars.* Chicago: University of Chicago Press, 2005.

———. 2015. *Freedom Time: Négritude, Decolonization, and the Future of the World.* Durham, NC: Duke University Press.

Ticketing, Signaling, and Watching:
A Reading Strategy for Times like These

Hugh R. Page Jr.

> I'll catch the next train,
> And I'll move on down the line
> > —Gary Clark Jr., "When My Train Pulls In"

Migration, economics, militarization, the exit of the United Kingdom from the European Union (Brexit), and the social and political upheaval following the general election of the United States in 2016—these and a host of other issues that shape disciplinary norms in tangible ways have always affected and will continue to shape biblical research and interpretation. Unfortunately, their influence, both direct and ancillary, has not been easy to detect at times because of the privileged spaces in which such work has tended to take place, as well as the genres in which it has typically been shared.

The principal domains of the Bible scholar have long been either academic or ecclesial. Whether focused on text criticism, philology, or theological exposition, the reading central to the craft of biblical scholarship is conducted in a way that tends not to make known the engagement of such themes. This reading can also disclose such themes selectively in various ways. It can do so in written fashion: in the prefatory or concluding matter of monographs, in footnotes, and in autobiographical musings.[1] It can also occur orally: in cocktail hours or coffeehouse banter at the meetings of professional organizations, such as the Society of Biblical Literature and the American Academy of Religion. At times, this reading is

---

1. The memoir of Cyrus Gordon (2000), for example, is particularly illustrative in this regard. One sees in it how myriad factors impact the selection of a scholarly focus, publishing, career trajectory, and the reception of new ideas.

-279-

280   Hugh R. Page Jr.

conducted using a *poetics of* concealment, which renders it accessible only to the initiated. It is written in a koine whose grammar and syntax only a small number are permitted to speak and understand.[2]

Furthermore, what one might term the prevailing disciplinary "politics of respectability" of biblical studies has discouraged posing context-specific questions to the scholars and texts foundational to it and its respective subfields. As a result, Bible scholars have long labored under the *illusion* that two of the distinguishing characteristics of solid, reliable, and mainstream investigative and hermeneutical work are objectivity and timelessness. Thus, for example, the movement of peoples, the fiscal and commercial dynamics that fuel the commodification of human bodies, or the blurring of boundaries between local police and the military should have little bearing on conversations either about the Bible or the tools used to make sense of it. Consequently, a responsible reading of Scripture must be dispassionate and revelatory only within a set of strict disciplinary or theological boundaries.[3]

Thankfully, this trend is being reversed by the work of a chorus of scholarly voices. Among these, I would mention the following, in alphabetical order: Cheryl Anderson (2009); Stacy Davis (2015); Randall Bailey, Tat-siong Benny Liew, and Fernando Segovia (2009); Brian Blount et al. (2007); Wil Gafney (2008); Teresa Hornsby and Deryn Guest (2016); Teresa Hornsby and Ken Stone (2011); Nyasha Junior (2015); Cheryl Kirk-Duggan and Tina Pippin (2009); Herbert Marbury (2015); Vincent Wimbush (2008, 2011, 2012); and Gale Yee, Hugh Page Jr., and Matthew Coomber (2014). All these scholars are championing a more inclusive and wide-ranging investigative agenda for biblical studies.

This is, for many of us, a heartening development, because we are facing challenges in these early decades of the twenty-first century that are unprecedented. These include government policies that inhibit the

---

2. In their provocative manifesto, *The Invention of the Biblical Scholar*, Moore and Sherwood (2011) predict that this specialized language is likely to grow as theoretical interventions in biblical research increase.

3. This impulse is clearly counterintuitive, given the many ways that context-specific elements of one sort or another can be seen to have helped shape the work of the acknowledged pioneers in biblical studies. I explore this theme elsewhere in relation to the Albright/Johns Hopkins University lineage (Page 2013, 3–13). A cursory perusal of topical entries in the *Dictionary of Biblical Interpretation* (Hayes 1999) is also illuminating in this regard.

free flow of those seeking freedom from tyranny or poverty across international borders, the impact of globalization on our ability to build sustainable and independent economies of scale, and the increasing prevalence of heavy armament within local police forces and among our general citizenry. These are all developments that can and should be part of the conversations we are having about how the First and Second Testaments are engaged. Such is particularly important given that the rationales for many of these developments, and the initiatives to challenge them, are at times bolstered by an array of biblical appeals.

Given these realities, my aim is to take a slightly different turn, toward the realm of the theoretical, and ask another set of questions. What species of reading commends itself to us given the social, political, and other real-world crises we currently face? What protocols for liberating encounters with the Bible should we be considering? Are there ways of *mining* our respective cultural traditions for home-grown interpretive tools, rather than relying on interventions external to the experiential domain of minoritized and subaltern peoples?

Some thirty-three years ago, Houston Baker (1984, 2–4, 7, 9, 12, 14, 202), in his monograph *Blues Ideology and Afro-American Literature*, suggested that the images of the train and the crossroads—both central to what he terms the blues matrix—might possess a particular poignance for literary and cultural criticism. He encourages scholars to embrace the creativity and freedom of movement elicited by these images (9). For him, the operational metaphor for scholars should be that of the rail-riding "hobo" (200). He encourages those intent on embracing this identity to conform their lives to the rhythms of the railroad, to be "trained," as it were (8, 10). He appears to mean this in the most literal sense.

In keeping with this notion, I propose a strategy for reading in these times that extends this trope by leveraging the evocative power of three related signifiers from the railroad milieu: the ticket, the signal, and the watch. Such is my way of channeling the "blues energy" and participating in the "unlimited play" that Baker (10–11, 202) identifies as necessary for those eschewing "fixity" and doing scholarship under the metaphorical railway crossing sign—at the crossroads—where various instantiations of Africana vernacular reality converge.

In this vein, reading, especially for those of us with homes in the church and the academy, involves acknowledging several truths. The first is that we have obtained access to an elite, though not always welcoming or affirming, space. The second is that a ticket, whether purchased or gifted, has granted us passage to a destination at best unknown and with uncertain benefits. We have access to all cars on this institutional train, at least in principle. Proficiency in research, teaching, and service carries with it the promise of preferred and somewhat permanent seating. Failing to meet the bar in any of these areas, or being judged to have participated in conversations that in any way cause consternation to other passengers, may result in our being asked to exit at one of many station stops. Reading in fraught times like ours necessitates, therefore, acknowledging the means by which our ticket was obtained, its cost, and its concomitant ambiguities.

Reading also involves attentiveness to signals alerting departure, crowding, transition, and trouble ahead. Some of these are as clear as the sound of a locomotive's horn or a stationmaster's voice. Others are far less easily discerned, such as the speed and smoothness of the ride or the quality of the track bed. Messaging about what research is considered marketable and capable of turning a profit in an increasingly digital marketplace is a signal. Faculty job compression is a signal. A substantial alteration in teaching load is a signal. The erosion of the tenure system is a signal. The increasing use of adjunct labor is a signal. Reading, according to this model, must elicit heightened sensitivity to the representational significance of, in a word, everything.

Finally, reading of the kind I have in mind requires temporal adroitness—an intuitive understanding of schedules, times, seasons, and patterns. In other words, one must have a timepiece and possess the ability to *watch*. Having lived for many years as a child and young adult in Baltimore, Maryland—and having ridden to destinations north, south, and west on trains with haunting names like the Silver Meteor, the Palmetto, and the old Montrealler—I came to appreciate the vagaries of scheduling and the controlling power of the watch.[4] Some of these East Coast trains rarely, if ever, arrived or departed on time. They seemed to exist in their own universe and operate according to their own norms. You had to know exactly when to show up at Pennsylvania Station. You needed to know how much leeway you might have, given the train, weather, and day of the week. Amtrak never issued inconvenience refunds if a train due in from Miami and bound for New York happened to be three hours late. If you wanted to ride, you had to be there when the train arrived. To be a passenger, you had to conform to railroad time. You had to watch. Reading

---

4. On some of these train names, see Cameron 2022.

Scripture today involves watching: that is, knowing when particular kinds of work are needed and *timely*, relying on occasional hunches or flashes of insight to make a particular kind of proposal or to shop an idea for an article- or monograph-length intervention. It also involves intuiting those moments when conscience dictates that one absent oneself, temporarily or permanently, as an academic railway passenger, when it might be prudent to utilize another mode of travel.

Viewing biblical hermeneutics as reading nuanced by an awareness of both the academy and the church as ideology-laden machines for the transport of ideas, status, bodies, and other commodities—as trains—enables us to ask whether, in what capacity, and for how long we wish to ride them. This is particularly so if we want the work we do to touch on social issues: draconian immigration policies in our country and elsewhere, which disproportionately affect people of color; deindustrialization and the new economic normal, which have decreased the viability of Midwestern urban centers such as Detroit; or even the use of police tactics grounded in the fear of Black bodies in South Carolina, Ohio, Missouri, and elsewhere. Many rightly fear the job-related fallout associated with hermeneutical forays of this kind that challenge the status quo.

To read in a way that questions the truth claims of authoritative texts, or to bring those texts into conversation with voices and artifacts considered outside the disciplinary mainstream, may not ensure tenure or guarantee the compassionate embrace of one's faith community. Reading against implicit and explicit rhetorics of exclusion in the Pentateuch and Pastoral Letters with an eye toward building just and sustainable communities within and beyond our borders may cause consternation among colleagues. Arguing against notions of Jesus as prosperity-oriented patron of venture capitalists the world over, as advocate of a good news oriented solely toward the acquisition of bling, or even as a church growth guru touting prepackaged strategies to fill pews and collection plates may limit preaching invitations. Seeing the haunting assertion in the Song of Songs that "Love is as strong as death itself" (8:6) as the center of gravity for the articulation of a theological grammar of connectedness through which the Bible and other ancient Near Eastern sources can be productively queried may raise eyebrows. Yet, apparently weird strategies such as these[5] may be the kinds of projects that enable

---

5. I use the adjective *weird* playfully and intentionally to suggest the *conjurational* and *numinous* propensities of such approaches.

us to hear anew the words of prophets such as Isaiah, Joel, and Micah, collectively repurpose our implements of destruction (Isa 2:4, Joel 3:10, Mic 4:3) for peaceful aims, and enable our guild of scholar-practitioners to enjoy greater relevance now and in the future.

Needless to say, this is dangerous and destabilizing work. It requires of those of us willing to take it on a capacity to become active and informed inside workers on those academic and ecclesial trains for which we have obtained tickets. It means being attentive to signals within the institutional cars we occupy. It means watching—that is, keeping track of time and being presciently aware of key moments when one must make pivotal decisions. Focusing attention on issues such as border security measures, rising hate crime statistics, electoral irregularities, and related issues today means that we must become more than academic tourists that watch the events of the world go by as we ourselves make that great pilgrimage to job security and success. It means sharing what we have come to know about struggle, injustice, and crisis from our respective points of departure. It means querying the sustainability of the natural vistas on which we gaze as our journeys unfold. It means pondering ways to rebuild the infrastructure of the forgotten parts of cities—the "Bad Avenues" immortalized by the late blues artist Koko Taylor (2007; see Baker 1984, 8, 10)—through which rail lines have been typically constructed, and with which both the church and academy should be in deeper dialogue.

It may well require telling our institutional conductors and engineers from time to time to stop their trains so that we can get off, read, feel, imagine, dream, rebuild, and restore those things shattered and forgotten, not simply as scholars but as ordinary folk and as friends. Furthermore, in terms of career planning, minoritized readers hoping to thrive in the academy or church while resisting forces inimical to our well-being may periodically need to determine when the time is right, in the words of Gary Clark Jr. (2011), to "catch the next train" and "move on down the line."

Works Cited

Anderson, Cheryl B. 2009. *Ancient Laws and Contemporary Controversies: The Need for Inclusive Interpretation*. New York: Oxford University Press.

Bailey, Randall C., Tat-Siong Benny Liew, and Fernando F. Segovia, eds. 2009. *They Were All Together in One Place? Toward Minority Biblical Criticism*. SemeiaSt 57. Atlanta: Society of Biblical Literature.

Baker, Houston A., Jr. 1984. *Blues, Ideology, and Afro-American Literature.* Chicago: University of Chicago Press.

Blount, Brian K., Cain Hope Felder, Clarice J. Martin, and Emerson B. Powery, eds. 2007. *True to Our Native Land: An African American New Testament Commentary.* Minneapolis: Fortress.

Cameron, Jim. 2022. "Why Do Trains Have Names?" CT Mirror. 12 June. https://tinyurl.com/SBLPress06106c2.

Clark, Gary, Jr. 2011. "When My Train Pulls In." Track 4 on *The Bright Lights EP.* Warner Brothers Records. "Extended Play" format.

Davis, Stacey N. 2015. *Haggai and Malachi.* Collegeville, MN: Liturgical.

Gafney, Wilda C. 2008. *Daughters of Miriam: Women Prophets in Ancient Israel.* Minneapolis: Fortress.

Gordon, Cyrus H. 2000. *A Scholar's Odyssey.* BSNA 20. Atlanta: Society of Biblical Literature.

Hayes, John H., ed. 1999. *Dictionary of Biblical Interpretation.* 2 vols. Nashville: Abingdon.

Hornsby, Teresa J., and Deryn Guest. 2016. *Transgender, Intersex, and Biblical Interpretation.* SemeiaSt 83. Atlanta: SBL Press.

Hornsby, Teresa J., and Ken Stone, eds. 2011. *Bible Trouble: Queer Reading at the Boundaries of Biblical Scholarship.* SemeiaSt 67. Atlanta: Society of Biblical Literature.

Junior, Nyasha. 2015. *An Introduction to Womanist Biblical Interpretation.* Louisville: Westminster John Knox.

Kirk-Duggan, Cheryl, and Tina Pippin, eds. 2009. *Mother Goose, Mother Jones, and Mommie Dearest: Biblical Mothers and Their Children.* SemeiaSt 61. Atlanta: Society of Biblical Literature.

Marbury, Herbert Robinson. 2015. *Pillars of Cloud and Fire: the Politics of Exodus in African American Biblical Interpretation.* New York: New York University Press.

Moore, Stephen D., and Yvonne Sherwood. 2011. *The Invention of the Biblical Scholar: A Critical Manifesto.* Minneapolis: Fortress.

Page, Hugh R., Jr. 2013. *Israel's Poetry of Resistance: Africana Perspectives on Early Hebrew Verse.* Minneapolis: Fortress.

Taylor, Koko. 2007. "Bad Avenue." Track 7 on *Old School.* Alligator Records.

Wimbush, Vincent, ed. 2008. *Theorizing Scriptures: New Critical Orientations to a Cultural Phenomenon.* New Brunswick, NJ: Rutgers University Press.

———. 2011. "Interpreters—Enslaving/Enslaved/Runagate." *JBL* 130:5–24.

286 Hugh R. Page Jr.

———. 2012. *White Men's Magic: Scripturalization as Slavery.* New York: Oxford University Press.

Yee, Gale A., Hugh R. Page Jr., and Matthew J. M. Coomber, eds. 2014. *Fortress Commentary on the Bible: The Old Testament and Apocrypha.* Minneapolis: Fortress.

Leer Para Hacer Lío/Reading to Raise a Ruckus: The Critical Task of Disruptive Reading in These Times

Jean-Pierre Ruiz

> Rabbi Tarfon and the Elders were once reclining in the upper story of Nithza's house, in Lod, when this question was posed to them: Which is greater, study or action? Rabbi Tarfon answered, saying: Action is greater. Rabbi Akiva answered, saying: study is greater. All the rest agreed with Akiva that study is greater than action because it leads to action.
> —b. Qiddushin 40b (cited in Dorfman n.d.)

Introduction: Vanity and Beyond

There is among academics—myself included, I should confess—a peculiar sort of vanity that is much aided and abetted by instant access to resources such as Google Scholar and its My Citations tool, which tells curious authors where and by whom something they have written has been cited. Beyond mere vanity, in some academic disciplines and in some colleges and universities, citation frequency and impact factor are metrics that are taken very seriously in deliberations over faculty reappointment, tenure, and promotion. According to that logic, the academic tree that falls in the forest without anyone to hear it—published in a little-known venue—hardly matters by comparison with an article that finds its way into the most selective peer-reviewed journal in the field, where it garners critical acclaim as a noteworthy contribution to the field and then makes its way into the footnotes and reference lists of still other articles and chapters and monographs published by prestigious university presses.

It is especially gratifying to find references that find merit in what we have written, yet it can also be rewarding when peers take the issues that we raise in our work seriously enough to consider alternate readings and arrive at different conclusions. The critical give-and-take of respectful

288 Jean-Pierre Ruiz

debate is, after all, according to the culture of the academy, the way in which new knowledge is produced and the path by which our disciplines advance. It was in a moment of academic vanity that I became aware of a quotation from my book, *Readings from the Edges: The Bible and People on the Move* in an essay by Hector Avalos (2017) titled "Minoritized Biblical Scholarship as Christian Missiology and Imperialism" (see Ruiz 2011).[1]

There Avalos (2017, 4) cites a sentence from the acknowledgments in which I explain, "I am convinced that the work of biblical studies and of theological scholarship is an ecclesial vocation, one that takes place at the heart of the church for the sake of its mission to witness to the goodness and the justice of God in the world." On the basis of this single sentence (for he makes no further reference to that book or to any other of my publications), Avalos (4–5) concludes, "In so doing, Ruiz and most other advocates of minoritized biblical scholarship are still carrying out another version of the Great Commission in Matt. 28:19: 'Go therefore and make disciples of all nations, baptizing them in the name of the Father and of the Son and of the Holy Spirit.'"

I was quite surprised to find myself listed among the academics whom Avalos understands to be engaging in minoritized biblical scholarship, which he charges to be a matter of "Christian missiology and imperialism." It is not my aim to cast this essay mainly as a response to Avalos, yet his citation of my work and his characterization of my intentions in those terms offers a salutary opportunity for careful and critical reflection on *how* I read and *why* I read as I do in these times. I *do* unabashedly and deliberately engage in "minoritized biblical scholarship," a critical perspective that grapples—as Avalos (1) quotes from *They Were All Together in One Place? Toward Minority Biblical Criticism*—with "'minoritization' or the process of unequal valorization of population groups, yielding dominant and minority formations and relations, within the context, and through the apparatus, of a nation or state as a result of migration, whether voluntary or coerced" (see Bailey, Liew, and Segovia 2009). More specifically, I read as a Latino, more specifically as a US-born Puerto Rican—a Nuyorican at that—and as a Roman Catholic Christian.

---

1. Avalos's essay is reprinted in this volume. I quote from the original version, Avalos 2017.

Leer Para Hacer Lío/Reading to Raise a Ruckus 289

Situating myself in that way makes me guilty as charged (by Avalos) of "religionism" and "bibliolatry." Religionism, according to Avalos (2017, 3), "refers to a position that regards religion as useful and necessary for human existence, and something that should be preserved and protected." For Avalos (3), bibliolatry is "the position that views the Bible as a privileged document that is worthy of more study or attention than many other ancient works that we can name." He contends, "Promoting the Bible as important for our civilization is another self-interested project because it also functions to preserve the employment of biblical scholars" (3).

While I am employed as a biblical scholar and am very conscious of the privilege that is mine as a tenured faculty member at a large university, I also count myself among those who are struggling "to re-imagine biblical studies as something more than a highly specialized academic discipline, considering the role of the sociopolitically engaged biblical scholar as a public intellectual whose responsibility for the production of new knowledge is neither ethically neutral nor inconsequential vis-a-vis the shaping of public opinion" (Ruiz 2011, 9; see also 34–53). This is quite different from what Avalos (2017, 4) claims to recognize as the intention of minoritized biblical scholarship, which he argues is "a missiological and pastoral endeavor, meant to retain or recruit minorities by persuading them that the Bible offers them some comfort or analogy to their experience that can be beneficial."

For Whom Do We Write?

Avalos raises the question of the audience(s) of minoritized biblical criticism, suggesting that our principal addressees are themselves members of minoritized communities. Matters are considerably more complicated in terms of the diverse publics for whom we write. To explicate this, I turn to the work of M. Daniel Carroll R. (2008), whose *Christians at the Border: Immigration, the Church and the Bible* also receives attention from Avalos (2017, 12) under the umbrella of "ethno-theology as colonialism." By discounting out-of-hand explicitly theological reading strategies such as Carroll R.'s and my own, Avalos fails to consider the intention of such reading strategies to engage communities for whom Christian faith and the Bible *already* matter a great deal.[2] Thus Carroll R. explains:

---

2. Avalos (2017, 3) writes, "Given my commitment to empirico-rationalism as the only approach to historical or literary biblical studies, I hold that theological approaches are academically unsound because I cannot evaluate theological claims."

My intention is to try to move Christians to reconsider their starting point in the immigration debate. Too often discussions of faith default to passionate ideological arguments, economic wrangling, or racial sentiments that dominate national discourse. Among Christians, my experience has been that there is little awareness of what might be the divine viewpoint on immigration. It is neither exhaustive nor comprehensive. Rather it is designed as a primer for a more biblically and theologically-informed approach to the topic. (2008, 19–20)

Christians at the Border is not an academic monograph, nor did Carroll R. intend it to be that sort of book at all. He readily admits, "This book is not an academic tome full of specialist jargon or bewildering charts" (20). It is instead explicitly intended to influence the ways in which evangelical Christians think about immigrants and immigration policies, leveraging the considerable influence that the Bible already has on that community. Avalos (3) maintains:

I am open to hearing sound legal or humanitarian arguments for being more liberal toward undocumented workers. I am open to hearing what biblical authors thought was a divine viewpoint about immigrants. But I do not know how to go about researching "what might be a divine viewpoint on immigration." I cannot verify what a divine viewpoint might be.

For Carroll R.'s intended audience, though, there is no doubt whatsoever that *the* divine viewpoint on what matters—including immigration—is to be found in the pages of the Bible.

In the United States, the privilege attributed to the Bible is a given. This was demonstrated emphatically on 20 January 2017, when Donald J. Trump took the presidential oath of office with his hand resting on *two* Bibles. One was used by Abraham Lincoln at his first inauguration in 1861, and the second was a Bible that Trump himself received from his mother in 1955, on the occasion of his graduation from Sunday school (Mettler 2017). This vividly challenges the claim Avalos (2017, 3; see also 2007) makes that "the supposed influence of the Bible in our civilization is an illusion created in part by biblical scholars, the professorial class, and ministers who wish to preserve their status in our society." If the influence of the Bible were merely illusory, why would Trump himself have claimed repeatedly during the 2016 presidential campaign that it was his favorite book (Bump 2016)?

Leer Para Hacer Lío/Reading to Raise a Ruckus 291

On the morning of Inauguration Day, during a prayer service that took place at St. John's Episcopal Church (Washington DC's so-called Church of Presidents), then President-elect Trump heard a sermon preached by Baptist pastor Robert Jeffress, who addressed him in these words:

> When I think of you, President-elect Trump, I am reminded of another great leader God chose thousands of years ago in Israel. The nation had been in bondage for decades, the infrastructure of the country was in shambles, and God raised up a powerful leader to restore the nation. And the man God chose was neither a politician nor a priest. Instead, God chose a builder whose name was Nehemiah.
>
> And the first step of rebuilding the nation was the building of a great wall. God instructed Nehemiah to build a wall around Jerusalem to protect its citizens from enemy attack. You see, God is NOT against building walls! ("Read the Sermon" 2017)

Besides claiming divine intervention on behalf of the president-elect and anointing him as a new Nehemiah, Jeffress found in Nehemiah's rebuilding of the walls of Jerusalem—though possibly somewhat tongue-in-cheek—divine warrant for Trump's well-known and highly controversial campaign promise to build a wall across the US border with Mexico.

With evangelicals such as Robert Jeffress wielding the Bible and its considerable authority in the public square in terms like this, biblical scholars such as Carroll R. have felt compelled to raise their voices to speak a different word that emerges from a very different take on the biblical text. Too-frequent appeals to the Bible in support of the current political and economic status quo—with Jeffress's Inauguration Day sermon as but one especially egregious instance—call for the sort of disruptive and even ruckus-raising readings that challenge the injustices of the present order. I offer three recent examples of such challenging readings by biblical scholars writing not for specialists but instead for broader publics.

I was proud to be a participant in the American Values, Religious Voices project. This national, nonpartisan campaign brought together scholars of religion from a broad range of traditions to send a one-page letter to President Trump, Vice President Mike Pence, the members of the cabinet, and the members of the 115th Congress on each of the first one hundred days of the new administration (American Values, Religious Voices 2017). My letter, sent on 27 January 2017, contested Jeffress's take on Nehemiah—both his claim that Trump's election was a matter of divine favor and his suggestion that God smiles on the border wall project. I suggested instead that "God smiles on all of God's children, both the meek and the mighty" and that "God calls on all of us to work together in building for the sake of the common good," yet we should be working together to build "not walls but bridges, roads, and communities" (Ruiz 2017).

Another example is found in the challenge of Joel Baden, professor of Hebrew Bible at Yale University Divinity School, to the efforts of evangelist Franklin Graham to put the Bible at the service of President Trump's immigration ban. Writing not in an academic journal but in the *Washington Post*, Baden explains, "Attempting to defend the ban from a religious point of view, evangelist Franklin Graham declared, 'That's not a Bible issue.'" Baden (2017) states it plainly: "He could not be more wrong. Both the Hebrew Bible and the New Testament are clear and consistent when it comes to how we are to treat the stranger.... The Bible consistently spells out that it is the responsibility of the citizen to ensure that the immigrant, the stranger, the refugee, is respected, welcomed and cared for."

A third example is the appeal of Eric D. Barreto, the Frederick and Margaret L. Weyerhaeuser Associate Professor of New Testament at Princeton Theological Seminary, to the authority of the Bible in support of preserving DACA, the Deferred Action for Childhood Arrivals. This was an immigration policy put into effect in 2012, during the administration of President Barack Obama, that offered certain protections to people brought into the United States as minors without authorization. That policy was rescinded by the Trump administration in September 2017. Barreto (2010) is the author of *Ethnic Negotiations: The Function of Race and Ethnicity in Acts 16*, a carefully argued study intended mainly for consideration intramurally among biblical scholars and published in a prestigious series by a major European scholarly publisher.

In a concise online publication for the Salt Collective, Barreto offers "The Biblical Case for Saving DACA," where he begins by insisting that, "If the Bible is clear about anything, it is crystal clear about our call to welcome the exile, the refugee, the stranger." In support of this argument, Barreto appeals to a variety of texts. These range from Deut 10:19, "You shall also love the stranger, for you were strangers in the land of Egypt," to Matt 25:35, "For I was hungry and you gave me food, I was thirsty and you gave me drink, I was a stranger and you welcomed me, I was homeless and you gave me a room" (Barreto 2017a). As is the case with Carroll R.'s *Christians at the Border*, Barreto's piece avoids the intramural jargon of biblical studies as he writes in support of justice

Leer Para Hacer Lío/Reading to Raise a Ruckus 293

for immigrants as an imperative for those who turn to the Bible as an ethical reference point.[3]

A Brief Lapse into Autobiography

The year 1989 remains a memorable year to me on account of two very different rites of passage that took place half a world away from each other at two different Jesuit universities, the convergence of which would take years to unfold in my vocation as a biblical scholar.[4] The first was a personal milestone: 1989 was the year I defended my doctoral dissertation at the Pontifical Gregorian University in Rome, thereby gaining admission into the ranks of the guild of academically credentialed, professional readers of the Bible. Just a few months after that personal academic rite of passage, thousands of miles away at the Universidad Centroamericana José Simeón Cañas in San Salvador, six Jesuit priests, together with their housekeeper and her daughter, endured another rite of passage as the cruel bullets of their assassins carried them through the door of this life's final passage.

To read in these times, in *our* times, calls for us to think long and hard about the work that words can do, words that have so often been written in the very blood, violently inscribed in the very flesh, of their authors. The martyrs of the Universidad Centroamericana were killed not because of what they did off-campus but precisely because of what they said in the classrooms and because of what they wrote at their desks: challenging words that spoke uncomfortable truth to the oppressive, death-dealing regime that ruled their nation. In contrast, when people grouse about university presidents in *these* times and in *this* country, it is more often than not about their astronomically high salaries that they are complaining. These are salaries that are many hundreds of times higher than the pittances paid to the growing ranks of the undercompensated, contingent faculty, who are shouldering more and more of the burden of undergraduate education in our colleges and universities.

Let us consider the words of Jesuit priest and philosopher Ignacio Ellacuría, the martyred president of Universidad Centroamericana, offered at the 1982 commencement ceremonies of the University of Santa Clara in Cal-

---

3. Barreto (2017b) also contributed to the American Values, Religious Voices project.

4. On autobiography, see Segovia 2000.

294   Jean-Pierre Ruiz

ifornia, when that Jesuit university bestowed an honorary doctorate on him. Ellacuría began by explaining, "Our university's work is oriented, obviously, on behalf of our Salvadoran culture, but above all, on behalf of a people who, oppressed by structural injustices, struggle for their self-determination— people often without liberty or human rights." He went on to explain:

> There are two aspects to every university. The first and most evident is that it deals with culture, with knowledge, the use of the intellect. The second, and not so evident, is that it must be concerned with the social reality—precisely because a university is inescapably a social force: it must transform and enlighten the society in which it lives. But how does it do that? How does a university transform the social reality of which it is so much a part?
>
> There is no abstract and consistent answer here. A university cannot always and in every place be the same. We must constantly look at our own peculiar historical reality. For us in El Salvador, the historical reality is that we are a part of the Third World which is itself the major portion of human kind. Unfortunately, the Third World is characterized more by oppression than by liberty, more by a terrible, grinding poverty than by abundance. (Ellacuría 1982)

As for what must be done and how a university is in a privileged position to do what must be done, Ellacuría (1982) asks and just as quickly answers:

> What then does a university do, immersed in this reality? Transform it? Yes. Do everything possible so that liberty is victorious over oppression, justice over injustice, love over hate? Yes. Without this overall commitment, we would not be a university....
>
> But how is this done? The university must carry out this general commitment with the means uniquely at its disposal: we as an intellectual community must analyze causes; use imagination and creativity together to discover the remedies to our problems; communicate to our constituencies a consciousness that inspires the freedom of self-determination; educate professionals with a conscience, who will be the immediate instruments of such a transformation; and constantly hone an educational institution that is both academically excellent and ethically oriented.

The Bible and the University: Reading to Raise a Ruckus

It is easy enough for me to repeat Ellacuría's words in these pages, sitting at my desk in the comfort and safety of my campus office, writing an essay

Leer Para Hacer Lío/Reading to Raise a Ruckus   295

for an intended audience of scholars who will not be too likely to push back against the words of a fellow academic who gave up his life rather than surrender his convictions. Yet what traction would accompany these words of Ellacuría if they were redeployed as a call for change in our own institutions of higher education, and in the discipline of biblical studies, yes, even in what we perhaps sometimes—with a wink and a nudge—refer to as "the guild"?

How much has *really* changed in this little province of academe since the 1987 Society of Biblical Literature presidential address delivered by Elisabeth Schüssler Fiorenza, an address titled "The Ethics of Biblical Interpretation: Decentering Biblical Scholarship"? *Before* Schüssler Fiorenza addressed our society at its Annual Meeting in Boston, one might have speculated that the ethics of biblical interpretation were mostly a matter of following the rules for civil discourse, of doing one's level best to avoid vulgarity and personal invective, and to scrupulously cite one's sources and thereby avoid even the appearance of plagiarism. Consider this memorable indictment:

> Only a few presidential addresses have reflected on their own political contexts and rhetorical strategies. If my research assistant is correct, in the past forty years, no president of SBL has used the opportunity of the presidential address for asking the membership to consider the political context of their scholarship and to reflect on its political accountability. Since 1947 no presidential address has explicitly reflected on world politics, global crises, human sufferings, or movements for change. Neither the civil rights movement nor the various liberation struggles of the so-called Third World, neither the assassination of Martin Luther King nor the Holocaust has become the rhetorical context for biblical studies. (Schüssler Fiorenza 1988, 7)

Let us pause for a moment to wonder about how much has changed and how much has stayed the same in the decades since those strong words were pronounced. In his 2010 presidential address, Vincent Wimbush (2011, 6–7) made it amply clear that,

> Although differently named and tweaked from decade to decade since 1880, those practices and discourses that define this professional Society have always been and are even now still fully imbricated in the general politics and emergent discourses of the larger period to which I refer. And the cultivated obliviousness to or silence about—if not also the ide-

ological reflection and validation of—the larger prevailing sociopolitical currents and dynamics marks the beginning and ongoing history of this Society (among other learned and professional societies, to be sure). With its fetishization of the rituals and games involving books and THE BOOK, its politics of feigning apolitical ideology, its still all-too-simple historicist agenda (masking in too many instances unacknowledged, theological-apologetic interests), its commitment to "sticking to the text," its orientation in reality has always contributed to and reflected a participation in "sticking it" to the gendered and racialized Others. The fragility of the fiction of the apolitical big tent holding us together is all too evident in the mind-numbingly general and vapid language we use to describe our varied practices and ideologies and orientations.

In his 2014 Society of Biblical Literature presidential address, Fernando F. Segovia proposed an ambitious interpretive project for our times. "The objective," he admitted, "is ambitious: to bring the field to bear upon the major crises of our post–Cold War times, in both individual and converging fashion" (Segovia 2015, 26). The first Society of Biblical Literature president from the Global South, Segovia challenged biblical critics to focus attention on extramural concerns and to adopt activist positions that brought all the resources of the discipline to bear in the deployment of a global-systemic critical paradigm. He called for a "conjunction of the scholarly and political" in the preoccupations of biblical critics, paraphrasing the great Chilean poet Pablo Neruda to urge, "We have all made a pact of love with criticism; let us now make a pact of blood with the world" (29). We academics are comfortable enough with ink, but talk of blood makes us awfully nervous, especially when it is our blood that is at stake.

Let us ask ourselves, then, does the noise outside the windows of our campus offices interrupt our reading? It is echoing all the way from campus of the University of Virginia at Charlottesville; does that make a difference? It is the undergraduate in our classroom who is wrestling with fear and uncertainty as DACA is rescinded; does that make a difference in our lectures for the day? It is the anguished cries of refugees whose lives are at risk on overcrowded wrecks of vessels on the Mediterranean Sea; can we still read what the Acts of the Apostles had to say about Paul's travels in the same way? It is the terrified voices of tens of thousands of Rohingya Muslims escaping to Bangladesh from persecution in Myanmar; does that make a difference in how we teach Exodus? What would it *really* take for the noise outside the windows of our campus offices to have an impact on how we read the Bible (other than to drown it out), on what we read in the

The Decentered University

Perhaps Ellacuría can help us think through these challenges as we consider his vision of a university with a center outside itself. Michael Lee (2013, 42) explains the transformation of the Universidad Centroamericana in the following terms:

> Originally founded in 1965, the UCA was viewed by the Salvadoran elite as a conservative haven from so-called secular and Marxist-inspired academics of the national university. Yet under the leadership of Ellacuría, the university was transformed in the 1970s and 1980s into one of the most outspoken critics of the brutal military regimes that governed El Salvador and of the social, political, and economic structures that undergirded the massive inequality that characterized Salvadoran society. This transformation sprang from UCA's commitment to serve the national reality, but to do so *universitariamente*, in the distinct manner of a university.

Lee (43) goes on to point out how "Ellacuría believed that a university cannot simply dedicate itself to the production of professionals or technicians who replicate the social structures already in place ... rather ... the university should serve as the 'critical and creative conscience [*conciencia*] of society.'" If a university is to challenge the status quo by doing those things that a university does, namely, teaching and research, it can do so— Ellacuría maintained—only when these two activities are grounded in what he called *proyección social*, social projection. As Lee (43) explains it:

> Social projection makes concrete the orientation of the university to the wider society and indicates how the university must have a center "outside itself" where that which is most conducive to satisfying the needs of the poor majority serves as the criterion and principle for determining research priorities and other university functions. Practically, social projection indicates the various ways that the university "projects" its knowledge to the wider society, but also allows the society, and particularly its poorest, to orient its activities.

As Michael C. McCarthy notes, Ellacuría was not alone in embracing a model of doing what a university does with a center outside itself. The

298 Jean-Pierre Ruiz

Jesuit confreres who shared his life and work at Universidad Centroamericana and who likewise shared a martyr's death with him on that November day dedicated their own scholarly efforts to the practice of teaching and research deeply rooted in social projection. He writes,

> For instance, the Rev. Ignacio Martín-Baró was a social psychologist whose research focused on the psychic conditions of living in a context of structural violence. The Rev. Segundo Montes taught anthropology with a view to the effects of social stratification and the displaced victims of the civil war. The Rev. Amando López Quintana was the chairman of the philosophy department but worked on weekends as a parish priest and championed a mass-literacy campaign. (McCarthy 2014)[5]

In a 2015 letter to the grand chancellor of the Pontifical Catholic University of Argentina, on the occasion of the centenary of its faculty of theology, Pope Francis (2015) insisted:

> At this time theology must address conflicts: not only those that we experience within the Church, but also those that concern the world as a whole and those which are lived on the streets of Latin America. Do not settle for a desktop theology. Your place for reflection is the frontier. Do not fall into the temptation to embellish, to add fragrance, to adjust them to some degree and domesticate them.

He went on to turn his attention to the student of theology, asking:

> Who then is the student of theology that the UCA is called to form? Certainly not a "museum" theologian who gathers data and information on Revelation without, however, really knowing what to do with it. Nor a passive onlooker on history. The theologian formed at the UCA should be a person capable of building humanity around him, passing on the divine Christian truth in a truly human dimension, and not a talentless intellectual, an ethicist lacking in goodwill, or a bureaucrat of the sacred. (2015)

The pontiff calls for the sort of theological research that raises a ruckus. He tells theologians that their place for reflection is the frontier and warns them against settling for the sort of theology that is bound to the desk-

---

5. See Ellacuría 2013 on Ellacuría's understanding of his own discipline.

top. "Even good theologians, like good shepherds, have the odour of the people and of the street," the pontiff counsels (2015). The same provocative counsel—that the academy should not be a place to hide from the world—is meant for the ears of biblical scholars as well. Francis challenges us to read so as to raise a ruckus, to borrow the Argentinian pope's advice to young people in Latin America: *¡Hagan lío!* In the classroom, then, we are charged to teach in such a way that our students will be well-equipped to raise a ruckus in their commitment to address the world's injustices. Addressing the young people of Paraguay, Pope Francis (2015) encouraged them to "Make a ruckus! But also help in cleaning it up. Two things: make a ruckus, but do a good job of it! A ruckus that brings a free heart, a ruckus that brings solidarity, a ruckus that brings us hope."

What might biblical studies look like with a center *outside itself*, if raising a ruckus happened to become part of our job descriptions? How differently might our discipline be reconfigured if the noise outside the windows of our campus offices came to be regarded not as an unwelcome distraction from our work on that next article, that next book review, or that next class lecture, but as the very reason for choosing to read as we do, for choosing to research and teach as we do, as we consider for whose sake it is we read and teach, research, and write—for the sake of the academy or for something more. What might the Society of Biblical Literature Annual Meeting program look like if that were the case?

I would venture to argue that the critical task of reading in *these* times, in *our* times, if what Ellacuría suggests has any bearing at all on biblical studies, is a matter of attending to two related dimensions of our work as critics. First, if ever there was a time when it was possible to imagine that reading could be a neutral and apolitical activity disengaged and insulated from whatever was happening off-campus, that time has passed. Ours are times of crisis in so many ways, for the world in which we read is deeply and gravely wounded by violence, by want, by inequalities too many to name. Second, to read in these times and to engage in close reading of the signs of these times in which we live calls for careful *krisis*, for the sort of judgment and discernment that can inform transformative action. The transformation of the Universidad Centroamericana by Ellacuría and his colleagues from a safe haven from what was happening outside its gates to the critical conscience of a nation gives us hope that the status quo in the academe of our time and place is not invincible. Yet what became of Ellacuría and his colleagues is a sobering warning that reading texts and times is not without its very real perils.

I have learned quite a lot from my Jesuit teachers, from high school through graduate school, interrupted only by my years away from them as an undergraduate. In fact, some of my Jesuit professors in graduate school had gotten themselves into trouble with the powers-that-were in Rome, for challenging the ecclesiastical status quo with respect to how they read the Bible. I still find myself learning from Jesuits, now from Ellacuría and his companions, who remind me of how deeply true are the words of Rabbi Tarfon that serve as the epigraph for this essay: study is greater than action when it leads to action. They remind my conscience that it should matter very little to me how often (or not) my work appears in other people's footnotes. It should matter much more that I am doing what I can as a biblical scholar to read so as to raise the sort of ruckus that makes a difference in these critical times.

Works Cited

American Values, Religious Voices: 100 Days, 100 Letters. 2017. http://www.valuesandvoices.com/.

Avalos, Hector. 2007. *The End of Biblical Studies*. Amherst, NY: Prometheus.

——. 2017. "Minoritized Biblical Scholarship as Christian Missiology and Imperialism." The Bible and Interpretation. https://tinyurl.com/SBL06106am.

Baden, Joel. 2017. "Franklin Graham Said Immigration Is 'Not A Bible Issue.' Here's What the Bible Says." *Washington Post*, 10 February. https://tinyurl.com/SBL06106an.

Bailey, Randall C., Tat-Siong Benny Liew, and Fernando F. Segovia, eds. 2009. *They Were All Together in One Place? Toward Minority Biblical Criticism*. SemeiaSt 57. Atlanta: Society of Biblical Literature.

Barreto, Eric D. 2010. *Ethnic Negotiations: The Function of Race and Ethnicity in Acts 16*. WUNT 2/294. Tübingen: Mohr Siebeck.

——. 2017a. "The Biblical Case for Saving DACA." *The Salt Collective* (blog). https://tinyurl.com/SBL06106c10.

——. 2017b. "Letter 3." American Values, Religious Voices: 100 Days, 100 Letters, 22 January. https://tinyurl.com/SBL06106ao.

Bump, Philip. 2016. "Trump Doesn't Have Time to Read—But If You Do, Here's What He Recommends." *Washington Post*, 17 March. https://tinyurl.com/SBL06106ap.

Carroll R., M. Daniel. 2008. *Christians at the Border: Immigration, the Church and the Bible*. Grand Rapids: Baker Academic.

Dorfman, Aaron. n.d. "Learning and Doing: The Relationship and Reconciliation of Two Jewish Values." My Jewish Learning. https://www.myjewishlearning.com/article/learning-amp-doing/.

Ellacuría, Ignacio. 1982. "Ignacio Ellacuría, S.J.'s June 1982 Commencement Address." Santa Clara University. https://tinyurl.com/SBL06106aq.

———. 2013. "The Liberating Function of Philosophy." Pages 93–122 in *Ellacuría: Essays on History, Liberation, and Salvation*. Edited by Michael E. Lee. Maryknoll, NY: Orbis Books.

Pope Francis. 2015. "Letter to the Grand Chancellor of the Pontifical Argentinian Catholic University for the 100th Anniversary of the Founding of the Faculty of Theology." 3 March. https://tinyurl.com/SBL06106ar.

Lee, Michael E. 2013. "Ignacio Ellacuría: Historical Reality, Liberation, and the Role of the University." Pages 41–44 in *A Critical Pedagogy of Resistance: Thirty-Four Pedagogues You Need to Know*. Edited by James Kirylo. Rotterdam: Sense.

McCarthy, Michael C. 2014. "A Jesuit Inspiration." *New York Times*, 15 November. https://tinyurl.com/SBL06106as.

Mettler, Katie. 2017. "The Symbolism of Trump's Two Inaugural Bible Choices, from Lincoln to His Mother." *Washington Post*, 18 January. https://tinyurl.com/SBL06106at.

"Read the Sermon Donald Trump Heard before Becoming President." 2017. *Time*, 20 January. https://tinyurl.com/SBL06106au.

Ruiz, Jean-Pierre. 2011. *Readings from the Edges: The Bible and People on the Move*. Maryknoll, NY: Orbis Books.

———. 2017. "Letter 8." American Values, Religious Voices: 100 Days, 100 Letters, 27 January. https://tinyurl.com/SBL06106av.

Schüssler Fiorenza, Elisabeth. 1988. "The Ethics of Biblical Interpretation: Decentering Biblical Scholarship." *JBL* 107:3–17.

Segovia, Fernando F. 2000. "My Personal Voice: The Making of a Postcolonial Critic." Pages 145–56 in *Decolonizing Biblical Studies: A View from the Margins*. Maryknoll, NY: Orbis Books.

———. 2015. "Criticism in Critical Times: Reflections on Vision and Task." *JBL* 134:6–29.

Wimbush, Vincent L. 2011. "Interpreters—Enslaving/Enslaved/Runagate." *JBL* 130:5–24.

Arrested Developments:
Dismantling the Disciplinary Network of a Surveillance State

Abraham Smith

> Today we have the highest rate of incarceration in the world. The prison population has increased from 300,000 people in the early 1970s to 2.3 million people today. There are nearly six million people on probation or on parole. One in every fifteen people born in the United States in 2001 is expected to go to jail or prison; one in every three black male babies born in this century is expected to be incarcerated.
> —Bryan Stevenson, *Just Mercy: A Story of Justice and Redemption*

The statistics cited in the epigraph by Bryan Stevenson, the founder of the Equal Justice Initiative, are astounding and alarming. They bespeak fundamental structural problems with the US justice system. To begin with, there is a disproportionate percentage of prisoners compared to the total population. According to John Pfaff (2017, 1), "The United States is home to 5 percent of the world's population but 25 percent of its prisoners. We have more total prisoners than any other country in the world, and we have the world's highest incarceration rate, one that is four to eight times higher than those in other liberal democracies, including Canada, England, and Germany." Second, there is a propensity to incapacitate the young rather than to educate them. According to Elizabeth Hinton (2016, 5), the "prison system costs taxpayers $80 billion annually, and has become such a permanent component of domestic social policy that states like California and Michigan spend more money on imprisoning young people than on educating them."

---

* The second part of this essay draws on the substance of my "Incarceration on Trial: The Imprisonment of Paul and Silas in Acts 16," *JBL* 140 (2021): 797–817.

304 Abraham Smith

Third, one finds racial disparities in policing, prosecuting, and sentencing (Mauer 2011). Fourth, one can point to voter disenfranchisement and legalized discrimination. (On voter disenfranchisement in some states, see Stevenson 2014, 1; on the denial of opportunities through "legalized discrimination in employment, housing, education, and public benefits," see Alexander 2010, 1–2.) Last, one can also point to the toll of social stigmatization, the collateral disruption of families, and tax dollar prodigality (Kilgore 2015, 1–2; for specific information on the collateral disruption of families, see deVuono-powell et al. 2015.) All of these structural features create the image that the United States has become a *surveillance state*, a state for which mass incarceration is but one of several mechanisms through which it seeks to discipline bodies, watch over those it does not trust, and secure order (Kilgore 2015, 1–2).

Surveillance states, though, did not begin with the United States. Despite Michel Foucault's protestations, ancient Rome was one of them.[1] Oddly, then, when scholars have examined Acts, few connections have been made between Rome and the United States as surveillance states. Not thinking about Rome as a surveillance state while reading Acts, though, might cause interpreters to miss much of what Luke seeks to do with the multiple prison references scattered in virtually every major section of this narrative.[2] This essay departs from previous studies of prison scenes in Acts in that it seeks to answer the question of whether the frequency

---

1. In his *Discipline and Punish*, Eve Taylor Bannet (1989, 101–2) states, "Foucault explores the methods of punishment and surveillance which have been used on those outside the law who have been imprisoned, to show that these methods of surveillance and punishment are also the law of the factory, the school and the institutions which control the lives of supposedly free, law-abiding citizens." The key factor that links all of the institutions is discipline, or the socialization of individuals in temporal and spatial regimens for which they received rewards for appropriate behavior and punishment for inappropriate behavior. In *Discipline and Punish*, moreover, Foucault presupposed that surveillance was not a factor in the world until the seventeenth century, when there emerged select social technologies of power (like the penitentiary and mental institutions) that regulated lives. Recent work on Rome, though, suggests that the sustained interest in maintaining Rome's *ordo* or system of social hierarchy required a larger system of surveillance that would keep "freedmen out of the curia [senate], knights out of the taverns, and slaves out of the bath water" (Fredrick 2002, 17–18).

2. The designation "Luke" is used for convenience and does not indicate a perspective on the flesh-and-blood author of the Gospel of Luke or Acts, about which there is not a scholarly consensus.

of such scenes in different geographical locations is a response to Rome's surveillance state. Proposed here, then, is the thesis that Acts is not an accommodationist work, as some scholars once thought.[3] Rather, given the role that incarceration played to convey Rome's dominance through security and surveillance, Luke acknowledges prisons as provincial signs of the ever-present empire and yet critiques such signs.

To see the surveillance-state nature of the US incarceration system and how Luke seeks to arrest the development of Rome's acts of carceral surveillance, three discussions will prove helpful. To begin with, I provide a brief history of incarceration in the United States. Then I go on to a brief history of scholarship on imprisonment in Acts. Last, I address Luke's critiques of Rome as a surveillance state. This third discussion, moreover, will examine how the narrative of Acts recasts the gaze of focalization and revisits the function of the ancient trial scene. A conclusion will follow that rewrites the narrative about justice. A reading of the Lukan author's "discrepant experience" (on this notion see David Mattingly 2011, 29) and approach to Rome will provide insight on the perennial need to rewrite narratives of justice in our own time.

A Brief History of Incarceration in the United States: The Rise of the Surveillance State

Even if *mass incarceration* began in the last quarter of the twentieth century, when the United States witnessed a spike in its incarceration rate from the mid-1970s to the present, incarceration on the shores of what would become the United States is as old as the colonial period (see Simon 2007). Beyond the colonial period but before the contemporary era, moreover, US incarceration included two phases. The first was penitential reformist, with the goal of reform ostensibly being the moral reclamation of the

---

3. Scholarship has not reached a consensus on the role of Luke-Acts with respect to empire. Some Lukan scholarship views Luke as an accommodationist, but there are other views. These range from the conciliatory positions of Henry Cadbury, Hans Conzelmann, Philip Esler, and Paul Walasky, to the resistance position of Richard Cassidy, and on to the mediating positions of Steve Walton, C. Kavin Rowe, and Gary Gilbert. In the case of mediating positions, such authors acknowledge Luke's counter-imperial claims but without suggesting that Luke does not also appear conciliatory at times. Noticing a subversive theme in the gospel, namely, its status reversals from the beginning to the end of the Gospels, Amanda C. Miller (2014, 14–19) argues that Luke is resistant but in ways that still negotiated with Rome.

306 Abraham Smith

imprisoned individual. The second was public safety reformist, with the goal being the individual's reform for the kind of public reentry that would ensure the protection of the public's safety.

Of course, the early period of colonial charters under British rule supported corporal or capital punishment—from fines and whips to "mechanisms of shame (the stock and public cage), banishment, and ... the gallows" for those convicted of a crime (Rothman 1995, 101). The crimes ranged from property offenses (for example, debt or theft) to moral offenses (for example, blasphemy or adultery), with the gallows (or scaffold for a public hanging) a recurring death sentence for various and sundry crimes, serving as "a powerful, theatrical tool to display state power and to try to exert state control" (Tarter and Bell 2012, 9; see Hirsch 1992, 6). The other aforementioned forms of punishment were equally humiliating, as if the ultimate aim of the punishments were to disfigure the body in "staged rituals designed to display to the public the rude power of the law" (Tarter and Bell 2012, 11). The ultimate goal of the aforementioned punishments was largely, then, to provide a deterrent (Rothman 1995, 101).

Furthermore, when offenders were placed in colonial *gaols* (or jails), the aim of the custodial control was "to facilitate pretrial and presentence detention" (Hirsch 1992, 7). The detention jail was "simply an institution for the 'safekeeping' of accused persons during the interval between meetings of the court" (Barnes 1922, 69). Custodial care also included workhouses, "which were utilized almost solely to repress vagrants and paupers and were not open for the reception of felons" (Barnes 1921, 36–37). Offenders did not wear a uniform, moreover, and socializing with one's family or associates until the meting out of corporal punishment was not restricted (Kealey 1984, 250).

Penitential Reformist Phase

In the wake of independence, however, the Enlightenment-informed framers of the young republic shifted from British retributivist laws about criminal justice to a concern for the reform of the individual (Rothman 1995, 103). According to Blake McKelvey (1977, 14), one influence on the young republic was eighteenth-century Italian jurist Cesare Beccaria, whose application of rationalistic "philosophical concepts of natural and equal rights" to crime led him to denounce both torture and capital punishment in "his famous essay *On Crimes and Punishments*." Pennsylvania printer William Bradford (1793, 5, quoted in Kealey 1984, 250) thought, for example, that English common law was brutish, replete with "sanguinary punishments, contrived in despotic and barbarous ages … the offspring of corrupted monarchy." In the case of Pennsylvania, perhaps the contribution of its founder William Penn has also to be considered. In 1682, Penn, who had found the province of Pennsylvania with a land charter under Charles II, tried to establish penal reform through a code that eradicated bloody punishments, but Queen Anne, Charles II's successor, reinstituted such sanguinary punishments (McKelvey 1977, 3). Thus, the turn away from public shaming or the gallows toward the long-term, privatized institutionalization of persons convicted of crimes in the United States in the 1780s was a part of a reformist ethic.

Barnes (1921, 42–46) charts the influence of various key figures. One was French political philosopher Charles-Louis Secondat, baron de Montesquieu (1689–1755). Another was Englishman John Howard (1726–1790), who denounced the deplorable prison conditions that he saw on his tour of workhouses and jails and inaugurated the prison-reform movement in England. Yet another was Jeremy Bentham (1748–1832), the author of *Panopticon*, on the rise of the reformist ethic in criminal jurisprudence, an ethic that was also influenced largely by the Quakers or by influential Pennsylvania citizens, from printer Benjamin Franklin to physician Benjamin Rush (1745–1813) and William Bradford (1755–1795).

Robert Abzug (1994, 11–29) also notes the influence of evangelical Protestantism on Rush's brand of penal reform. Franklin and Rush were members of a reform organization known as the Philadelphia Society for Alleviating the Miseries of Public Prisons, which began in 1787 to correct abuses that inmates were receiving at Philadelphia's Walnut Street Jail (Kahan 2012, 13). In that year, for example, Rush argued that various types of public punishment "tend to make bad men worse, and to increase crimes, by their influence upon society" (quoted in Schorb 2014, 84). According to Kahan (2012, xii), the organization "worked to reform Philadelphia's notorious Walnut Street Jail and then to build Eastern State Penitentiary. The PSAMPP placed great faith in the reformative possibilities of educational programs and put this faith into practice at the Walnut Street Jail between 1790 and 1810."

That is, with several acts of agitation by the organization, the Walnut Street Jail was converted into the Walnut Street prison (with the construction of a new building of solitary cells). The Walnut Street prison became "America's first penitentiary" and thus the precursor for the Eastern State Penitentiary, which began construction in 1822 and was opened in 1829

308   Abraham Smith

(Kahan 2012, 14). In truth, though, the first prison of hard labor (though it was not called a penitentiary) was at Castle Island, which was approved by the Massachusetts legislature in 1785 (Hirsch 1992, 11; Kealey 1984, 251). (On the earlier incarnation of the Philadelphia Society for the Relief of Distressed Prisoners, which was established in 1776, see Schorb 2014, 4.)

In the early 1800s, as this first, reformist stage of the United States incarceration grew stronger, two management models of incarceration developed. One featured solitary confinement, even when prisoners were working. This was known as the Philadelphia system. Eastern State Penitentiary, which opened in 1829, represents an example of this system: the inmates' continuous seclusion was supposed to lead them to think inwardly about their lives and to reform them. The other model allowed prisoners to congregate with each other during the day, though they were kept in separate cells at night. This was known as the Auburn system. Two examples of it are Auburn State Prison in Auburn, New York, which opened in 1817, and Sing Sing, the nation's first maximum-security prison, which opened at Ossining, New York, on the Hudson River in 1825. (See Schorb 2014, 98; Rothman 1995, 104–5; Simon 2007, 476–81.)[4]

Given that the Philadelphia system actually began with the Walnut Street Prison (1790), the Auburn system in its precursor form (with the Newgate Prison, 1797) and in the construction of the Auburn State Prison itself was an attempt to respond to the problems of the Philadelphia model's sedentary confinement, for example, insanity and pulmonary disease (Christianson 1998, 114). As prison systems grew from state to state, moreover, so did the debate over the prison models "across the early decades of the nineteenth century," with most adopting the Auburn model, which was the more cost-efficient model (Schorb 2014, 98).

Both models survived for a while, though, because they shared the philosophy that incarceration, the rule of silence, and "monastic seclusion" at one level or another could correct bad habits, even if that correction was enforced by the harsh punishment of wardens and prison guards.[5]

---

4. According to Scott Christianson (1998, 132), the Pennsylvania Eastern State Penitentiary, which opened in 1829, was constructed to "separate offenders from all forms of earthly corruption, contamination or infection and enable them to repent and be reformed. Thus, the term 'penitentiary.'" Again, though, the Pennsylvania Eastern State Penitentiary was heir to the penitentiary model of the Walnut Street prison.

5. On the rule of silence, see Schorb 2014, 99. On "monastic seclusion," Hill (2016, 129–30; see Rothman 1995, 109) writes, "The belief was that the criminal

Arrested Developments 309

State legislatures also supported both systems, and neither model had yet to face the problem of overcrowding that mushroomed from the 1820s to the 1860s (Rothman 1995, 109; see also Rotman 1995, 152).[6] Local or county jails, however, were not totally replaced by these two penitentiary (or reformatory) models. Rather, at least in the South, these became the venues through which slave masters subcontracted the "corporate punishment for chattel slaves throughout the antebellum era" (Tarter and Bell 2012, 21–22; see O'Donovan 2012, 129).

Local jails, when they did not serve the subversive purposes of the enslaved themselves, such as the unsupervised communication of vital information about escape routes and abolitionists stations, were also venues for other purposes as well. These included the detention of fugitives or insurrectionists, as with Denmark Vesey's co-conspirators in 1822 and Nat Turner and his followers in 1831; the private sale of the enslaved; or in some cases the kidnapping and enslavement of free Blacks, as with Solomon Northrup (Christianson 1998, 153; O'Donovan 2012, 125–32; see Northrup's [2014] memoirs, *Twelve Years a Slave*). Furthermore, during the Civil War period, camps on both sides of the divide—for example Elmira, New York, and Point Lookout, Maryland, in the north; and Cahaba, Alabama, and Andersonville, Georgia, in the south—detained prisoners of war (Christianson 1998, 164–68).

Public Safety Reformist Phase

In historiographies about the US penal code, a second phase, the public safety reformist phase (aka the modernization phase), developed after the Civil War. As David Rothman (1995, 112) notes, by the 1870s and 1880s prisons "became modern, that is, characterized by overcrowding, brutality, and disorder." Yet, this modernization period also had three distinguish-

---

needed monastic isolation to reflect on the crimes he had committed and, by so reflecting, he would be cured of his defect. In this sense, the American prison became the epitome of the social theory of crime—change the criminal's environment and you will change the criminal. And yet, at the same time, prisons were a clear demonstration of the principle of equality; people were people, whatever their origins, and if they ran astray, they merely needed a 'correction' to be restored to a place of equivalence with their neighbor."

6. On the cost efficiency of the Auburn model and the conflict between the two models, see Barnes 1921, 55–58.

310 Abraham Smith

ing features: (1) critiques of the penitentiary as a rehabilitative reform system; (2) correctives that issued out of the newly burgeoning social sciences, whose primary interests were reform for the sake of public safety; and (3) challenges that emerged or persisted in the reformist period over the near-century between the 1860s and the 1970s.

Critiques

As for the critiques, some had come earlier, before the 1860s. In effect, already in the earlier, reformist phase, mild and harsh forms of critiques of the penitentiary system came from abroad. There was a mild critique, from Frenchmen Gustave de Beaumont and Alexis de Tocqueville (in 1831–1832), who preferred the Philadelphia model but saw both systems as more despotic than rehabilitative. There was a harsh critique, from Charles Dickens (in 1842), the English novelist, who judged the Eastern State Penitentiary to be a place of mental injury with respect to the prisoners and of mental incompetence with respect to the administrative personnel (Rothman 1995, 112).

Having corresponded with Beaumont and Tocqueville, moreover, Enoch Cobb Wines (1806–1879) and Theodore W. Wright (1822–1892) offered extensive stateside critiques of the penitentiary system in 1867, especially as the system continued into the new phase. They argued that, by the 1860s, the penitentiary functioned more to incapacitate than rehabilitate the prisoner (Rothman 1995, 112). Indeed, by this time, prisons had become overcrowded and had capitulated to custodial control; further, increasingly, the prison system was drawing its population from the immigrant pool, for which state legislatures lacked much compassion (112–14).

Corrections

As for the corrections, most of the lasting changes that reframed the reformist model in the modernization period were influenced by the reformers of the Progressive Era. These reformers relied on the then-emerging behavioral sciences, such as psychology and sociology, arguing that a better way to reform the prisoners was through psychotherapy at the hands of a psychiatrist, on the one hand, or through vocational training programs at the hands of a social caseworker, on the other (Rotman 1995, 158–62). Progressives also developed what is known as the "Big House," which was "a new type of prison managed by professionals instead of short-term political appointees

Arrested Developments

and designed to eliminate the abusive forms of corporal punishment and prison labor prevailing at the time" (165). Furthermore, while the progressives pushed adamantly for the liberalization of the rule of silence that had prevailed in both the Philadelphia and Auburn systems, they also pushed against the military regimentation (such as lockstep marching or the use of striped uniforms) that had marked the Auburn system (165). So, prisoners could now communicate with one another, and the routine of prison life could be interrupted either by diversions in prison life or by contact and correspondence with family and friends from the outside (165).

To stem the swelling tide of the overcrowded prisons, moreover, the progressives also pushed for incarceration alternatives, such as the regularizing of probation (or detention release, with supervision) and the federalizing of indeterminate sentencing (through eligibility for parole or early release; 162–63). Indeterminate sentencing and probation, for example, were hallmarks of the Elmira Reformatory, "where vocational education and preparation for reentry into society were emphasized" (Hill 2016, 131). As emphasized by Zebulon Brockway, who directed the Elmira Reformatory, though, the preparation of the individual for reentry was ultimately to protect the society (Lindsey 1925, 20).

Yet, the progressive-era scientists also advanced a surveillance mode into Black life. In the late nineteenth and early twentieth centuries, scientists such as Nathaniel Southgate Shaler and Frederick Hoffman, for example, were influenced by what came to be known as social Darwinism. While not coined as such until the twentieth century, the traits behind this belief were present already in the nineteenth century (Foner 1998, 121). They presupposed the inferiority of Blacks and tried to use demographics and vital statistics—which they saw as infallible proof—to cast reported crimes among Blacks as a group-level pathology, as opposed to an individual failing (see Muhammad 2011, 54). As Khalil Muhammad (6) notes:

> For all the ways in which poor Irish immigrants of the mid-nineteenth century were labeled members of the dangerous classes, criminalized by Anglo-Saxon police, and over-incarcerated in the nation's failing prisons, Progressive era social scientists used statistics and sociology to create a pathway for their redemption and rehabilitation. A generation before the Chicago School of Sociology systematically destroyed the immigrant house of pathology built by social Darwinists and eugenicists, Progressive era social scientists were innovating environmental theories of crime and delinquency while using crime statistics to demonstrate the assimilability of the Irish, the Italian, and the Jew by explicit contrast to the Negro.

312   Abraham Smith

Challenges

As for the challenges, there were several. For one, most prisons still had deplorable conditions and corrupt, if not also incompetent, personnel. The administrators of penal systems thought more about social control than they did about reform, and they thought more about costs than about rehabilitation (Rotman 1995, 152). Furthermore, within this modernization, postslavery phase, African Americans were greatly affected, because a legal loophole in the Thirteenth Amendment paved the way for African Americans to be subjected to slave-like conditions directly after having been released from slavery. That is, while the Thirteenth Amendment made slavery and involuntary servitude illegal, it included an exception clause: "Neither slavery nor involuntary servitude, *except as a punishment for crime whereof the party shall have been duly convicted*, shall exist within the United States, or any place subject to their jurisdiction" (emphasis added). The exception clause thus legally made it possible to subject anyone convicted of a crime to involuntary labor. Thus, when free Black labor was no longer available through slavery, the exception clause was used to reenslave Black persons, who were convicted for vagrancy and subjected to debt peonage and convict leasing because they were unable to pay a loitering or vagrancy fine.

From the 1920s to the 1970s, the incarceration rate did not spike (Clear and Frost 2014, 1, 28). In the 1920s, for example, there were only

Another challenge was a lack of prisoner rights, at least until a series of riots in the 1950s and 1960s and the era of civil rights in general led to a 1961 decision by the Warren Supreme Court to revoke the federal government's hands-off policy. This meant that prison plaintiffs could sue for their constitutional rights before the generally more-lenient federal courts as opposed to state courts; inmates had rebelled, for example, through "sit-down strikes or isolated acts of escape and self-mutilation" (Rotman 1995, 171–72). Subsequent decisions by the Warren court included the exclusionary rule that banned the use of unreasonable search evidence in state criminal proceedings (1961) and the rights to an attorney and to be silent (1966), aka the Miranda rights. Ironically, it was Chief Justice Earl Warren, when he was the attorney general of California, who advocated what he later came to regret, namely, the forced evacuation and later internment of some 120,000 Japanese Americans. Such evacuations and internments went into effect through Executive Order 9066 by President Franklin D. Roosevelt, which he signed on 9 February 1942 (Neier 1995, 359).

93,000 prisoners in a population of 121 million, and in the early 1950s there were only 166,000 in a population of 151 million (US Department of Justice 1982, 1–2). However, a series of law-and-order campaigns resulted in mass incarceration, with a 600 percent increase in imprisonment from the 1970s to 2014 (Clear and Frost 2014, 25–45).

Such law-and-order rhetoric can be readily traced. It was used initially in 1964 by antistatist Barry Goldwater, the Republican candidate for president. His appeal for "social stability" in an era of "civil rights and student demonstrations, ghetto riots, and rising urban crime rates" helped him to carry five Deep South states—states traditionally loyal to the Democratic Party (Foner 1998, 313). Subsequently, avowed segregationist George Wallace attained much popularity in 1968, garnering nearly ten million votes on an independent ticket. Conservatives now knew that "politicians could strike electoral gold by appealing to white uneasiness with civil rights gains, an uneasiness by no means confined to the South" (315). Thus, Nixon reclaimed the White House for the Republicans in 1968 with the so-called Southern Strategy, an appeal to white racial resentment with a racially coded anticrime platform that used racial prejudice to divide poor and working-class whites from Blacks.

The law-and-order campaigns included the war on crime, directed at violent crimes; the war on drugs, targeted against drug possession with certain amounts and against drug suppliers; and a series of punitive sentencing laws—mandatory sentencing, "truth-in-sentencing" directives, and the three-strikes laws.

War on Crime. While many date the War on Crime to Nixon, Elizabeth Hinton convincingly argues that it began as early as Johnson's administration. She argues that Johnson's Law Enforcement Assistance Act, which "established a role for the federal government in local police operations," was presented to Congress on 8 March 1965, with the hope of beginning—in Johnson's words—a "thorough, intelligent, and effective war against crime" (Hinton 2016, 27; see Johnson 1965). The act and Johnson's Commission on Crime were largely a response to the riots of the 1960s. Johnson's growing views about Blacks in urban areas were largely influenced by the Moynihan Report of 1965. So, even while Johnson began his war on poverty, he linked it with a war on crime. That is, he increasingly thought that pathology, not poverty, was the principal problem for urban Blacks.

While Daniel Moynihan later worked for the Nixon administration, he is best known for his "Report on the Negro Family: The Case for National

314   Abraham Smith

Action," given in 1965 during the Johnson administration (Steinberg 1995, 100–104). The report, while noting the "cycle of poverty and deprivation" that continued to hurt African Americans, placed the blame on the Black family itself rather than the inequities of the social structure (119). Furthermore, it assigned the apparent "anti-social behaviors" of the Black family to a purported basic pathology fostered by slavery itself, as if the continuing structures of inequity played no role at all (119). That purported pathology was the "myth of matriarchal black family" (Ward 1999, 42).

Moynihan's report was the catalyst for a flurry of historical and social-scientific scholarship on the Black family, especially on Black cultural resistance despite the otherwise devastating effects of slavery. Such works included Herbert Gutman's *The Black Family in Slavery and Freedom*, John Blassingame's *The Slave Community*, Eugene Genovese's *Roll, Jordan, Roll: The World the Slaves Made*, Albert Raboteau's *Slave Religion*, and Lawrence Levine's *Black Culture and Black Consciousness* (Steinberg 1995, 121; Banks 1996, 171). Ironically, however, the report actually was the basis for Johnson's 4 June 1965 speech to Howard University, a speech that set the stage for affirmative action (Troy 2002, 78).

War on Drugs. The war on drugs had two iterations: the first, initiated in 1971 by Richard Nixon, who deemed drug abuse to be "public enemy number one"; and the second, initiated in 1982 by Ronald Reagan, who launched it as a part of his get-tough-on-crime initiatives, even before crack became an epidemic (Alexander 2010, 47–48). According to James Kilgore (2015, 60), "Despite the militaristic rhetoric [of Nixon's war on drugs], the majority of funding under Nixon went toward treatment rather than law enforcement." Nixon's resignation deaccelerated the war on drugs until Ronald Reagan. With a media blitz, the gifting of military hardware to local law enforcement (aka the 1033 Program), and the incentivizing of drug raids through the Asset Forfeiture Program, Reagan put it back into full force even at a time, in the 1980s, when drug use was down (61–65).

Punitive Sentencing Laws. Mandatory sentencing began with the so-called Rockefeller drug laws. Some of the drug legislation criminalized drug addiction, which was a departure from Rockefeller's earlier rehabilitative approach to drug addiction (through program treatment or methadone clinics as opposed to imprisonment). Formerly, Rockefeller had seen drug users as disease infected, but he later viewed them as disease infectors of the body politic (Kohler-Hausman 2010, 74, 82). In part, Rockefeller changed

Arrested Developments

course because of a series of challenges he faced in the late 1960s: from revolutionary protests to a wave of prison protests, including the most notorious Attica rebellion (1971). Rockefeller thus "blamed the uprising on a permissive criminal justice system, linking rebelliousness and criminality to increasing illegal drug use" (Kilgore 2015, 40). In part, Rockefeller changed course because of his own political—though unfulfilled—aspirations for the presidency. Thus, he joined the wave of law-and-order politicians—from Goldwater to Nixon—who looked for opportunities to brandish their sword-wielding, get-tough policies for political ends (Kohler-Hausman 2010, 82). Some of the drug legislation also advocated for stiffer penalties for drug pushers by advocating mandatory sentences, over which judges would have no control and for which the possibility of parole would not be possible for those sentenced to life (Kilgore 2015, 40). These harsh laws were then replicated across the country and upgraded by Reagan's own war on drugs, with the result that incarceration rates skyrocketed (Thompson 2010, 709–16; see Hill 2016, 132–40).

Both the truth-in-sentencing directives and the three-strikes laws were factors of the 1994 Omnibus Crime bill signed by President Clinton. On the one hand, the bill incentivized states with $9.7 billion dollars to build new prisons, if those states passed truth-in-sentencing legislation, which meant that those convicted would have to serve 85 percent of their sentences before being eligible for parole (Kilgore 2015, 31, 43). On the other hand, the bill advocated harsh mandatory minimums—in some cases twenty-five-years to life sentences—for recidivists newly convicted of a felony (44). Twenty-four states took up such three-strikes measures from 1993–1995 (Clear and Frost 2014, 88).

Strikingly, the rate of incarceration has largely continued to increase despite the fall of violent and property crime rates in the last decade or so (Clear and Frost 2014, 35). Rationalizing such rise, then, has been what Todd R. Clear and Natasha A. Frost (2) call the punishment imperative.[7]

Prison Industrial Complex Phase

Thus, a third phase could be called the era of the prison industrial complex, which has linked social services to a growing surveillance on urban Blacks, wedded the state to industry, rejected the rehabilitative principle,

---

7. On sentencing reform, see https://tinyurl.com/SBLPress06106c1.

316 Abraham Smith

and resulted in direct and collateral damage for multiple groups, not just inner-city Blacks alone. Following an online Critical Resistance publication, Marc Lamont Hill (2016, 150; see Critical Resistance n.d.) defines the prison industrial complex as "the overlapping interests of government and industry that use surveillance, policing, and imprisonment as solutions to economic, social, and political problems."

While a significant amount of the legislation that passed as a part of John F. Kennedy's New Frontier program and Lyndon Johnson's Great Society program fought poverty, such programs also linked social services to surveillance programs. The architects of such programs presupposed that the root cause of crime was a dysfunctional family life and that such life was the cause of unrest among urban Blacks. Consequently, they "introduced various forms of surveillance into social welfare programs, labeled entire groups of Americans as likely criminals and targeted them with undercover and decoy squads, ran sting operations that created underground economies, and combated gangs with militarized police forces and severe sentencing guidelines" (Hinton 2016, 10–11).

Through the FBI, surveillance, of course, was also directed at Black radicals or groups, such as the Black Panthers, deemed radical by J. Edgar Hoover (16). Surveillance also increased through Nixon's preemptive strikes against crime policies, which included "broad wiretapping authority" and the right to conduct "'no knock' raids" (157). Reagan's War on Drugs also advanced surveillance techniques "by increasing the scale of the raids, stings, and tactical police units that had characterized the urban landscape from the Nixon administration onward" (309). With the war on terror, more surveillance came into play through "street-level interrogations, dramatic night raids" in the borderland areas, and the data-mining surveillance of the National Security Administration (Hernández, Muhammad, and Thompson 2015, 19; Harcourt 2018, 157–58). While all of the aforementioned programs and policies have contributed to the swelling ranks of confinement and the construction of new prisons, none has done so more recently than immigrant detention. As Kelly Lytle Hernández, Khalil Gibran Muhammad, and Heather Ann Thompson (2015, 19) note, "Immigrant detention—that is, the process of forcibly confining immigrants during deportation proceedings—is now the largest system of human caging operated by the U.S. government."

While many prisons remain under public management, a spate of them are now run privately. This ties the sustenance of the economies—and even the political clout—of some cities or rural areas to prison construction or prison maintenance and diverts away funding that could address the social ills of the day, whether those ills have an origin in mental-health matters, homelessness, or general poverty altogether (Hill 2016, 150–52). Privatization, of course, is not new. The aforementioned prisoner-leasing system is an early form of it, as Douglas Blackmon asserts in his work *Slavery by Another Name* (Kilgore 2015, 167).

While protests in the early twentieth century all but placed nails in the coffin of privatization, privatization saw new life again in various modes (Hill 2016, 149; Kilgore 2015, 167–78). One involved the halfway houses constructed under the Prison Industry Enhancement Certification Program (1979). Another saw the construction of immigration detention centers, which grew slightly in the 1980s but flourished after 9/11. A third had to do with publicly traded prison management firms whose goal was to maximize their shareholders' wealth through the trimming of fiscal fat, even if such cuts result in a lower quality of services or resources for the incarcerated.

That the managers of prisons would focus on the free market at all over the question of what is moral or ethical reinforces the idea that the third period of incarceration had shifted from the rehabilitative principle that was a fundamental goal of both earlier postrepublic periods (Hill 2016, 132, 149). The shift occurred, at the least, from the time of Nixon on, when the prison population became increasingly Black or Latino and the Nixon administration had less interest in rehabilitation and more interest in "prioritizing the construction of maximum security facilities" (Hinton 2016, 169). The orientation, then, was purely punitive and purely intended to protect the body politic. The goal was management or discipline, not rehabilitation (170).

The shift may have occurred, philosophically speaking, because of a frustration with the Great Society principle. That principle presupposed that an individual had problems only because the wider society was not fair and egalitarian. Thus, if the Great Society offered services that would make society fairer, individuals involved in crime would integrate better in the society (Clear and Frost 2014, 64). In the 1970s, however, criminological theories, such as those advanced by Robert Martinson's "What Works? Questions and Answers about Prison-Reform" and James Q. Wilson's *Thinking about Crime*, located the cause of crime in personal choices of irresponsibility and focused on incarceration as a way not to *rehabilitate* but to *stop* crime (58–65).

Mass incarceration does not just affect the generations of unskilled Black men and Latinos arrested since the 1970s for their involvement in

318   Abraham Smith

one form of an underground economy or another in order to earn a living, because inner-city jobs disappeared or social welfare safety nets narrowed (Kilgore 2015, 138–41). Other groups have also been affected: spouses or significant others who bear the brunt of the financial burdens to visit or otherwise support the incarcerated; children who lack educational drive because of emotional hurt or community stigmatization; the homeless among the LGBTQ community, caught in the throes of incarceration because of the poverty-arrest trap; women who often face sexual abuse before and after their arrests; and, finally, immigrant groups held at detention centers because the country has failed to establish comprehensive immigration reform legislation (141–48, 178–81, 87).

A Brief History of Previous Scholarship on Prisons in the Book of Acts

Given the history of incarceration in the United States, would Luke's response to Rome offer any answers on dismantling the machinery or network of surveillance in any surveillance state? Scholars of Acts have certainly noticed the prevalence of imprisonment scenes in Acts (Rapske 1994). Broadly speaking, scholarship on prisons, imprisonment, and prisoners in Acts has proffered helpful treatises in three areas: (1) the harsh conditions of ancient incarceration, (2) the occurrence and function of recurring prison-escape/release type-scenes, and (3) the literary function(s) of Paul's imprisonment and detention scenes.

Before addressing these treatises, a word on the unity of Luke-Acts is in order. Mikeal Parsons and Richard Pervo[8] (1993) challenge the unity of the Gospel of Luke and Acts on a number of fronts; that is, they insist that it is possible to read the Gospel of Luke as a complete text without considering Acts as a prereading interpretive constraint. Parsons and Pervo's provocative study critiques the hyphenated "Luke-Acts" thesis, a thesis first brought into prominence at least with Henry J. Cadbury's (1927, 8–11) groundbreaking studies on Luke in the 1920s. Preferring to speak of Acts as a self-contained sequel to the Gospel of Luke, Parsons and Pervo take to task the three assumed unities—narrative unity, generic unity, and theological unity.

From an audience-oriented perspective, the quibble may not be of much consequence, especially if one assumes that the authorial audience of

---

8. By citing Richard Pervo's work, I am neither ignoring nor minimizing his serious criminal offense.

Acts—the audience Luke likely had in mind when composing Acts—was expected to know the Gospel of Luke. Acts 1:1 refers directly to the former book, as if the audience of Acts knows it. Furthermore, Theophilus, whoever he is or whatever the name means, is the addressee in both works. The thesis of the individual narrative unities of each book is an acceptable argument within the aesthetic canons of ancient audiences. From an authorial audience perspective, however, knowledge of previous self-contained texts is not problematic. That is, the authorial audience of Acts could well know the Third Gospel. The authorial audience of Acts certainly knows the LXX (and several books within it). Furthermore, Parsons and Pervo's arguments against narrative unity depend too heavily on assumptions about narratives based on studies of modern secular narratives. Though there may be similarities in all narratives, one could hardly assume that ancient audiences would recognize the intricate aspects of narratives (or the distinctions between types of narratives) proposed by Parsons and Pervo.

Generic unity falls or rests on one's definition of genre and on what we know about the possible prototypes of Luke's day. From an authorial audience's perspective, the genre of a work is a fluid set of conventions shared between author and audience—not a static, fixed constellation for which Luke or Acts must be made to fit. Some genres (such as ancient novelistic literature), moreover, did not evolve into a single form. Rather, the genre was synthetic enough to have biographical, historiographical, and dramatic elements within it. Parsons and Pervo are right to insist that we learn about several genres of that period and that the authorial audience of Acts need not expect Acts to follow all of the generic features of the Gospel of Luke. Still, the intertextual proclivity of ancient novelistic literature could support a careful reading of both the Gospel of Luke and Acts construed according to the popular conventions of this broad genre.

Theological unity is not actually denied by the authors; rather, they insist that we should not facilely seek a theological synthesis for the two books. Yet, the authorial audience of Acts would find it difficult to avoid synthesis, especially when the author recalls and summarizes the earlier book (Acts 1:1) before beginning the second one. Parsons and Pervo are right to suggest, however, that we need not think of Luke writing the first book with a second book in mind. At the same time, we need not think of Luke writing a second book to the addressee of a previous book without expecting the authorial audience of the second one to draw on the theological texture of the previous one. (For the latest on this debate, see Gregory and Rowe 2010.)

320   Abraham Smith

Harsh Conditions of Ancient Incarceration

Some studies wholly or partially devoted to Acts—for example, the works
of Brian Rapske (1994) or Craig Wansink (1996)—expose the harsh,
brutal, and shameful conditions of prison life in antiquity, especially in the
first-century CE world.

In the case of *The Book of Acts and Paul in Roman Custody*, Rapske
notes both the frequency of depictions of Paul in custody (Philippi, Jerusalem, Caesarea, and Rome) and the physical and psychological conditions
of his imprisonment. In general, to be taken into custody was to be subjected possibly to limited mobility and overcrowding, stifling air and
stench, intense and brooding isolation, limited bedding or bedclothes (if
at all), multiple privations (such as the absence of natural light), and the
incessant weight and noisy clanging of chains (Rapske 1994, 196–209).

He also notes that there were six reasons for taking someone into
custody: protection from the threats of others, remand to guarantee an
appearance at a trial, confinement before sentencing, confinement after
sentencing (for execution), pretrial coercion by a magistrate, and in some
cases punishment (10–20). Further, he adds, the severity of the punishment—from the most severe, such as the state prisons and stone quarries,
to the less severe, such as military custody, custody entrustment to a civil-
ian, or release on one's own recognizance—depended on the status of the
imprisoned, with each custody type also having various degrees of severity
(20–35). Magistrates' decisions to send a person into custody was a factor
of the charges, the status of the defendants, and the level of authority and
discretion available to the magistrate (39–70).

In a chapter titled "The Shame of Bonds," Rapske writes about the
shame of imprisonment both for the prisoner and for his associates.
Imprisonment itself was a source of shame because a prison was viewed
as a place for "social deviants" (288). Thus, to be hauled into a prison
brought public exposure and was—with enchainment, forced nakedness,
and flogging—a "status degradation ritual" (288–97). Imprisonment also
had wider implications. While it could bring shame to one's family, it also
could cause one's family and friends to avoid contact because of "communal shunning" (292–94).

Paul appears to have suffered in both ways. Paul must have faced
physical terror, because the text of Acts speaks about how "Paul must
suffer (Acts 9:16) for the name and that 'prison and hardships' (δεσμὰ καὶ
θλίψεις: Acts 20:23) await Paul in Jerusalem" (Rapske 1994, 195). With

Arrested Developments 321

respect to Paul, moreover, multiple privations are evident. In Philippi, he and Silas were beaten and "confined in stocks in the inner cell (Acts 16:24) of the prison" (202). That the jailer must call for lights suggests that the inner cell was dark (203–4). Whether in Philippi, Caesarea, or en route to Rome, Paul would have experienced the weight, noisy clanking, or limiting mobility of chains (206–9). Each of the imprisonment scenes in which Paul is involved also includes elements of shame: torn clothes and a flogging in Philippi, a beating and a binding with two chains in Jerusalem, an appearance in chains before an esteemed audience in Caesarea, the detention of a military guard on the way to Rome (288–309).

In the case of *Chained in Christ*, Wansink also speaks about the physical and psychological conditions of imprisonment, though he considers both Acts and Paul's own letters. He dispels the notion that all ancient prisons were holding tanks. Thus, while some scholarship suggests that ancient prisons were just holding tanks or that "there was no such thing as long-term incarceration in the ancient world," Wansink (1996, 28–29) argues that prisons could detain the incarcerated for lengthy periods of time. In truth, he points out, some prisons were holding tanks, "for those [who were] awaiting a trial," but some prisons still kept prisoners for a long time, even for life (30–32; Cicero, *Cat.* 4.7; see Pseudo-Plutarch, *Mor.* 11A; Josephus, *B.J.* 6.434; Sallust, *Bell. Jug.* 14.15).

The "physical conditions" included "suffering, beatings, chains, darkness and squalor" (Wansink 1996, 33). With respect to chains, which "signified, among other things, shame and humiliation," "prisoners appear to have been chained almost all the time and at night they were often put in stocks or some other type of intensified restraint" (47–48). There were differences, though, depending on the "prisoners' status." In general, a prisoner was treated with more respect if the prisoner had a higher status. Ironically, though, some were punished for claiming high status (41–43).

Occurrence and Function of Recurring Prison-Escape/Release Type-Scenes

Some studies in Luke-Acts have examined the prison-escape/release scenes (aka *Befreiungswunder* scenes). These studies include both historical-critical (in this instance, form-critical) analyses, as in the work of Richard I. Pervo, and myth-critical approaches, as in the work of John B. Weaver (2004).

The most recent of these, Weaver's (2004) *Plots of Epiphany: Prison-Escapes in Acts of the Apostles*, reads the prison releases in Acts 1–7, 12,

322   Abraham Smith

and 16 in the light of a resistance myth. This involves a structural pattern or set of types scenes in which a minoritized religious/political cult legitimates its work, either in its own territory or elsewhere as it emigrates to newer territories, through references to divine epiphanies (especially through angels). In effect, a deity's vouchsafing of the rescue/release of members of a cult—as in the Dionysian myths, the Jewish writer's legendary tale of Moses's prison escape, or the prison release of Jews from the clutches of the hubristic tyrant Philopator—becomes a sign that the deity legitimates the group. The group may be part of a larger aggregate or religious/political community, as with the early minoritized Jewish subset that came be known as Christians, if the subset is compared to the established Jewish authorities. The group may also be an immigrant group, as again with the early Christians, whose work outside Jerusalem made them migrant workers taking the gospel to new territories.

Thus, when Weaver (2004, 144–45) examines Acts 1–7, he sees the angel's release of the apostles (Acts 5:19) as legitimizing their work in Jerusalem, as the established Jewish leaders are stylized as tyrannical brutes who act with rage (5:33) and even proceed to flog the apostles shortly before they release them (5:40). Weaver's examination of Acts 12 does not simply reveal a contrast between an angelic response to Peter's imprisonment (namely, release) and an angelic response to the tyrannical arrogance of Herod Agrippa I (namely, regicide). Rather, the analysis also confirms Jerusalem as a base for the work of the Christian cult (149–217).

Then, when he examines the release of Paul and Silas from the Philippi dungeon (Acts 16), Weaver highlights two dimensions. On the one hand, the release exposes the customary polemics made against ancient immigrant cults that moved into new territories: "They are peace disturbers and proclaim 'customs' [ἔθη] we are not allowed to receive or do" (Acts 16:20–21). On the other hand, the presence of yet another prison-escape epiphany—but now one outside Jerusalem and one produced by a supernatural event (an earthquake)—reflects a familiar colonizing legitimation device when a cult from one territory wanted to show its right to colonize and propagate its cult in another territory (Weaver 2004, 233–69). The colonizing group simply resorted to an epiphany to make its case. (Weaver also has some reflections on Acts 21–27, but what he says is similar to Matthew Skinner's [2003] *Locating Paul*, which I will take up shortly.)

Arrested Developments

Literary Function(s) of Paul's Imprisonment and Detention Scenes

Some studies, such as those of Richard Pervo (1987) and Matthew Skinner (2003), discuss the literary function(s) of Paul's imprisonment and detention scenes. In *Profit with Delight*, Pervo notes the functions of arrests in the ancient Greek novels, namely, to evoke sympathy and to serve as an impetus for travel. Then he goes on to say, "Luke uses arrest, or the threat of arrest, as the mainspring by which Paul is propelled from Damascus to Jerusalem and on through Pisidian Antioch, Philippi, and Corinth, from Jerusalem to Rome" (Pervo 1987, 19). In *Locating Paul: Places of Custody as Narrative Settings in Acts 21–28*, Matthew Skinner (2003, 79, 77–88; like Rapske and Wansink before him) assesses the "conditions of custody in ancient literature" before turning to the function of the long detention of Paul in Acts 21–28.

Ancient literature, he notes, is important to establish the extratextual repertoire that audiences would likely have had about prisons before Paul's arrest in Acts 21, namely, that "life in custody" is "bleak and oppressive." Skinner (2003, 88–105) suggests, though, that the intratextual repertoire (everything about prisons or prison escapes in Acts 1–20 or the expectation that Paul will suffer [20:17–38; 21:8–14]) would also have created an impression that a long imprisonment would also spell a bleak, restrictive, and disastrous end for Paul. Acts 21–28, though, does not depart from the ideological drive of the rest of Acts. The shift in settings—now without the possibility of a miraculous release—still allows Paul to be successful. Now, though, God does not work to release the protagonists to do the will of God. Rather, God works through the venue of detention itself to allow Paul to challenge the established powers of the day. Thus, an erstwhile difficult and shame-filled setting of prison could yet be a place of redirection, for Paul still found a way to confront systems "with all openness of speech and without hindrance" (Acts 28:31) (175–201).

Arresting the Development of a Surveillance State in Acts

That Luke-Acts frequently uses the sensory metaphors of seeing and hearing is generally accepted among Lukan scholars, even if the prominence of one or the other of these sensory metaphors is still in dispute (see Wilson 2016). Could the focus on the sensory metaphor of seeing in Acts, though, have been understood by ancient audiences as a response to Rome's own mechanisms of surveillance? This final discussion answers that question

324   Abraham Smith

first by noticing the attention Luke gives to sight terminology in the narrative's diction about prisons, before showing that the narrative's widened gaze on prisons raises questions about the function of the larger trial scenes of which the imprisonment scenes are features. Then, given the putative claim that trial scenes should be about justice, the conclusion will treat the narrative's perspective on justice. That is, the trial imprisonment systems, as surveillance mechanisms, are themselves placed on trial, with the narrative claiming that justice lies only with the Just One whose deity vouchsafes the travels of the protagonists and ultimately vindicates the openness of the movement of the early followers of Jesus. Justice is best seen, then, when transparency is apparent, when "nothing is done in a corner" (Acts 26:26).

Recasting the Gaze in Acts

The Lukan author's focus on the sensory metaphor of sight has not drawn sufficient attention to the narrative's use of sight terminology to describe the prisons or prison keepers in the several imprisonment scenes that dart the narrative landscape. While Luke certainly uses δεσμωτήριον (a place for keeping a δέσμιος or prisoner—literally, "a bound one") in the larger narrative, two of Luke's terms—φῠλᾰκή and τήρησις—more directly indicate a *watching*, especially the latter. Thus, when Luke uses such terms, Luke refers to a place where the confined are watched or guarded as they are held in detention. As the chart below reveals, Luke not only deploys such τηρέω terms in every account of imprisonment (Acts 4–5, 12, 16, and 24– 25), but Luke also deploys compound terms that bring the root δέσμιος and τηρέω together, as in the case of δεσμωτήριον:

Acts 4–5	τήρησις (4:3)	τηρήσει (5:18)	δεσμωτήριον (5:21, 23)
Acts 12	ἐτηρεῖτο (12:5)	ἐτήρουν (12:6)	
Acts 16	τηρεῖν (16:23)	δεσμωτηρίου (16:26)	
Acts 24–25	τηρεῖσθαι (24:23)	τηρεῖσθαι (25:4)	τηρηθῆναι, τηρεῖσθαι (24:21)

Why give such prominence to a prison as a place that is guarded? Why speak as well of a prison as a place where a prisoner is watched or guarded? In alignment with the well-known Lukan reversal theme, Luke appears to

Arrested Developments 325

recast the gaze. A prison is often a place of surveillance, where the gaze of others is cast exclusively on the prisoners. In Acts, however, a special comparative spatialization reveals both what happens inside the prisons to the protagonists and what happens outside to those who seek to detain or harm the protagonists. The wide focal range of spatialization thus suggests that more than the inside of the prisons receives scrutiny. Luke's audience has a chance to see and hear those who are supposedly in charge of the protagonists' detention, even those who supposedly are charged with *watching* over them.

In the case of Acts 4–5, which may be taken together because both reflect the council's private deliberations about the arrested parties (4:15, 5:34), the authorial audience (over)hears the private deliberations of the council and observes the discovery of the temple police, who go to the prison expecting to find prisoners who have already been released (5:22–26).[9] Thus, the locked doors were opened for the disciples (5:19) and then found locked securely by guards who were standing nearby when the prisoners escaped (5:23). Evidently, all the apostles (compared to the imprisonment of Peter and John in Acts 4) were imprisoned, but the guards neither saw nor heard anything as the apostles were set free.

In the case of Acts 12, the audience can see both the action of the angel of the Lord in rescuing Peter and the action of the angel of the Lord in killing Herod Agrippa I. In both instances, Luke deploys forms of the same Greek word (πατάσσω)—in one instance, to indicate the angel's *touch* of Peter on his side (12:7), and in the other to indicate the same angel's *striking* of Herod Agrippa I to kill him (12:23). Thus, the gaze widens beyond that of Peter's imprisonment. Even in the case of Peter's release, moreover, the authorial audience sees—in ways similar to what happens in Acts 5—four squads of soldiers who seemingly can neither see nor hear any of Peter's release activity (12:4–11). The irony is that Peter was sleeping between two of the guards who hear and see nothing (12:6), not even with a light shining in the cell. Peter also escapes the notice of the other two

---

9. The "authorial audience," a term coined by Peter Rabinowitz (1977, 126), is the hypothetical construct of the audience an author was likely to have had in mind when composing a work. In line with Rabinowitz's discussion is the work of Hans Jauss (1982, 18–19), which insists on the reconstruction of the horizon of expectations in the original readers, largely through a reconstruction of the literary environment "which the author could expect his contemporary public to know either explicitly or implicitly."

326   Abraham Smith

guards, and neither, evidently, can hear the opening of what likely was a noisy iron gate. The gaze has been recast.

In the case of Acts 16, the comparative spatialization reveals the different responses to the earthquake from two different quarters. One involves the quarters of the jailer, who is ready to take his own life because of his assumptions that open prison doors mean escaped prisoners. The other has to do with the quarters of Paul, in the innermost part of a cell, who without lights still knows that the jailer is preparing to take his own life. The Lukan author's play on the inner and outer spaces (16:24, 30), moreover, deconstructs the notion that such spaces are fully different. Indeed, the earthquake affects everyone, for it shakes the foundations of the prison (16:26).

In the case of Acts 24–25, the comparative spatialization reveals Paul's custody under two governors after his earlier arrest in the temple in Jerusalem (21:27; see 22–25; 12). The first is the pretrial conversation that governor Festus has with King Agrippa (Herod Agrippa II) and Bernice (25:13–22). The second is the actual defense of Paul (25:23–26; 29) and the departure of the governor and his guests (26:30). That the audience can see a wide temporal range of scenes and a wide spatial range suggests that what is really at stake is not simply Paul's placement in custody but the degree to which the parties holding him act responsibly.

Revisiting the Function of the Trial Scene

The function of Luke's recasting of the gaze within the larger Lukan reversal motif is to draw attention to the larger trial narratives of Acts. Luke's interest in forensics is clear. According to Saundra Schwartz (2003, 116), the text includes fourteen trial scenes. Even if scholars could quibble about the frequency of such scenes, Luke also signals the trial motif with select forensic diction: (1) witness diction, (2) spatial forensic terminology, and (3) a flurry of diction about interrogation, accusation, and defense.

So, Luke describes Jesus's "apostles" as witnesses (Acts 1:8, 22; 2:32; 3:15; 5:32; 10:39, 41; 13:31; see 4:33) but applies the term to others as well: from Stephen (22:20) to Saul/Paul (22:15; see 20:26; 22:18; 23:11; 26:16, 22). The flurry of such terms throughout Acts, along with the gospel's use of the term (12:11, 21:12–19, 24:48), suggests that the work of a witness is a key role to be adopted by those who seek properly to hear and see acts of God in their lives. As John A. Darr (1994, 87) states, "The primary pur-

Arrested Developments 327

pose of Luke-Acts is to form its readers [or auditors] into ideal witnesses of and to sacred history."

Acts also includes forensic spatial terminology: from μέσον, which was the place from which a "judicial inquiry" could be made (5:40), to the βῆμα (or tribunal rostrum), which was located at the center of each Greek city's agora (18:12, 16, 17; Trites 1974, 279, 281). Even the language of bringing a defendant forth or out for examination (προάγειν, 25:26; or ἀπάγειν, 23:17) or standing to make one's case (παραστῆναι, 27:24) plays a role in Acts's trial motif (Trites 1974).

Finally, in each of the aforementioned prison scenes, what is clear is that the protagonists are being examined, being accused, requesting to know the charge, offering a defense, or receiving a judgment. Thus, when Peter and John are made to stand in the μέσον, Peter speaks of the two being examined (ἀνακρινόμεθα, 4:9; see 24:8, 28:18) as if to defend themselves. In Acts 12, Herod Agrippa I evidently sentences James to death and wants to kill Peter. Not succeeding, though, he examines (ἀνακρίνας) the guards and orders their deaths (12:18–19). In Acts 16, after the release of Paul and Silas from prison, Paul responds to the release by noting that he and Silas, though Roman citizens, were subjected to a public beating and arrest without being charged (ἀκατακρίτους, 16:37). In Acts 24–25, the diction of accusation (κατηγόρει) appears (24:8 [2x]; 25:16 [2x]; 25:18), with such diction also appearing earlier in 23:30, 35. In Acts 25:18, 27, requests are made to know the charge (αἰτίαν) that Paul's opponents might make against him. Furthermore, in Acts 24–25, apologia terminology also appears (24:10; 25:8, 16). Such diction appeared earlier in 19:33 and 22:1, 16, and will also appear later as Paul offers his defense before King Agrippa II, Bernice, and Festus (26:1, 2, 24).

Apparently, then, the prison scenes cannot be separated from the trial terminology. The gaze of the protagonists on the handlers, then, could draw attention to the trial motif so that the authorial audience can begin to raise questions about the tyrannical posturing or the incompetence of such handlers. The early prisons scenes within their trial framework— Acts 4–5 and 12—evoke well-known motifs of tyrants. The later scenes vividly demonstrate the incompetence of the handlers. (On the tyrannical posture of the opponents in Acts 4–5 and 12, see Yamazaki-Ransom 2011; on how the jailer in Acts 16 may or may not be viewed as incompetent, see Weaver 2004, 266 n. 168.)

328 Abraham Smith

Conclusion: Rewriting the Narrative about Justice

Several scholars have noted that Acts has an interest in vindicating the work of Jesus's followers. James R. McConnell Jr. (2014), for example, argues that in the whole of Luke-Acts God provides testimonial proof through words (for example, prophetic oracles) or deeds (for example, signs or portents) that both Jesus and his followers are just. Allen Trites (1974, 284) argues that "the frequent use of legal language in connection with real courts of law is germane to Luke's presentation.... The claims of Christ are being debated, and Luke intends by the use of the lawcourt scenes and legal language to draw attention to this fact." Two points regarding the prison and trial scenes should be noted. On the one hand, they are not haphazardly arranged but are linked with Jesus's own arrest, detention, and trial. On the other hand, they raise questions about justice related either to a lack of discipline or to a lack of competence. These suggest that such scenes could have been heard by first-century audiences as the narrative's attempt to rewrite the narrative about justice or to recast the nature and meaning of justice.[10]

The Romans certainly spoke about justice repeatedly to legitimate their claims to rule the world. Cicero calls justice "the crowning glory of the virtues" (*Off.* 1.20). In Virgil's *Aeneid* (6.853), Anchises, the father of Aeneas, declares that Aeneas will "crown peace with justice." In his reporting of Jupiter's prophecy about Augustus, Ovid (*Metam.* 15.832) marks justice as a new-age blessing. In *Ex Ponto* (1.2.97), Ovid also reckons Augustus as the "most just" of all the gods. The honorific shield placed in the Curia Julia in 27 BCE included justice as one of its four virtues (Res gest. divi Aug. 34.2).

Using δίκαιος or δικαιοσύνη expressions, Luke also relies heavily on justice or righteous living diction in the Gospel of Luke (1:6, 17, 75; 2:25; 5:32; 10:35; 12:57; 13:10; 14:14; 15:7; 17:31; 18:9; 20:20; 23:47, 50) and in Acts (3:14; 4:19; 7:52; 10:22; 22:14, 15). In a network of prison scenes and trial

---

10. That there are similarities between the sufferings of Jesus and that of the protagonist in Acts is clear. For example, according to Richard Pervo, both Jesus and Paul have "four trials. In the case of Jesus, he has such trials before the Sanhedrin (22:66–71), Governor Pilate (23:1–5), the Herodian King Antipas (23:6–12) and again Governor Pilate (23:13–25). In the case of Paul, he has trials before the Sanhedrin (Acts 22:30–23:10), Governor Felix (24:1–22), the Herodian King Agrippa (26), and Governor Festus (Acts 25:6–12)" (Pervo 2008, 107).

Arrested Developments

329

scenes, the emphasis on justice could echo, then, what is needed and yet not apparent in the behavior of those who oppose the principal protagonists. Such is the case with regard to Jesus, whose arrest and trial represent a travesty of justice, as well as with regard to the disciples Stephen and Paul, who constantly face difficulty in their defense of the "righteous one" (Acts 3:14, 7:52, 22:14). Further, in the episode of the two criminals, the penitent criminal, who gets a chance to be "with" Jesus, speaks of the just (δίκαιος) punishment that he and the other criminal receive, that is, the punishment that fits or is worth (ἀξία) their deeds (ἐπράξαμεν). Yet he adds that Jesus has done (ἔπραξεν) nothing wrong (23:40–41). Pilate also says that Jesus has done nothing worthy (ἄξιον, 23:15) of death. Of course, the centurion declares Jesus to be just/righteous/innocent (δίκαιος, 23:47).

Furthermore, a telling sign of the absence of justice in the prison and trial scenes is that the protagonists' opponents operate covertly. In the first trial, the protagonists speak openly, wanting their words and deeds to become known to all (4:10) and declaring their inability not to speak what they have seen and heard (4:20). After their initial release, they pray for boldness of speech (or better, for frankness of speech, παρρησία) as they face ineludible opposition (4:29, 31). (Marrow [1982, 434] asserts that the word παρρησία was often used in Cynic literature to indicate a philosopher's "boldness and openness of speech.") Likewise, in the second trial, the protagonists acknowledge the necessity of their role as "witnesses" (5:29–32). They simply cannot do otherwise, and, as the narrator reveals, even after they receive a "dishonorable" (ἀτιμασθῆναι) beating, they do not cease proclaiming Jesus as Christ (5:42).

The council officials, on the other hand, constantly worry about their image before the people (4:22, 26), and the narrator aptly depicts Gamaliel as one "honored" (τίμιος) by all the people (5:34). The council's apprehension about its image before the people leads the council, therefore, to maintain two different impressions of itself—one of nonviolence before the people (4:26) and one of mounting fury inside their closed council chambers (5:33, 40). Worse than that, however, the council, twice desiring to assure itself of totally concealed deliberations, orders the witnesses out of their chambers (4:15, 5:34), one instance of which is occasioned by Gamaliel himself (5:34).

The argument of David Gowler (1991) that Gamaliel's point of view lies close to the view of the narrator needs nuancing because he does not see the narrator's ideological contrasting of characters on the basis of Luke's secrecy-openness theme. That is, he does not recognize the contrast

330   Abraham Smith

between the council's hiddenness and the witnesses' openness with respect to the favor of the people. Indeed, the exception to Luke's thematic rule is telling, for the one time in the triple-unit sequence when the council does not defer to private deliberations is when the council has no fear for their image before the people, for the people, in this instance, are stirred against one of the protagonists, namely, Stephen (6:12). Consequently, the council's fury (διεπρίοντο), once exhibited behind closed doors, for the sake of the people (5:33; see 5:26), is now openly displayed by all of Stephen's opponents (the leaders and people alike; see διεπρίοντο, 7:54), and the desire (ἐβούλοντο) to kill (ἀνελεῖν) the apostles finally leads to the murdering (ἀναιρέσει, 8:1) of Stephen.

Moreover, the narrator's description of Gamaliel as "honored" by all the people stands in contrast to the narrator's description of the disciples as characters willing to suffer "dishonor" for the sake of Jesus (5:41). A similar contrast is made earlier. Note that the neutrally described "rulers [ἄρχοντες] of the people" (4:8), of which Gamaliel is a member, is later negatively depicted in the witnesses' prayer, where they constitute, along with all the peoples (λαοί), the opponents of Jesus (4:26). Yet the witnesses describe themselves as slaves (δοῦλοι, 4:29). The point is that the lowly, slave-like, and dishonored witnesses continue their public proclamation (4:31, 5:42), while the lofty figures (such as all of the rulers and the honored Gamaliel) operate clandestinely.

Thus, the authorial audience readily interprets the clandestine character of the council as dysphoric, in part because the hiddenness-versus-openness contrast reverts back to Jesus's teachings about insincerity in the first volume (Luke 11:33–12:12) and in part because the second volume's episode of Ananias and Sapphira (Acts 5:1–11) graphically illustrates the Lukan deity's wrath against secrecy and deception. Moreover, that the private deliberations are not inaccessible to the authorial audience all the more suggests the witlessness of the officials. Their closet feelings are in truth *exposed*. Like the earlier witnesses, Paul preaches openly (9:27, 13:46, 14:3, 19:8, 26:26). In contrast to the earlier witnesses, however, Paul's stylized Jewish or gentile opponents continue the pattern of the earlier provincial council: they work plotting trouble for him in secret (20:3, 20; 23:12; 25:3).

The flurry of παρρησία terms in Acts leads Abraham Malherbe to several conclusions. First, he argues that Luke's contemporaries saw fearless speech as a philosophic ideal worthy of imitation. Second, he adds that the term παρρησία in Acts is used as a part of Luke's apologetic to show that the church's leaders, especially Paul, far from exhibiting characteristics of

Arrested Developments

morally irresponsible charlatans, actually manifested philosophical ideals, particularly in their willingness to speak publicly without fear (Malherbe 1985, 197). Thus, Malherbe (201–210) reads Acts 26:26 as a tagline that philosophers used to show the integrity of their witness in being willing to speak publicly and not hide their witness. What may also be the case, though, is that the narrative rewrites justice as transparency. No books are hidden. Nothing is done "in a corner" (26:26). True justice has nothing to hide. The same is no less true today.

Works Cited

Abzug, Robert H. 1994. *Cosmos Crumbling: American Reform and the Religious Imagination*. New York: Oxford University Press.

Alexander, Michelle. 2010. *The New Jim Crow: Mass Incarceration in the Age of Colorblindness*. New York: New Press.

Banks, William M. 1996. *Black Intellectuals: Race and Responsibility in American Life*. New York: Norton.

Bannet, Eve Taylor. 1989. *Structuralism and the Logic of Dissent: Barthes, Derrida, Foucault, Lacan*. Urbana: University of Illinois Press.

Barnes, Harry E. 1921. "The Historical Origin of the Prison System in America." *JCLC* 12:35–60.

———. 1922. "The Criminal Codes and Penal Institutions of Colonial Pennsylvania." *BFHSP* 11.2:68–84.

Bradford, William. 1793. *An Enquiry [on] How Far the Punishment of Death Is Necessary in Pennsylvania*. Philadelphia: Dobson.

Cadbury, Henry J. 1927. *The Making of Luke-Acts*. New York: Macmillan.

Christianson, Scott. 1998. *With Liberty for Some: Five Hundred Years of Imprisonment in America*. Boston: Northeastern University Press.

Clear, Todd R., and Natasha A. Frost. 2014. *The Punishment Imperative: The Rise and Failure of Mass Incarceration in America*. New York: New York University Press.

Critical Resistance. N.d. "What Is the PIC? What Is Abolition?" https://tinyurl.com/SBL06106aw.

Darr, John A. 1994. "'Watch How You Listen' (Luke 8:18): Jesus and the Rhetoric of Perception in Luke-Acts." Pages 84–107 in *The New Literary Criticism and the New Testament*. Edited by Edgar V. McKnight and Elizabeth Struthers Malbon. Valley Forge, PA: Trinity Press International.

deVuono-powell, Saneta, Chris Schweidler, Alicia Walters, and Azadeh Zohrabi. 2015. "Who Pays? The True Cost of Incarceration on Families." Ella Baker Center, Forward Together, Research Action Design. https://tinyurl.com/SBL06106ax.

Foner, Eric. 1998. *The Story of American Freedom*. New York: Norton.

Fredrick, David. 2002. "Introduction: Invisible Rome." Pages 1–30 in *The Roman Gaze: Vision, Power, and the Body*. Edited by David Fredrick. Baltimore: Johns Hopkins University Press.

Gowler, David. 1991. *Host, Guest, Enemy and Friend: Portraits of the Pharisees in Luke and Acts*. Emory Studies in Early Christianity. New York: Lang.

Gregory, Andrew F., and C. Kavin Rowe, eds. 2010. *Rethinking the Unity and Reception of Luke and Acts*. Columbia: University of South Carolina Press.

Harcourt, Bernard E. 2018. *The Counterrevolution: How Our Government Went to War against Its Own Citizens*. New York: Basic Books.

Hernández, Kelly Lytle, Khalil Gibran Muhammad, and Heather Ann Thompson. 2015. "Introduction: Constructing the Carceral State." *JAH* 102:18–24.

Hill, Marc Lamont. 2016. *Nobody: Casualties of America's War on the Vulnerable, from Ferguson to Flint and Beyond*. New York: Atria Books.

Hinton, Elizabeth. 2016. *From the War on Poverty to the War on Crime: The Making of Mass Incarceration in America*. Cambridge: Harvard University Press.

Hirsch, Adam J. 1992. *The Rise of the Penitentiary: Prisons and Punishment in Early America*. New Haven: Yale University Press.

Jauss, Hans. 1982. "Literary History as a Challenge to Literary Theory." Pages 3–45 in *Toward an Aesthetic of Reception*. Translated by Timothy Bahti. Minneapolis: University of Minnesota Press.

Johnson, Lyndon B. 1965. "Special Message to the Congress on Law Enforcement and the Administration of Justice." 8 March. The American Presidency Project. https://tinyurl.com/SBL06106ay.

Kahan, Paul. 2012. *Seminary of Virtue: The Ideology and Practice of Inmate Reform at Eastern State Penitentiary, 1829–1971*. New York: Lang.

Kealey, Linda. 1984. "Punishment at Hard Labor: Stephen Burroughs and the Castle Island Prison, 1785–1798." *NEQ* 57:249–54.

Kilgore, James William. 2015. *Understanding Mass Incarceration*. New York: Free Press.

Kohler-Hausman, Julilly. 2010. "'The Attila the Hun Law': New York's Rockefeller Drug Laws and the Making of a Punitive State." *JSH* 44:71–95.

Lindsey, Edward. 1925. "Historical Sketch of the Indeterminate Sentence." *JCLC* 16:9–69.

Malherbe, Abraham. 1985. "'Not in a Corner': Early Christian Apologetic in Acts 26:26." *SecCent* 5.4:193–210.

Marrow, Stanley. 1982. "Parrhesia in the New Testament." *CBQ* 44:431–46.

Mattingly, David. 2011. *Imperialism, Power, and Identity: Experiencing the Roman Empire*. Princeton: Princeton University Press.

Mauer, Marc. 2011. "Addressing Racial Disparities in Incarceration." *PJ* 91.3:87–101.

McConnell, James R., Jr. 2014. *The Topos of Divine Testimony in Luke-Acts*. Eugene, OR: Pickwick.

McKelvey, Blake. 1977. *American Prisons: A History of Good Intentions*. Montclair, NJ: Patterson Smith.

Miller, Amanda C. 2014. *Rumors of Resistance: Status Reversals and Hidden Transcripts in the Gospel of Luke*. Emerging Scholars. Minneapolis: Fortress.

Muhammad, Khalil Gibran. 2011. *Condemnation of the Black Race: Race, Crime, and the Making of Modern Urban America*. Cambridge: Harvard University Press.

Neier, Aryeh. 1995. "Confining Dissent: The Political Prison." Pages 350–80 in *The Oxford History of the Prison: The Practice of Punishment in Western Society*. Edited by Norval Morris and David J. Rothman. New York: Oxford University Press.

Northrup, Solomon. 2014. *Twelve Years a Slave*. Mineola, NY: Dover.

O'Donovan, Susan Eva. 2012. "Universities of Social and Political Change: Slaves in Jail in Antebellum America." Pages 124–48 in *Buried Lives: Incarcerated in Early America*. Edited by Michele Lise Tarker and Richard Bell. Athens: University of Georgia Press.

Parsons, Mikeal, and Richard I. Pervo. 1993. *Rethinking the Unity of Luke and Acts*. Minneapolis: Fortress.

Pervo, Richard I. 1987. *Profit with Delight: The Literary Genre of the Acts of the Apostles*. Minneapolis: Fortress.

———. 2008. *The Mystery of Acts: Unraveling its Story*. Santa Rosa, CA: Polebridge.

Pfaff, John. 2017. *Locked In: The True Causes of Mass Incarceration—and How to Achieve Real Reform*. New York: Basic Books.

Rabinowitz, Peter. 1977. "Truth in Fiction: A Reexamination of Audience." *CI* 4:121–41.

Rapske, Brian. 1994. *The Book of Acts and Paul in Roman Custody*. Vol. 3 of *The Book of Acts in Its First-Century Setting*. Grand Rapids: Eerdmans.

Rothman, David. 1995. "Perfecting the Prison: United States, 1789–1865." Pages 111–29 in *The Oxford Handbook of the Prison: The Practice of Punishment in Western Society*. Edited by Norval Morris and David J. Rothman. New York: Oxford University Press.

Rotman, Edgardo. 1995. "The Failure of Reform: United States, 1865–1965." Pages 151–77 in *The Oxford History of the Prison: The Practice of Punishment in Western Society*. Edited by Norval Morris and David J. Rothman. New York: Oxford University Press.

Schorb, Jodi. 2014. *Reading Prisoners: Literature Literacy, and the Transformation of American Punishment, 1700–1845*. New Brunswick, NJ: Rutgers University Press.

Schwartz, Saundra. 2003. "The Trial Scene in the Greek Novels and in Acts." Pages 103–305 in *Contextualizing Acts: Lukan Narrative and Greco-Roman Discourse*. Edited by Todd C. Penner and Caroline Vander Stichele. Leiden: Brill.

Skinner, Matthew L. 2003. *Locating Paul: Places of Custody as Narrative Settings in Acts 21–28*. AcBib 13. Atlanta: Society of Biblical Literature.

Simon, Jonathan, 2007. "Rise of the Carceral State." *SocRes* 74:471–508.

Smith, Abraham. "Incarceration on Trial: The Imprisonment of Paul and Silas in Acts 16." *JBL* 140 (2021): 797–817.

Steinberg, Stephen. 1995. *Turning Back: The Retreat from Racial Justice in American Thought and Policy*. Boston: Beacon.

Stevenson, Bryan. 2014. *Just Mercy: A Story of Justice and Redemption*. New York: Random House.

Tarter, Michele Lise, and Richard Bell. 2012. "Introduction." Pages 1–34 in *Buried Lives: Incarcerated in Early America*. Edited by Michele Lise Tarter and Richard Bell. Athens: University of Georgia Press.

Thompson, Heather. 2010. "Why Mass Incarceration Matters: Rethinking Crisis, Decline, and Transformation in Postwar American History." *JAH* 97:703–34.

Trites, Allen. 1974. "The Importance of Legal Scenes and Language in the Book of Acts." *NovT* 16.4:278–84.

Troy, Tevi. 2002. *Intellectuals and the American Presidency: Philosophers, Jesters, or Technicians*. Lanham, MD: Rowman & Littlefield.

US Department of Justice. 1982. *Bureau of Justice Statistics Bulletin.* December.

Wansink, Craig S. 1996. *Chained in Christ: The Experience and Rhetoric of Paul's Imprisonments.* JSNTSup. Sheffield: Sheffield Academic.

Ward, Brian. 1999. "Sex Machines and Prisoners of Love: Male Rhythm and Blues, Sexual Politics and the Black Freedom Struggle." Pages 41–68 in *Gender in the Civil Rights Movement.* Edited by Peter J. Ling and Sharon Monteith. New York: Garland.

Weaver, John B. 2004. *Plots of Epiphany: Prison-Escape in Acts of the Apostles.* Berlin: de Gruyter.

Wilson, Brittany E. 2016. "Hearing the Word and Seeing the Light: Voice and Vision in Acts." *JSNT* 38:456–81.

Yamazaki-Ransom, Kazuhiko. 2011. "Paul, Agrippa I, and Antiochus IV: Two Persecutors in Light of 2 Macc. 9." Pages 107–21 in *Luke-Acts and Empire: Essays in Honor of Robert L. Brawley.* Edited by David Rhoads, David Esterline, and Jae Won Lee. PTMS. Eugene, OR: Wipf & Stock.

"Talkin' 'bout Somethin'":
Scripturalization—Or, a
Transgressive Politics of the Word

Vincent L. Wimbush

In every society the production of discourse is at once controlled, selected, organized and redistributed according to a certain number of procedures, whose role is to avert its powers and its dangers, to cope with chance events, to evade its ponderous, awesome materiality.... We must conceive discourse as a violence that we do to things, or, at all events, as a practice we impose upon them; it is in this practice that the events of discourse find the principle of their regularity.
> —Michel Foucault, "The Discourse on Language"

I don't read such small stuff as letters; I read men and nations.
> —Sojourner Truth

The time will come again when the study of the word will condition the study of nature. But at this juncture we are still in the shadows.
> —Aimé Césaire, "Poetry and Knowledge"

Boko Haram as a movement of scriptural (de)formation; ISIL as a reading formation in orientation to Abu Bakr Naji's treatise "Management of Savagery"; Justice Scalia's constitutional originalism; the Florida-based, Qu'ran-burning pastor Terry Jones and his claims to be the protector of the one true book; the Sanskritization movement in India and its threats to freedom of expression in book publishing; the skirmishes in the United States over same-sex marriage and abortion as right and wrong biblical interpretation; the gendering of scriptural authority and the policing of women's bodies and sexual activities; the Western-culture congratulatory 2011 celebration, led by the National Endowment for the Humanities, of

-337-

338   Vincent L. Wimbush

the four hundredth anniversary of the King James Bible in the rhetorical
key of "manifold greatness"; the book-canonical construction and politics
of academic fields; the perduring mystification of *auctoritas* in the form
of ascetical, literate males in the world of Roman Catholicism; Mormons'
recent efforts to reinforce and harden doctrinal boundaries in their pro-
nouncements about children of same-sex families; the cultural-scriptural
overdetermination of colored peoples; and so forth. These are some examples of modern and contemporary refractions and politics having to do
with the scriptural—the politics of the word, written and otherwise. The
refractions and politics here are of a sort that would appear to construct
and/or project mostly male dominance.

Yet there are also, concurrently and sometimes in the same spaces,
mimetic-signifying-resisting movements, dynamics, practices. Among
these, the following examples can be mentioned: book-reading/discus-
sion groups among women; mixed-race and mixed-social-status house
churches; academic feminist criticism of scriptures; in the African diaspora, the ring-shout, the chant sermon, the Haitian *vévés*, jazz and blues
and their riffing on canonical performances, the music that is poignantly
called gospel; the development of Yoruba and other Black Atlantic religions; and so on.

All of the examples in the two groupings above are layered social
movements, dynamics, practices, and politics. All have to do complexly
with the word, the scriptural. They are dynamics and issues of our history and present that beg—even scream for—sensitive but also ex-centric
critical analysis, far beyond the normally assumed apolitical but actually
unacknowledged conservative-apologetic interest in the (field-construed)
exegetical.

The terms *scriptures, scriptural,* and *the word* I use to register much
more than text. These terms have to do with the cross-cultural phenomenon
of the word. They register oddly, poignantly, ironically, metonymically—as
site of problematics having to do with language/discourse/knowledge and
power—the *ordo verborum*, the order of things, as pertains to the word
(Wynter 1997; Foucault 1994). To such terms we need to turn again, to
challenge ourselves to think more about, to dig more deeply into how and
with what consequences we make ourselves humans, how we, differently
and in what patterns and strategies, orient ourselves to ourselves and to
everything around us.

We are in a world that could profit from the challenge advanced by
Aimé Césaire (1990, xxix) and Sylvia Wynter (1997, 162–63) toward con-

"Talkin' 'bout Somethin'" 339

struction of a "science of the word." This challenge is especially poignant because we are situated in that world, a world that is constructed, consolidated, and overdetermined by, among other things, the productions, practices, politics, and social psychology having to do with the word—written and otherwise. The publication of the project that the famous philologist/Sanskritist F. Max Müller supervised and edited, called *Sacred Books of the East*, helps make the case for the challenge.

This enormous work, fifty volumes in total, was put together between 1879 and 1910. This period represents the height of European colonialist expansion and violence as well as the making of the world we know, with the creation and carving up of nation-states. The work has come to reflect and determine much about how we understand and negotiate the world. It reflected and modeled, as well as consolidated, what I now call the ideology of *scripturalism* and its projection as discursive regime over the modern world, or *scripturalization*. Billed as a collection of the sacred texts of the world—scandalously excepting the books of the Jewish-Christian religion as those books not to be signified and interrogated on the same terms—Müller's project firmly consolidated and legitimized the "aristocracy of the book religion." He made clear the framing agenda of dominance and violence of his project. In his own description of the work as a reflection of his project in the classification of religion as a classification of language and culture and races, he used the old empire-world expression *divide et impera*, shockingly, bluntly, and honestly translated by him as "classify and conquer" (Masuzawa 2005, 216).

We see the picture here. The books of the Christian West are not to be classified, not to be the focus of critical inquiry, not to be interrogated, alongside all other scriptural "religions" (Hinduism, Buddhism, etc.) that have been invented by scholars. Like the construction of whiteness itself in the modern world, Christianism—or the sometimes extended, constructed, fraught, complex Jewish-Christianism or sometimes Judaism-Christianity-Islam (the so-called family of Abrahamic religions)—was not to be interrogated or even acknowledged on the same terms, that is, as a projection/production of texts to be viewed as sources for critical inquiry. In the same way that whiteness is to be left unacknowledged and uninterrogated, so the texts of Christianism are to be *exegeted*, their truths decoded and re-presented to the religio-culturalist flock by certified/authorized high clerics—religious/academic/cultural.

Drawing on the *Sacred Books of the East* project as touchstone, as one important marker, I contend that we now live in the time of the consoli-

340   Vincent L. Wimbush

dation of the ideology of scripturalism and the social-cultural-political regimes of scripturalization. Moreover, we have hardly begun the hard work of taking stock of what it means to be situated in such a world—whether we call it by my term, *scripturalization*, or some other term. To advance the point of argument, it is worth our taking note of another more recent publication, the four-thousand-plus-page *Norton Anthology of World Religions*, edited by Jack Miles (2014; along with a corps of established scholars), hailed in reviews as a magisterial and authoritative project. This project, I suggest, represents pretty much for the first part of the twenty-first century further confirmation and consolidation of what Müller's colonialist project of the late nineteenth century signified. The claims of Miles's *Norton Anthology of World Religions* project to broader representativeness in the texts selected hardly makes it less problematic in conceptual-political terms. For the globalized twenty-first century, it is arguably far more problematic in its very conceptualization. Without a critical perspective on what the very concept of world/scriptural religions means and what it has wrought among us, the drawing up of more texts cannot be sufficient.

I have, after so many years of effort, come to agree with anxiety-filled critics that my orientation to criticism and my critical project do not fit. My perspectives and presuppositions and orientation are in sharp conflict with the reigning programs and paradigms within and beyond the academy, insofar as the latter—obviously, including biblical studies as metonymic field and discourse—continue to turn around the generally apolitical (meaning conservative-apologetic textualist-historicist-theological) practices and orientation to the text. I see the failure to problematize word/discourse/scriptures in critical-cultural terms as an influence and/ or controlling factor of unacknowledged, mostly unrecognized apologetics for white/colonialist dominance. I do not get the point—on the part of anyone, much less "minority" scholars—of continuing to engage the fields absent the addressing of these problems.

Several years ago, I approached that point of break in consciousness that brings me to the argument being made here. I would like to think that point approximates where Amiri Baraka was in psychic terms when he promoted the concept of the scream (Benston 2000, 204–7). I was also seemingly channeling James Carville, Bill Clinton's campaign aide, with his mantra regarding the need to focus "like a laser beam" on what is important (for him it was the economy), when I began several years ago to scream (*to myself!*) in both affirmation and refusal: "It's *scripturalization*, stupid!" It is *not* the text in itself. *Not* the obfuscating and mystifying appearance of the books/texts in the form of authorized-canonical-publication (the anthology/reference work as canon). *Not* the philological-exegetical engagement (the lexical-content-meaning—liberal or conservative-fundamentalist) of the text. *Not* the assessment of the text's soaring rhetoric or literary features and turns. *Not* the establishment of its more-or-less accurate historical background (whether Jesus was married or Black …). *Not the* proclamations about it as high culturalist achievement. And so forth.

No. What the scream is about is a different orientation to meaning itself. It raises the most basic but disturbing question about it, including what the "it" represents. It raises questions about that mystifying instrument of communication of meaning—word, words, scriptures (Smith 1993). It uses the engagement of scriptures to think with and to pursue a critical intellectual project and initiative around such engagement. In effect, it involves excavating: scripturalization as social-cultural-discursive and political regime or formation, scripturalism as the ideology turning around the politics of the written, and scripturalizing as reference to ongoing cultural practices with the word, with attendant complex politics and effects. With these concepts I advance a challenge for critical interpretation that is transgressive—far beyond any one current field or discipline.

No, it is *not* biblical studies. However, biblical studies, I think, should be in the forefront in responding to this challenge and be remapped and reoriented. It is essentially a challenge to invent and model a different transdisciplinary field of critical studies, scrambling and upending the traditional fields and disciplines that serve to mask sophisticated (religion- and culture-based) apologetics that are widely played out. What I propose here is thicker and more layered than the analysis of the rigid interplay of domination and resistance found in James C. Scott's (1990) *Domination and the Arts of Resistance*. It is consonant with but more expansive and fluid than Benedict Anderson's (2006) focus on the constitution of the nation, in his *Imagined Communities*. Using my own research on African/African diaspora experiences and expressivities as touchstone, as portal, and as analytical wedge, this critical intellectual project I call *signifying (on) scriptures*. The matrix and safe space for it—necessarily, for the time being, located outside the traditional academy—is the research organization I have founded, called the Institute for Signifying Scriptures (signifyingscriptures.org).

As fraught shorthand, Scriptures desperately need to be exploded, refracted, to be examined on terms befitting the complexity of the situation and dynamics—namely, the level of the metalexical and meta-discursive, the sociocultural and sociopolitical, the psycho-social and ethnographic—that they represent. What we mean by the term *scriptures* and by the dynamics associated with such at the most profound level point to more than a text—this or that canonical text. The shorthand points to the ultimate politics of the word, of language, part of the establishment and management of meaning as part of the making and striving of the human. Fears and anxieties inspire scriptures, as the latter are made to stoke and more broadly manage these fears and anxieties.

In *White Men's Magic: Scripturalization as Slavery*, I argue, using Olaudah Equiano's (2003) signifying on early modern Britain in his *Interesting Narrative*, about what should be the focus of critical attention (Wimbush 2012). One of the earliest and most complex anglophone slave narratives, Equiano's self-storying is a provocative text to think with about the formation of the modern, especially with its complex engagement of the text that was the British Bible or Scriptures. Among the issues taken up by Equiano were the funny dynamics and phenomena he observed among the British. These dynamics and phenomena—what he called "white men's magic"—I call scripturalization.

The latter term is more expansive than—even as it includes—religion and text. Certainly, it is at least beyond religion as conceptualized and delimited and put in its sphere or domain by the religion-allergic and -anxious "enlightened" figures. Further, ironically, scripturalization must be conceptualized in critical expansive terms so as to be understood as itself a product, if not a syndrome, of the Enlightenment. What can be referred to as scripturalization facilitates some differences and conflicts among us, but it also *paradoxically and ironically* binds us together—into the "universe of the undiscussed" (Bourdieu 1977, 168). So scripturalization can be argued to be a chief characteristic, if not the defining orientation, of at least the modern anglophone world, certainly, and arguably the North Atlantic world. This is a world of the word, a texted/textured world, the semiosphere, for moderns (Lotman 2001, 2).

The period in which scripturalization was most firmly constructed as a reality and consolidated as a regime—with much psychosocial, cultural, political and other forms of violence and toxicity as strategy and as fallout—was that of the first contacts between "civilization" and the "savage," the West and the Other. Columbus's voyages can serve as very useful historical marker and node for theorizing and critical analysis (Wynter 1997, 141–52).

Although it does not have its original impetus in his work, my conceptualization of scripturalization is complimentary of and complementary to—and is in many respects an invited elaboration on—French theorist Michel de Certeau's notion of scriptural economy and of scriptural practice/reading among the everyday practices that define social life. Advanced in his phenomenal book *The Practice of Everyday Life*, his focus on the scriptural remained at the level of broad and general theorizing (de Certeau 1984). Although not without poignant examples here and there, the work clearly assumed modern-era and, most important, racially and ethnically homogenous (namely, pan-white) Europe as singular if not supreme example and context—or, perhaps, more accurately, with France as the most obviously practical focus. At any rate, I certainly read de Certeau's work as an invitation to probe further and more deeply into others' practices, problems, and contexts—historical and contemporary.

However, I arrogate to myself the right to use, in direct defiance of and conflict with traditional scholarly works that have to do with the subject here at hand, dispossessed peoples, especially Black peoples, to think with. Following the language and arguments set forth in Toni Morrison's (1992, 90) now-famous provocative essay, I aim to practice a type of criticism that is commensurate with her notion of "playing in the dark," the agenda and interests of which are neither "too polite [n]or too fearful" to take note of, or indeed, embrace, "disrupting darkness."

Now back to Equiano, in order to demonstrate what window Equiano's story about himself opens onto this fraught phenomenon of scripturalization and critical thinking about such. In his chapter 11, Equiano is depicted on one of his many sailing adventures. This time he records himself in flagrant imitation of Columbus, no less, lording it over those he and his party come upon in Jamaica and call—what else—"Indians."

> Recollecting a passage I had read in the life of Columbus, when he was amongst the Indians in Jamaica, where, on some occasion, he frightened them, by telling them of certain events in the heavens, I had recourse to the same expedient, and it succeeded beyond my most sanguine expectations. When I had formed my determination, I went in the midst of them ... I pointed up to the heavens ... I told them God lived there, and he was angry with them ... and if they did not leave off, and go away quietly, I would take the book (pointing to the bible), read, and *tell* God to make them dead. This was something like magic. (Equiano 2003, 208)

344 Vincent L. Wimbush

Here it is in all its poignancy—the wielding of the word, scriptures used as culturalist-discursive/nationalist weapon. As white men's magic—used by a Black man, to show himself "almost a white man." Here is scripturalization as part of the regime of meaning-transcendent, as part of meaning-making and meaning-management, a system in which the (stable) meaning is actually in the performance of ownership and control. Content-meaning to be gained from the book is secondary, controlled by the metatextual meaning in actually pointing out and pointing to the book.

Nevertheless, the regime Equiano mimics occludes the full onslaught, the underlying framing meaning—involving the meaning of whiteness and its various European (especially here Spanish and English), early Manichaean-style opposites—*indios, negras/negros* (Fanon 1963, 1967; Wynter 1997, 159). Only an ex-centric, a stranger, in this case a Black stranger, could signify on the word, on scriptures, on the word in/as a system, in this way. Equiano's mimetics beg the question—How did this politics of language involving the performance of the scriptural come about?

That the self-understandings, practices and performances, politics and orientations of complexly minoritized communities—that is, those racially hypersignified—throughout the circum-Atlantic worlds have much to teach us about the formation and deformation of the human should not startle or surprise. From their different forced positionalities on the margins, these minoritized colored peoples open wide windows onto the challenges of human striving. These include their experiences of pressures (even if never realized) to conform to white men's conventional-canonical construals of language forms of communication, representation, and embodiment (or mimicry); opportunities taken to speak back to and confront and overturn conventionality (or interruptions); and the need to experience ongoing, meaningful relationships (or accommodation/orientation) to white-centering politics, practices, and myths that define the burgeoning nation-states.

I am with these arguments in agreement with literary critic Srinivas Aravamudan's (1999, 233–34) important challenge that we put focus on the strangers, the dispossessed, as "tropicopolitans" and on their "tropicopolizations"—that is, how these subalterns, Equiano as one of his powerful examples, read and "make do (*fait faire*)," with the dominant world. I argue in *White Men's Magic* that Equiano read, as Sojourner Truth later made the point, not (merely) the content-lexical-meaning of the English Scriptures but the scripturalizing practices/the scripturalism/the scripturalization of the English elite, who, as inventors and wielders of the nationalizing-

"Talkin' 'bout Somethin'"   345

cultural texts, exercised "*unbounded influence* over the credulity and superstition of the people" (Wimbush 2012). It was just such influence, or magic, that was understood by Equiano to function much like the magic he *imagined* had been obtained among the Igbo priests and magicians of his homeland (if not land of birth).

The notion of influence in Equiano's text is important; it has disturbed me for some time. The language is problematic—at once too obvious and easy and hard to fathom, both apt and incongruent, both familiar and odd. Who speaks this way, in what contexts, reflective of what politics? I grant that one of the main points of Equiano's narrative was to demonstrate that he could talk that talk, could make the book speak, and so forth. However, in seeking, as he does in his chapter 1, to draw a parallel between white men's ways and the ways of his people, the Igbos, he aims to show that the latter had mechanisms and protocols for divining meaning (magical ways with words, a type of scriptural system like the white men), but he overreaches.

He presses his ethnic-tribal-cultural ecumenism and religious comparativism too hard. "Unbounded influence" is the language and/or ideology not of any local tribe or village, Igbo or otherwise. It is the language and ideology of the extensive civilizations, the empires or modern European nations and their reflections and projections of state-inflected world religions and the scriptural economies/fundamentalisms refracted by such. The language of "unbounded influence" seems out of step with the textures of life in the scale of social organization that was the real or partly constructed Igboland. It was the anxiety around such issues that was the basis of the comparison made by Equiano in relationship to the white man.

This problem of misapplication raises some other important issues and questions. Given what is known about ways of knowing and patterns of authority in tribal and village societies throughout the world, the Igbo priests and magicians, like their counterparts in other tribal groups, especially in African societies, were very unlikely to have been thought to possess unchecked authority (Thornton 1996, ch. 9). What, then, does Equiano's thinking here suggest about the differences in construals of knowing and authority, discourse and power, and the politics of language in European and African worlds? If Equiano's point of comparison is unsurprisingly, even compellingly, fictionalized history, historical fiction, what reality does it nonetheless reflect? What issues—about human consciousness and knowing—are reflected in the politics of the comparison?

346   Vincent L. Wimbush

The most profound challenge of Equiano's narrative is to help the reader see the reality of white men's magic, indeed, to see whiteness as construction or in terms of performance, the performance that is scripturalization, which is part of the evolutionary dynamics of knowledge or meaning management. Scripturalization, as it appears in Equiano's world, is not different from our own in its most significant respect, given the invention of writing and the printing press. It is the discursive/ideological playing field onto which we all are now, more or less, forced. It has a wide if not global reach; it is not of local Igbo priests and wise men but of unbounded influence; it represents stable meaning. We have in Equiano's narrative a window onto what such a construction makes of Equiano, and, through him, not only all Black strangers but all, even if to different degrees and in some respects, who live, or are made to live, within scriptural civilizations. We must ask, as his narrative provokes us to ask: How did it come to be so? What follows it or is determined by it? What do the dispossessed have to do with it? I should like in this essay to try to begin to account for scripturalization as the dominant and extensive regime of language use and authorized stable forms of knowing. I want also to try to position the phenomenon within an historical schema of meaning management.

Including scripturalization as a phenomenon reflective of whiteness as ideological-political orientation as well as the baseline on which dominant standard discourse rests, I isolate three types of *reading formations* as types of systems of language use, knowledge claims, stages in the structures of consciousness or meaning and orientations to the world. The first type encompasses the totalistic ways of knowing of traditional local cultures, organized around ritual and oral traditions, including the masking (literally and otherwise) of meaning. The second represents the stable, totalistic-universal knowledge of ways of knowing of extensive hierarchical societies, with the cultivation of meaning-transcendent reflected in their invention and advancement of the scriptural. The third type refers to the mimetics, interruptions, and interrogations of the extensive-totalistic-universal and its orientations and politicism by dispossessed or humiliated peoples, namely, signifying (on) scriptures, including ideological-psychical marronage, resulting in the radical degrading of meaning itself. The middle or second reading formation—scripturalization—is my starting point or touchstone for analysis of the other two as part of the larger schema. *Reading* here is understood rather expansively—in terms of a system of communication and collective knowing.

The first reading-formation—notwithstanding its association with oral and local cultures—is not simply chronologically *prior* and psychosocially anachronistic to the dominant reading that is scripturalization. It is a baseline formation, whence we all developed. It is also complexly perduring in our time, but dislocated and muted, carried and translated by the outliers, the subaltern, and denied by all others. It cannot now be recovered in any simple manner. It need not be reached for in nostalgic or apologetic terms. It reflects basic fears and anxieties and carries its own set of politics, especially the politics of mostly male-specific anxieties over sexual performance and death.

Yet it may provide possibilities for turning back onto, checking, challenging, and denaturalizing the second long-dominant formation that is scripturalization. Examples of this first reading or knowing formation may be found in scientific evolutionary schemas and theories, the most recent and comprehensive of which is Robert Bellah's (2011) magisterial book, *Religion in Human Evolution*. Equiano describes only faintly this traditional village world of the Igbos in his story. Chinua Achebe's (2009) *Things Fall Apart* is a more extended, fascinating, and richer-textured historical fiction, using the village of Umuofia, at the height of the onset of British colonialism in Equiano's homeland, as window (Wimbush 2017).

The third formation—associated with the disruption that is voice-finding and agency and the arrogation of its practice among the humiliated—represents ongoing reiterations and construals of scripturalization. Yet, it also provides openings and possibilities for its own upending, for moving beyond it, in marronage, to a state in which meaning is ruptured, made not mean (at least on traditional terms).

These three turns in and types of formation should not be understood to be chronologically successive or to represent mutually exclusive temporalities. They overlap in time and in all but the earliest, barely recoverable historical situations, for example, before the onset and fairly widespread popular practices of writing and reading. Insofar as these formations represent forms or structures of consciousness and social psychologies and orientations, they are more than ideas about ideas, concepts about concepts, or abstract abstractions. I understand them to be more fundamentally about social textures and psychosocial dynamics, orientations of the embodied, everyday practices of ordinary lives that are scripted, namely, made to mean.

What does focus on the Black subject/body do or add to this theory? What must not be lost sight of is that the modern world in which the Black

348   Vincent L. Wimbush

self/Black body has been race-d, overdetermined in racial terms, is itself the major impetus for, or reflection of, the phenomenon of scripturalization. The Black body, as Charles Long (1986, 4) puts it, has been "signified," or, according to my framework here, scripturalized. "In America, it is traditional to destroy the black body—*it is heritage.*" So, in wrenching notes impossible to respond to, argues Ta-Nehisi Coates (2015) in *Between the World and Me.* This phenomenon of scripturalization as the violence of construction of meaning—that is, Black always necessarily to mean lack or deficit—requires persistent defense or management of meaning as the way to exercise and maintain control. *Scriptures*, then, is here shorthand for the refractions of social-cultural domains and practices that represent a mechanism or protocol for the control or stabilization of meaning.

What is this meaning to be controlled? It is sadly this—*that Black and white exist* and *how white and Black mean in the modern world.* Frantz Fanon taught us much about this situation with his argument about the lie that is the tight, epistemic, Manichean structure that colonial dominance sets up in the modern world (Sekyi-Out 1996, 33–35). The modern ideology that is generative of scriptures as object and as cultural practices—what I call scripturalism—is metareligious, pan-cultural, universal. The regime in which scriptures are made to work or operate is reflected in John Locke's politics of language or "purification"—what I call here scripturalization (Bauman and Briggs 2003, 18, passim; Wimbush 2012, 173–74). Whatever the interests at point of origin, it has devolved into the violent—controlling, suffocating, enslaving, and policing. It cannot be ignored or simply played with and played off, through fancy methods and approaches to texts of different domains—academy, law, politics, economics, and so forth. It has to be met—as Fanon (1967) and others make plain—with alternate forms of conscientization.

What the Black subject represents in this tight situation is *difference* (as in Equiano's difference from Englishmen, and his difference from the Indians as his mimetics/performance of white men shows). Further, there is in this difference the potential to model a turn in human knowing or consciousness—what Fanon (1963, 9) calls relativism, "new humanism"; Du Bois (1989, ch. 14), the "gift"; and I, the radical *rupture of meaning* (Wimbush 2017). It is so only in complex reaction to the enslavement of meaning that is scripturalization. It is contingent politics in response to what is before us. This refusal of meaning is to be distinguished from postmodernism's tight ideological principle of indifference to stable meaning. What we are confronted with among the dispossessed of the

"Talkin' 'bout Somethin'"   349

world is rather the harsh reality of the politically contingent need to be made aware that the meaning constructed by dominants cannot hold sway, that it must be refused, and that unmeaning is to be embraced like air for breathing. This consciousness is reached first through the experience of the pulverization of meaning through slavery and the ensuing contempt in which slaves and their seed are held. This experience serves as potential springboard into transmuting and theorizing the world's contempt into *contemptus mundi* and translating it into the practices and politics of radical marronage, with its strange sounds and silences and gestures (Wimbush 2000, introduction).

A now-classic example of the phenomenon involved here, which provokes hard thinking on our part, is found in Frederick Douglass's first autobiography, his 1845 *Narrative of the Life of Frederick Douglass, an American Slave.* The writerly Douglass looks back on an incident from his youthful years when he was a slave. This look back reflects already a conceit about differences and consciousness. The incident he reports was likely a recurring one, but he makes it read like a singular pointed incident for the sake of heightened narratological effect. The famous and riveting incident can now teach us much about thinking about meaning and the experience:

> The slaves selected to go to the Great House Farm ... would make the dense woods, for miles around, reverberate with their wild songs, revealing at once the highest joy and the deepest sadness.... Especially would they do this, when leaving home. They would then sing most exultingly ... words which to many would seem *unmeaning jargon*, but which, nevertheless, were full of meaning to themselves.... I did not, when a slave, understand the deep meaning of those *rude and apparently incoherent songs*. (quoted in Andrews 1996, 37–38)

Reflecting on the situation of black slaves—including his memory of his own slave self—Douglass thinks in terms of what literary critic Kimberly Benston (2000, 293) calls "site" sanctioning "insight." He thinks in terms of different types of consciousness and speech corresponding to or determined by different positionalities: the enslaving, meaning the Great House Farm; the group of the enslaved; and the runagate, the Douglass of the story, yes, but also at a remove Douglass the writer. He begins with physical Black enslavement on the way to a problematization of what others have described in different ways. In effect, what he does resonates with what Houston Baker (1984, 144–55), following the argument of Stephen

350 Vincent L. Wimbush

Henderson, called the "black (w)hole," what Howard Thurman (1965) thought about in terms of luminous darkness, and what critical studies scholar Abdul JanMohammed (2005) theorized about Richard Wright's work in terms of the death-bound subject and the archaeology of death.

Yet it is precisely at this point, I believe, that one finds the issue that Douglass touches on but does not fully grasp (who can, really, given the issues, the forces to contend with here?), the larger critical issue for an understanding of the consciousness of the dispossessed. It was precisely in that discursive psychosocial space—*between home and the Great House Farm*—where the "unmeaning jargon" and the "rude and incoherent songs" were made and heard, and where meaning of the sort associated with the Great House Farm was enscripturalized even as it was ruptured, refused, and signified on (Benston 2000). It is resonant of that zone that theorist and critic Sekyi-Otu (1996, 54), following Fanon, calls "non-being, an extraordinarily arid and sterile region, an utterly naked declivity where an authentic upheaval can be born." It is the space between the stable secure house, in which masters sit and manage meaning, and that volatile expanse of jargon and wild freedom, representing the edge and fragmentation of culture, and the possibility of something new.

In light of these phenomena and dynamics, I should like to call for a criticism of "unmeaning jargon" as part of this critical consciousness-raising project, complementing literary critic Houston Baker's (1988, 88–110) call for a "criticism of silence," in his "Lowground and Inaudible Valleys: Reflections on Afro-American Spirit Work." The function of the omissions and silences and of the jargon is not passivity but an active ascetics of refusal of the traditional uses and forms of language. This resonates with Toni Morrison's (1998, 306) language about "br[eaking] the back of words" and with other critics' analysis of what takes place in several domains and contexts—science, education, politics—so infected by anti-Black racialism (Long 1986).

It also resonates powerfully with philosopher Susan Buck-Morss's (2009) argument in her book *Hegel, Haiti, and Universal History*, in which she draws on literary critic Joan Dayan's (1998) brilliant work *Haiti, History, and the Gods*. First, African diaspora expressivities, especially in religious rituals, are said to reflect persistent loss and dispossession. Further, with such loss of culture and nation and body, these rituals are said to translate not the intact traditions that mark so much nationalist-ideological analysis straining desperately to identify intact traditions from the African continent, but now the "shreds of bodies come back" and the

"Talkin' 'bout Somethin'" 351

resultant "decay of meanings" (Buck-Morss 2009, 127 n. 112; Dayan 1998, 35–37).

With African diasporas, we are faced with peoples whose collective body/spirit was pulverized, a people who, according to writer Derek Walcott (1993, n.p.), have "no nation now but imagination," who are fragments, "the cracked heirlooms whose restoration shows its white scars." How could history be other than absurd? This stark orientation suggests the potential that can be gained from finding agency in the expressivities of those who speak in other words, outside the symbolic order or meaning machine. With its need and tendency, as Pierre Bourdieu (1977, 170) puts it, to "occult the aphasia," to veil the veiling, dominant Western discourse must now be ripped, as Du Bois and Morrison might put it, made to be seen to be what it is (Wimbush 2008).

Concluding Comments

Finally, we are brought back to the matter of the Black Atlantic, reading and signifying, difference and mimetics. This is the "mimetic excess" that Michael Taussig (1993) argues, following Horkheimer and Adorno, breaks the normally violent repressed and closed circle of mimetics. It is "reflexive awareness"—an awareness of the play, as if it were real, as if artifice were natural. This excess is now situated precisely—compellingly, necessarily—in the situations of postcoloniality, or postslavery and Jim Crow-ism, in which the historically dispossessed and humiliated take hold of the tools and magical tricks that historically had been exclusively in the hands of the overground, the male elites, including political-economic, academic-intellectual, and religio-cultic virtuosi. It becomes a type of radical agency—a capacity "to live subjunctively," that is, the "freedom to live reality as really made-up" (Taussig 1993, 254–55). "Black is ... and black ain't.... Blackness will make you and unmake you," Ellison (1995, 9) taught us. Anything goes, as Richard Wright's Fred Daniels came to understand in the underground, because one sees that what went on in the overground worlds was all made up. Equiano showed us that white men were scripturalized constructions, that the world religions and their fundamentalisms and supernationalist orientations of the sort that we take for granted are the construction produced by white men's magic/scripturalism, not by Black folks.

This means that Black and other dispossessed folk were also constructions. Indeed, their constructions were the impetus for early modern intensifications of constructivism; they were intended to mean according to their already-forced positioning in the larger construction that is scripturalization. Those dispossessed folk, all made to be Black, now with their varied scripturalizing practices—reflective of some agency in the sense that, according to Zora Neale Hurston (1990, xxi), even the Bible was "made over to suit their vivid imagination"—may teach us something. Are we not all, should we not all be, now located in that space between "home and the Great House Farm"? That discursive space in which we must navigate between the stable, secure Great House Farm (of discourse) and that volatile expanse of unmeaning jargon and wild freedom, which represents the edge and end of culture, that place beyond (the categories of) religion, tribe, and nation, and their nexus? We have, historically, mostly been forced to mean according to the directives and tight circumstances of the Great House Farm, but how might we now *not* mean in this fraught space that is our current circumstance? The space is frightening, not only because of the policing and death inherent in it but also because it facilitates radical agency.

We have, in my view, hardly begun to recognize and to act on as much. My challenge to readers is that we commit ourselves as promiscuous, transgressive collectives—across ethnic enclaves, national boundaries, academic field-discursive prisons, religious affiliations—to the hard but compelling work before us: to learn for our problems and opportunities of our times *what* to read and what it means to read/signify/inflect. Now we simply must learn to read scripturalization (as part of our formation and enslavement) and thereby learn to scripturalize the human (as part of de-/re-formation, agency, and power).

Have we the resolve and commitment to be other than the minoritized critics an academic field needs for its decidedly modernist and corrosive politics? Have we the courage to declare with Fanon that we will henceforth not be prisoners of history/meaning—whether white colonial or Afrocentric, disciplinary or denominational, home or school, political party or nation, and the several other vectors of scripturalization? That we will be among those dissident intellectuals who, through hard successive choices, in each Jeffersonian generation, defy meaning and find radical freedom to find a way to a new story, to a new humanism. One in which we learn—as Sojourner Truth by tradition encourages us—to read not letters but "men and nations." One in which, following the pressing politics reflected in the vernacular of the folk, might we finally begin "talkin' 'bout somethin'" (Wimbush 2011, 9, 24)?

"Talkin' 'bout Somethin'"   353

Works Cited

Achebe, Chinua. 2009. *Things Fall Apart: Authoritative Text, Contexts and Criticism.* Edited by Francis Abiola Irele. New York: Norton.

Anderson, Bernard. 2006. *Imagined Communities: Reflections on the Origin and Spread of Nationalism.* Rev. ed. New York: Verso.

Andrews, William L., ed. 1996. *The Oxford Frederick Douglass Reader.* New York: Oxford University Press.

Aravamudan, Srinivas. 1999. *Tropicopolitans: Colonialism and Agency, 1688–1804.* Durham, NC: Duke University Press.

Baker, Houston A., Jr. 1984. *Blues, Ideology, and Afro-American Literature: A Vernacular Theory.* Chicago: University of Chicago Press.

———. 1988. *Afro-American Poetics: Revisions of Harlem and the Black Aesthetic.* Madison: University of Wisconsin Press.

Bauman, Richard, and Charles L. Briggs. 2003. *Voices of Modernity: Language Ideologies and the Politics of Inequality.* New York: Cambridge University Press.

Bellah, Robert N. 2011. *Religion in Human Evolution: From the Paleolithic to the Axial Age.* Cambridge, MA: Belknap.

Benston, Kimberly W. 2000. *Performing Blackness: Enactments of African-American Modernism.* New York: Routledge.

Bourdieu, Pierre. 1977. *Outline of a Theory of Practice.* Cambridge: Cambridge University Press.

Buck-Morss, Susan. 2009. *Hegel, Haiti, and Universal History.* Pittsburgh: University of Pittsburgh Press.

Certeau, Michel de. 1984. *The Practice of Everyday Life.* Berkeley: University of California Press.

Césaire, Aimé. 1990. "Poetry and Knowledge." In *Lyric and Dramatic Poetry: 1946–82.* Translated by Clayton Eshleman and Annette Smith. Charlottesville: University Press of Virginia.

Coates, Ta-Nehesi. 2015. *Between the World and Me.* New York: Spiegel & Grau.

Dayan, Joan. 1998. *Haiti, History, and the Gods.* Berkeley: University of California Press.

Du Bois, W. E. B. 1989. *The Souls of Black Folk.* New York: Bantam Books.

Ellison, Ralph. 1995. *Invisible Man.* New York: Vintage Books.

Equiano, Olaudah. 2003. *Olaudah Equiano: The Interesting Narrative and Other Writings.* Edited by Vincent Carretta. New York: Penguin.

Fanon, Frantz. 1963. *Wretched of the Earth.* New York: Grove.

354 Vincent L. Wimbush

———. 1967. *Black Skin, White Masks*. New York: Grove.

Foucault, Michel. 1994. *The Order of Things: An Archaeology of the Human Sciences*. New York: Vintage Books.

Hurston, Zora Neale. 1990. *Mules and Men*. New York: Perennial Library.

JanMohammed, Abdul R. 2005. *The Death-Bound-Subject: Richard Wright's Archaeology of Death*. Durham, NC: Duke University Press.

Long, Charles H. 1986. *Significations: Signs, Symbols, and Images in the Interpretation of Religion*. Philadelphia: Fortress.

Lotman, Yuri M. 2001. *Universe of the Mind: A Semiotic Theory of Culture*. London: Taurus.

Masuzawa, Tomoko. 2005. *The Invention of the World Religions: Or, How European Universalism Was Preserved in the Language of Pluralism*. Chicago: University of Chicago Press.

Miles, Jack, Wendy Doniger, Donald S. Lopez Jr., and James Robson, eds. 2014. *The Norton Anthology of World Religions*. New York: Norton.

Morrison, Toni. 1992. *Playing in the Dark: Whiteness and the Literary Imagination*. Cambridge: Harvard University Press.

———. 1998. *Beloved: A Novel*. New York: Vintage.

Scott, James C. 1990. *Domination and the Arts of Resistance: Hidden Transcripts*. New Haven: Yale University Press.

Sekyi-Otu, Ato. 1996. *Fanon's Dialectic of Experience*. Cambridge: Harvard University Press.

Smith, Wilfred Cantwell. 1993. *What Is Scripture? A Comparative Approach*. Philadelphia: Fortress.

Taussig, Michael. 1993. *Mimesis and Alterity: A Particular History of the Senses*. New York: Routledge.

Thornton, John K. 1996. *Africa and Africans in the Making of the Atlantic World, 1400–1800*. Cambridge: Cambridge University Press.

Thurman, Howard. 1965. *The Luminous Darkness: A Personal Interpretation of the Anatomy of Segregation and the Ground of Hope*. New York: Harper & Row.

Walcott, Derek. 1993. *The Antilles: Fragments of Epic Memory*. New York: Farrar, Straus & Giroux.

Wimbush, Vincent L., ed. 2000. *African Americans and the Bible: Sacred Texts and Social Textures*. New York: Continuum International.

———. 2008. "'Naturally Veiled and Half Articulate': Scriptures, Modernity, and the Formation of African America." Pages 56–68 in *Still at the Margins: Biblical Scholarship Fifteen Years after the Voices from the Margin*. Edited by Rasiah S. Sugirtharajah. Maryknoll, NY: Orbis Books.

———. 2011. "Interpreters—Enslaving/Enslaved/Runagate." *JBL* 130:5–24.

———. 2012. *White Men's Magic: Scripturalization as Slavery*. New York: Oxford University Press.

———. 2017. *Scripturalectics: The Management of Meaning*. New York: Oxford University Press.

Wynter, Sylvia. 1997. "Columbus, the Ocean Blue, and Fables That Stir the Mind: To Reinvent the Study of Letters." Pages 141–64 in *Poetics of the Americas: Race, Founding, and Textuality*. Edited by Bainard Cowan and Jefferson Humphries. Baton Rouge: Louisiana State University Press.

Part 3
Conclusion

On the Threshold of End Times:
Paths and Agendas of Minoritized Criticism

Fernando F. Segovia

In 2014, during my term as president of the Society of Biblical Literature, I devoted the presidential address to the topic of critical posture (Segovia 2015). I sought to ponder, as the title indicates, the vision and task of criticism, and biblical criticism in particular, in the light of the times at hand. Such times I portrayed as critical, insofar as I perceived a set of major crises bearing down, individually as well as collectively, on the world. I had no inkling then of how steep and frightening the deterioration of the global scene would be in but a few years' time. The latter part of the 2010s brought about—or, better, forced—a radical overhaul in my assessment regarding the state of affairs of the world. Such revisioning came about as a result of a conjunction of fateful developments. None of them was novel by any means, having long trajectories behind them, but they had all reached a striking point of inflection. Regardless of original point of eruption or primary area of impact, these developments have all crossed and will continue to cross borders, leaving no one and no place unaffected. I have three such developments in mind, which I present in chronological order.

The first development involves the United States, the American empire, as the epicenter of the global order and artificer of the Pax Americana that followed World War II. The years 2017–2021 represent the term of office corresponding to Donald J. Trump as president of the United States. Over the course of the quatrennium, this administration unleashed, in sustained and escalating fashion, a social-cultural upheaval of alarming proportions in the country. As is always the way of empire, this upheaval had multiple and direct ramifications for the rest of the world. The other two developments have to do with the global scene as a whole. First, toward the end of the quatrennium, a sudden and swift outbreak of infectious disease set off a medical convulsion of enormous and lethal magnitude throughout the world. Then, soon after the end of the quatrennium, an unprecedented and widespread outbreak of weather events brought about an environmental convulsion of dire proportions for the world. As is the way of such phenomena, these developments of nature had bleak repercussions for the United States as well. This confluence of developments reached a climax during the first half of 2021, with many more and much worse turning points to come in the future. The result is a situation, a crossroads, that may justifiably be described as an overture or portal to end times, to times of apocalyptic dystopia.

What had transpired in the space of seven years was remarkable. In 2014 I had foregrounded the crisis of global economics, in the light of the global meltdown of 2008 and its still palpable consequences, especially for the Global South. I placed it alongside two others, a crisis of climate change and a crisis of worldwide migration, which I viewed as primary at the time, while mentioning a number of others in passing—geopolitical competition, political breakdown, explosion of violence. This global context, I argued, was widely perceived as "uniquely critical, beyond all critical times of the twentieth century, severe as these were," an evaluation with which I found myself in full concurrence (Segovia 2015, 16–17). Only seven years later, I find myself having to go beyond this assessment, to take it up a notch, to see the present juncture as more critical still. This I have sought to convey by invoking an aura of apocalyptic unease.

As with all moments of end-times foreboding, the present juncture conveys a twofold revelation. On the one hand, an unveiling of what lies in store takes place—a glimpse at the future, catastrophic and inevitable. On the other hand, there is also an unveiling of what stands in place—an insight into the present, awry and frightening. This juncture I should like to unfold further by way of the singular developments, the major crises, mentioned above. As phenomena that spread across countries and affect large numbers of people, these may be said to constitute a confluence of pandemics. In what follows I proceed in order of gravity.

A Confluence of Pandemics

Foremost among these stands the environmental-climatological pandemic, marked by the irruption of weather extremes throughout the world, in the Global South and the Global North alike. To be sure, the crisis of climate change has been anticipated for quite some time, and signs of its

On the Threshold of End Times   361

presence have already been detected for years in no uncertain ways. Now, however, it has arrived in full force, much earlier than expected, making itself felt in widespread and terrifying ways in 2021. That a feared threshold in the Anthropocene epoch, a point of no return, has been reached, there can be no doubt (Plummer and Fountain 2001).[1] All that remains now, it would seem, is containment, for prevention has been rendered out of the question. I present this crisis as foremost, as most acute, because it lays open a future of radical uncertainty and looming peril for all humanity. Of course, as is always the case, this future will prove far more grievous for some than for others, at least in its initial stages, and in this regard the Global South will suffer much.

The second pandemic bears a nationalist-exceptionalist stamp, involving a panoply of distinctive features: white in ethnic-racial identity, supremacist in social-cultural constitution, nativist in attitude toward and treatment of the Other, and messianic in religious-theological orientation. This crisis of populist nationalism I would characterize as unnerving and reverberating. It has been simmering for years in the Global North, particularly in the West, as a result of repeated waves of migration from the Global South and the economic detritus left behind by the economic recession of 2008. While the former yielded acute resentment of the Other, given their expanding presence in their midst, the latter led to intense distrust of the state, given the policies that led to their plight. This crisis came to full expression, protracted and mounting, with the phenomenon of Trump and the crusade of Make America Great Again from 2017 to 2021.

Then, following the electoral defeat of the leader-savior, the crisis reached a decided point of inflection on 6 January 2021, when the movement mounted an open insurrection against the state, seeking a violent interruption of the electoral process, while invoking a narrative of a stolen election by a deep state. In keeping with the feast of the day in the Christian liturgical calendar, this date represents a veritable epiphany of the crisis: a manifestation of its far-reaching roots and its will to triumph. This crisis I have classified as unsettling, insofar as it heightens the sense of uncertainty and peril regarding the future at the heart of the American empire. Such reverberations of insecurity at the center of power will have,

---

1. For a sobering assessment, see Solnit 2021. For a reflection on its repercussions, including the possibility of a final exit for humanity, see Žižek 2021.

362 Fernando F. Segovia

as always, grievous consequences for everyone else in the future, nowhere more so than in the Global South.

Foundational among the crises lies the medical-virological pandemic, signified by the irruption of COVID-19. This crisis of human welfare emerged in the People's Republic of China in the winter of 2019–2020, spread rapidly around the globe through 2020, and now presents a series of ongoing surges and variants in 2021. This is certainly not the first pandemic that has afflicted the human species, nor will it be the last. It has, however, been the most extensive in over a hundred years, since the great influenza of 1918, and has wreaked much havoc throughout, in both the Global North and the Global South.

Now, with the arrival of the Delta variant in early 2021, the virus has turned far more contagious and aggressive, marking a clear point of inflection. That the virus has come to stay, in one form or another, despite spectacular successes in prevention and treatment, seems beyond doubt as well. I present this crisis as foundational, because, over and beyond its medical dimension, it has brought to the surface, with trenchant clarity, the many differential chasms that cut across society and culture everywhere, within states as well as across states. As a result, the crisis further enhances the sense of uncertainty and peril surrounding the future that already hovers over all humanity. The combination of lethal consequences and conscientization of disparity will make, as is always the case, for grievous ramifications everywhere, especially in the Global South, which always fares worse and where such effects are only now beginning to be felt.

A Confluence Interactive

In speaking of confluence, it is imperative not to think of these developments simply along individual and separate lines. It is essential, rather, to see them as interrelated and interdependent, indeed closely so, interfeeding and interpropelling one another. Thus, what happens in one case alters the rest, nourishing and intensifying the other pandemics as well. On this point, I find a recent opinion piece, "Apocalypse or Cooperation," published in *Project Syndicate* by Jayati Ghosh (2021), professor of economics at the University of Massachusetts Amherst, to be most relevant and instructive. The first sentence is striking: "The Apocalypse is now." Such is the message, she argues, presented by the "perfect storm of COVID-19 and climate change that has broken." This perfect storm is actually expanded to include a third component, namely, economics, given the massive loss of employment and the dramatic spike in inequality already underway throughout.

The consequences of climate change, which is portrayed as "playing out in real time" and involving "irreversible" climatic trends, will affect—as it has already begun to do—all parts of the world, any number of natural species, and the conditions of human life itself—drastically so. The consequences of COVID-19, which is described as "unlikely to end for years" as the virus mutates into "increasingly transmissible and drug-resistant variants," will bring about—as it has already begun to occur—"substantial income losses, declining access to basic needs, acute deprivation, and hunger"—at levels unimaginable. Such conditions will prove simply unsustainable and will yield social and political turbulence throughout—severely so. Standing at the brink, for Ghosh there is only one way forward: international cooperation, about which she is less than optimistic. The last sentence is no less striking: otherwise will "future species wonder why we chose to participate actively in our own destruction?"

Reflecting on Critical Posture

Any reflection on critical identity and function at this time cannot but begin with this coming together of pandemics, especially since all of them are here to stay for the future. Not just the proximate future, with eventual return to the old normal, the situation ante quem, but a future long-lasting, with the dawn of a new normal, a situation post quem. At the same time, these are not the only major crises that are having an impact on the global scene at present. Revolving around these, a number of others can be readily discerned. One of these I had previously foregrounded: global economics; this, as outlined earlier, Ghosh places at the top of the agenda as well. Another I had highlighted: transnational migration. Three others I had identified: geopolitical disorder, state breakdown, systemic violence. Two others I would now add as well: total surveillance and ethnic-racial othering (the other side of the crisis of populist-nationalism). Alongside the irruption of the pandemics, all of these major crises have become more severe and more consequential in recent years as well.

A number of observations regarding this global scenario are in order. First, each crisis is multidimensional in causes and manifestations, involving, therefore, a variety of constitutive factors and distinctive features. The nomenclature assigned to each, such as climate change, is thus meant as an abstract designation encompassing manifold and related components.

364 Fernando F. Segovia

Further, as already noted earlier with respect to the pandemics, all of these crises stand to one another in interconnected fashion. While each may be examined in its own terms and from a particular trajectory of studies, all may be analyzed in relation to the others and hence as a network. Here, too, it may be said that what happens in one crisis does alter the course of the others, nourishing and intensifying one another throughout, though perhaps some more than others at any one moment. Last, in the light of such a network of interrelationships, the set of crises as a whole may be approached and examined as a phenomenon in its own right. Given the process of interfeeding and interpropelling, the set itself grows in scope as well as in power, setting the stage thereby for what could be characterized as a crisis of the world-system as such. It is for such reasons that I have referred to our times as a portal to apocalyptic dystopia.

It is, then, in the face of this overarching global scenario, not just the coming together of the pandemics highlighted but also the expansive framework of all concomitant crises, that a discussion of critical posture must perforce take place. What I propose to do in what follows is to think through the problematic with the wisdom, the acumen and the resolution, of the participants in the project. What this amounts to is an exercise of reflection *en conjunto*, in joint or collaborative fashion. This is a critical strategy that has been in use for some time now in Latinx American theology, signifying a coming together, from a variety of contexts and perspectives, to shed light on a particular issue or set of issues, with distinct goals in mind. While such goals will vary from conversation to conversation, at the heart of such dialogue in common always lies a perceived need for and acknowledged benefit of diversity—a coming together of multidimensional backgrounds and knowledges, insights and dispositions, expectations and resolutions.

This strategy was put to work in a previous volume of the overall project on minoritized ethnic-racial criticism, *Reading Biblical Texts Together*. Critics from various ethnic-racial strands were asked to interpret the same biblical passage and to discuss the variety of readings produced. Thereupon, I brought together all of the participants in an exercise of joint reflection on the pursuit of minoritized interpretation. What resulted was a rich and sophisticated layout of the dynamics and mechanics at work in ethnic-racial criticism as well as the frameworks and motivations behind such models and strategies.

In this next stage of the project, critics have again been asked to address the same text: not a literary production as such but rather the problematic of critical posture in our times. I will pursue the strategy of collaborative reflection as follows. I begin by securing a sense of how the various critics regard and execute their task in these times, foregrounding a set of key factors and problematics—the reading of the times at hand, the configuration of the task envisioned, and the sense of Scripture at play. I continue by drawing critical mappings in each of the problematics analyzed, providing thereby a spectrum of positions for critical understanding and orientation. I conclude with a beginning exposition of my own take on critical posture, marking a position within each mapping, in the light of my introductory comments on a sense of the end times.

Reading in These Times: Variations on Critical Posture

This first part of the problematic I pursue, as anticipated above, by way of a threefold inquiry. As a first step, I address how these critics discern and assess our present times. My objective here is to determine the major forces and currents that they, as minoritized voices, find as impinging on their lives as academic-professional scholars as well as on the lives of their respective ethnic-racial groups or any set of such groups. Toward this end, I will call on the grid of major crises that I have outlined above in my own analysis of the times. In a second step, I investigate the critical posture that these critics construct and advance for their work as minoritized scholars. My aim in this regard is to ascertain the dynamics and mechanics of interpretation that they deem imperative, given their reading of the times. As a final step, I analyze how these critics look on and appeal to the biblical texts and contexts. My objective here is to establish their position regarding the Bible, its status and role, in the light of their proposed approaches with the present times in mind.

In this process of bringing together critical voices in collaborative reflection, much stands to be learned about critical identity and function in and for minoritized criticism. Indeed, such is the case not only for today but also with respect to the past as well as with the future in mind. In laying out readings of the present, glimpses of both past and present are inevitably tendered. Thus, with regard to the past, a reading of the present may and usually does reveal a sense of trajectory, of the whence and the why. Similarly, with regard to the future, a reading of the present may and usually does discloses a sense of direction, of a whereto and a how. With the latter, utopian impulses, whether envisioned as feasible or as ideal, provide paths out of dystopian circumstances. While such thinking-through

366   Fernando F. Segovia

en conjunto can be pursued in various ways, I have opted for the following
order of presentation. I begin by examining the various proposals by way
of ethnic-racial formation; then, I continue in alphabetical order, within
each group.

African American Critics

Cheryl Anderson: HIV/AIDS Pandemic and African-Descent Reading

Anderson devotes her attention to the crisis of human welfare and, in so
doing, reminds us that this crisis is far broader than the outbreak of the
Covid-19 pandemic. The latter certainly captures and channels attention
today, and with good reason, given its global reach, its facile transmission,
its lethal threat, and its social repercussions, above all in the economic
realm. Nevertheless, many other currents and forces contribute to this
crisis, among which one could readily mention the climbing usage of opi-
oids and the rising rate of mental disorders, such as depression and anxiety.
As an African American critic, Anderson's concern lies with another medical-virological crisis, the HIV/AIDS pandemic: the cross-borders spread
of HIV, the human immunodeficiency virus, and, if untreated, the late-
stage disease of AIDS, acquired immunodeficiency syndrome. HIV/AIDS
was first detected and diagnosed in the early 1980s, and the Minority HIV-
AIDS Fund describes the virus "as the cause of one of humanity's deadliest
and most persistent epidemics."[2]

That Anderson should focus on this ongoing pandemic can be read-
ily understood in light of the statistics provided, which reveal a lopsided
impact on peoples of African origins and descent. Thus, two-thirds of all
HIV infections worldwide are to be found in sub-Saharan Africa, with
South Africa as the country with the highest number of cases in the world.
Further, more than half of new cases in the United States take place among
African Americans, who constitute about 13 percent of the national popu-
lation. That she should do so as a critic can be readily explained as well in

---

2. This description is taken from HIV.gov, an official US government website
managed by the US Department of Health and Human Services and supported by the
Minority HIV/AIDS Fund. See https://tinyurl.com/SBL06106az. The virus, it should be
recalled, spreads by contact with bodily fluids from an HIV-infected person, primarily
through unprotected sexual contact or sharing injection drug paraphernalia. While there
is no cure for it yet, effective medical treatment can prevent the development of AIDS.

On the Threshold of End Times   367

light of her academic-scholarly research, in process for some time now, on how Christian communities of African descent read the Bible in the face of such critical times. This work involves not just surfacing, the creation of a spectrum of approaches, but also critique, the evaluation of models in light of the grave circumstances and needs of such communities. While not emphasized or surfaced as such, Anderson undertakes such work as a critic grounded in and informed by the religious-theological tradition of African American Christianity.[3] As a critic, therefore, she is committed to the social-cultural enlightenment and advancement of the minoritized ethnic-racial formation to which she belongs.

What emerges from Anderson's work is a divided trajectory of inter-pretation, present in ecclesial communities as well as in critical circles: traditional approaches that work to the detriment of African-descent peo-ples and resistant approaches that work to their benefit. The difference is whether an approach takes the historical experiences and the social con-text of African-descent formation into consideration. Those that do not lead to a reading from and for a privileged perspective—with the Israelites, with a literalist lens, with white hegemony, from alienation. Those that do yield a reading from an oppressed perspective—with the Canaanites, with a social justice lens, with Black resistance, from conscientization. The result is a view of interpretation as conflicted, which, from a minoritized perspective, demands ideological reading with liberation in mind. Toward this goal, the work of African American hermeneutics, anticolonial think-ing, and liberationist psychology prove most helpful.[4]

Vanessa Lovelace: Racial Violence and Ideological Reading

Lovelace foregrounds, jointly, the crisis of populist nationalism and the crisis of ethnic-racial othering, with a primary focus on the United

---

3. This matrix is best captured by a declaration made as part of the discussion on the psychological effects of colonization: "For me," Anderson states, "a founda-tional Christian belief is the existence of a God who acts in history and sides with the oppressed."

4. Anderson suggests a variety of measures toward such a posture. One is to keep together the notions of individual and collective freedom and well-being. Another is to replace traditional discourse with a new discourse, more diversified. Yet another is to include in this new discourse all voices, especially those of excluded or marginalized subgroups. All of these are worth keeping in mind by ethnic-racial critics of all stripes.

States. Recent expressions of this dialectical relationship represent, she argues, but the latest manifestations of a long trajectory of white supremacy in the country. Insofar as such expressions, like their historical antecedents, are steeped in violence, there is a further connection to the crisis of systemic violence, but this link is not developed as such. As an African American critic, Lovelace highlights the violence directed at Blackness, "symbolic and material," in particular. In so doing, however, she does bear in mind other targets of ethnic-racial violence at the hands of whiteness, both in the country, such as the Native Americans, and around the world, such as the indigenous peoples under Western colonization. Behind the study lies the steep rise in violence against the Black body through the 2010s, alluding to the spate of deaths involving Black men at the hands of law enforcement officials and the mass shooting of Black congregants during a Bible study meeting at Emanuel African Methodist Episcopal Church in Charleston, South Carolina, in June 2015.

As a critic, Lovelace addresses a foundational correspondence between the texts of the Bible and the claims of white supremacy. This relation centers on the concept of election: just as the Deuteronomist tradition casts Israel as the chosen of God, so does white America view itself as the chosen of God. This concept has consequences: the preservation of election by distantiation from and annihilation of the Other, who stands for moral deviance and religious perversion, leading to the decline of self. For Israel, the Other was, among many, the Canaanites; for America, the Other was, among many, the Blacks. In this ideological mapping, two connections are advanced: the Israelites and Canaanites of yore with the whites and Blacks of today, respectively.[5] Behind white supremacy and violence against Blackness lies, therefore, a biblical grounding and project. Yet, Lovelace points out, this relation remains largely unknown in both white and Black settings. Such a state of affairs is most problematic, but especially so for African Americans, given their self-perception as children of Abraham, through Jesus, and their embrace of chosenness through identification with the Israelites. For her, therefore, an essential task of the minoritized critic is ideological exposé.

---

5. This connection is secured through a variety of interpretive moves: the curse of Cain by God, who comes to represent Blackness; the curse of Canaan by Ham, who is made to represent the peoples of African descent; and a kinship link between Cain and Canaan, through a depiction of Ham as a relation of Cain.

On the Threshold of End Times   369

For Lovelace, as a biblical critic "of African descent," the texts of the Bible emerge as problematic as the interpretation of these texts. Ideological critique is of the essence in both regards. It is imperative to surface the project of the divine election of Israel in the texts and its nefarious consequences for those outside the circle of the chosen. It is no less imperative to expose the claim to divine election, through identification with Israel, in the interpretive traditions of white supremacy and its devastating repercussions for those outside the circle of the chosen. In this task, a recourse to readings, of any stripe, that run against the grain, that raise fundamental questions of ethnic-racial identity, is necessary. While not presented as such, Lovelace speaks from the perspective of the Christian tradition. It is important, she states, for "Christians of all racial/ethnic categories" to acknowledge that "the church's doctrine of election has been used to exclude" and to abandon any notion of the United States as God's "chosen nation with power and privilege over other peoples of nations."[6]

Aliou Cissé Niang: Transnational Migration and Négritude Reading

Aliou Cissé Niang approaches the call of the minoritized voice today by way of transnational migration, in conjunction with ethnic-racial othering and geopolitical world order. The focus is on the path of migration from the Republic of Senegal to the United States, as embodied in his own life. At the same time, this path is viewed as structurally parallel to other such paths: from the rest of Africa and from throughout the Global South into the United States—and ultimately the Global North. This focus is pursued in mostly discursive fashion, yet Niang is by no means unmindful of the material dimensions surrounding such migrations. Thus, he writes

---

6. It should be noted in this regard that behind this study lies—besides the escalation of violence against Black bodies in present-day America—the growing threat of religious-theological movements rooted in white supremacy, with a radically opposite interpretation of the Bible. Lovelace points to the example of Christian Identity. Its religious-political agenda is well laid out: (1) election—whites constitute the chosen people of God today; (2) greatness—whites are superior to all other races; (3) nationalism—America is the homeland of whites and the site of the kingdom of God; (4) exclusionism—nonwhites must be strategically managed; (5) destiny—a racial apocalypse is in the offing. For a succinct summary of this ideology, see the description by the Anti-Defamation League, https://tinyurl.com/SBL06106ba. For a description of its religious system, see Quarles 2004, 89–104 (ch. 4, "Christian Identity Religious Beliefs").

370 Fernando F. Segovia

with historical-political frameworks in mind: the wreckage of imperial presence in Africa and the movement of Black Lives Matter in the
United States. Foremost in mind, however, stands the cultural onslaught
unleashed on African culture, both in the continent and in the diaspora.
Thus, in the case of his native Senegal, he refers to the "colonial shambles"
left behind by the colonial project of France, an occupation described as
having "nearly obliterated Senegalese culture and faith traditions." From
this detritus of colonization, Niang argues for a poetics of postcolonial
biblical criticism, a project that has "immigrants and transnationals alike"
in mind and is thus of universal import.

This poetics signifies a sharp departure from his training as a biblical
scholar, which involved a mode of interpretation that had "little to do"
with either his context in Senegal or his status as a transnational migrant
in the United States. Its grounding is twofold. Theoretically, it calls for
constructive appropriation of the social space assigned to minoritized
groups and scholars, marked by alienation throughout. The appropriation
envisioned seeks to turn a site of subordination into an "alternative space"
offering "endless possibilities for socioeconomic, political, and religious
freedom." Culturally, it calls for creative integration of the driving spirit
behind the movement of Négritude fashioned by an earlier generation of
migrant intellectuals from Senegal, alongside colleagues from the West
Indies and the United States, in France during the 1930s and hence in the
colonial era.[7] The integration sought seeks a reimagination of this project
appropriate for today. This poetics involves a twofold movement: freedom,
over against assimilation and the dictates of dominant culture, and repositioning, through decolonization and the incorporation of minoritized
culture. Its objective is well captured by Niang: a "hopeful vision of life ...
that overcomes despair and repositions objectified people to live and proclaim liberty." For Niang, therefore, what the program of Négritude sought
to do then remains valid today, duly reconceptualized. Such a sense of
correspondence is due to the enduring dynamics and mechanics in transnational migration—an othering that involves not only Africans in the
United States but also the Global South in the Global North.

This poetics of postcolonial biblical criticism inherits a distinctive
religious-theological dimension from the project of Négritude as crafted

---

7. More specifically, Niang highlights the figure and work of Leópold Sédar Senghor, one of the luminaries of the anticolonial movement prior to the era of decolonization and one of the political leaders of Africa in the era of liberation and independence.

On the Threshold of End Times   371

by Leópold Sédar Senghor. In its initial formulation, Niang points out, the movement of freedom and repositioning was posited not as oppositional but as dialogical, yielding a symbiosis of the cultural values of the West as represented by France and the cultural values of Africa as embodied in Senegal. This symbiosis is formulated as follows. First, the alternative space signals the concept of "life together," whereby identity is conceived and constructed in relational terms. Second, life together constitutes an expression of the "vital force" that stands behind and brings together the many forces that make up the universe—a force that emanates from God and yields a "mystical *divine-human-cosmos* relationship." Third, this force underlies both the traditional religions of Africa and the religion of Christianity—this force finds its "goal and crown" in Jesus Christ. Last, the Scriptures convey the dynamics and mechanics of this vital force and thus prove most fruitful for the project of freedom and repositioning. The end result is not a decolonization based on "hatred and revenge," but rather on "a subversive, resilient invitation for reconciliation." This vision Niang embraces and names "redemptive activism"—outright opposition to injustice alongside unwavering espousal of rapprochement.

Hugh Page: Critical Alienation and Train-Like Reading

In a succinct but incisive reading of our times, Hugh Page offers a large catalog of crises wreaking havoc, of one sort or another, around the world. Many of these have to do with the United States; some involve other countries or areas of the world; others affect the global scene as a whole. In this last set three come to the fore: transnational migration, global economics, and ethnic-racial othering. No one development channels the discussion. What captures Page's critical attention is the constellation of such forces and currents, which conveys a sense of a world under siege and in travail—a world confronting "challenges in these early decades of the twenty-first century that are unprecedented." In the face of such circumstances, Page turns to a different sort of crisis, having to do with the academy in general but above all with the field in particular. This discussion takes center stage throughout. This crisis emerges as a combination of epistemic blindness and critical silence: a looking away from or laying aside of contextual developments in the pursuit of the critical task.

As a critic, Page finds such a state of affairs unacceptable, on two counts: first, insofar as the Bible is oftentimes invoked as a source of affirmation or resistance regarding such developments; second, because such

372 Fernando F. Segovia

developments have always shaped "disciplinary norms in tangible ways." As an African American critic, he proceeds to expose the problematic behind this type of criticism. The dominant model in the field eschews, under pain of marginalization, explicit and active engagement with contextual forces and currents. Attention to such matters is regarded as a violation of the fundamental principles of interpretation—objectivity and timelessness. What is needed instead is a model of full engagement: putting aside the "politics of respectability" and the "illusions" under which the ruling model labors, while embracing "a more inclusive and wide-ranging investigative agenda." While this call is applicable to all, the focus is on minoritized critics: it is imperative to draw on the cultural traditions and critical tools of "minoritized and subaltern peoples." Only then will "liberating encounters with the Bible prove possible." This move Page demonstrates by adopting a strategy of what I would call reading trains, grounded in African American discursive and material life. [8]

This strategy calls for attention to various dimensions of the railroad metaphor: ticketing—taking account of the demands of access to elite status; signaling—paying attention to all aspects of professional life; and watching—weighing what to do at any one time and how to do it. [9] In laying out the parameters of this critical scenario, Page offers a glimpse into his position regarding the Bible. First, he portrays himself as a critic, like many others, with "homes in the church and the academy"—an interpreter with a twofold footing. Second, through the strategy of train reading, he reveals an attitude of critique by speaking of church and academy alike as "ideology-laden machines." Consequently, the critical task implies and entails "dangerous and destabilizing work," insofar as the interpreter scrutinizes and challenges not only academic-

---

8. Page draws on the discursive and material traditions of African American life. On the one hand, he derives the strategy of train reading from the work of Houston Baker, Distinguished University Professor and professor of English at Vanderbilt University. Baker proposed the railroad as model for literary and cultural criticism and the "hobo" as a working model for scholars, given the sense of movement and freedom conveyed by such images. On the other hand, he expands on this model by drawing on his own experience with trains in his early years in the Northeast.

9. For minoritized critics, such reading in fraught times entails, in terms of ticketing, awareness of how it was secured, what it cost, and what ambiguities it bears; with respect to signaling, attention to how all components of professional life are represented; in terms of watching, insight into how all elements of academic life are regarded at any one time and when it might be in order to act otherwise.

On the Threshold of End Times   373

professional norms but also religious-theological texts and traditions. For minoritized critics, such work of critique means "sharing what we have come to know about struggle, injustice, and crisis from our respective points of view," and this will have consequences in all aspects of train reading.

Abraham Smith: Surveillance State and Gazing-Back Reading

With Abraham Smith the focus turns to the crisis of totalizing surveillance, which is tied closely to that of ethnic-racial othering. This refers to the emplacement of a variety of gazing mechanisms by a state for the purpose of keeping its population under close scrutiny and tight supervision.[10] As a critic, Smith addresses the use of one such mechanism in the United States: the practice of incarceration. He outlines its historical development from colonial times to present times in terms of shifting ideological frameworks, which yields a set of three major phases. What drives the study is the key dimension behind the present phase of this practice, the prison industrial complex, which begins with the last quarter of the twentieth century. This is the phenomenon of mass incarceration, which emerged in reaction to the social turmoil of the 1960s, driven by a series of law-and-order crusades undertaken by successive presidential administrations. For Smith, this model exposes not only the fundamental problems of the judicial system but also the role of the United States as a surveillance state—a state that seeks "to discipline bodies, watch over those it does not trust, and secure order."

---

10. Raúl Zibechi, a leading political theorist of Latin America and professor at the Multiversidad Franciscana de América Latina, views the project of social control as reaching a new level altogether in the twenty-first century. As enforced by states and business alike, in close collusion, social control has mutated into "una malla tan fina que atrapa y sujeta todas las manifestaciones de la vida cotidiana" ("a mesh ever so thin that it captures and holds all manifestations of daily life"). The result, he argues, is the decline of democracy as the rule of law and the rise of democracy as authoritarian or totalitarian. See, e.g., Zibechi 2019. Surveillance exhibits a wide range of mechanisms. For heuristic purposes, these may be arranged in three categories. First, there are the traditional measures of containment, such as the criminalization and confinement of a particular population group. Second, one also finds the standard strategies of espionage, such as the recruitment of moles and the spread of misinformation. Third, there is the use of technological devices, ever more sophisticated, such as electronic eavesdropping and massive data gathering.

374 Fernando F. Segovia

As an African American critic, Smith foregrounds another key dimension of mass incarceration: a sharp racial disparity throughout, which affects the Black bodies of African Americans in particular. This, he points out, the mechanism of incarceration has always done, but now ever more so, accompanied as it is by the imputation of a pathology, along familial and personal rather than social and economic lines, on the group as a whole.[11] As a biblical critic, Smith turns to the Bible, through Acts, to see what wisdom it has to offer on this matter. Such a move is grounded on two historical stances: first, a view of the Roman Empire as a surveillance state, and second, the use of incarceration by Rome as a mechanism of surveillance. Given the prominence of trials and prisons in the narrative, Acts is approached as a source for guidance on political incarceration and surveillance. In effect, argues Smith, "Luke both acknowledges prisons as provincial signs of the ever-present empire and yet critiques such signs."

With regard to the Bible, therefore, what Smith deploys is a fundamental correspondence between the past of construction and the present of reception: both the Roman Empire and the United States classify as surveillance states and use incarceration as one among multiple mechanisms of surveillance. In so doing, Smith offers no insight regarding his stance on the nature and authority of the Bible. What he does is to use the Bible as a critical lens for analysis of the present state of affairs. Toward this end, he undertakes a literary analysis of the prison narratives in Acts with strong historicist and ideological dimensions. What emerges is a view of Acts as a narrative of resistance, turning the gaze on the dynamics and mechanics of the empire in order to belie its claims to peace and justice and expose its real disposition and comportment. In so doing, it shows the need to speak without reservation and without ambiguity. "The same," Smith concludes, "is no less true today." This is, in effect, what Smith does: to recast the gaze on the United States, from a minoritized ethnic-racial perspective, laying bare its true character as a surveillance state with a deeply flawed system of justice.

---

11. It should be noted that, while Smith's focus lies primarily on the differential fate of African Americans in the historical development of incarceration, Smith is keenly aware that other bodies emerge as primary targets and/or victims as well in the era of mass incarceration. Besides the brown bodies of Latinx Americans, he mentions the family of the incarcerated, the homeless in the LGBTQ community, women who suffer sexual abuse before and after arrest, and immigrant groups who are confined in detention centers.

On the Threshold of End Times 375

Vincent Wimbush: Systemic Subordination and Transgressive Reading

With Vincent Wimbush it is the crisis of ethnic-racial othering that prevails, with a slight connection to the crisis of geopolitical order. The problematic is presented not so much in material terms, such as violence against the body, as in discursive terms, through subordination to the system, although such a "politics of the word" does entail material consequences of all sorts, including violence. Further, the problematic is pursued for the most part with respect to peoples of African descent, though it ultimately applies to all those lying outside the system—"dispossessed folk" or "historically dispossessed and humiliated." With regard to the former, the angle of vision certainly includes African Americans in the United States, but it also comprehends the whole of Black experience in the Black Atlantic. The system in question refers to the cultural and political construction of a world, a discursive framework, by "white/colonialist dominance." This is a world designed to the benefit of those who construct it, those who espouse "whiteness as ideological-political orientation," and to the detriment of those who are ensnared by it, those who are captured by the strategies of "white magic." This ideological construction Wimbush names the project of scripturalization.

In his role as a critic, Wimbush sees the Bible as a key component in the project of scripturalization, given the way in which the tradition of interpretation, the set of "reigning programs and paradigms within and beyond the academy," has subscribed to the white politics of the word. What this entails parallels the charges commonly lodged for some time now against approaches of a historicist-contextualist bent: apolitical concentration on and isolation of the past. As an African American critic, Wimbush argues, what is needed instead is an approach that focuses on the social-cultural and historical-political ramifications of the Bible as part of the system of world construction. This task minoritized critics in particular should take up, breaking ties in so doing with the fixation on history and text of a field of studies that needs and uses such critics "for its decidedly modernist and corrosive politics."

Wimbush's concern as a critic, therefore, lies not so much with analysis of the biblical texts and contexts as such. In fact, from the study it is hard to discern his position regarding the religious-theological character and import of the Bible. What does emerge is an overriding concern with the ideological usage of the Bible as a dimension of the project of white-colonialist world construction. In interrupting, not only exposing but also

376 Fernando F. Segovia

contesting, such usage, critics pursue a "transgressive" politics of the word, leading to the construction of an alternative world or system, marked by a "radical rupture of meaning." In this new discursive framework, this new-found freedom, the question before critics—above all Black critics and minoritized critics but ultimately all critics—is how to proceed, how to write a new story and a new sense of the human, in the light of the circumstances of our times—"*what* to read and what it means to read/signify/inflect."

Asian American Critics

Tat-siong Benny Liew: Neoliberal Progress and Grief Reading

Liew's vision of the times is complex, involving a variety of crises bringing about death and disorder on the world, individually as well as concurrently. Among these, four emerge as prominent: neoliberalism, imperialism, whiteness, and racism. These are what I would call, respectively, global free-market economics, geopolitical-military order, nationalist-exceptionalist populism, and ethnic-racial othering. All such developments are brought together under the umbrella signifier of neoliberalism, as conveyed by his description of our times as "these times of neoliberalism." In effect, these four major forces and currents come together as a project of domination and subordination, reinforcing and pushing one another in the process. For the most part, this project is dissected in terms of the United States, and thus with reference to its consequences for minoritized populations. At the same time, Liew is keenly aware of its global compass as well, and hence of its implications for the Global South in particular. A peculiar component of the project provides a point of departure for a vision of minoritized criticism in such circumstances—its conception of time.

For Liew this multisided project of neoliberalism is grounded in a conception of time that is linear and progressive, setting itself up as the ideal to which all should aspire, putting aside any elements that might occlude or challenge such supremacy, and adopting a narrative of transcendence and "innocence." What he proposes instead, from the perspective of the minoritized, is a sense of time that involves "multiple temporalities"—above all, a sense of time that does not erase the inconvenient past but appropriates it as consequential for and as enduring in the present, yielding a "politics of mourning." In so doing, the minoritized disturb and expose the project of the dominant, enabling an alternative project of political activism and alliances, a "melancholic freedom," that leads to identity construction and a "politics of resistance"—and, ultimately, hope. In this project, Liew sees an important role for biblical criticism. This role is made possible by what amounts to a strategy of historical correspondence: on the one hand, the minoritized under the project of neoliberalism, among whom stand minoritized critics; on the other hand, the colonized under the project of the Roman Empire, among whom lie the early Christian communities and their writings.

The texts of the Bible can thus serve today, by means of a "blatantly anachronistic reading" of the past within the "squeezed and accelerated time of neoliberalism," in interrupting, revealing, and bypassing the project of the dominant insofar as they convey similar raids on and visions beyond the Pax Romana on the part of the early Christians. Such indeed, for Liew, is what the Gospel of John furnishes by way of the figure of Jesus, whose "scars" and "wounds" may remind readers, through "affective transfers," of the injustice and the violence of empire. In this regard, no "authority or supremacy" need be attributed to the Bible; what suffices is the character of the ancient text as contestatory in its own imperial-colonial context. What works for the critic in dealing with the texts, moreover, is not so much a sense of religious-theological affiliation but a sense of "ethical responsibility and political agency" within the critic's own context, put into effect through the exercise of anachronistic reading.

Yii-Jan Lin: Unmarked Hermeneutics and Marked Reading

Lin deals with the crisis of ethnic-racial othering, in discursive rather than material terms. Thus, one finds no reference to a trajectory of ethnicization-racialization in the country or to a present-day concretization of a process of othering, although both lie clearly in the background. What one does come across is a powerful sense of the challenges and travails that minoritized ethnic-racial scholars face in both the world of the academy and the circles of biblical criticism. There are two crises in view here. The former has a distinct material bearing: the profession is facing difficult times, signified by highly unstable patterns of work and highly uncertain prospects of employment. Minoritized scholars are not spared by such circumstances. The latter is decidedly discursive in tone: the field is marked by sharp division, signified by unequal formations and relations of power in its repertoire of critical approaches. Minoritized scholars are directly

378 Fernando F. Segovia

affected in such configuration. It is this latter situation that Lin pursues in the study.

The world of criticism, she argues, reveals a hierarchical structure; this she unveils and critiques, not so much by way of answers but rather by way of questions.[12] There is a dominant tradition that sets itself, and is viewed, as authoritative, "unquestionably central and essential." There are also traditions that are rendered and regarded by the dominant tradition as subordinate, characterized as "special interest, marginal, or simply not *Wissenschaftliche*." The former, deemed "unmarked," proceeds to do what it does without any sense of a need for justification or definition. This Liu equates with historical criticism. The latter, "marked" as they are, foreground questions of identity and context, authenticity and representation, as they seek to "define and justify" what they do. Among these belong the variations of ethnic-racial criticism. Their modus operandi proceeds by way of difference, stressing opposition to the dominant, as well as *différance*, emphasizing ambiguity and diversity within themselves. Through pointed comments and repeated questions, Lin problematizes concepts of authenticity and representation, essentialism and boundaries, on both sides of the divide. In the end, the hierarchy stands undone. Both central and marginal traditions rely on "theoretical premises of epistemology and semiotics"—all reading emerges thereby as "marked" and complex, decidedly hybrid and in flux. The result is the "possibility for new creativity" regarding the configuration of field and guild alike.

The status and role of the Bible are not directly addressed by Lin. Indirectly, the subject does arise in the light of what lies outside the circles of criticism, which she explores by way of pointed questions. Looking out, what does critical scholarship have to do with the majority of people who read the Bible as the word of God, for whom "the bedside Bible and the preaching on Sunday serve as their daily bread"? Should minoritized eth-

---

12. This differential configuration of the field Lin adroitly describes, in what she characterizes as a "more-whimsical meditation," through an appeal to the world of gastronomy, which is analyzed along similar lines of division. On the one hand, one finds a tradition that presents itself and is regarded as dominant, which any aspiring chef must master, the classical cuisine of France—properly codified and duly imparted. On the other hand, one finds any number of other traditions (ranging from the regional to the national) that are seen and assigned as subordinate—open to fusion with the classical tradition. Thereby, fundamental questions of identity and context, authenticity and mixture, are shown as parallel in another field and thus as shedding light on the dynamics and mechanics of the field of biblical criticism.

On the Threshold of End Times   379

nic-racial critics attend solely or primarily to the guild, given the trying conditions faced in such quarters? Looking in, what does the reading of the Bible outside our circles, "the street food" that is "nourishing" and "beautiful," have to contribute to critical scholarship? Should minoritized ethnic-racial critics, who owe much to "experiences outside and excluded from the academy," not continue this dialogue? In posing such questions, alongside their traditional repertoire of questions, minoritized ethnic-racial criticism should, she concludes, "lead the way forward."

Roger Nam: Transnational Migration and Repatriate Reading

In reflecting on reading in these times, Roger Nam attends to the crisis of transnational migration, which he pursues in connection with that of ethnic-racial othering. This he does with reference to the reality and experience of the Korean American population group. At the same time, this state of affairs he regards as representative, in broad strokes, of all ethnic-racial minoritized groups—and, ultimately, of all transnational movements. This pattern is addressed from two directions: incoming, as Koreans undergo the process of becoming Korean Americans, and out-going, as Korean Americans undertake the process of repatriation in Korea. In both regards, the processes in question involve dynamics and mechanics of ethnic-racial othering, though in different ways. In terms of immigration, Nam points to the context of "ethnic heterogeneity" encountered in the United States—a social-cultural framework that yields "power struggles and marginalization" for migrants. In terms of emigra-tion, he refers to the context of "nationalism and ethnic purity" existing in Korea—a social-cultural framework that engenders issues having to do with "trauma, power, identity, and hope" among returnees. Both processes bring about a negotiation of "identity across borders" and the emergence of "new complex understandings of self." Nam draws on both dimensions of Korean American transnational migration to anchor and advance the work of minoritized biblical criticism, using these as points of entry into the task of interpretation.

From both reading strategies are developed. Thus Nam argues for the validity and richness of minoritized reading by way of what I would characterize as diasporic reading. This he does in reaction to historical criticism and its foundational principles—reconstruction of contexts and texts, application of "objective and scientific" approaches, suspension of critical introspection. What minoritized criticism offers instead is a sense

380 Fernando F. Segovia

of the fluidity of texts—a pattern at work within the biblical corpus itself—in other contexts, popular and professional alike. As such, it moves beyond original meaning to ongoing function—"within communities across spatial and temporal boundaries."[13] In so doing, minoritized criticism offers relevance beyond the academy; broad dialectical engagement, allowing for the empowerment of "moral and ethical directives" in our world; and commitment to interdisciplinary research. Similarly, Nam upholds the insight and value of minoritized reading by way of what he calls repatriate reading. This he does by showing how, beyond temporal and spatial variations, a set of major structural elements can be identified across transnational migrations—traumatic experiences, power negotiations, identity reconfigurations, and hopes for the future. Consequently, such elements as they arise in the context of Korea repatriation can shed light on the context of Judean repatriation, and vice versa.

In Nam's advocacy of minoritized criticism and its reading strategies, no explicit religious-theological reflections are offered. Various traces are nonetheless to be found. The first is personal. In describing his social location, he points to his upbringing in the Protestant tradition for his initial interest in the biblical texts. The second is ecclesial. Nam refers to the institutional difficulties faced by minoritized critics. Since their work is "often tied to our own communities of faith," readings that challenge tradition may lead to exclusion "from their own social group." The third is theoretical. His interest as a minoritized critic, he explains, is to bring together the historical focus of traditional criticism and the reader focus of minoritized approaches into an "ideal theoretical platform" for a reading of the Bible that is fruitful for both "our minoritized communities" and "the broader society in which we dwell."[14] The final trace is methodological. Out of this

---

13. This approach derives its inspiration from the critical movement of reception criticism, whereby the meaning of the text is perceived not as settled once and for all in its original moment of production but rather as the sum of all meanings advanced through the trajectory of consumption. The specific channel adduced for this type of criticism is the work of Brennan Breed and his concept of the nomadic text, with its interest in the question of the function played by the text across time and space. The religious-theological context of this proposal comes across in the way that Nam presents—in palpable approval—such work: dialectic approaches serve to "ultimately widen[ing] the possibilities for biblical theology" and to foster learning about the "versions and meanings and contexts" of other communities for "sacred scripture" (Breed 2014).

14. Here Nam seeks to build directly on a tradition of presidential addresses in the Society of Biblical Literature delivered by minoritized ethnic-racial critics, Vin-

On the Threshold of End Times 381

vision of an ideal platform comes the deployment of the principle of correspondence between past and present, making it possible for communities and society alike to attain a "better understanding of the religious dimensions of our texts." Underlying the proposal, therefore, there is a distinct sense of religious-theological attachment and import.

Latinx American Critics

Hector Avalos: Christian Imperialism and Secularist Reading

In pondering the pressing task of minoritized critics, Hector Avalos centers on ethnic-racial othering, with eyes set on both the national and the international frameworks. In so doing, he favors the discursive dimension over the material. To be sure, he is distinctly aware of the social situation of minoritized groups in such contexts. With regard to the United States, various elements of such conscientization can be readily distinguished. Thus, he takes for granted the process of othering that yields the division of dominant and minority formations. Further, he looks with approval on the study of how minoritized groups, such as the Latinx American formation, approach the Bible in light of their situation. Last, he points to his own expertise and trajectory in Latinx studies, which he has pursued at length through the optic of religious experience. With regard to the world, he notes the process of othering that leads to a division between dominant Christianity and other minoritized religions, whereby the latter are targeted as an object of mission. On none of these situations does Avalos provide much elaboration. What he does pursue intently instead is the cultural dimension at work in such processes of othering, and this he does with the formulation of a minoritized hermeneutics in mind, yet one that has nothing to with the ethnic-racial problematic.

This hermeneutics is advanced in dialectical fashion to what he identifies as the established path of minoritized criticism. While the latter has developed along the lines of constructive theology, his proposal calls for proceeding along the lines of historical and sociological analysis. Further,

---

cent Wimbush (2011) and Fernando Segovia (2015). These he views as embodying key features and strategies envisioned for minoritized reading, calling as they do for broad impact on society, broad dialogue with diversity, and broad interdisciplinarity in research. In so doing, he argues, they point criticism away from entrenched sterility and toward reinvigoration—the path sought for repatriate reading.

382   Fernando F. Segovia

while minoritized criticism is represented as a variant on the project of "Christian missiology and imperialism," his objective, he argues, is "to expose and undermine imperialism." This radical opposition is created by a twofold move, which one could describe as essentialism and exceptionalism.[15] First, minoritized criticism is bent on claiming a unique lens for and forging a unique approach to scholarship. Second, minoritized criticism is grounded on a religious-theological view of the Bible as the word of God, whereby the critical task emerges as a way of affirming and promoting such authority. Over against such ascribed positions, Avalos espouses a criticism on two planes. First and foremost, it must be historicist-contextualist as well as secular-humanist in character—seeking the authorial intent and social location of the texts, while following an empirical-rationalist approach to the texts. Secondarily, it may include a sociological component as well—analyzing the appeal to the texts today and hence their "influence in the modern world."

In the formulation of this proposal, Avalos presents a most explicit expression of attitude toward the status and role of the Bible, crafted along the lines of religious studies. Indeed, from the outset Avalos defines himself as an "atheist." His aim, he explains, is to avoid two pitfalls present in biblical criticism, to which minoritized criticism has altogether succumbed: religionism and bibliolatry. On the one hand, it does not regard religion as "useful or necessary for human existence," and hence in no way as "something that should be preserved and protected." It is imperative to move "past any sort of religious thinking." On the other hand, it does not view the Bible as a "privileged document" or "important for our civilization," and thus as in no way meriting more attention than all other texts of antiquity. It is imperative to give similar attention to all such remains, whether "from Mesoamerica, Ugarit, Mesopotamia, Egypt, and

---

15. Avalos pursues this evaluation of minoritized criticism in considerable detail, undertaking a critical overview of the range of positions taken by such critics. This overview is informed by a set of strategies identified as common in such work. The first of these is one variously deployed in the present volume: the positing of transhistorical analogies between the biblical texts and the minoritized experience. The other three are identified as follows: representativism, involving the inclusion and exclusion of biblical evidence as convenient; ethno-theologizing, whereby a divine viewpoint is named or an essentialist view of a population group is adopted; and interpretive flexibility, involving a sense of universal significance and applicability. All such strategies constitute "simply religionist and bibliolatrous variants of ... Eurocentric or nonminoritized" criticism.

On the Threshold of End Times 383

other places." In so doing, as with the Bible, the need for ideological and ethical evaluation is presupposed. It is such a hermeneutics that is truly minoritized, emerging from the circles of the "most marginalized minority" in the ranks of biblical critics, paying attention to all texts and places "devalued and marginalized by biblical scholars," and representing a truly "radical or transformative" break with standard criticism.

Jacqueline Hidalgo: Biblical Identification and Unauthorized Reading

Jacqueline Hidalgo's reading of our times attends to the crisis of transnational migration, which she examines in conjunction with two others, populist nationalism and ethnic-racial othering. In analyzing migration, her focus rests primarily on the United States, though she is quite aware of the global dimensions of the crisis. With respect to the United States, her focus lies primarily on the flow of unauthorized migrants from Mexico and Latin America, yet she is keenly aware that this migration is much wider in scope. In terms of populist nationalism and ethnic-racial othering, Hidalgo situates herself in the aftermath of the Trump presidency, citing its recourse to the tradition of "xenophobic US nationalism" and its activation of a rhetoric of "racialized and Christian supremacist discrimination." What this project reveals, she argues, is a politics of citizenship excess—the status and authority inherent in the concept of citizenship. On the one hand, this involves the political capital attached to the claim to citizenship—the "privileges" of citizens as distinct from noncitizens. On the other hand, this entails a process of differential accumulation regarding political capital among citizens—the power some citizens wield over other citizens. Despite its prevalence in conservative circles, Hidalgo notes, such politics often underlie as well the rhetoric and agenda of liberal circles, welcoming and compassionate as such politics may wish to be.

As a critic, what captures Hidalgo's attention is the salient role assigned to the Bible in such politics. Indeed, in the wake of the Trump onslaught, the situation now facing minoritized critics is described as involving "greater challenges than ever before." In response, she undertakes an exercise in cultural biblical criticism: critical analysis of the appeal to the Bible in citizenship excess alongside a constructive proposal for an alternative reading. The analysis surfaces a process of identification on the part of dominant formations today with dominant formations in the biblical texts, be it the Hebrew writings or the Christian writings. Thus, the political privileges and powers abiding in such formations are appropri-

384   Fernando F. Segovia

ated as their own in the present, whether as the people of God or the sheep of Jesus. Thereby ideological justification and authorization are secured for their political capital as elite citizens, yielding marginalization of the other—whether unauthorized migrants as noncitizens or minoritized groups as subaltern citizens. The proposal envisions a different approach to the Bible—a reading beyond identification.

This approach reveals a view of interpretation as ideological, multidimensional, and perspectival. It calls for a reading that is variously attuned to the ideological thrust of texts—the dynamics of identity; the complex character of texts—the ambiguities of texts and resultant variety of interpretations; and the perspective of the reader—the variety of options regarding standpoint. This approach also conveys an external criterion for ideological critique. It calls for a reading that favors not the rights of citizens in nations but the rights of all individuals as human beings. Human rights would thus sit in judgment over texts and interpreters alike. Within such a framework, no one would emerge as possessing citizenship excess, no one would be regarded as "unauthorized," whether as migrant or as minoritized, and no crisis of transnational migration would be posited as such. Consequently, no group would be allowed to cast itself, along the lines of citizenship excess, as "the people of God" or "the more legitimate sheep for inheriting the kingdom"—whether in the Bible or in continuity with the Bible. What the proposal contemplates instead is a "future without boundaries between citizens and migrants."

Francisco Lozada: Recognition Politics and Equality Reading

Francisco Lozada's take on the times is panoramic rather than pointed. Instead of a particular moment of crisis, circumscribed in terms of components and parameters, what he pursues is a crisis ongoing, with a long historical trajectory and an undiminished contemporary incarnation. This is the crisis of ethnic-racial othering. The focus lies on the reality and experience of the Latinx population in the United States. He approaches the project of othering from the point of view of recognition by the dominant formation: the failure to acknowledge the "existence and epistemology" of the Latinx group "as equal to all others." As a result, the full range of identities and expressions are "marginalized, devalued, or despised." At the same time, this politics of recognition is viewed as expansive, affecting not only all other minoritized ethnic-racial groups but also groups minoritized

On the Threshold of End Times   385

on other grounds. In the face of such withdrawal of recognition, Lozada argues for a politics of equality.

This project of resistance aims to counteract the twofold thrust of non-recognition. On the one hand, it highlights the minoritized existence of the Latinx population, approaching their constructions of identity as on a par with all others. On the other hand, it advances the minoritized epistemology that emerges from the Latinx formation, presenting their productions of knowledge as on a par with all others. In so doing, the project moves beyond the existing binomial of acknowledgment and belonging toward equality. This project Lozada assumes by way of Latinx biblical criticism. Toward this end, he has recourse to Latinx studies, entering into critical dialogue with various analyses of Latinx life, all highly interdisciplinary in nature. These studies show how the life of the group intersects with and forms part of American life in general.[16] It is this sense of interrelationship and mutual belonging that he has in mind for biblical criticism: a vision of Latinx criticism alongside others on a spectrum of equals. Latinx criticism would thereby intersect with and form part of criticism in general, not along the traditional perception of visiting but rather along an alternative perception of belonging to the field.

At no point in the exposition of this counterpolitics of recognition does Lozada address the religious-theological character or import of the Bible. With regard to character, what emerges is a view of the Bible more along the lines of a social-cultural artifact that is open to any number of interpretations, all of which constitute social-cultural artifacts in their own right. Thus, the entire range of interpretations merits attention and engagement on an equal footing. This position entails significant ramifications: no one tradition is allowed to set itself up as superior, while deeming all others as inferior; no one tradition is to be regarded as the natural or assigned province of that formation from which it has emerged; and all traditions are to engage with and learn from one another, nurturing a desire to entertain a "different point of view" as well as the "possibility of change." With regard to import, what results proceeds on a social-cultural key as well. In effect, what Latinx criticism seeks to do is no different from what the studies in Latinx studies do: to retrieve the past in dialogue with the Latinx issues of the present, such as

---

16. These volumes analyze different dimensions of Latinx life—the process of ethnic-racial construction, the world of media communications, and the ideological construction of migration patterns.

386 Fernando F. Segovia

"immigration, the sense of belonging, and colonialism"—a relationship of correspondence.

Jean-Pierre Ruiz: Inward-Looking Scholarship and Disruptive Reading

At present, for Jean-Pierre Ruiz, the world, both at the national and the global level, stands in a state of crisis, "deeply and gravely wounded by violence, by want, by inequalities too many to name." Foremost in this regard lies the crisis of transnational migration, which appears through the lenses of two other crises—populist nationalism and ethnic-racial othering. The former is directly addressed. Its representation revolves around the presidency of Donald Trump and its harsh stance on migration, especially with regard to the southern border with Mexico. The latter lies mostly in the background, but palpably so. At one point, various strands of it are named. Inside the country, Ruiz points to two dimensions of Latin American migration, both involving individuals without papers: those who venture to cross the border and the children who struggle to belong for the rest of their lives. Outside, he refers to two large-scale phenomena: the African migrants who attempt to cross the Mediterranean Sea and the Rohingya Muslim migrants who leave Myanmar for Bangladesh. All such migrations involve anguish and terror. Such circumstances point, for Ruiz, to another crisis, discursive in nature, which functions as the center of critical attention.

This crisis is defined as the failure, on the part of the academy in general and the field in particular, to peer outside its "windows" and to hear the "noise"—"to read the signs of these times in which we live." As a Latinx American critic, Ruiz espouses a different model: the critic as a "public intellectual" who is "sociopolitically engaged," and a mode of scholarship that is concerned with ethics and with the public sphere.[17] Such a shift

---

17. The model advanced is based on two discursive frameworks. One current is academic-institutional in nature. This has to do with university studies: the problematic of the status and role of the university, and indeed the academic-intellectual world in general, in society and culture. Here Ruiz draws on the reflections of Ignacio Ellacuría, the former president of the Universidad Centroamericana José Simeón Cañas in San Salvador, El Salvador, who was assassinated, along with several of his Jesuit confrères, by the forces of the state in 1989. It was precisely the conception and the work of the university as a site of social projection that led to such a tragic end. The other current is academic-professional in character. This involves the tradition of presidential addresses in the Society of Biblical Literature: the critique undertaken by

he regards as imperative, given the appeal to the Bible by the forces of nationalism and othering in support of the status quo, political and economic alike. In opposition, the model calls for a reading that is "disruptive and even ruckus-raising" in order to challenge "the injustices of the present order." This type of criticism demands a center of orientation outside itself—in the scholarly guild, inside the windows, but in social projection, outside the windows. In so doing, it would foreground throughout the disadvantaged and have "transformative action" as its goal; consequently, it would also labor under threat at all times, for "reading texts and times is not without its very real perils."

Without expanding on the character of the Bible as such, Ruiz's proposal regarding the task of biblical criticism is religious-theological to the core.[18] To begin with, the Bible is related to the church as institution. He holds to a vision of criticism that has the church as its matrix and the mission of the church as its raison d'être, described as "giving witness to the goodness and the justice of God in the world." Further, the Bible is tied to ecclesial communities as audience. For Ruiz, the Bible represents the key source for orientation and direction, as in the case of migration. Last, the Bible is related to the world as a site of struggle, as evident in the discussion of migration. It can be used to uphold the interests of elite groups. This he shows in the way that a number of pastors have invoked it not only to defend the antimigration project of Trumpism but also to exalt the figure of former President Trump himself as a ruler chosen by God. It can also be used to defend the interests of the othered groups, such as migrants. This he demonstrates through the work of voices and institutions committed to "careful *krisis*"—"the sort of judgment and discernment that can inform transformative action." With this latter stance it is that Ruiz casts his lot, seeking "to read so as to raise the sort of ruckus that makes a difference in these critical times.

---

a succession of recent presidents, all from outside traditional circles of the membership, who call, in one way or another, for such a project of external projection.

18. Indeed, it is written in direct response to the severe critique of minoritized criticism advanced by a fellow member of the Latinx American formation, Hector Avalos. The program of disruptive reading outlined is presented as by no means a continuing exercise in the traditional missionary and imperialist project of Christianity. It is minoritized, it is church-rooted, it is community-minded—yet, its objective is not to promote conversion but to challenge the injustices and transform the structures of the world.

388 Fernando F. Segovia

Reading in These Times: A Cartography of Critical Postures

The reflections on critical posture, as analyzed, lay out a rich variety of positions on the constitutive components of the inquiry: the state of affairs, the critical task, and the nature of the texts. With regard to the times, the reflections set forth assessments of the historical-political context, the nation as well as the world, as decidedly awry and utterly disconcerting. In so doing, emphasis is placed sometimes on the nation and sometimes on the world. Yet, no matter how weighted, the two frameworks are, in one way or another, taken as imbricated. In terms of interpretation, such evaluations of the times elicit critical responses, ways of approaching the texts, that are specifically designed for the historical frameworks as represented. For the most part, such approaches involve trenchant critique of traditional-dominant models alongside constructive proposals for models of a contextual-perspectival and political-ethical bent. With regard to the Bible, these alternative projects of interpretation bear underlying conceptions regarding the religious-theological status and role of the texts. Such stances are sometimes rendered as quite explicit and sometimes left as largely implicit. Regardless, they involve, in one mode or another, a tendering of historical correlations between times then and times now.

Such a wealth of positions can yield, by way of comparative analysis, highly instructive as well as highly useful cartographies of the critical terrain in each category. These mappings provide, on the one hand, a keen sense of the social-cultural, theoretical-methodological, and religious-theological standpoint of minoritized ethnic-racial criticism at this point in time. These mappings also present, on the other hand, a ready repertoire of systemic visions, critical approaches, and ideological convictions for the continued pursuit of such criticism with the future in mind—especially so in the face of such freighted times as ours. In what follows, I proceed to the construction of such cartographies.

In These Times: The State of Affairs

With respect to the state of affairs in our times, what emerges from the reflections is a wide array of diagnostic assessments. For a workable grasp of the scope in question, I would propose a range of evaluations extending from a comprehensive pole to a punctiliar pole. Toward the former end, I would place visions that refer to a multiplicity of crises, all regarded as more or less linked to one another and having a similar impact. Toward

On the Threshold of End Times   389

the latter end, I would situate visions that identify an overriding crisis, not perhaps without mentioning others but certainly expanding on the one foregrounded. In the middle section of the spectrum, I would place those visions that identify a distinct set of crises, all of which are taken as related and consequential in more or less equal fashion. The result is a revealing cartography of our times, national and global, as perceived from the optic of minoritized ethnic-racial criticism.

At the comprehensive end of the spectrum, there are two visions that involve an expansive set of crises. While Page points to any number of crises as bearing down on the world, including the United States, Liew identifies a particular set of crises, taken from among many, that come together to form a driving project, emanating from the Global North, particularly the United States, but affecting the whole of the Global South. This is the project of neoliberalism, which is presented as resting on four pillars—free-market economy, military imperialism, racial supremacy, and racial othering. For both, the harsh material consequences of such historical-political currents are duly noted. In both cases, however, it is a discursive dimension that is pursued. For Page, it is the blindness and the silence regarding such developments in the academy and the field alike; for Liew, it is the conception of time, linear and progressive, that lies at the core of the dominant project.

At the punctiliar end of the spectrum, a variety of visions point to a number of overriding crises. First, Anderson brings up the crisis of human welfare by way of a pandemic, the HIV/AIDS virus, approached as a global phenomenon. Second, Smith raises the issue of totalizing surveillance, with a focus on the program of mass incarceration in the United States. Last, a number of others foreground the agenda of ethnic-racial othering: Wimbush, Lin, Avalos, Lozada. I hasten to add that both Anderson and Smith are keenly aware of the ethnic-racial dimensions of the crises discussed, insofar as both the pandemic of HIV/AIDS and the mechanism of surveillance via incarceration affect in highly differential terms African Americans in particular and minoritized populations in general. At the punctiliar end of the spectrum, clearly the crisis of ethnic-racial othering shines prominently.

How it does so is worth examining. In all four cases, it is a discursive dimension that prevails. For Wimbush, othering is approached in terms of a global system of white domination that demands submission. Its impact lies heavily on all those of African descent, but it also includes all colonized subjects as well. With regard to Lin, othering is discussed in

390   Fernando F. Segovia

terms of an academic realm that works to the detriment of the minoritized, with a focus on the United States. With respect to Avalos, othering is pursued by way of an essentialist construction of minoritized hermeneutics, also focused on the United States. For Lozada, othering has to do with a system of domination that presses down on the identities and knowledges of the minoritized. While the focus rests primarily on the Latinx community, the situation is taken to affect all other minoritized groups in the United States.

In the middle, one finds a set of visions that, while favoring a particular historical-political development, tie such a crisis quite closely to others—Lovelace, Niang, Nam, Hidalgo, Ruiz. To one side, there lies Lovelace, who addresses the dialectic of populist nationalism and ethnic-racial othering: the system of white supremacy that engenders violence against the African American body—and the bodies of other minoritized in the United States and among the colonized. To the other side, the other critics highlight the phenomenon of transnational migration, closely intertwined with ethnic-racial othering. Thus, Nam points to the travails and reconfigurations of identity in migration, with reference to Koreans in the United States but all such migrations as well. Niang adds geopolitical disorder as well: migrations of Africans—and others from the Global South—as a result of imperial wreckage and cultural onslaught. Hidalgo and Ruiz also bring in populist nationalism. She reflects on the inclusive-exclusive character of citizenship, heavily focused on Latinx in the United States but with reference to the world as well. He underlines the terror and the anguish present in all migrations, with reference to Latinx in the United States but applicable to such movements anywhere.

In conclusion, while pointing to any number of historical-political developments hovering over the nation and the world, it is the agenda of ethnic-racial othering that rises over the others and marks the overall mapping of the times as decidedly awry. This is a project that is seen at work in any number of ways, with severe ramifications, material as well as discursive, for all the groups in question.

Reading: The Critical Task

With regard to the critical task demanded by the times, the reflections offer an extensive arsenal of interpretive paths. In order to capture a functional pulse of the field, I would construct a range of approaches encompassed by a traditionalist pole and a dissenting pole. At the former end, I would posit a continued espousal of dominant models of interpretation, though with a significant twist. The call here is for an unrelenting focus on the past as the proper domain of criticism. At the latter end, I would place a pressing demand for alternative models, along various lines. Here the call is for pointed engagement with the present on the part of criticism. Taking up the central section of the spectrum, I would situate a couple of orientations. These would all identify with the need for alternative models of interpretation involving interaction with the social-cultural context of the day. Their focus, however, would lie not so much on the structural framework as such but more on the ongoing relevance of the texts. The resultant cartography of critical function proves equally insightful with respect to the angle of vision in minoritized ethnic-racial criticism.

At the traditionalist pole of the spectrum, one finds but a single vision. For Avalos, the critical task to be undertaken by minoritized scholars proves no different from that followed by traditional criticism: a combination of historicist-contextualist and realist-objectivist analysis. The twist lies in a concomitant call for radically diminishing the significance attached to these texts. At the dissenting pole, the field proves quite crowded, bringing together a total of seven critics. All argue, in forceful opposition to the traditional focus on the past and omission of the present, for direct and active engagement with the times, conceived along the lines of a comprehensive system.

In the case of Page and Ruiz, it is the social-material context that figures prominently. Both argue, in similar ways, for the need to bring the objectives and strategies of minoritized criticism to bear on our historical-political framework, including the field of studies. With respect to Wimbush, Liew, and Lozada, it is the cultural-discursive context that is highlighted. All espouse engagement with what they identify as the core of the dominant framework: submission of the Other (Wimbush), a notion of time that sidelines the Other (Liew), and the downplaying of the Other (Lozada). In response, they seek considered attention to the deployment of the Bible (Wimbush), pointed interruption through integration of the notion of time of the Other (Liew), and a vision of equality for the Other (Lozada). In the case of Lin and Hidalgo, the focus is on the field: while Lin calls for a view of all approaches as dealing in one way or another with identity and thus as marked, Hidalgo argues for the criterion of human rights to govern all correlations established with the texts.

In the central section, two lines of argument can be identified with regard to the ongoing relevance of the texts. One set of proposals argues for sharp ideological critique of the texts. Here stand Anderson and Lovelace: ready identification with the biblical past must be exposed in the light of consequences for those left aside in the process—both with social justice as objective. The other set of proposals argues for supportive application of the texts. Here lie Niang, Smith, and Nam: the texts have much to offer, properly recalibrated, for the present—all with social amelioration in mind.

In sum, given the salient priority attached to the crisis of ethnic-racial othering in the evaluation of historical-political frameworks, it is the call for interaction that prevails in the crafting of critical responses. While the mode envisioned for such an undertaking varies considerably, all approaches but one agree on resistance with transformation in mind of one type or another, so that the driving concerns and principles of minoritized formations can be brought to bear on all aspects of the field of study. Most popular in this regard stands the thorough critique of the dominant system represented as in force.

The Bible: The Nature of the Texts

With respect to the nature of the texts conveyed by the interpretive paths advocated, what the reflections disclose is a wide array of stances on the question of religious-theological import. With a guiding grasp of the terrain in mind, I would propose a range of opinion proceeding from a secularist pole to a scripturalist pole. At the former end, I would place positions that dispense with religious-theological appropriation of any sort and adopt instead a humanist-rationalist approach. Here there would be no room for any scriptural vision of the texts as representing the word of God. At the latter end, I would bring together positions that subscribe to a religious-theological embrace of the texts. The emphasis here would be on their scriptural character as the word of God. In the middle section of the spectrum, I would arrange a variety of positions that express, in varying ways as well as degrees, acknowledgment of the religious-theological dimensions of the texts, but without a formal position on the question of Scripture. The result is a revealing cartography of positions regarding the Bible as a religious-theological artifact through the lens of minoritized ethnic-racial criticism.

At the secularist pole of the spectrum, there lies the voice of Avalos. Defining himself explicitly as an atheist, Avalos views criticism, whether the traditionalist approach he favors or the minoritized approach he questions, as espousing religionism and bibliolatry. What he advocates instead is to move beyond religious-theological thinking altogether and to treat the biblical texts as no different from those of other traditions. At the scripturalist pole, two strong voices come to the fore, Niang and Ruiz. The more explicit is that of Niang: the texts embody the divine vital force of life together that circulates throughout the universe, finding its fullest expression in Jesus. That of Ruiz proves more implicit but no less forceful: the texts are intrinsically related to the mission of the institutional church and the life of ecclesial communities in the world, giving witness to the justice of God. In both cases, it is incumbent on criticism to bring this out, with transformation in mind.

Between these two poles, there stands a crowded field, where the other voices refrain from a formal position on the Bible as word of God. I would distinguish three tendencies at work: toward the scripturalist pole, a set of voices bring the religious-theological dimension into consideration, in varying degrees; toward the secularist pole, a set of voices approach the texts from a social-cultural perspective, in different ways; between them, a set of voices do refer, without expansion, to religious-theological traditions and convictions.

To begin with, a number of critics attach value to religious-theological frameworks. In the case of Page, criticism involves a double home in the academy and the church and demands a view of both as ideological frameworks, which calls for critique in the name of justice. For Smith, the ideological critique undertaken by the texts in the past can serve, through historical correspondence, toward a critique of the present. For Lin, the way forward for criticism includes paying attention to modes of interpretation outside the academic realm, among both ecclesial communities and popular venues. In the case of Nam, the craft of criticism is to focus on ongoing function, through correspondence, for the welfare of both minoritized groups and society at large.

Somewhat at a distance, two critics do acknowledge religious-theological affiliation, with specific reference to communities of African descent. Such is the case with Anderson. In arguing for approaches grounded in context and correspondence with oppressed formations, she declares, in passing, her own belief in a God who takes the side of the oppressed in history. It is also the case with Lovelace. In arguing against the ideology of election, and any appropriation of it through correspondence, she emphasizes the need for all Christians to abandon any such exclusivist claim regarding the Other or the state.

394 Fernando F. Segovia

Last, a number of critics place the value of the texts along other lines. Thus, Wimbush, with a grounding in transgressive geopolitics, calls for ideological attention to the use of the texts in the system and politics of whiteness, with redirection in mind. Liew looks instead, out of a sense of ethical responsibility, to use the texts, through correspondence, to challenge any unproblematic notion of time in a dominant system, with muddying as a goal. Hidalgo, working from the tradition of human rights, seeks to read the texts with emphasis on multidimensionality as a way beyond group appropriation through correspondence, in order to avoid any dialectic of inclusion-exclusion. Finally, Lozada, drawing on a politics of recognition rooted in cultural studies, calls for a view of texts and interpretations via correspondence as cultural artifacts, with equality of voices in mind.

In conclusion, behind the various critical approaches advanced toward critical engagement with the historical-political frameworks identified, the predominant stance to be found regarding the religious-theological problematic of the Bible as Scripture can be best characterized as noncommittal. At the same time, such a formal stance of nondisclosure is accompanied by a pointed sense of value regarding the significance and relevance of the texts for our times. Toward this end, a recurrent strategy should be noted: the recourse to historical analogies or correlations between the past of the texts and the present of minoritized groups, activated for the purpose of furthering the status and role of the minoritized in the midst of forbidding times.

Concluding Comments

I have drawn above, as proposed, mappings of the various positions on critical posture by way of the key components of interpretation selected for comparative analysis. This I have done for the sake of both reconnoitering and advancing—establishing the lay of the terrain as traversed by the set of minoritized critics and providing an array of directions for the ongoing pursuit of minoritized criticism. I should like to take advantage of this analysis to offer a sense of my own bearings in such mappings. This I do by way of initial venture. It is my hope to take up such matters at greater length in the future, not just as a desideratum but rather as an imperative.

With respect to the first axis of interpretation, the reading of the times at hand, I find myself, within the comprehensive-punctiliar spectrum drawn, beyond the former pole. My position extends beyond those of Page and Benny Liew insofar as I not only refer to a multiplicity of crises but also point to a conjunction of such crises in interdependent fashion, yielding a crisis of the world-system as known. I do agree with them that the damage wrought thereby is universal in scope, but I would emphasize that the fate suffered by the Global South—within which I include minoritized ethnic-racial formations in the Global North—is much worse in every regard. At the same time, I agree with all critics across the spectrum that ethnic-racial othering constitutes a primary crisis of our times, with harsh social and cultural ramifications for the groups in question, and this phenomenon I see at work not only in the United States but also throughout the world.

Regarding the second axis, the formulation of a critical task for our times, I situate myself, within the traditionalist-dissenting pole outlined, at the latter pole. At this point, given all the theoretical and methodological developments that have taken place in biblical studies as well as in historical studies, I find the traditionalist stance demanded by Avalos altogether unacceptable. To argue for a focus solely on the realm of production, supported by principles of historical empiricism and epistemic objectivity, proves unviable. I do sympathize, in principle, with the call to relativize the unique significance bestowed on the biblical texts, although, in practice, I recognize any number of strategic reasons, historical and political, for so doing. My path, therefore, is that of dissent. With the majority of critics at that pole, I see critical engagement with present times as imperative, materially as well as discursively. Further, with those in the center, I regard critical engagement with past times as no less essential, with full embrace of ideological critique. In both regards, I also agree that the axis of ethnic-racial identity figures prominently across the whole of society and culture and must be engaged as such.

With respect to the third axis of interpretation, the status accorded to the biblical texts in the critical project set forth for our times, I find myself, within the securalist-scripturalist spectrum drawn, at the former pole, but on a different footing from that of Avalos. In using these texts, I do not see myself as espousing religionism and bibliolatry, nor do I see myself as opting with the majority of critics for a noncommittal stance. On the question of status as word of God, I take a decidedly low path, with a view of the texts as attempts to come to terms with the ways of the world and the ways of the deity. Thus, rather than signifiers of revelation, inspiration, and normativity, I approach them as artifacts of enormous historical and cultural significance as well as resources of great potential for utopian thinking. My position is to value the possible contributions, duly subject to ideological analysis, of religious-theological traditions toward a vision of a better world, indeed not only for human beings but also for nonhuman life.

All three cartographies have consequences. The first mapping regarding the state of our times impresses on me the need to address, in ever more extensive and sophisticated fashion, the unfolding crisis of ethnic-racial othering embraced by all critics, its optic and its agenda, as an urgent priority. With the second mapping involving critical task, it is the need to foreground the problematic of racial-ethnic identity at all levels that compels itself on me, with ideological critique as lens and social justice as objective. The third cartography, regarding the status of the texts, foregrounds for me the need to resort to religious-theological traditions, alongside secular-humanist traditions, in confronting the constellation of crises in our times and, in so doing, to render explicit what religious-theological principles lie behind any such endeavor. Needless to say, all such consequences bear further exploration. Such are the gifts of ethnic-racial minoritized criticism.

Works Cited

Anti-Defamation League. 2017. "Christian Identity." 5 April. https://tinyurl.com/SBL06106ba.

Breed, Brennan. 2014. *Nomadic Texts: A Theory of Biblical Reception History*. Bloomington: Indiana University Press.

Ghosh, Jayati. 2021. "Apocalypse or Cooperation." Project Syndicate, 19 August. https://tinyurl.com/SBL06106bc.

HIV.gov. 2023. "What Are HIV and AIDS?" 13 January. https://tinyurl.com/SBL06106az.

Plummer, Brad, and Henry Fountain. 2001. "A Hotter Future Is Certain, Climate Panel Warns. How Hot Is Up to Us." *New York Times*, 9 August. https://tinyurl.com/SBL06106bd.

Quarles, Chester R. 2004. *Christian Identity: The Aryan American Bloodline Religion*. Jefferson, NC: McFarland.

Segovia, Fernando F. 2015. "Criticism in Critical Times: Reflections on Vision and Task." *JBL* 134:6–29.

Solnit, Rebecca. 2021. "Our Climate Change Turning Point Is Right Here, Right Now." *Guardian*, 12 July. https://tinyurl.com/SBL06106be.

Wimbush, Vincent. 2011. "Interpreters—Enslaving/Enslaved/Runagate." *JBL* 130:5–24.

Žižek, Slavoj. 2021. "Last Exit to Socialism." *Jacobin*, 21 July. https://tinyurl .com/SBL06106bf.

Zibechi, Raúl. 2019. "Control social, designio del siglo XXI." *Jorn.* 12 April. https://tinyurl.com/SBL06106bb.

Contributors

Cheryl B. Anderson, professor emerita of Old Testament, Garrett-Evangelical Theological Seminary, Evanston, Illinois

†Hector Avalos, professor of religious studies, Department of Philosophy and Religious Studies, Iowa State University, Ames, Iowa

Jacqueline M. Hidalgo, associate dean for institutional diversity, equity and inclusion; chair and professor of Latina/o studies; and professor of religion, Williams College, Williamstown, Massachusetts

Tat-siong Benny Liew, 1956 Chair in New Testament Studies, Department of Religious Studies, College of the Holy Cross, Worcester, Massachusetts

Yii-Jan Lin, associate professor of New Testament, Yale Divinity School, Yale University, New Haven, Connecticut

Vanessa Lovelace, associate dean, associate professor of Hebrew Bible/Old Testament, Lancaster Theological Seminary, Lancaster, Pennsylvania

Francisco Lozada Jr., Vice President for Faculty Affairs and Dean of the Faculty, Professor of New Testament Studies, Christian Theological Seminary, Indianapolis, Indiana

Roger S. Nam, professor of Hebrew Bible, Candler School of Theology, Emory University, Atlanta, Georgia

Aliou Cissé Niang, associate professor of New Testament, Union Theological Seminary, New York City

400   Contributors

Hugh R. Page Jr., vice president for institutional transformation and advisor to the president; professor of Theology and Africana studies, University of Notre Dame, South Bend, Indiana

Jean-Pierre Ruiz, associate professor and senior research fellow, Department of Theology and Religious Studies, St. John's University, Queens, New York

Fernando F. Segovia, Oberlin Graduate Professor of New Testament and Early Christianity, The Divinity School, Vanderbilt University, Nashville

Abraham Smith, professor of New Testament, Perkins School of Theology, Southern Methodist University, Dallas, Texas

Vincent L. Wimbush, scholar of religion and director of Institute for Signifying Scriptures, Decatur, Georgia

Names Index

Abraham, Ibrahim 192, 204
Abusch, Tzvi 113, 122
Abzug, Robert H. 307, 331
Achebe, Chinua 347, 353
Ahmed, Sara 56–57, 70, 76, 78–79, 81, 145–46, 148, 151–52, 154–55, 160–63
Ahn, John 249, 252
Alexander, M. Jacqui 69, 81
Alexander, Michelle 75, 81, 304, 314, 331
Amaya, Hector 126, 130–31, 138
Amin, Samir 70, 81
Anderson, Bernard 341, 353
Anderson, Cheryl B. 93, 280, 284, 366–67, 389, 392–93
Andrews, Williams L. 165, 349, 353
Annas, Max 146, 260, 275
Aparicio, Frances R. 210, 233
Aravamudan, Srinivas 344, 353
Arendt, Hannah 66, 78, 81, 248, 252
Armstrong, Richard H. 147, 164
Arsenault, Lisa 85
Ashcroft, Bill 108, 122
Ashton, John 151, 164
Atanasoski, Neda 69–70, 81
Avalos, Hector 105, 108–9, 115–16, 118, 120–122, 124, 288–90, 300, 381–82, 387, 389–92, 395
Aymer, Margaret 104, 137–39
Azuma, Eiichiro 72, 81
Bâ, Sylvia 262, 275
Bacevich, Andrew J. 63, 81
Baden, Joel 292, 300
Bahng, Aimee 65, 81
Bailey, Amy Kate 195, 204

Bailey, Randall C. 3, 57, 62, 81, 96–97, 103, 105–6, 121–22, 198, 200, 204, 280, 284, 288, 300
Baird, William 181, 186
Baker, Houston A., Jr. 281, 284–85, 349–50, 353, 372
Baldwin, James 75, 81
Banks, William M. 314, 331
Bannet, Eve Taylor 304, 331
Barkun, Michael 200–201, 204
Barnes, Harry E. 306–7, 309, 331
Barreto, Eric D. 292–93, 300
Barreto, José-Manuel 43–44, 50, 57
Barthes, Roland 62, 81, 331
Barton, John 239, 252
Bartram, David 245, 252
Bauman, Richard 348, 353
Bauman, Zygmunt 23, 67–68, 81
Becking, Bob 249, 252
Behdad, Ali 74, 81
Bell, Richard 306, 309, 334
Bellah, Robert N. 347, 353
Beltrán, Cristina 125, 131, 138
Benjamin, Walter 71, 74, 76, 78, 82, 150–51, 164
Benston, Kimberly W. 340, 349–350, 353
Bergner, Gwen 98, 103
Berlant, Lauren 62, 82
Berry, Wendell 74, 82
Bhabha, Homi 93, 103, 147, 150, 163–64, 183, 239, 259–60, 263, 275
Bierman, Noah 126, 138
Blaxter, Loraine 208, 233
Blount, Brian K. 280, 285

-401-

Names Index

Boer, Roland 192, 204
Boris, Eileen 65, 82
Boschma, Janie 67, 82
Bourdieu, Pierre 233, 342, 351, 353 B
Bradford, William 306–307, 331
Braedley, Susan 64, 82
Breed, Brennan 240, 242, 252, 380, 396
Briggs, Charles L. 348, 353
Brodie, Thomas L. 157, 164
Brooks, Rosa 63, 82
Brown, Wendy 62, 64–65, 72–73, 82
Browne, Malcolm W. 149, 164
Brueggemann, Walter 198–199, 204
Brysk, Alison 66, 82
Buck, Christopher 202, 204
Buck-Morss, Susan 350–51, 353
Buell, Denise Kimber 148, 160, 164
Bultmann, Rudolf 157, 164
Bump, Philip 290, 300
Busch, Annett 260, 275
Bush, George W. 37–38, 63
Butler, Judith 73, 77–78, 80, 82, 149, 151, 162–64
Cadbury, Henry J. 305, 318, 331
Callahan, Allen D. 96, 103
Cameron, Jim 282, 285
Carr, David M. 248, 252
Carroll R., M. Daniel 116–17, 122, 129, 138, 289–92, 301
Carter, Warren 88, 134, 136, 139
Caruth, Cathy 162, 164, 248, 252
Casey, Edward 74, 82
Casillas, Dolores Inés 218–224, 231, 233
Cerase, Fernando 245, 252
Certeau, Michel de 343, 353
Césaire, Aimé 257, 260, 262–64, 267, 274–75, 277, 337–38, 353
Chakrabarty, Dipesh 69–70, 82
Chang, David 174–75, 186–87
Chardin, Pierre Teilhard de 270, 272, 275
Chavers, Linda 74, 83
Cheng, Anne Anlin 76–77, 83
Cherry, Conrad 132, 139

Chiu, Lily V. 146, 164
Cho, Grace M. 73–74, 83, 158, 164
Choi, Jin Young 169, 172, 174, 177, 186
Christianson, Scott 308–9, 331
Christou, Anastasia 246, 252
Chu, Jocelyn 85
Clark, Gary, Jr. 279, 284–85
Clear, Todd R. 312–13, 315, 317, 326–328, 331
Coates, Ta-Nehisi 189, 348, 353
Cobham, Alex 66, 83
Coburn, Noah 63, 83
Coffey, Mary K. 77, 83
Collins, John 237, 252
Connolly, William 67, 83
Coomber, Matthew J. M. 280, 286
Cortés-Fuentes, David 134–37, 139
Critchley, Simon 67, 84
Cuéllar, Gregory Lee 110–13, 115, 122
Culpepper, R. Alan 157–158, 164
Cvetkovich, Ann 79, 83, 149, 165
Daise, Michael A. 161, 165
Damas, Léon-Gontran 260, 263–64, 267, 277–78
Darr, John A. 326, 331
Davies, Phillip 245, 252
Davies, William 65, 83
Davis, Stacy 192, 204, 280, 285
Dayan, Joan 350–51, 353
De Paris, Mairie 274–75
De Wit, Hans 118, 123–24
deClaissé-Walford, Nancy L. 151, 165
Depestre, René 265, 275
Derrida, Jacques 23, 63, 83, 239, 331
deSilva, David A. 134–135, 139
Desmond, Matthew 67, 83
Diagne, Souleymane Bachir 262, 268–69, 275
Diallo, Samba 258, 272
Díaz-Quiñones, Arcadio 227, 233
Dignam, Pierce 167
Dionisopoulos, George N. 149, 168
Diop, Cheikh Anta 271, 276
Diop, Mamadou 274, 276
Dodd, Charles H. 157, 165

Names Index

Donaldson, Laura E. 116, 123, 198–200, 205
Doniger, Wendy 354
Dooling, Sarah 64, 83
Dorfman, Aaron 287, 301
Douglass, Frederick 154–55, 161, 165, 241, 253, 349–50
Dowd-Arrow, Benjamin 167
Drescher, Hans-Georg 237, 253
Du Bois, W.E.B. 66, 76, 83, 143, 156, 165, 348, 351, 353
Duménil, Gérard 65, 83
Dunlop, Fuschia 173, 186
Dunn, Timothy J. 127, 139
DuRocher, Kristina 194, 205
Dyk, Janet 118, 123
Edelman, Diana V. 245, 253
Elizondo, Virgilio 117–18, 123
Ellacuría, Ignacio 293–95, 297–301, 386
Ellison, Ralph 71, 76, 83, 156, 351, 353
Eng, David L. 76–78, 82–84, 142, 164–65
Equiano, Olaudah 342–48, 351, 353
Erichsen, Kristen 167
Escoffier, George Auguste 172–73, 179–81, 186
Espiritu, Yên Lê 78, 84
Estes, Douglas 157, 165
Evans, Brad 67, 84
Fabian, Johannes 69, 84
Fabre, Michel 267, 276
Fanon, Frantz 26, 57, 59, 75, 84, 97–98, 100–4, 147, 163, 262–63, 265, 273–74, 276–77, 344, 348, 350, 352–54
Faría, Carlos Ramiréz 70, 84
FBI, Counterterrorism Divison 205
Fehribach, Adeline 160, 165
Felder, Cain Hope 96, 103–4, 241, 253, 285
Fewell, Danna Nolan 96, 103
Fishbane, Michael 119, 123
Foner, Eric 311, 313, 332
Foner, Nancy 244, 253
Fontevecchia, Jorge 47–48, 57
Fortna, Robert T. 157, 165

Foucault, Michel 23, 64, 75, 84, 161, 165–66, 304, 331, 337–38, 354
Fountain, Henry 361, 396
Fraser, Nancy 208, 221, 233
Frederick, David 332
Frei, Peter 249, 253
Freud, Sigmund 77–78, 84, 147, 149, 164–65
Frey, Sylvia R. 200, 205
Frost, Natasha A. 312–13, 315, 317, 331
Gadamer, Hans-Georg 119–20, 123–24
Gadjigo, Samba 260, 276
Gafney, Wilda C. 280, 285
Gaines, Stanley O., Jr. 101, 103
Gasparetti, Fedora 266, 276
Gates, Henry Louis, Jr. 98, 103
Gentile, Haley 167
Ghosh, Jayati 362–63, 396
Gibson, Nigel 101, 103
Gilman, Sander 147, 165
Gilmore, Ruth Wilson 143, 165
Gmelc, George 244, 253
Gold, Steven J. 244, 253, 313
Goldberg, David Theo 73, 84
Goldenberg, David M. 191–92, 205
Gordon, Avery F. 78, 84, 150, 163, 166
Gordon, Cyrus 279, 285
Gordon, Robert J. 109, 124
Gowler, David 329, 332
Gramsci, Antonio 30, 68, 85
Greenhouse, Carol 64, 85
Greer, Rowan A. 119, 123
Gregg, Melissa 151, 168
Gregory, Andrew F. 319, 332
Griffiths, Gareth 108, 122
Guerrero, Andrés G. 117, 123
Guest, Deryn 280, 285
Guibbory, Achsah 200, 205
Guilmette, Lauren 161, 166
Gutiérrez-Rodríguez, Encarnacion 65, 85
Hacker, Karen 63, 85
Hahn, Sharon K. 236
Hale, Grace Elizabeth 73, 85
Han, Shinhee 83, 142, 165

Names Index

Hanchard, Michael 70, 85
Haraway, Donna J. 160, 166
Harcourt, Bernard E. 316, 332
Hartman, Geoffrey 162, 166
Hartung, William D. 63, 85
Harvey, David 24, 72, 85
Hasegawa, Tsuyoshi 73, 85
Hayes, John H. 280, 285
Hegel, Georg Wilhelm Friedrich 62, 69, 85
Heidegger, Martin 61, 85
Hernández, Kelly Lytle 316, 332
Hidalgo, Jacqueline M. 125, 383, 390–91, 394
Hill, Marc Lamont 308, 311, 315–17, 332
Hinton, Elizabeth 303, 313, 316–17, 332
Hirsch, Adam J. 306, 308, 333
Hirsch, Marianne 153, 166
Holden-Smith, Barbara 193–194, 205
Holloway, Karla F.C. 77, 85, 141, 148, 166
Hong, Cathy Park 76, 85, 146, 153, 166
Honneth, Axel 208, 233
hooks, bell 141, 258, 276
Hornsby, Teresa 188, 280, 285
Hughes, Christina 208, 233, 267
Hurston, Zora Neale 352, 354
Hutcheon, Linda 163, 166
Ioanide, Paula 163, 166
Islam, Md Saidul 64
James, Kenneth 172, 186
JanMohammed, Abdul R. 350, 354
Jauss, Hans 325, 332
Jean-Georges 175, 186
Jen, Gish 74, 85
Jenkins, Richard 249, 253
Jobson, Richard 192, 205
Johnson, Lyndon B. 150, 313–15, 316, 332
Johnson, Sylvester A. 130, 137, 139
Johnston, Ron J. 64, 83, 85
Jones, Ian 205, 285, 337
Jonkers, Louis 249, 253
Judis, John B. 200, 205
Junior, Nyasha 240, 280, 285

Kahan, Paul 307–308, 332
Kaminsky, Joel S. 132–133, 139
Kane, Cheikh Hamidou 257–58, 260–61, 264, 266, 268, 272, 276
Kane, Ousmane Oumar 266–67, 276
Kang, Miliann 65, 85
Kaplan, Sara Clarke 77, 86, 160, 166, 201, 205
Karlsson, Bengt G. 65, 86
Kasper, Lynn Rossetto 174, 186
Kavanaugh, Emma 205
Kazanjian, David 76–78, 82, 84, 164
Kealey, Linda 306, 308, 332
Kelly, Raina 186
Kendi, Ibram X. 76, 86
Kesteloot, Lylian 262, 276
Keyder, Çağlar 26–27, 57
Khoser, Khalid 244, 253
Kikon, Dolly 65, 86
Kilgore, James William 304, 314–15, 317–18, 332
Kim, David Kyuman 76, 78, 86
Kim, Jinah 73, 76–79, 86, 146, 152 163, 166
Kim, Nadia Y. 246, 253
King, Sallie B. 166
Kinkupu, Leonard Santedi 273, 276
Kirk-Duggan, Cheryl 201, 205, 280, 285
Kittredge, Cynthia Briggs 95, 103–4, 138–39
Klein, Naomi 66, 86
Knoppers, Gary 249, 253
Kohler-Hausman, Julilly 314–15, 333
Korstanje, Maximiliano E. 58, 66, 86–88
Kugel, James L. 119, 123,
Laburthe-Tolra, Philippe 271, 276
LaCapra, Dominick 71, 86, 162, 166
Latham, Michael E. 63, 86
Leary, John Patrick 70, 86
Lee, James Kyung-Jin 5, 57, 261, 335
Lee, Jung Young 258, 276
Lee, Michael E. 297, 301
Leeman, Richard 70, 86
Legaspi, Michael 236, 253
León-Portilla, Miguel 111, 123

Names Index

Levy, Dominiqué 65, 83
Li, Xiaobing 73, 86
Liew, Tat-siong Benny 3–4, 55–57, 61–62, 81, 87, 105–6, 121–22, 141–43, 147, 153, 166–67, 170, 186, 207–8, 232–33, 236, 243, 253, 280, 284, 288, 300, 376–77, 389, 391, 394–95
Lin, Yii-Jan 169, 172–73, 182, 187, 377–78, 389, 391, 393
Lindsey, Edward 311, 333
Litchfield, Chelsea 190, 205
LoBianco, Tom 125, 139
Locke, Alain 263, 276, 348
Lohr, Joel N. 196, 200, 205
Long, Charles H. 348, 350, 354
López, Alfred J. 20, 57
Lopez, Donald S., Jr. 354
Los Tigres del Norte 112, 123
Lotman, Yuri M. 342, 354
Lovelace, Vanessa 189, 367–69, 390, 392–93
Lowe, Lisa 74–75, 87
Lozada, Francisco, Jr. 121–23, 207, 384–85, 389–91, 394
Lozano, Adele 207, 233
Lu, Sidney Xu 73, 87
Luxton, Meg 64, 82
M'Baye, Babacar 267, 277
MacFarquar, Larissa 174, 187
Malherbe, Abraham 330–331, 333
Mandel, Ruth 246, 254
Mann, Thomas 114, 121, 123
Marbury, Herbert Robinson 96, 104, 280, 285
Marín, Luis Muñoz 225–229
Marquez, John 63, 87
Marrow, Stanley 329, 333
Marshall, Wesley C. 64, 87
Martin, Clarice J. 195, 206
Martín-Baró, Ignacio 99–100, 104, 298
Martinez, Michael 127, 139
Masuzawa, Tomoko 339, 354
Matejowsky, Ty 184, 187
Mattingly, David 305, 333
Mauer, Marc 304, 333

Mbembe, Achille 65, 87
Mbiti, John 268, 277
McCarthy, Michael C. 297–98, 301
McConnell, James R., Jr. 328, 333
McCoy, Alfred W. 74, 87
McKelvey, Blake 306–7, 333
McWilliams, Mark 175, 187
Meads, Mallory 63, 87
Medina, Néstor 131, 139
Mehta, Seema 126, 138
Memmi, Albert 99–100, 104
Mennell, Stephen 180, 187
Merrill, Curt 67, 82
Mettler, Katie 290, 301
Middleton, Stephen 107, 123
Miles, Jack 340, 354
Miller, Amanda C. 305, 333
Miller, Elise 141, 167
Mintz, Sidney W. 177, 180, 187
Mohanty, Chandra Talpade 69, 80, 87, 158, 167
Molina, Natalia 210–17, 230–31, 233
Momofuku 174, 186–187
Monforte, Pierre 245, 252
Monroe, Irene 101–2, 104
Moore, Stephen D. 80, 87, 142, 161, 167, 280, 285
Morrison, Toni 74, 80, 87, 141, 143, 156, 158, 167, 343, 350–51, 354
Moshe, Mira 55, 57, 68–69, 75, 87
Moskin, Julia 176, 187
Moss, Candida 144–46, 151, 160, 167
Most, Glenn W. 144, 151–52, 159, 167
Mphahlele, Ezekiel 265, 277
Muhammad, Khalil Gibran 311, 316, 332–33
Muñoz-Larrondo, Rubén 109, 123
Murphy-Teixidor, John 67, 82
Myers, Alicia D. 161, 167
N'Dong, Henri Biram 274, 277
Nam, Roger S. 235, 243, 254, 379–80, 390, 392–93
Napolitano, Marcos 43, 58
Neier, Aryeh 312, 333
Nguyen, Viet Thanh 154, 163, 167

406 Names Index

Niang, Aliou Cissé 257–58, 277, 369–71, 390, 392–93
Nietzsche, Friedrich Wilhelm 80, 84, 87
Northrup, Solomon 309, 333
Novick, Peter 61, 87
Nwel, Pierre Titi 271, 277
O'Connor, Kathleen 248, 254
O'Donovan, Susan Eva 309, 333
Obama, Barack 70, 73, 86, 218, 292
Oeming, Manfred 250, 254
Oliver, Kelly 162–63, 167
Olsen, Niklas 72, 87
Omi, Michael 213, 233
Osborne, Jaquelyn 205
Padios, Jan M. 65, 88
Page, Hugh R., Jr. 279–80, 285–86, 371–72, 389, 391, 393–94
Parker, L. Evelyn 5, 58
Parreñas, Rhacel Salazar 65, 82
Parsons, Mikeal 318–19, 333
Patler, Nicholas 150, 167
Patrick, Deval 127–131, 133, 135–39
Pelikan, Jaroslav 118, 123
Pervo, Richard I. 318–19, 321, 323, 328, 333
Pfaelzer, Jean 74, 88
Pfaff, John 303, 333
Phillips, Andrew 72, 88
Phoenix, Davin L. 163, 167
Pieters, Jürgen 162, 167
Piore, Michael J. 245, 254
Pippin, Tina 280, 285
Pisani, Elizabeth 95, 104
Plummer, Brad 361, 396
Poole, Stafford 117–18, 124
Poros, Maritsa 245, 252
Portes, Alexandro 266, 277
Powery, Emerson B. 285
Pritchard, James B. 115, 124
Quarles, Chester R. 369, 396
Quinones, Ricardo 191–92, 206
Rabaka, Reiland 260, 265, 277
Rabinowitz, Peter 325, 334
Ramose, Mogobe B. 268, 274, 277

Raposo, Jacqueline 176, 187
Rapske, Brian 318, 320, 323, 334
Ray, Philippe 271, 277
Reiner, Erica 113, 124
Renault, Matthieu 101, 104
Rhodes, Robert 244, 254
Rich, Adrienne 61, 88
Ristau, Kenneth A. 249, 253
Rivera, Mayra 5, 58
Robin, Corey 66, 88
Robson, James 354
Rody, Caroline 158, 167
Roediger, David R. 107, 123
Rogin, Michael 74, 88
Rosaldo, Renato 219, 233
Ross, Andrew 66, 88
Rothman, David 306, 308–10, 334
Rotman, Edgardo 309–10, 312, 334
Rowan, Carl T. 202–3, 206
Rowe, C. Kavin 305, 319, 332
Rowland, Christopher 157, 168
Rudrappa, Sharmila 65, 88
Ruether, Rosemary Radford 204, 206
Ruhlman, Michael 175, 187
Ruiz, Jean-Pierre 109, 124, 136, 139, 287, 288–89, 292, 301, 386–87, 390–91, 393
Rumbaut, Ruben G. 244, 253–54
Russell, Letty M. 203, 206
Said, Edward W. 78, 88, 163, 242, 254, 259–60, 262, 265, 277
Salinas, Cristobal, Jr. 207, 233
Sarkozy, Nicolas 271, 273
Sartre, Jean-Paul 264–65, 277
Schaeffer, Francis A. 269–70, 277
Scharff, Christina 64, 88
Schechner, Richard 150, 167
Scheffer, Gabriel 245, 254
Schipani, Daniel 118–120, 124
Schliefer, Theodore 126, 139
Schorb, Jodi 307–8, 334
Schrock, Douglas 163, 167
Schuchard, Bruce G. 161, 167
Schwartz, Saundra 326, 334
Schweidler, Chris 332

Names Index

407

Scott, Catherine V. 64, 88
Scott, James C. 341, 354
Scribano, Adrian 65, 68, 88
Segovia, Fernando F. 3–4, 57, 61–62, 66, 81, 87–88, 93–94, 104–106, 121–23, 170, 187, 207, 209–10, 224, 234, 236, 238, 241–42, 254, 280, 284, 288, 293, 296, 300–301, 359–60, 381, 396
Seidman, Steven 22–25, 30, 52, 58
Seigworth, Gregory J. 151, 168
Sekyi-Otu, Ato 350, 354
Senghor, Léopold Sédar 257–78, 370–71
Serequeberhan, Tsenay 273, 278
Shaffer, Donald M. 107, 123
Shalev, Eran 132, 139
Sharman, Jason C. 72, 88
Sherwood, Yvonne 280, 285
Shin, Gi-Wook 246, 254
Shockley, Martin 114, 121, 124
Shoenberg, Shira 129, 140
Shorris, Earl 111, 123
Shulman, Helene 98, 104
Simon, Gregory 64, 83
Simon, Jonathan 305, 308, 334
Singh, Nikhil 73, 89
Singleton, Jermaine 74, 77, 89, 146, 153, 168
Sison, Bree 129, 140
Sitkoff, Harvard 194, 206
Ska, Jean-Louise 249, 254
Skinner, Matthew L. 322–23, 334
Skoll, Geoffrey R. 66, 89
Skonieczny, Amy 163, 168
Skow, Lisa M. 149, 168
Slobodian, Quinn 64, 89
Smith, Abraham 303, 334, 373–74, 389, 392–93
Smith, D. Moody 157, 168
Smith, Mitzi J. 169, 187
Smith, Paul 66, 88
Smith, Wilfred Cantwell 341, 354
Smith-Christopher, Daniel L. 116, 124, 248, 254
Snedker, Karen A. 195, 204
Snider, Laureen 64, 89

Solender, Andrew 75, 89
Solnit, Rebecca 361, 396
Sousa Santos, Boaventura de 25, 40–54, 56–59
Southern Poverty Law Center 201, 206
Soyinka, Wole 265, 278
Spillers, Hortense 62, 89
Spivak, Gayatri Chakravorty 69, 89, 259–60, 278
Steinberg, Stephen 314, 334
Stevenson, Bryan 303–4, 334
Stohl, Michael 63, 89
Stoler, Ann Laura 73, 78, 89
Stone, Ken 280, 285
Stonebridge, Lyndsey 158, 168
Stutzman, Rene 189, 206
Suárez Findlay, Eileen J. 224–32, 234
Tabone, Mark A. 158, 168
Tarter, Michele Lise 306, 309, 334
Taussig, Michael 351, 354
Taylor, Diana 74–75, 78, 89, 153, 162–63, 168
Taylor, Koko 284–85
Taylor, Peter J. 64, 85
Tezózomoc, Fernando Alvarado 111
Theophanidis, Philippe 67–68, 72, 89
Thiong'O, Ngũgĩ wa 264, 278
Thiselton, Anthony C. 120, 124
Thomas, Dominic 266, 278
Thornton, John K. 345, 354
Thurman, Howard 350, 354
Tiffin, Helen 108, 122
Tilley, Helen 109, 124
Tolbert, Mary Ann 61, 88, 104
Tracy, David 80, 89
Trites, Allen 327–28, 334
Troeltsch, Ernst 237, 253, 255
Troy, Tevi 314, 334
Trubek, Amy B. 177, 180–81, 183, 187
Trudy 171, 187
Trump, Donald J. 21, 63–66, 73–74, 85, 87–89, 125–27, 138–40, 163, 166–68, 290–92, 300–301, 359, 361, 383, 386–87
Tumarkin, Maria 76, 89

Names Index

Tuvel, Rebecca 171, 187
Ulla, Gabe 176, 187
Vaillant, Janet 260, 262–63, 268, 278
Vega, Cecilia 126, 140
Ventura, Patricia 64, 89
Vesey, Denmark 200–201, 309
Via, Dan O. 134, 140
Viego, Antonio 77, 90
Villalobos, Manuel 177–78, 188
Walcott, Derek 351, 354
Walker, Alice 171, 188
Wallerstein, Immanuel 24–40, 52–54, 56–58
Walters, Alicia 332
Wansink, Craig S. 320–21, 323, 335
Ward, Brian 314, 335
Warrior, Robert Allen 132, 140, 198–99, 206
Watkins, Mary 98, 104
Watts, Michael J. 64, 85
Weaver, John B. 321–22, 327, 335
Wehellye, Alexander G. 80, 90
Wexler, Stuart 202–203, 206
Wilder, Gary 262, 278
Wilentz, Gay 143, 168
Williams, Catrin H. 157, 168
Williams, Raymond 77, 90, 153, 168
Wilson, Brittany E. 323, 335
Wimbush, Vincent L. 96–97, 104, 236, 241–42, 255, 280, 285, 295, 301, 337, 342, 345, 347–49, 351–52, 354, 375, 381, 389, 391, 394, 397
Winant, Howard 213, 233
Winters, Joseph R. 70, 74, 77, 79, 90, 142, 154, 156, 162–63, 168
Wood, Amy Louise 194, 206
Wylie, Sara Ann 67, 90
Wynter, Sylvia 338, 342, 344, 355
Yamazaki-Ransom Kazuhiko 327, 335
Yan, Holly 127, 139
Yancy, George 190, 193, 206
Yang, Michelle Murray 149–151, 163, 168
Yates, Heather E. 163, 168

Yee, Gale A. 103, 110, 113–14, 124, 157, 168, 235, 280, 286
Young, Harvey 193, 206
Young, Jason R. 143, 168
Zamir, Shamoon 156, 168
Zarembka, Paul 64, 90
Zavella, Pat 222, 234
Zerubavel, Yael 245, 255
Ziai, Aram 42, 45, 59
Zibechi, Raúl 373, 397
Žižek, Slavoj 361, 397
Zohrabi, Azadeh 332
Zvi, Ehud Ben 245, 253

Subject Index

abolition, 89, 331
abuse, 314, 318, 374
abyssal line, 44–50, 53, 56
adroitness, 282
affective transfer, 141, 148, 155, 161
  scars, 54, 144–46, 151, 351, 377
  wounds, 55, 74, 78, 143–52, 159
African American, 62, 77, 85, 89, 93, 95–96, 103–4, 109, 137, 139, 141, 148, 156, 166–68, 176, 189–90, 195, 198, 232, 253, 267, 285, 366–68, 372, 374–75, 390
African descent, 93–94, 96–97, 190–91, 273, 367–69, 375, 389, 393
Africana, 281, 285
Afrocentric, 198, 200, 265, 352
agency, 39, 61, 76, 86, 143, 172, 347, 351–53, 377
alienation, 36, 98, 259, 367, 370–71
alterity, 259, 354
  subaltern, 44, 89, 281, 347, 372, 384
America of the South, 17–18
American Academy of Religion, 279
American Values, Religious Voices, 291, 293, 300–1
Amtrak, 282
Ancient Near East, 121, 124
antiquity, 8–12, 54, 144, 147, 164, 204, 237, 320, 382
anxiety, 54, 66, 72, 131, 133, 168, 254, 340, 342, 345, 347, 366
apocalypse, 61, 202, 362, 369, 396
archives, 222, 231
arrest, 146, 303–9, 311, 313, 315, 317–19, 321, 323, 325–29, 331, 333, 335, 374

Asian American, 76, 85, 166, 169–72, 174, 176, 186, 253, 376
assimilation, 83, 133, 173, 241, 246, 250, 257, 260, 262, 267, 370
atheism, 105, 122, 238, 382, 392
Atlantic, 93, 96, 344, 354
  Black Atlantic, 338, 351, 375
  North Atlantic, 342
Auburn system, 308, 311
authorial, 318–319, 325, 327, 330, 382
authority, 8, 83, 109, 137, 147, 160, 193, 241, 249, 291, 316, 320, 337, 345, 377, 382, 383
  authorized, 63, 131, 339, 341, 346
  unauthorized, 125, 127, 130, 137, 383–84
autobiography, 114, 123, 258, 293, 349
awareness, 20, 101, 105–6, 117, 190, 260, 283, 290, 351, 372
belonging, 129–33, 172, 209–10, 214, 217–220, 223–24, 229, 231–33, 248, 254, 385–86
biblical chosenness, 189–91, 193, 195, 197–99, 201, 203, 205, 368
bibliolatry, 109, 116, 121, 289, 382, 393, 395
  definition, 108
  idolatry, 42, 96, 192, 198
Black, Blackness, 62–63, 65, 73–74, 83, 87, 90, 94–97, 99, 100–101, 103, 141–43, 156, 165, 167–68, 184, 197–99, 201–3, 205, 211–15, 222, 225, 241, 265, 268, 273–78, 311–12, 314, 316, 331, 333, 335, 338, 341, 343, 346–47, 349, 350–54, 367, 370, 375–76

-409-

410 Subject Index

Black, Blackness (cont.)
  Black bodies, 102, 189–90, 192–93, 206, 283, 348, 368–69, 374
  Black men, 98, 189, 194, 264, 303, 317, 344, 368
  Black students, 257, 262
  Black women, 102, 170–71
border, 17, 125, 127, 211–12, 216–18, 284, 289–92, 301, 386
bridge, 193, 242
Britain, 108, 200–1, 306, 342, 347
Canaanites, 96, 140, 192, 196–99, 205–6, 367–68
capitalism, 24–27, 45, 47–48, 50, 53, 56, 64, 66, 74, 76, 78, 86, 89, 100, 156, 212
  capital, 29–30, 33, 35–37, 50, 64–65, 72–73, 126–27, 130, 233, 247, 306, 383–84
  disaster capitalism, 64, 66, 86
cartography, 388–89, 391–92, 396
children, 114–15, 127–30, 139–40, 168, 193–94, 197, 200, 202, 205, 227, 235, 246, 250, 266, 272, 276, 285, 292, 318, 338, 368, 386
China, 37, 39, 48–50, 95, 216, 362
Christian identity, 109, 189, 191, 193, 195, 197, 199–205, 369, 396
Christian missiology, 105–9, 111, 115, 117, 119, 123, 300, 382
  civilization, 27, 50, 77, 99, 263, 265, 271, 274, 278, 289, 290
  missions, 113, 120, 202, 260, 269, 272, 274, 387
  savage, 337, 342
citizen, 112, 126, 132, 150, 260, 292
  citizenship, 125–33, 135–38, 200, 216, 219–20, 222, 230–31, 233, 254, 383–84, 390
  naturalization, 130, 211, 214, 217
classical cuisine, 172, 174–76, 179–80, 182–83, 185, 378
colonialism, 47, 50, 69, 72, 81, 87, 108, 117, 131, 139, 147, 159, 164, 177, 183, 209, 225–27, 228, 230, 263, 289, 347, 353, 386

colonialism (cont.)
  anticolonial, 367, 370
  decolonial, 18–19, 26, 34, 85, 273, 277–78, 370–71
  neocolonial, 70, 73
  postcolonial, 43–44, 82, 86, 88, 93, 98, 100, 103–4, 108, 120, 122, 166–67, 169, 171–72, 174, 178, 183, 186, 204, 257, 259, 262, 269, 301, 351, 370
comparison, 78, 172–73, 176, 182, 186, 192, 287, 345
conscientization, 17, 19, 348, 362, 367, 381
consciousness, 5, 58, 69, 172, 177, 241, 263, 270, 294, 314, 340, 345–50
conservative, 34, 297, 338, 383
  movement, 37, 42
  tradition, 8, 101, 340–41
covenant, 196–98
criminalization, 373
  criminality, 194, 315
crisis, 7, 17–21, 25, 31, 42, 44–45, 47–48, 50, 52, 59, 62, 65, 89, 110, 125, 128, 137, 149, 165, 229, 238, 242, 248, 281, 284, 295–96, 299, 334, 359, 361, 364–68, 371, 373, 375–77, 379, 383–84, 386, 388–90, 392
  climate change, 19, 67, 360, 362–63, 396
  structural crisis, 28, 36, 38, 53–54, 56
Crónica Mexicáyotl, 111–12
crucifixion, 134, 143–44, 151–52, 155, 273
  the cross, 146–48, 271, 338, 366
cultural memory, 89, 168, 245
dark, 17, 73, 82, 155, 168, 193, 343
  darkness, 264, 321, 350, 354
death, 25–28, 40, 65–67, 76, 79, 95, 98, 116, 141, 143, 148–50, 152–53, 155, 157–60, 167, 253, 272, 283, 293, 298, 306, 327, 329, 331, 347, 350, 352, 354, 376
deep state, 361
democracy, 50, 53, 56, 64, 130, 138–39, 233, 303, 373

Subject Index

desktop theology, 298
diaspora, 17, 83, 85, 122, 136, 138, 164, 224, 228, 230, 232, 246, 250–52, 254, 259, 267–68, 274–75, 338, 341, 350–51, 370
différance, 169–70, 378
disability, 105, 145, 171, 208
discourse, 15, 20, 24, 44, 86, 104, 125, 136, 146–48, 157, 168, 207, 223, 225, 229, 232, 242, 259, 262, 267–68, 275, 278, 290, 295, 334, 337–38, 340, 345–46, 351–52, 367
discrimination, 47, 126, 190, 203, 275, 304, 383
dish, 173, 175, 178, 187
divinity, 95, 99, 109, 117, 118, 132, 137, 167, 195, 251, 269, 270, 271, 290, 298, 333
    deity, 137, 191–92, 196–200, 322, 324, 330, 395
    God, 58, 95, 99–100, 102, 109, 111–12, 116, 119, 131, 133, 137, 139, 142, 148, 151, 154, 158, 168–69, 184, 187, 227, 249–51, 269–72, 288, 291–92, 323, 326, 328, 343, 367–69, 371, 378, 382, 384, 387, 392–93, 395
    life-force, 269
    sacred, 8–9, 118–20, 240, 269, 298, 327, 339, 380
ecclesial
    church communities, 97, 99–100, 103, 109, 117, 122, 129, 174, 200–1, 203, 205, 228, 238, 262, 274, 281, 283–84, 288–89, 291, 298, 301, 330, 368–69, 372, 387, 393
economy, 22, 24, 27–30, 32, 37, 48–49, 52–53, 56, 59, 63, 65, 224, 246, 318, 340, 343, 389
ecumenism, 345
El Salvador, 99, 119, 294, 297, 386
elite, 36, 113, 121, 131, 180, 184, 224–25, 267, 281, 297, 344, 372, 384, 387
emotion, 56–57, 79, 81, 145–46, 154–55, 160–63, 168

emotion (cont.)
    feeling, 66, 77, 87, 147, 153, 161, 167, 258
empire, 29, 45, 58, 72–73, 81, 88–89, 108, 112–13, 122, 134, 162–63, 204–5, 238, 244, 249–51, 267, 272–73, 305, 333, 335, 339, 359, 361, 374, 377
    sovereign, 24, 65, 67, 83, 87
en conjunto, 364, 366
enterprise, 106, 110, 120, 185, 199, 237
environmental destruction, 64
epiphany, 321–22, 335, 361
episteme, 78, 162
    epistemology, 40, 45, 84, 165, 182, 208–10, 378, 384–85
ethics, 43, 109, 122, 139, 166, 262, 295, 301, 386
ethnic-racial biblical criticism, 57
    African American biblical hermeneutics, 3–6, 8–15, 18, 21, 55, 61–62, 93, 114, 127, 132, 135, 163, 170, 182, 190, 195, 203, 208–9, 236, 238, 240–43, 247, 257, 262–65, 267, 270, 275, 278, 296–97, 299, 301, 340, 344, 349–50, 352, 364–69, 371–77, 379–83, 386, 390–91, 393–96
    Asian biblical hermeneutics, 3, 6, 8–11, 13–15, 55, 61–62, 127, 132, 163, 170, 186, 190, 195, 203, 209, 242, 253, 278, 301, 344, 349–50, 366–69, 371–77, 380, 383, 386
    Latino/a biblical hermeneutics, 122–23, 170, 187, 207–8, 233
ethnic-racial othering, 363, 367, 369, 371, 373, 375–77, 379, 381, 383–84, 386, 389–90, 395
ethno-theology, 106, 110, 117, 289
ethnography, 170, 205, 222
Euro-American, 113–14, 121, 175
Eurocentrism, 43–45, 69, 106–7, 109–10, 120, 183, 265, 382
European, 17, 22, 58–59, 80, 106–7, 109, 114, 116, 118–121, 124, 126, 175, 181, 192, 205, 225, 233, 263, 265, 273–74, 279, 292, 339, 344–45, 354

412   Subject Index

evangelical, 100–101, 194, 198, 269, 290, 307

exceptionalism, 46–47, 70, 200, 361, 376, 382

exile, 110–1, 113–15, 173, 178, 198, 235, 247, 250, 260, 264, 266, 292

exploitation, 26, 29–30, 50, 66, 70, 74, 96, 224, 228

Ezra-Nehemiah, 235–37, 239, 241, 243, 245–51, 253–55

faculty, 26–27, 185–86, 235, 238, 282, 287, 289, 293, 298, 301

fear, 36, 47, 66, 72, 88–89, 111–12, 148, 153, 178, 216, 229, 283, 296, 330–31, 343

focalization, 305

food, 33, 173–79, 182, 184–85, 187, 224, 292, 379

forensic, 326–27

Forum for Theological Exploration, 238

France, 30, 84, 98, 172, 181, 187, 258, 261, 262, 265–67, 271–74, 277, 278, 343, 370, 371, 378
    French colonization, 259
    French education, 263, 266
    French school, 260, 268

fundamentalism, 100

gaze, 179, 190, 264, 284, 305, 324–27, 332, 374

gender and sexuality studies
    feminist, 23, 87, 123, 145, 165, 167, 169, 171, 186, 219, 226, 230–31, 233, 338
    heterosexual, 24, 101–2, 126
    LGBTQ, 24, 66, 78–79, 102, 104, 145, 177, 188, 285, 318, 374
    masculinity, 23, 224–28, 232, 234
    paternalism, 227, 229–30
    patriarchy, 45, 47, 50, 101, 116, 169, 222, 227, 229–30
    sex, sexual, sexuality, 35, 66, 81, 83, 95–96, 190, 192, 195, 198, 204, 207–8, 218, 223, 238, 335, 337–38, 347, 366

geopolitical, 16, 18–19, 25, 31–35, 37–40,

geopolitical (*cont.*)
    44, 53, 59, 64, 259, 268, 360, 363, 369, 375–76, 390, 394

ghost, 73–74, 76, 78, 84, 100, 143–44, 152, 163, 166

globalization, 20, 24, 36, 40, 45, 48–49, 82, 89, 221, 244, 281

Great Commission, the, 109, 135, 288

Great House Farm, 349–50, 352

Great Recession, the, 19, 31, 36, 48, 53, 361

grief, 17, 56, 74–81, 83, 86, 141–42, 145, 150, 153, 155–56, 158–63, 166, 376
    colonial grief, 149, 159

hate, 142–43, 154, 200–201, 272, 284, 294, 371

hegemony, 30–32, 35, 37–38, 55, 73, 108, 243, 367
    counterhegemony, 94, 99
    domination, 26, 50, 52, 73, 112–13, 149, 194, 248, 259, 341, 354, 376, 389–90 subjugation, 160

historical criticism, 9, 13, 181–83, 226, 237, 239–40, 252, 378–79, 395

historiography, 10, 237, 253–54, 259

homecoming, 248
    settlement, 130
    unsettled, 154, 194, 235, 248

hope, 47, 62, 76, 86, 90, 103–4, 154–55, 163, 168, 185, 188, 202, 227, 238, 246, 250–51, 253, 258, 264, 285, 299, 313, 354, 377, 379, 394

hospitality, 83, 125, 127, 206

humanitarian, humanity
    dehumanization, 130, 154, 171, 258
    humanism, 265, 278, 348, 352
    humanistic, 244

humiliation, 321, 346–47, 351, 375

ideology, 10–11, 13, 20, 31–33, 35, 39, 42, 53–55, 89, 100, 204, 246, 259, 268, 281–85, 290, 296, 323, 329, 332, 339, 340–41, 345–46, 348, 350, 353, 367–69, 372–75, 383–85, 388, 392–96

Igbo, 345–46

imagination, 72, 78, 84, 86, 89, 134, 166, 252, 294, 331, 351–52, 354

Subject Index

imperialism, 15, 24, 54–56, 69, 73, 76–77, 105–10, 121, 132, 151, 152, 249, 253, 254, 263, 265, 278, 288, 370, 376, 377, 381, 382, 389, 390
  conquest, 109, 120, 199, 206
  expansion, 12–13, 17, 27, 32–34, 37, 59, 120, 177, 221, 339, 393
incarceration, 127, 130, 136–37, 303–5, 308, 311–13, 315, 317–18, 320–21, 373–74, 389
India, 44, 72, 86, 88, 337
indigenous, 51, 86, 96, 110–12, 118, 120, 192, 196–97, 199, 225, 230, 368
insecurity, 19, 66, 361
interpretive flexibility, 110, 118–21, 382
interregnum, 67–68, 72, 81, 89
intertextuality, 319
invent, 265, 280, 285, 341, 346, 354
Islam, 192, 204, 205, 274, 277, 339
  Islamic state and law, 116
  Muslim, 116, 125–26, 258, 296, 386
Israelites, 96, 114, 131–33, 138, 195–98, 200, 367–68
Jamaica, 343
Jesuit, 99, 270, 293–94, 298, 300–1, 386
Jesus, 109, 113, 128, 134–35, 138, 141–153, 155–60, 163, 177–78, 197, 200, 202, 270–74, 283, 321, 324, 326, 328, 335, 341, 368, 371, 377, 384, 393
Jew, 106, 112, 135, 147, 162, 202–5, 211, 311, 322
  Jewish, 120, 128, 132, 136, 157, 165, 168, 200, 238, 250, 252, 301, 322, 330, 339
Johnson-Reed Act of 1924, the, 211
justice, 22–23, 41, 44–45, 109, 119, 156, 227, 288, 292, 305–6, 312–13, 324, 328–29, 331–34, 335, 337, 387, 393
  injustice, 47, 75, 145–46, 217, 226, 273, 284, 294, 371, 373, 377
  justice system, 303, 315, 374
  social justice, 97, 102, 233, 367, 392, 396
kingdom, 30, 34, 56, 115, 134, 137, 202, 252, 279, 369, 384

Korea, 37–38, 73, 83, 164, 169, 174–75, 251, 254, 380
  Korean American, 77, 236, 239, 246–47, 379
labor, 29, 85, 114, 185, 188, 212, 216, 254, 282, 308, 311–12, 332, 387
  bregar, 227–29, 233
  income, 65, 224, 363
  markets, 38, 48, 64, 221
  unions, 64, 211
  workers, 49–50, 83, 117, 228, 245, 284, 290, 322
Latin America, 17, 34, 44–6, 100, 220, 223, 298–99, 373, 383
  Latino/a studies, 105, 109, 116, 207–10, 212–15, 219, 221, 223–25, 227, 229–31, 233
  Latinx, 4, 15, 20, 77, 135–36, 169, 171, 176, 178, 207, 233, 364, 374, 381, 384–87, 390
least of these, the, 125, 127–29, 131, 133, 135–39
liberal studies, 8, 24, 42, 57, 87, 117, 129–30, 226, 290, 303, 341, 383
  liberalism, 35, 59
  neoliberalism, 20, 34, 36, 38, 47–50, 53–56, 62, 64–69, 72–77, 80, 126, 163, 376–77, 389
liberation, 33–34, 70, 99, 101, 103–4, 108, 132, 176, 198–99, 201, 204, 206, 262, 301, 367
  freedom, 22–23, 37, 63–64, 74, 76, 86, 96, 113, 139, 152, 187, 199–200, 225, 227, 244, 259, 263–65, 267, 272, 278, 281, 294, 314, 332, 335, 337, 350–52, 370–72, 376–77
  liberation theology, 99, 176, 199, 206
liminality, 245, 259–60
love, 128–29, 132, 175, 196, 283, 292, 294, 296, 335
lynching, 189, 193–94, 204–6
marginality, marginalization, 24, 43, 70, 100, 110, 115, 122, 129, 169, 236, 259–60, 275–76, 301, 344, 354, 372, 379, 384

414   Subject Index

martyr, 293, 298

Marxism, 42–44, 71, 89, 167, 269–70, 297

material, materiality, 11, 34, 46, 100, 132, 144, 160, 215, 240, 269, 337, 368–69, 372, 375, 377, 381, 389–91

    discursivity and, 7, 10, 13, 16–17, 390, 395

media studies, 126–30, 149, 189–90, 219–20, 222, 224, 231, 314

    images, 69, 70, 111, 151, 225, 229, 270, 273, 281, 304, 330, 354, 372

    radio, 186, 218–24, 231, 233

melancholy, melancholia, 76–79, 84, 86, 147, 149, 156

    melancholic freedom, 76, 86, 377

methodology, 10, 18, 84, 87, 93, 103, 106, 119, 123, 165, 167, 174, 176, 180–82, 193, 236, 241–42, 270, 380, 388, 395

Mexico, 118, 125, 127, 139, 177, 210–14, 218, 230, 291, 383, 386

    Mexica, 111–12

    Mexican, 109–13, 115, 122–25, 127, 173, 178–79, 207, 210–17, 222, 226, 228–29

    Mexican American, 105, 109–110, 112, 117, 215–17

migration, 15–16, 18–19, 65, 85–87, 105, 133, 136–37, 224–28, 234, 242, 249, 288, 360–61

    deportation, 125–26, 138–39, 217–18, 316

    immigration, 17, 66, 70, 81, 110, 112–17, 122–27, 129–30, 138–40, 173–74, 176, 209–14, 216–20, 223, 230, 233, 235, 241, 244, 252–54, 258–60, 262–64, 267–68, 272–73, 277–78, 283, 289–90, 292, 300–301, 310–11, 316–18, 322, 374, 379

    refugees, 84, 127–28, 245, 296

    transnational migration, 266, 363, 369–71, 379, 383–84, 386, 390

militarism, 17, 30, 32, 35, 38, 43, 58, 64–66, 72, 76–77, 81–82, 89, 129, 146, 150, 177, 184, 246, 280, 297, 311, 320–21, 376, 389

militarism (cont.)

    militarization, 63, 70, 78, 84, 87, 127, 139, 217, 279, 314, 316

mimicry, 183, 344

    imitation, 330, 343

    mimetic, 11, 227, 338, 346, 348, 351

minoritized biblical criticism, 57, 62, 106, 108, 121, 172, 184–85, 236, 243, 289, 379

    minoritized approaches, 105–6, 110, 236, 239–40, 380

    minoritized ethnic-racial criticism, 3–4, 7–8, 16, 21, 25, 54–57, 361, 363–69, 371, 373–81, 383–86, 388–92, 395–96

modernism, 353

    Enlightenment, 22, 25, 169, 236, 306, 342, 367

    modernity, 24, 44–45, 52–54, 80, 85, 225, 227, 353–54

    postmodernity, 22–23, 43–44, 69, 93, 252, 348

mourning, 62, 77–79, 81–82, 84–86, 89, 141–42, 147, 151, 155, 158–64, 166–68, 376

movement, 37, 44, 65, 69, 100, 133, 150, 163, 175, 190, 199, 201, 203–4, 226, 244, 246, 248, 250, 257–58, 261–62, 266–67, 270, 274–75, 277, 280–81, 295, 307, 324, 335, 337, 361, 370–72, 380

myth, 70, 74, 83, 137, 139, 204, 269–71, 278, 314, 321–22, 344

narrative, 20, 55–56, 70, 73–74, 77, 93–96, 101, 110–12, 131–32, 137, 143–45, 148–49, 151–52, 156–60, 162, 164–65, 168, 178, 190, 196, 199, 217, 240–41, 245, 249, 251, 253, 304–5, 318–19, 323–24, 326, 328, 331, 334, 342, 345–46, 349, 353, 361, 374, 376

nation, 22, 24, 67, 70, 74, 81, 85, 88, 98, 105, 131–33, 138, 160, 190, 195–98, 200–206, 229–30, 278, 288, 291, 293, 299, 308, 311, 339, 341, 350–52, 388

Subject Index

415

nation (cont.)
 nationalist, nationalism, 17, 26, 42, 89, 109, 125, 135, 137, 177, 246, 254, 344, 350, 353, 361, 363, 367, 369, 376, 379, 383, 386–87, 390
National Association for the Advancement of Colored People, 194
Native American, 140, 195, 199
Négritude, 257–65, 267–70, 272–75, 369, 370
 Senghorian Négritude, 259–60, 262, 269–70, 273–75
Negro, 81, 217, 262–64, 269–70, 274, 276, 278, 311, 313
non-European, 106, 120, 265, 274
objectification, 98, 193, 268, 274
 objectivity, 22, 24, 46, 61, 87, 237, 280, 372, 395
oppression, 22, 44, 47, 50, 66, 96–98, 103, 114, 149, 153, 160, 171, 242, 273, 294
Orientalism, 114, 175, 183, 259, 277
pandemic, 48, 50, 53, 93–97, 102, 360–64
 COVID-19, 47, 62, 66, 125, 362–63, 366
 HIV/AIDS, 93–96, 102, 389
Persian Empire, 164, 235, 238, 240, 244–45, 248–51, 253–54
philology, 182–83, 237, 279
poetics of concealment, 280
police, 42, 63, 65, 87, 146, 201, 217, 280–81, 283, 311, 313, 316, 325
politicians, 65, 218, 273, 313, 315
politics of respectability, 280, 372
populism, 10, 34, 56, 64, 163, 168, 224–226, 361, 363, 367, 376, 383, 386, 390
positionality, 131
poverty, 29, 43, 68, 83, 201, 206, 224–25, 228, 230, 281, 294, 313–14, 316–18, 332
prejudice, 67, 115, 234, 313
priest, 99, 111, 117, 153, 178, 201, 206, 250, 273, 291, 293, 298, 345–46
prison, 42, 70, 75, 85, 113, 130, 134, 265, 303–4, 307–13, 316–18, 320–29, 335, 352, 374

prison (cont.)
 confinement, 308, 316, 320, 373
 parole, 271, 303, 311, 315
 prison reform, 39, 47, 219, 226–27, 257, 262, 305–10, 312, 315, 317–18, 331–34
privatization, 36, 48–49, 64, 317
profit, 29, 33, 37, 40, 49, 52, 63, 66, 83, 282, 323, 333, 338
progress, 22–23, 43, 46, 55–56, 69–71, 73–75, 77, 80, 90, 145, 155–57, 160, 168, 376
Protestant, 117, 196, 200, 238–39, 380
proyección social, 297–298, 386–387
psychology, 99, 103–4, 310, 339, 347, 367
 psychosocial, 342, 347, 350
Puerto Rico, 224–26, 228–30, 232, 234, 288
punishment, 95, 134, 155, 191, 304, 306–9, 311–12, 315, 320, 329, 331–34
purity, 203
 ethnic purity, 246, 379
 racial purity, 194, 202
race, 23–26, 35, 40, 63, 65, 74, 83–85, 89–90, 104, 123, 126, 139, 147, 156, 165–68, 173–74, 190, 202–6, 208, 215, 218, 222, 225, 230–31, 246, 250, 253, 264, 276, 292, 300, 331, 338, 348, 355
 racial disparities, 304, 333
 racial scripts, 215–17, 233
 racialization, 76, 193, 210, 213, 217, 220, 377
reality, 11, 28, 46, 50, 62, 69, 76, 119, 152, 170, 172, 185, 209, 232, 236, 251–52, 268, 271, 281, 294, 296, 297, 301, 342, 345–46, 349, 351, 379, 384
 dystopia, 51, 360, 364
 utopia, 54, 56, 248, 365, 395
redemptive activism, 273, 371
rehabilitation, 311–12, 317
religionism, 70, 109, 121, 289, 382, 393–95
 definition, 107
repatriate reading, repatriation, 202, 235–37, 239, 241, 243–51, 253, 255, 379–81

416   Subject Index

representativism, 110, 116, 382

resistance, 17, 35, 37–38, 46–47, 51, 77, 94, 96–99, 110, 145, 153, 158, 160, 205, 246, 258, 285, 301, 305, 314, 316, 322, 331, 333, 341, 354, 363, 367, 371, 374, 377, 385, 392

resurrection, 143, 145, 152–53, 157, 159, 164, 270

revelation, 8, 270–71, 298, 360, 395

revolution, 35–36, 47, 71, 82–84, 86, 90, 139, 168, 257, 262

ritual, 89, 168, 178, 184, 193–94, 274, 296, 306, 320, 346, 350

Roman, 268, 327, 332–34, 338, 377
    Empire, 29, 146–47, 153, 162
    execution, 142, 144, 152
    law, 67
    Rome, 148, 151, 274, 293, 300, 304–5, 318, 320–21, 323, 374
    Roman Catholic, 100, 117–18, 149–50, 200, 228, 238, 260, 288, 298, 301

ruckus-raising reading, 287, 291, 294, 298–99, 301, 387

scream, 338, 340–41

scripturalization, 286, 337, 339, 340–44, 346–48, 352, 355, 375
    scripturalism, 9, 197, 337–41, 343–45, 351, 392

secular-humanist, 8–9, 382, 396

segregation, 85, 195, 201, 354

seminary, 9, 108, 184, 195, 292

Senegal, 257–58, 260–62, 266–67, 269–70, 272–73, 275–77, 369–71

sensory metaphor, 323–24

settler, 72, 81, 87, 131–32

shame, 76, 83, 164, 306, 320–21, 323

sheep, 131, 133–37, 143, 152, 384

sign, 102, 111, 123, 177, 281, 322, 329
    signify, 36, 45, 50, 207, 236, 338, 341–42, 344, 346, 351–52, 364, 376
    the signal, 281

silence, 9–10, 14–15, 146, 154, 269, 295, 308, 311, 350, 371, 389

slave, slavery, 70, 95, 97, 143, 154–56, 165, 168, 200–201, 205, 225, 241, 253, 263,

slave, slavery (cont.)
    271, 286, 309, 312, 314, 317, 330, 333, 342, 349, 355

Society of Biblical Literature, 15, 61, 105, 176, 183–85, 236, 238, 241–42, 279, 293, 295–96, 299, 359, 378–80, 386–87

sojourner, 116, 133

stigmatization, 147, 304, 318

stranger, 128–29, 131, 133–34, 292, 344

subjectivity, 44, 73, 76–77, 93
    subject, 15, 24, 39, 44, 49, 64–65, 68, 73, 78, 98–99, 107, 113, 116, 136, 142, 149, 154, 160, 173, 190, 196, 209–10, 212, 217, 219, 230, 232, 259–60, 312, 343, 348, 350, 378, 389, 396

surveillance, 222, 303–5, 311, 315–16, 318, 324–25, 363, 389
    surveillance state, 303–5, 318, 323, 373–74

terrorism, 63, 66–67, 74, 125–26, 151–52, 316, 320, 386, 390

textual criticism, 172, 182, 187

theological studies, 5, 9

ticket, 281–82, 313

time, 5, 7, 12, 15–16, 25, 28, 31, 33–34, 36, 42–43, 46, 51–53, 67–73, 78, 94–95, 97, 99, 102, 130, 140, 142, 146, 147, 151, 155–57, 159, 161–62, 180, 183–84, 193, 195, 199, 210–11, 213–14, 221–23, 227–32, 239, 257, 260, 262, 264, 270, 274, 278, 284, 298–301, 305, 309–11, 314, 317, 319, 321, 330, 359, 363–64, 367, 369, 375–77, 379, 384, 388–89, 391, 394–95
    spatiality, 325–26
    temporal, 55–56, 75, 77–81, 83, 85, 87, 89, 134, 141, 145, 156–58, 160, 165, 240, 244–45, 282, 304, 326, 380
    timelessness, 80, 280, 372

Torah, 133, 240, 249–50, 253–54

train reading, 176, 269, 279, 281–85, 371–73

transcendent, 167, 344, 346

Subject Index

transdisciplinary, 41, 341

transgressive politics, 337

trauma, 15, 70, 83, 86, 93–94, 100, 102, 146, 148, 151, 153, 155, 158–59, 162–66, 247–48, 250–52, 379–80

colonial trauma, 148, 151, 153, 159

trial, 51, 303, 305, 320–21, 324, 326–29, 334

tribal, 69, 345

triumphalism, 36–37, 48, 55, 71, 73–74, 167, 361

Union of Soviet Socialist Republics, the, 18–19, 30–33, 35–36, 48

United States, 3–7, 17, 19, 21, 24, 26–27, 30–35, 37–38, 41–43, 53, 55, 63–74, 76–77, 81, 86, 88, 94–95, 99–100, 104–5, 112, 122, 125–30, 132–33, 139, 142, 149–50, 160, 173–74, 176, 185, 188, 194–95, 201–2, 204–5, 208, 210–22, 224–25, 227–31, 233, 244, 246, 252, 254, 257, 260, 266, 279, 290, 292, 303–5, 307–8, 312, 316, 318, 334, 337, 359–60, 366, 369–71, 373–76, 379, 381, 383–84, 389–90, 395

Universidad Centroamericana, 293, 297–99, 386

university, 9, 22, 26–27, 41–42, 55, 57–59, 81–90, 98, 103–5, 123–24, 138–39, 150, 163–68, 186–87, 204–6, 209, 233–35, 252–55, 257–58, 273, 275–76, 278, 280, 284–87, 289, 292–94, 296–98, 301, 314, 331–34, 353–55, 362, 372, 386, 396

vanity, 287–288

violence, 16, 19, 65, 71, 76, 78, 81–82, 84, 95, 125, 132, 137, 151, 152, 189–95, 197–206, 252, 273, 298–99, 337, 339, 342, 348, 360, 367–69, 375, 377, 386, 390

systemic violence, 363, 368

vision, 3–6, 11, 19, 25, 37, 43–44, 47–48, 54, 62, 88, 103, 123, 139, 202, 210, 222, 231–32, 248, 254, 264, 268, 270, 273, 275, 297, 301, 332, 335, 370–71, 375–76, 381, 385, 387, 391–92, 396

vision (cont.)

revision, 8, 14, 16, 22, 237, 359

virus, 62, 67, 95, 102, 362–63, 366, 389

wall, 125, 143, 184, 248–50, 254, 291–92

War on Drugs, 87, 313–16

warfare, 16, 73

wars, 33, 63, 73–74, 86, 166, 278

Civil War, 139, 298, 309

Cold War, 7, 16, 18–19, 25, 31, 52, 69, 71, 73, 85–86, 242, 296

First World War, 16, 27

Second World War, 16, 22, 30–31, 33, 55, 73, 130, 201, 225, 359

watch, the, 281–82

wealth, 29, 31–32, 36, 64, 118, 128, 184, 317, 388

West Indies, 265, 267, 370

white, whiteness, 23, 69–70, 74, 76, 83, 85, 96, 98, 102–3, 107, 118, 123, 138, 170, 175–76, 189–94, 201–3, 205–6, 210–16, 222, 230, 238, 241, 264, 273, 276, 313, 339–40, 343–46, 352, 354–55, 361, 367, 375–76, 389, 394

white men, 174, 286, 342, 344–46, 348, 351, 355

white supremacy, 5, 63, 73, 160, 172, 193, 195, 201, 265, 368–69, 390

witness, 109, 148, 155, 160, 162, 193, 288, 326, 331, 387, 393

womanism, 169, 171, 184, 187–88, 206, 285

world order, 20–25, 52–54, 57, 369

worlds

Global South, 16–22, 25, 40, 43–45, 52, 57, 64–66, 241, 296, 360–62, 369–70, 376, 389–90, 395

Second World, 16, 22, 31, 33, 40, 73

the West, Global North, 16–22, 24–25, 27, 35, 40, 44–46, 49, 52, 66, 69, 82, 114, 194, 221, 247, 267, 342, 360–62, 369–71, 389, 395

Third World, 17–18, 32–33, 35–36, 40, 140, 276, 294–95

xenophobia, 20, 125–26, 250, 383

www.ingramcontent.com/pod-product-compliance
Lightning Source LLC
LaVergne TN
LVHW042343010825
817679LV00032B/676